Augustus J. C. Hare

IN MY
SOLITARY LIFE

BEING AN ABRIDGEMENT OF THE
LAST THREE VOLUMES OF
THE STORY OF MY LIFE

Edited with
Notes and Introduction
by
MALCOLM BARNES

London
GEORGE ALLEN & UNWIN LTD
RUSKIN HOUSE · MUSEUM STREET

Originally published by
George Allen
in three volumes
1900

Abridged edition, 1953

Printed in Great Britain
in 12 pt. Fournier type
by C. Tinling & Co., Ltd.,
Liverpool, London and Prescot

INTRODUCTION

❧❧

IN *My Solitary Life* is the title I have given to an abridgement of
the second half of Augustus Hare's autobiography, which originally
appeared—as *The Story of My Life*—in two instalments, in 1896
and 1900 respectively. Its author, who was born in 1834 and according to
his own statement began this work which eventually totalled over 3,000
pages—more than three-quarters of a million words—in 1878, died in
1903; and although his memoirs form a completed work as published,
Hare continued to keep a voluminous journal and, according to Mr.
Somerset Maugham, was still at work on his autobiography towards the
end of his life. Of this later material I have been able to find nothing in
a finished condition, but I have been fortunate in having access to his
last diary, in which he was writing on the night before his death, and of
this I have included the more interesting entries as an Appendix to
the present volume. There still remains a gap, however, between the
published *Story* and the diary of some two years, which is impossible
to fill.

The first half of the autobiography I have already abridged and it
is available to readers under the title *The Years With Mother*, which I
chose because its author's almost maudlin devotion to Maria Hare, his
adoptive mother, widow of his uncle Augustus, was in fact the keynote
of the period which ended with her death in 1870.

In the Introduction to that book I very briefly set forth the salient
facts of the author's origin and career, more with a view to explaining
why I thought this story worth the modern reader's attention than to
recapitulating the events of which he himself has given us so many
details. I do not intend to repeat that summary here; I can only commend
the reader who has missed it to a work which, apart from its immense
fund of fascinating fact and anecdote concerning many famous persons
and places of the mid-Victorian era, has given us an almost unequalled
record of those times in three distinct and alternating aspects. These
were: the English rural middle-class, pious to the point of hypocrisy,
but comfortably endowed with this world's goods, typified by those
whose circle centred upon the Rectory at Hurstmonceaux in Sussex,
where Augustus's uncle Julius, the Archdeacon, presided with his harsh-
tempered wife Esther, sister of Frederick D. Maurice; the cosmopolitan

and snobbish crowd that thronged the cities of Italy—especially Rome—
and the French Riviera, where Augustus and his mother passed many
weeks each year, enabling him to record the almost medieval pomp of
the Papal State; lastly, the life of the English landed gentry and aristocracy, of the great homes of England, still mostly occupied by their
hereditary owners and stuffed with historic and artistic treasure, which
Hare was enabled to observe through his many cousinships in these
families, which he exploited during his early efforts at compiling guide-
books for John Murray.

He gave us, too, a vivid—and to some an incredible—account of his
sufferings as a child, mostly in the name of religion, of the picturesque
adventures of his sister 'Esmeralda' and his real mother 'Italima', of
conditions of travel in Europe before the network of railways was laid
down and the *vetturino* (a large hackney carriage) was the normal means
of long-distance transport, and of men and scenes in Rome before the
Sardinian government had got to work in its cleaning up of the city
and its destruction of much of its character. Augustus deeply deplored
the Sardinian government's efforts, and indeed much of the work—like
the removal of the vegetation from the ruins of the Coliseum and other
ancient relics—was unnecessary; but one has to recall the plagues of
cholera and typhus and other diseases of which he himself was a witness,
and remember that these could not have been brought to an end without
a very broad measure of modernisation.

Such was the substance of the first three volumes which, by ruth-
lessly excluding all that has lost its value with the years and all that was
sheer padding, I reduced to about a third of their length and called *The
Years With Mother*.

Maria, the adoptive mother, died when Hare was thirty-six, when he
imagined in his grief that his own life must there end too, so deeply
devoted were they and so intricately involved their lives. Of course, he
did not die. Indeed, after quite a brief interval the pattern of living
already established was developed on a more extensive scale. The literary
career which had always been his ambition and of which his family did
not approve—nor Maria, who had planned for him a life in the Church—
was now taken up in all earnestness. His European travels were continued and widened. Relieved of the burden of his semi-invalid mother—
who suffered from a strange malady of a largely hysterical character
which successfully tied Augustus to her side—he plunged very deeply
into the social life of the day, extended his already broad acquaintance,
moved in the season from one house-party to another, busied himself
at Holmhurst and the Athenaeum in the endless compilation of guide-

books and massive memoirs of worthy ladies, and became, despite defects of manner and aspect, a familiar figure.

Of his writing life I have already given a full account and a complete bibliography is included in *The Years With Mother*. He was by no means unsuccessful: one or two of his works, especially the *Memorials of a Quiet Life*, became famous and ran into many editions. He was an industrious worker, though not gifted with any great originality, since his guide-books are largely constructed of copious quotations from other writers and his ,memoirs of equally copious extracts from journals and letters; nevertheless, he was painstaking, thorough and methodical, and his reading was vast.

I have already alluded to his complaints that he never made anything out of his books; but George Allen's accounts show that in later years at least he made a substantial income by the standards of his day. Indeed, indiscreet in many aspects of his memoirs, he is more than shy about money, and his few statements are confusing and contradictory. He complained of his poverty, of the little that his mother left him, of the swindlings of his publishers; yet he was still able to travel widely, to live very comfortably both at Holmhurst and in London, to lose quite large sums in speculation, and to leave, according to the will which can be examined at Somerset House, an estate first valued at £22,157 and subsequently resworn, for no stated reason, at £31,900. Therefore, I cannot think that all his publishers behaved so badly; George Allen, as I have said, certainly did not, for he allocated of the profits on each book two-thirds to the author and only one-third to himself. Profit-sharing agreements are rare today, but such as there are usually apportion the profits equally.

But shyness about one's wealth is not uncommon even today, when we are more inclined to overstate than otherwise; few of us are honest about it, as if there was some guilt attached to the possession of money, provoking some of us to shame and others to boasting. However, it has been put to me that, because Hare was misleading in this particular, he cannot be believed at all, more especially with regard to his childhood's misery. I cannot agree. Consciously or otherwise, we are all of us liars some of the time in the effort to impress our personalities upon the world, and do not always deceive those we wish to influence in our favour, but that does not mean that nothing we say can ever be believed. Hare's story of his early years, as recounted in *The Years With Mother*, can be believed because it is fully in keeping with the manners of those days; the novels of many eminent authors of Hare's own generation are full of similar stories which are clearly founded upon observed or experienced fact. Moreover, as an entry in this present volume shows, Hare did find a very reliable witness to the most shocking of the incidents recorded of life at Hurstmonceaux: the hanging of his cat. Canon Douglas Gordon assures us he was there when it took place.

In fact, when the first three volumes of the autobiography had been published, few people really doubted his story. They had no reason to, being so close themselves to the time when such things were common; many could have told similar tales. What angered both reviewers and readers was that Hare should have been so indiscreet as to have mentioned these matters at all. In Matilda Lucas's book, *Two English Women in Rome, 1871–1900*, is a letter dated November 6th 1896: 'We are now reading Augustus Hare's reminiscences. We cannot help being amused, but it is strange that he should publish such unguarded statements about his own people and others.' This was typical comment: he was abused not for what he said, but for having said it. Most critics wrote that he was 'wholly without delicacy' or 'wanting in propriety'. *Blackwood's* went so far as to describe the first three volumes as a 'foam of super-annuated wrath . . . . this vicious and personal onslaught . . . . Mr. Hare's paragraphs plump like drops of concentrated venom over the dinted page. Such a cold rage of vituperation is seldom to be met with'. Even the author was surprised by this attack. The modern reader will understand even less the anger of such reviews.

Yet it was not wholly in respect of his own people that Hare was indiscreet, as readers of *The Years With Mother* will have discovered. Sir Osbert Sitwell records the effect of his disclosures in *Left Hand, Right Hand*; when Augustus appeared at a garden party at Renishaw, for fear that he might put them into his next book, the ladies held their hats to their heads and fled for the house. This occurred shortly after the publication of the first three volumes of the autobiography.

No: I do not believe that Hare was ever deliberately mendacious; certainly not in respect of his own experiences and observations. But he was obviously credulous: his love of a story, his taste for the dramatic and the bizarre, led him sometimes to pass on as a fact what was merely gossip, without reflection on its probability. Hence, for instance, his story of Queen Victoria's scream at the Prince Consort's deathbed, which could not have 'echoed all over the castle', having regard to the thickness of the walls. But that was the sort of story Victorians readily believed, and of this and similar tales Hare, I think, was not the inventor but only the recorder.

By this time, however, the generation which Hare had valued and which had respected him was rapidly dying out. He himself was past his sixtieth year. Many of his friends—like Lady Waterford—were dead, and society at the turn of the century was revealing tastes which he despised and manners which he regarded with contempt. The young Maugham was even reproved for speaking of a 'bus' instead of an 'omnibus'. He complains that conversation is not what it was, that the dinner parties are no longer worth recording, that social life in London has become a waste of time. I suspect that, though he was still to be met at some London houses, invitations were becoming fewer, and that to the young people and to those mercantile classes who were replacing the aristocracy that Hare, in his snobbery, regarded as his proper *milieu* he was a slightly ridiculous figure, if not a bore, as elderly snobs are inclined to be when they insist that the world is no longer what it was when they were young. So London saw less of him and Holmhurst saw more.

He had never married, of course, and his last years, as friends and servants passed away, were rather solitary, except for occasional guests. Readers of *The Years With Mother* will remember that in 1864 he hinted that he had considered marriage but had abandoned the idea as incompatible with his entire devotion to his mother. Rather wistfully, he added: 'These things do not—cannot—recur'. It is interesting, however, that in the book by Matilda Lucas, already quoted, there is the following entry dated 'Rome, 1879': 'Augustus Hare is reported to be engaged, but denies it indignantly and says he will never marry.' At that time he was very busy conducting Prince Gustav of Sweden about the city and there is, indeed, no hint in his book of a romance.

Only a few weeks before that entry, Miss Lucas had seen Hare for the first time and she describes him as follows (December 1878): '. . . a little dark-haired man who sits near us in church. He is not at all good-looking. His forehead is good, but the lower part of his face is weak. He has black hair and moustache and piercing eyes. He speaks deliberately and through his nose.' Eighteen years later, in 1896, they met again: 'Augustus Hare came in . . . and talked a little about the pictures. Mrs. Gaunt did not catch his name and thought him a dandy because of the extreme glossiness of his hat . . . he has an affected manner and rather trying voice. . . . He is small and round-shouldered, with hair as glossy as his hat and a very prominent nose."

As to the darkness and glossiness of his hair at the age of sixty-two, I am told there was gossip that he wore a wig; but I can naturally find no proof, though his last portrait does suggest that the gossip was well founded; he was certainly vain enough and sensitive enough about his age (note his constant reference to how young he feels) to have taken

A*

to a wig if necessary. It is also said, on what evidence I know not, that he painted his face to conceal the marks of time.

Because of his relative retirement after the turn of the century, there are few references to him in the reminiscences of the time. For a picture of the man and his surroundings one must go therefore to Mr. Maugham's essay in the book *In Vagrant Mood*; its author, probably the only living person apart from Queen Mary who ever met Hare, was a guest at Holm-hurst following the publication of his first book, and Hare was giving the young author some encouragement. Mr. Maugham gives an impression of a household of considerable comfort without ostentation, and of a plain but copious board, the day being divided into a very regular and slightly pompous routine. One of the entertaining stories in Mr. Maugham's essay, which is illuminating in respect of Hare's religious beliefs and social outlook, concerns the prayers which he read before the assembled guests and servants at breakfast. It was noticed by the young author that the prayers as read by Hare did not exactly correspond to those he re-membered in the prayer-book, and the older man explained that as no gentleman liked being praised to his face, and as he was certain that God was a gentleman, he had excised all such passages. I think myself that Hare was in religious matters only a formalist; his experience of religious people in his childhood had probably turned him into something of an agnostic, though he would not have acknowledged the fact because 'gentleman' and 'agnostic' were undoubtedly incom-patible terms.

The house, judging from photographs, was full of bric-à-brac, the accumulation of his lifetime's travels and his inherited treasures; the garden, too, seems to have been well filled with oddments of masonry and statuary brought from near and far. There was the surround of a well brought from Italy, the statue of Queen Anne from St. Paul's, and a large ornamental portal with *Ave* on the outside to greet his visitors and *Vale* on the inside to speed their departure, and much besides. In those days it was well outside the built-up area of Hastings and had an uninterrupted view of the sea, across pasture and parkland, from its hilly position. The gardens appear to have been cunningly contrived to give an exaggerated idea of their extent.

For some years he had suffered from an affection of the heart, and one morning, early in 1903, his servant found him in his nightshirt, dead upon the floor of his room. He had lived long enough to see a greater change in society than he cared for, but he was saved the sight of what he would have regarded as its rapid deterioration in the Edwardian era. His life had covered very closely the whole reign of Victoria; he was a typical representative of his age and his memoirs have preserved aspects of it that cannot be found in the history books.

His will contained a codicil of about eighty items, by which he left some memento to each of his surviving friends and acquaintances—a picture or some similar treasured possession—and in detailing each item, he was careful to record its history and even, in the case of a picture, to mention whether or not he regarded as correct its attribution to a named artist.

In my first acquaintance with this long autobiography I regarded its author with some slight amusement, considering him to be a prig and an unadulterated snob. But in time I have come to regard him with considerable affection. Shane Leslie says of him that he has made himself interesting because he has preserved so much that is interesting in others; which is true enough, but I think he is an interesting figure in his own right and lovable behind his affectations, many of which have their origin in his severely repressed youth. As the French say, to understand is to forgive.

As in the preceding volume, I have included a selection of the attractive engravings that embellished the original edition; they were made from his own water-colours. He was one of the best amateur water-colourists of his time, and curiously was not at all conceited about it. I have also retained most of his excellent uncanny stories, for which he was quite famous, being invited to tell them wherever he went. The reminiscences of his contemporaries contain references to his skill and repute as a raconteur.

I have not repeated here the details of his family tree, which are as interesting as they are intricate. For this I must refer the reader to *The Years With Mother*. As regards my excisions, I have refrained from indicating where they have been made because they are too many, except in the few cases where there is an obvious break in continuity. And as in the previous volume, I have, where I thought it useful, added footnotes concerning many of the persons mentioned; to some readers these notes may seem to contain very obvious information and I ask their indulgence because I think that to others they may be helpful. As in the previous volume, where I have rendered into English a passage unnecessarily recorded in French by the author, I have indicated the fact by simply inserting the symbol [Fr.]. Square brackets in the text indicate the few interpolations of the editor.

Malcolm Barnes

July 1952

CONTENTS

ILLUSTRATIONS

PLATES

ILLUSTRATIONS IN THE TEXT

IN MY SOLITARY LIFE

1870–73

❧

I SPENT the greater part of the fiercely cold winter of 1870–71 in complete seclusion at Holmhurst, entirely engrossed in the work of the *Memorials*, which had been the last keen interest of my Mother's life. In calling up the vivid image of long-ago days spent with her, I seemed to live those days over again, and I found constant proof of her loving forethought for the first months of my solitude in the materials which, without my knowledge, and without then the slightest idea of publication, she must have frequently devoted herself to arranging during the last few years of her life. As each day passed, and the work unravelled itself, I was increasingly convinced of the wisdom of her death-bed decision that until the book was quite finished I should give it to none of the family to read. They must judge of it as a whole.

Unfortunately this decision greatly ruffled the sensibilities of my Stanley cousins, especially of Arthur Stanley and his sister Mary, who from the first threatened me with legal proceedings if I gave them the smallest loop-hole for them, by publishing a word of their own mother's writing without their consent, which from the first, also, they declared they would withhold.

My other cousins did not at first approve of the plan of the *Memorials*, but when once completed, convinced that it had been their dear aunt's wish, they withdrew all opposition. Still the harshness with which I was now continually treated and spoken of by those with whom I had always hitherto lived on terms of the utmost intimacy was a bitter trial. In a time when a single great grief pervades every hour, unreasonable demands, cruel words, and taunting sneers are more difficult to bear than when life is rippling on in an even course. I was by no means blameless: I wrote sharp letters: I made harsh speeches; but that it was my duty to fight in behalf of the fulfilment of the solemn duty which had devolved upon me, I never doubted then, and I have never doubted since.

A vivid impression that I had a very short time to live made me more eager about the *rapid* fulfilment of my task. I thought of the Spanish proverb, 'By-and-by is always too late,' and I often worked at the book for twelve hours a day. My Mother had long thought, and latterly often said, that it was impossible I could long survive her: that when two lives were so closely entwined as ours, one could not go on alone. It was partly owing to the strong impression in her mind that I could not survive her that my Mother had failed to make the usual arrangements for my future provision. As she had never allowed any money to be placed in my name,

HIGHCLIFFE, THE KING'S ORIEL

I had—being no legal relation to her—to pay a stranger's duty of £10 per cent on all she possessed, and this amounted to a large sum, when extended to a duty on every picture, even every garden implement, &c.[1] Not only this, but during her lifetime she had been induced by various members of the family to sign away a large portion of her fortune, and in the intricate difficulties which arose I was assured that I should have nothing whatever left to live upon beyond £60 a year, and the rent of Holmhurst (fortunately secured), if it could be let. I was urged by the Stanleys to submit at once to my fate, and to sell Holmhurst; yet I could

---

[1] I had to pay a duty of 10 per cent, even on all my own money and savings, as it had been unfortunately invested in her name.

not help hoping for better days, which came with the publication of *Walks in Rome*.

Meanwhile, half distracted by the unsought 'advice' which was poured upon me from all sides, and worn-out with the genuine distress of my old servants, I went away in March, just as far as I could. I was so very miserable and so miserably preoccupied at this time, that I have no distinct recollection of these visits, beyond the image on my mind of the grand chrysoprase seas of Cornwall and the stupendous rocks against which they beat, especially at Tol Pedn Penwith.

In May I paid the first of many visits to my dear Lady Waterford at Highcliffe, her fairy palace by the sea, on the Hampshire coast, near Christ Church, and though I was still too sad to enter into the full charm of the place and the life, which I have enjoyed so much since, I was greatly refreshed by the mental tonic, and by the kindness and sympathy which I have never failed to receive from Lady Waterford and her friend Lady Jane Ellice. For many years after this, Highcliffe was more familiar to me than any other place except my own home, and I am attached to every stone of it. The house was the old Mayor's house of Les Andelys, removed from Normandy by Lord Stuart de Rothesay, but a drawing shows the building as it was in France, producing a far finer effect than as it was put up in England by Pugin, the really fine parts, especially the great window, being lower down in the building, and more made of. In the room to which that window belonged, Antoyne de Bourbon, King of Navarre, died. The original house of Highcliffe was built on land sold to Lord Stuart by a Mr. Penlees, who had had a legacy of bank-notes left him in the case of a cocked-hat—it was quite full of them. Mr. Penlees had built a very ugly house, the present 'old rooms,' which Lord Stuart cased over. Then he said that, while Lady Stuart was away, he would add a few rooms. When she came back, to her intense consternation, she found the new palace of Highcliffe: all the ornaments, windows, &c., from Les Andelys having been landed close by upon the coast.[1]

I have put down a few notes from the conversation at Highcliffe this year.

Mr. M. was remonstrated with because he would not admire Louis Philippe's régime. He said, 'No, I cannot; I have known him before so well. I am like the peasant who, when he was remonstrated with because he would not take off his hat to a new wooden cross that was put up, said he couldn't *parceque je l'ai connu poirier* [because I have known it as a peartree]'.

Lady Anne Barnard[2] was at a party in France, and her carriage never came to take

---

[1] The palace has been considerably altered since Lady Waterford's day.—*Ed.*

[2] Daughter of the 5th Earl of Balcarres. Cf. Madeleine Masson, *Lady Anne Barnard.*—*Ed.*

her away. A certain Duke who was there begged to have the honour of taking her home, and she accepted, but on the way felt rather awkward and thought he was too affectionate and gallant. Suddenly she was horrified to see the Duke on his knees at the bottom of the carriage, and was putting out her hands and warding him off, when he exclaimed, '*Taisez-vous, Madame, voilà le bon Dieu qui passe*'. It was a great blow to her vanity.

Old Lord Malmesbury[1] used to invent the most extraordinary stories and tell them so well; indeed, he told them till he quite believed them. One was called 'The Moth-eaten Clergyman'; it was about a very poor clergyman, a Roman he was, who had some small parish in Southern Germany, and was a very good man, quite excellent, absolutely devoted to the good of his people. There was, however, one thing which militated against his having all the influence amongst his flock which he ought to have had, and this was that he was constantly observed to steal out of his house in the late evening with two bags in his hand, and to bury the contents in the garden; and yet when people came afterwards by stealth and dug for the treasures, they found nothing at all, and this was thought, well . . . not quite canny.

Now the diocesan of that poor clergyman, who happened to be the Archbishop of Mayence, was much distressed at this, that the influence of so good a man should thus be marred. Soon afterwards he went on his visitation tour, and he stopped at the clergyman's house for the night. He arrived with outriders, and two postillions, and four fat horses and four fat pug-dogs, which was not very convenient. However, the poor clergyman received them all very hospitably, and did the best he could for them. But the Archbishop thought it was a great opportunity for putting an end to all the rumours that were about, and with a view to this he gave orders that the doors should be fastened and locked, so that no one should go out.

When morning came, the windows of the priest's house were not opened, and no one emerged, and at last the parishioners became alarmed, for there was no sound at all. But when they broke open the doors, volleys upon volleys of moths of every kind and hue poured out; but of the poor clergyman, or of the Archbishop of Mayence, or of the outriders and postillions, or of the four fat horses, or of the four pug-dogs, came out nothing at all, for they were all eaten up. For the fact was that the poor clergyman really had the most dreadful disease which bred myriads of moths; if he could bury their eggs at night, he kept them under, but when he was locked up, and he could do nothing, they were too much for him. Now there is a moral in this story, because if the people and the Archbishop had looked to the fruits of that excellent man's life and not attended to foolish reports with which they had no concern whatever, these things would never have happened.

I have said little for many years of the George Sheffield who was the dearest friend of my boyhood. He had been attaché at Munich, Washington, Constantinople, and now at Paris as secretary to Lord Lyons. In this my first desolate year he also had a sorrow, which wonderfully reunited us, and we became perhaps greater friends than we had been before.

I needed all the support my friends could give me, for the family feud about the *Memorials* was not the only trouble that pressed upon me at this time.

[1] James Edward, 2nd Earl.

It will be recollected that, in my sister's death-bed will, she had bequeathed to me her claims to a portrait by Sir Joshua Reynolds. It was the very fact of this bequest which in 1871 made my poor Aunt Eleanor (Miss Paul) set up a counter-claim to the picture, which was valued at £2,000. Five-and-twenty years before, the picture had been entrusted for a time to Sir John Paul, who unfortunately, from some small vanity, allowed it to be exhibted in his own name instead of that of the owner. But I never remember the time when it was not at Hurstmonceaux after 1845, when it was sent there.

THE CHURCHYARD, HURSTMONCEAUX

For the whole of November I was in London, expecting the trial every day, but it was not till the evening of the 6th of December that I heard that it was to be the next morning in the law-court off Westminster Hall. The court was crowded. My counsel, Mr. Pollock, began his speech with a tremendous exordium. 'Gentlemen of the jury, in a neighbouring court the world is sitting silent before the stupendous excitement of the Tichborne trial: gentlemen of the jury, *that* case pales into insignificance —pales into the most *utter* insignificance before the thrilling interest of the present occasion. On the narrow stage of this domestic drama, all the historic characters of the last century and all the literary personages of the present seem to be marching in a solemn procession.' And he proceeded to tell the really romantic history of the picture—how Benjamin Franklin saw it painted, &c. The trial continued for several hours, yet when the court adjourned for luncheon I believed all was going well. It was a terrible moment when afterwards Judge Mellor summed up dead against us.

Then the jury came back and gave a verdict for . . . the defendant! It took everybody by surprise, and it was the most triumphant moment I ever remember. All the Pauls sank down as if they were shot. The trial took the whole day, the court sitting longer than usual on account of it. The enemy immediately applied for a new trial, which caused us much anxiety, but this time I was not required to appear in person. The second trial took place on the 16th of January 1872, before the Lord Chief Justice, Judge Blackburn, Judge Mellor, and Judge Hannen, and, after a long discussion, was given triumphantly in my favour.

As both trials were gained by me, the enemy had nominally to pay all the costs, but still the expenses were most heavy. It was just at the time when I was poorest, when my adopted mother's will was still in abeyance. There were also other aspirants for the picture, in the shape of the creditors of my brother Francis, who claimed as representing my father (not my mother). It was therefore thought wiser by all that I should assent to the portrait being sold, and be content to retain only in its place a beautiful copy which had been made for me by the kindness of my cousin Madeleine Shaw-Lefevre. The portrait by Sir Joshua Reynolds was sold at Christie's in the summer of 1872 for £2,200, and is now in the National Gallery of America at New York.

A week after the trial, on the 13th of December, I left England for Spain. It had at first been intended that a party of five should pass the winter there together, but one after another fell off, till none remained except Miss Wright, who joined me in Paris.

To Miss Leycester.

Paris, Dec. 14, 1871.—How different France and England! At Holmhurst I left a green garden bright with chrysanthemums and everlastings: here, a pathless waste of snow up to the tops of the hedges became so deep near Creil that, as day broke, we remained fixed for an hour and a half in the midst of a forest, neither able to move backwards or forwards. And by the side of the rail were remains of a frightful accident of yesterday—engine smashed to bits, carriages cut in half, the linings hanging in rags, cushions lying about, &c. The guard was not encouraging—'*Oui, il y avait des victimes, pas beaucoup, mais il y a toujours des victimes* [Yes, there were victims; not many, but there are always victims].' . . . The state of Paris is unspeakably wretched, hillocks of snow, uncarted away and as high as your shoulder, filling the sides of the streets, with a pond in the intervening space. The Tuileries (after the Commune) looks far worse than I expected—restorable, but for the present it has lost all its form and character. We went inside this morning, but were soon warned out on account of the falling walls weakened by the frost.

Convent of Montserrat, in Catalonia, Jan. 4, 1872.—At the best of times you would never have been able to travel in Spain, for great as is the delight of this unspeakably glorious place, I must confess we paid dear for it in the sufferings of the way. The first day introduced us to plenty of small hardships, as, a train being taken off *al improviso*, we had to wade through muddy lanes—and the Navarre mud is *such* mud—in pitch darkness, to a wretched hovel, where we passed the night with a number of others, in fierce cold, no fires or comforts of any kind. From thence (Alasua) we got on to Pamplona, our first picturesque Spanish town, where we spent part of Christmas Day, and then went on to Tudela, where we had another wretched *posada*; no fires; milk, coffee, and butter quite unknown, and the meat stewed in oil and garlic; and this has been the case everywhere except here, with other and worse in-*conveniences*.

At Zaragoza we were first a little repaid by the wonderful beauty of the Moorish architecture—like lace in brick and stone, and the people as well as the place made a new world for us; but oh! the cold!—blocks of ice in the streets and the fiercest of winds raging. . . . No words certainly can describe the awful, the hideous ugliness of the railway the whole way here: not a tree, not a blade of grass to be seen, but cease-less wind-stricken swamps of brown mud—featureless, hopeless, utterly uncultivated.

We have been four days in the convent. I never saw anything anywhere so beauti-ful or so astonishing as this place, where we are miles and miles above every living thing except the monks, amid the most stupendous precipices of 3,000 feet perpen-dicular, and yet in such a wealth of loveliness in arbutus, box, lentisc, smilax, and jessa-mine, as you can scarcely imagine. Though it is so high, and we have no fires or even *brasieros*, we scarcely feel the cold, the air is so still and the situation so sheltered, and on the sunlit terraces, which overlook the whole of Catalonia like a map, it is really too hot. The monks give us lodging and we have excellent food at a *fonda* within the convent walls, and are quite comfortable, though it must be confessed that my room is so narrow a cell, that when I go in it is impossible to turn round, and I have to hoist myself on the little bed sideways.

To MARY LEA GIDMAN.

Barcelona, Jan. 17.—We have good rooms now, but everywhere the food is shock-ing. At the *table-d'hôte* one of the favourite dishes is snail-soup, and as the snails are cooked in their shells, it does not look very tempting. If the food were improved, this coast would be better for invalids in winter than the Riviera, as it is such a splendid climate—almost too dry, as it scarcely ever rains for more than fifty days out of the 365. The late Queen Isabella II ordered every tree in the whole of Spain which did not bear fruit to be cut down, so the whole country is quite bare, and so parched and rocky that often for fifty miles you do not see a shrub, but in some places there are palms, olives, oranges, and caroubas.

We are very thankful for the tea which Miss Wright's maid makes for us in a saucepan.

To MISS LEYCESTER.

Cordova, Feb. 6.—We broke the dreadful journey from Valencia to Alicante by sleeping at Xativa, a lovely city of palms and rushing fountains with a mountain back-ground, but the inn so disgusting we could not stay. Alicante, on the other hand, had no attraction except its excellent hotel, with dry sheets, bearable smells, no garlic, and butter. The whole district is burnt, tawny, and desolate beyond words—houses, walls, and castle alike dust-colour, but the climate is delicious, and a long palm avenue fringes the sea, with scarlet geraniums in flower. With Elche we were perfectly en-raptured—the forests of palms quite glorious, many sixty feet high and laden with golden dates; the whole place so Moorish, and the people with perfectly Oriental hospitality and manners.

We were disappointed with Murcia, though its figures reach a climax of grotesque magnificence, every plough-boy in the colours of Solomon's temple. But though we had expected to find Cordova only very interesting, it is also most beautiful—the immense court before the mosque filled with fountains and old orange-trees laden with fruit, and the mosque itself, with its forest of pillars, as solemn as it is picturesque.

To Mary Lea Gidman.

Seville, Feb. 10.—The dirt and discomfort of the railway journey to Cordova was quite indescribable, but the mosque is glorious. We made a large drawing in the court with its grove of oranges, cypresses, and palms, and you would have been quite aghast at the horrible beggars who crowded round us—people with two fingers and people with none; people with no legs and people with no noses, or people with their eyes and mouths quite in the wrong place.

The present King (Amadeo) is much disliked and not likely to reign long.[1] Here at Seville, in the Carnival, they made a little image of him, which bowed and nodded its head, as kings do, when it was carried through the street, and all the great people went out to meet it and bring it into the town in mockery; and yesterday it was strangled like a common criminal on a scaffold in the public square; and to-day tens of thousands of people are come into the town to attend its funeral.

The Duchess de Montpensier,[2] who lives here, does a great deal of good, but she is very superstitious, and, when her daughter was ill, she walked barefoot through all the streets of Seville: the child died notwithstanding. She and all the great ladies of Seville wear low dresses and flowers in their hair when they are out walking on the promenade, but at large evening parties they wear high dresses, which is rather con-trary to English fashions. Miss Wright's bonnet made her so stared at and followed about, that now she, and her maid also, have been obliged to get mantillas to wear on their heads instead, which does much better, and prevents their attracting any attention.

To Miss Leycester.

Seville, Feb. 13.—Ever since we entered Andalusia it has poured in torrents, but even in fine weather I think we must have been disappointed with Seville. With such a grand cathedral interior and such beautiful pictures, it seems hard to complain, but there never was anything less picturesque than the narrow streets of whitewashed houses, uglier than the exterior of the cathedral, or duller than the surrounding country. Being Carnival, the streets are full of masks, many of them not very civil to the clergy—the Pope being led along by a devil with a long tail, &c. . . . When we first came, we actually engaged lodgings in the Alcazar, the great palace of the Moorish

[1] Isabella II, daughter of Ferdinand VII by his fourth wife, Marie Cristina of Naples, was forced to resign the throne at the age of 36 after a reign of 22 years in which she tried, like her mother, to rule as a despot. But Spain was not prepared for a republic and various kings were suggested. At last Amadeo of Savoy consented to be a candidate, was elected in November 1870, but was forced to flee in 1873 (Feb.). It was a pitiful business; he became the tool of the politicians and by all others was regarded as an intruder. A short republic followed his fall and then Alfonso XII (Isabella's son) became king.—*Ed.*

[2] See *The Years With Mother*, pp. 117–8.

kings, but, partly from the mosquitoes and partly from the ghosts, soon gave them up again.

Algeciras, Feb. 25.—What a dull place Cadiz is. Nothing to make a feature but the general distant effect of the dazzling white lines of houses rising above a sapphire sea.

Gibraltar, March 2.—It was strange, when we crossed from Algeciras, to come suddenly in among an English-talking, pipe-smoking, beer-drinking community in this swarming place, where 5,000 soldiers are quartered in addition to the crowded English and Spanish population. The main street of the town might be a slice cut out of the ugliest part of Dover, if it were not for the numbers of Moors stalking about in turbans, yellow slippers, and blue or white burnooses.

The Governor, Sir Fenwick Williams, has been excessively civil to us, but our principal acquaintance here is quite romantic. The first day when we went down to the *table-d'hôte*, there were only two others present, a Scotch commercial traveller, and, below him, a rather well-looking Spaniard, evidently a gentleman, but with an odd short figure and squeaky voice. He bowed very civilly as we came in, and we returned it. In the middle of dinner a band of Scotch bagpipers came playing under the window, and I was seized with a desire to jump up and look at them. Involuntarily I looked across the table to see what the others were going to do, when the unknown gave a strange bow and wave of *permission!* With that wave came back to my mind a picture in the Duchesse de Montpensier's bedroom at Seville: it was her brother-in-law, Don Francisco d'Assise, ex-King of Spain! Since then we have breakfasted and dined with him every day, and seen him constantly besides. This afternoon I sat out with him in the gardens, and we have had endless talk—the result of which is that I certainly do not believe a word of the stories against him, and think that, though not clever and rather eccentric, he is by no means an idiot, but a very kind-hearted, well-intentioned person. He is kept here waiting for a steamer to take him to Marseilles, as he cannot land at any of the Spanish ports. He calls himself the Comte de Balsaño, and is quite alone here, and evidently quite separated from Queen Isabella.[1]

The King says that of all the things which astonish him in England, that which astonishes him most is that the Anglo-Catholics (so called), who are free to do as they please, are seeking to have confession—'the bane of the Roman Catholic religion, which has brought misery and disunion into so many Spanish homes.'

Hôtel Siete Suelos, Granada, March 19.—We had a dreadful journey here—rail to Las Salinas and then the most extraordinary diligence journey, in a carriage drawn by eight mules, at midnight, over no road, but rocks, marshes, and along the edge of precipices—quite frightful. Why we were *not* overturned I cannot imagine. I could get no place except at the top, and held on with the greatest difficulty in the fearful lunges.

How lovely was the morning awakening! our rooms looking down long arcades of high arching elms, with fountains foaming in the openings of the woods, birds singing, and violets scenting the whole air. It is indeed alike the paradise of nature and art. Through the first day I never entered the Alhambra, but sat restfully satisfied

---

[1] Isabella, daughter of Cristina, became Queen in 1833, at the age of 3, with her mother as regent. Her marriage to Francisco d'Assise (who was 'notoriously incapable of having heirs') was arranged by Louis Philippe, who saw advantage in an alliance between a Bourbon Spain and a Bourbon France. On the same day, Isabella's younger sister married Louis Phillipe's son, the Duke of Montpensier. This is the Duchess referred to in these pages.—*Ed.*

with the absorbing loveliness of the surrounding gorges, and sketched the venerable Gate of Justice, glowing in gorgeous golden light. This morning we went early to the Moorish palace. It is beyond all imagination of beauty. As you cross the threshold you pass out of fact into fairyland. I sat six hours drawing the Court of Blessing without moving, and then we climbed the heights of S. Nicholas and overlooked the whole palace, with the grand snow peaks of Sierra Nevada rising behind.

Toledo, April 11.—We had twelve hours' diligence from Granada, saw Jaen Cathedral on the way, and joined the railroad at the little station of Mengibar. Next morning found us at Aranjuez, a sort of Spanish Hampton Court, rather quaint and pleasant, four-fifths of the place being taken up by the palace and its belongings, so beloved by Isabella (II), but since deserted. We went to bed for four hours, and spent the rest of the day in surveying half-furnished palaces, unkempt gardens, and dried-up fountains, yet pleasant from the winding Tagus, lilacs and Judas-trees, in full bloom, and birds singing. It was a nice primitive little inn, and the landlord sat on the wooden gallery in the evening and played the guitar, and all his men and maids sang round him in patriarchal family fashion.

Madrid, April 20.—We like Madrid better than we expected. It is a poor miniature of Paris, the Prado like the Champs Elysées, the Museo answering to the Louvre, though all on the smallest possible scale. It has been everything to us having our kind friends Don Juan and Doña Emilia de Riaño here, and we have seen a great deal of them. They have a beautiful house, full of books and pictures, and every day she has come to take us out, and has gone with us everywhere. . . . She gives a dreadful picture of the immorality of society in Madrid under the Italian King, the want of law, the hopelessness of redress; that everything is gained by influence in high places, nothing by right. A revolution is expected any day, and then the King must go. The aristocratic Madrilenians all speak of him as 'the little Italian wretch', though they pity his pretty amiable Queen. All seem to want to get rid of him, and, whatever is said by English newspapers, we have never seen any one in Spain who was not hankering after the Bourbons and the handsome young Prince of Asturias, who is sure to be king soon.

Segovia, April 28.—It was a dreadful journey here. The road was cut through the snow, but there was fifteen feet of it on either side the way on the top of the Guadarama. However, our ten mules dragged us safely along. Segovia is gloriously picturesque, and the hotel a very tolerable—pothouse.

Salamanca, May 5.—May-day we spent at La Granja, one of the many royal palaces, and one which would quite enchant you. It is a quaint old French château in lovely woods full of fountains and waterfalls, quite close under the snow mountains; and the high peaks, one glittering mass of snow, rise through the trees before the windows. The inhabitants were longing there to have the Bourbons back, and only spoke of the present King as 'the inoffensive Italian.' Even Cristina and Isabella will be cordially welcomed if they return with the young Alfonso.

On May 2nd we left Segovia and went for one night to the Escurial. Then we were a day at Avila, at an English inn kept by Mr. John Smith and his daughter—kindly, hearty people. Avila is a paradise for artists, and has remains in plenty of Ferdinand and Isabella, in whose intimate companionship one seems to live during one's whole tour in Spain.

I shall be *very* glad now to get home again. It is such an immense separation from every one one has ever seen or heard of, and such a long time to be so excessively uncomfortable as one must be at even the best places in Spain. Five o'clock tea, which we occasionally cook in a saucepan—without milk of course—is a prime luxury, and is to be indulged in to-day as it is Sunday.

Biarritz, May 12.—We are thankful to be safe here, having seen Zamora, Valladolid, and Burgos since we left Salamanca. The stations were in an excited state, the platforms crowded with people waiting for news or giving it, but we met with no difficulties. I cannot say with what a thrill of pleasure I crossed the Bidassoa and left the great discomforts of Spain behind. What a luxury this morning to see once more tea! butter!! cow's milk!!!

Dover Station, May 23.—On Monday George [Sheffield] drove me in one of the open carriages of the Embassy through the Bois de Boulogne to S. Cloud, and I thought the woods rather improved by the war injuries than otherwise, the bits cut down sprouting up so quickly in bright green acacia, and forming a pleasant contrast with the darker groves beyond. We strolled round the ruined château, and George showed the room whither he went to meet the council, and offer British interference just before war was declared, in vain, and now it is a heap of ruins—blackened walls, broken caryatides.[1] What a lovely view it is of Paris from the terrace: I had never seen it before. Pretty young French ladies were begging at all the park gates for the dishoused poor of the place, as they do at the Exhibition for the payment of the Prussian debt. George was as delightful as only he can be when he likes, and we were perfectly happy together. At 7 P.M. I went again to the Embassy. All the lower rooms were lighted and full of flowers, the corridors all pink geraniums with a mist of white spirea over them. The Duchesse de la Tremouille was there, as hideous as people of historic name usually are. Little fat Lord Lyons was most amiable, but his figure is like a pumpkin with an apple on the top. It is difficult to believe he is as clever as he is supposed to be. He is sometimes amusing, however. Of his diplomatic relations with the Pope he says, 'It is so difficult to deal diplomatically with the Holy Spirit.' He boasts that he arrived at the Embassy with all he wanted contained in a single portmanteau, and that if he were called upon to leave it for ever to-day, the same would suffice. He has collected and acquired—nothing! [2]

It is partly the relief I experienced after Spain and the animation of ever-changing society which make me look back upon the summer of 1872 as one of the happiest I have spent at Holmhurst. A constant succession of guests filled our little chambers, every one was pleased, and the weather was glorious. I was away also for several short but very pleasant glimpses of London, and began to feel how little the virulence of some of my family signified when there was still so much friendship and affection left to me.

---

[1] It has since been entirely destroyed.

[2] Richard Bickerton Pemell Lyons, second Baron and first Earl Lyons, 1817–1887, son of Admiral Lyons. In 1865 he was appointed ambassador at Constantinople, and two years later at Paris, where he remained for twenty years. He died immediately after his resignation. He got into trouble for fleeing from Paris in 1870 with the provisional government and so identifying himself with that authority; but events justified his action. He was preparing to become a Roman Catholic when he died.—*Ed.*

To MISS WRIGHT.

Holmhurst, June 25.—I have been made very ill-tempered all day because Murray, during my absence in Spain, has published a second edition of my Oxfordshire Handbook, *greatly* altered, without consulting me, and it seems to me utterly spoilt and vulgarised. He is obliged by his contract to give me £40, but I would a great deal rather have seen the book uninjured and received nothing.

In the beginning of October I was at Ford with Lady Waterford, meeting the Ellices, Lady Marion Alford, and Lady Herbert of Lea, who

FORD CASTLE, THE LIBRARY

had much to tell of La Palma, the *estatica* of Brindisi, who had the stigmata, and could tell wonderful truths to people about their past and future. Lady Herbert had been to America, Trinidad, Africa—in fact, everywhere, and in each country had, or thought she had, the most astonishing adventures—living with bandits in a cave, overturned on a precipice, &c. She had travelled in Spain and was brimful of its delights. She had armed herself with a Papal permit to enter all monasteries and convents. She had annexed the Bishop of Salamanca and driven in his coach to Alva, the scene of S. Teresa's later life. The nuns refused to let her come in, and the abbess declared it was unheard of; but when Lady Herbert produced the bishop and the Papal brief, she got in, and the nuns were so captivated that they not only showed her S. Teresa's dead body, but dressed her up in all S. Teresa's clothes, and set her in S. Teresa's arm-chair, and gave her her supper out of S. Teresa's porringer and platter.

The first evening she was at Ford Lady Herbert said :—

Did you never hear the story of '*La Jolie Jambe*'? Well, then, I will tell it you. Robert, my brother-in-law, told me. He knew the old lady it was all about in Paris, and had very often gone to sit with her.

It was an old lady who lived at *le pavillon dans le jardin*. The great house in the Faubourg was given up to the son, you know, and she lived in the *pavillon*. It was a very small house, only five or six rooms, and was magnificently furnished, for the old lady was very rich indeed, and had a great many jewels and other valuable things. She lived quite alone in the *pavillon* with her maid, but it was considered quite safe in that high-terraced garden, raised above everything else, and which could only be approached through the house.

However, one morning the old lady was found murdered, and all her jewels and valuables were gone. Of course suspicion fell upon the maid, for who else could it be? She was taken up and tried. The evidence was insufficient to convict her, and she was released, but every one believed her guilty. Of course she could get no other place, and she was so shunned and pointed at as a murderess that her life was a burden to her.

One day, eleven years after, the maid was walking down a street when she met a man, who, as she passed, looked suddenly at her and exclaimed, '*Oh, la jolie jambe!*' She immediately rushed up to a sergeant-de-ville and exclaimed, '*Arretez-moi cet homme.*' The man was confused and hesitated, but she continued in an agony, '*Arretez-le, je vous dis: je l'accuse, je l'accuse du meurtre de ma maîtresse.*' Meanwhile the man had made off, but he was pursued and taken.

The maid said at the trial, that, on the night of the murder, the windows of the *pavillon* had been open down to the ground; that they were so when she was going to bed; that as she was getting into bed she sat for a minute on its edge to admire her legs, looked at them, patted one of them complacently, and exclaimed, '*Oh, la jolie iambe!*'

The man then confessed that while he had been hidden in the bushes of the garden waiting to commit his crime, he had seen the maid and heard her, and that, when he met her in the street, the scene and the words rushed back upon his mind so suddenly, that, as if under an irresistible impulse, his lips framed the words '*Oh, la jolie jambe.*' The man was executed.

Lady Marion Alford[1] is a real *grande dame*. Some one, Miss Mary Boyle, I think, wrote a little book called the *Court of Queen Marion*, descriptive of her and her intimate circle. She was delightful with her reminiscences of Italy :—

Once when I was spending the summer in Italy I wanted models, and I was told by an old general, a friend of mine, that I had better advertise, send up to the priests in the mountains, and tell them to send down all the prettiest children in their villages

[1] Marianne Margaret Alford (1817–1888), daughter of the 2nd Marquis of Northampton and wife of Viscount Alford. Artist. Assisted in founding the Royal School of Needlework.—*Ed.*

to be looked at: the lady wanted models; those she chose she should pay, the others should each have sixpence and a cake. I was told I had better prepare for a good many—perhaps a hundred might come. When the day came, I never shall forget our old servant's face when he rushed in —'Miladi, Miladi, the lane is full of them.' There were seven hundred. It was very difficult to choose. We made them pass in at one door of the villa and out at the other. Those we selected we sent into the garden, and from these we chose again. Some were perfect monsters, for every mother thought her own child perfection. Those we selected to come first were a lovely family of three children with their mother. They were to come on a Wednesday. The day came, and they never appeared: the next, and still they did not come. Then we asked our old general about it, and he said, 'The fact is, I have kicked my carpenter downstairs this morning because he said you were sending for the children to suck their blood, and they all think so.' They none of them ever came.

We used to hear Teresa talking to our other maid, and they boasted of the number of times they had been beaten by their husbands. One day—it was during the French occupation, when the bread was doled out—Teresa took her tambourine with her when she went to get it, for they all loved flirting with the soldiers; and when her husband asked her what it was for, she said it was to bring back the bread in. But when she got inside the circle of soldiers, they had a merry *saltarello*. The husband was kept back outside the circle, and stood there furious. At first she laughed at him, but when he went away and came back again, she got really frightened. And when she came out of the circle he flogged her with a whip all the way back to the Trastevere, and she ran before him screaming.

About ghosts Lady Marion was very amusing :—

When I went to Belvoir with Lady Caroline Cust, they danced in the evening. I went upstairs early, for I was tired. As I was going to my room, Lady Jersey—it was wrong of her, I think—said, 'Oh, I see you are put into the ghost-room.' I said, 'I am quite happy; there are no real ghosts here, I think'—'Well,' said Lady Jersey, 'I can only say Miss Drummond slept there last night, and she received letters of importance this morning and left before breakfast.' Well, I went into my room, and lit the candles and made up the fire, but very soon I gave a great jump, for I heard the most dreadful noise close at my elbow—'Oh-o-oo-oo!' I thought of course that it was a practical joke, and began to examine every corner of the room, thinking some one must be hidden there; then I rang my bell. When my maid came in I said, 'Now don't be frightened, but there is some one hidden in this room somewhere, and you must help me to find him.' Very soon the noise came again. Then Lady Caroline came, and she heard it: then her maid came. The noise occurred about every five minutes. We examined everything and stood in each corner of the room. The noise then seemed close to each of us. At last Lady Caroline said, 'I can stand this no longer, and I must go,' and she and her maid went away and shut themselves into the next room. Then I said to my maid, 'If you are frightened you had better go,' but she protested that she would rather stay where she was; after what she had heard, anything would be better than facing the long lonely passages alone. However, just at that moment 'Oh-o-oo-oo!' went off again close to her ear, and with one spring she darted out of the room and ran off as hard as ever she could. I went courageously to bed and determined to brave it out. But the thing went to bed too, and went off at intervals on the pillow close to my face. And at last it grated on my nerves to such a degree that I could bear it no longer, and I dragged a mattress into Lady Caroline's room and slept there till dawn. The next morning I also received letters of importance and left before breakfast.

Before I left, I sent for the housekeeper, and said, 'You really should not put people into that room,' and told her what had happened. She was much distressed, and told me that there really was no other room in the house then, but confessed it had often happened so before. Some time after, I went over to Belvoir with some friends who wanted to see the castle, and the housekeeper then told me that the same thing had happened again in that room, which was now permanently shut up.

To MISS WRIGHT.

Crook Hall, Lancashire, Oct. 20, 1872.—My *Memorials*[1] are out! Ere this all will have it. I know there will be much abuse and many varieties of opinion, but I am conscious of having carried out the book as I believe to be best for others, not for myself, and in this consciousness can bear what is said. One thing I dread is, that people should think I am a better person than I am, on reading the book: for I suppose it is always the fact that a man's book is the best of him, his thought better than his life. But in any case, it is a relief to have it out (as Arthur and Mary Stanley, at the last moment, persuaded Mr. Murray to go to my publishers to try to stop the publication), yet it is also a wrench to part with the occupation and chief thought of two desolate years.

Dalton Hall, Oct. 28.—A second edition of the *Memorials* was called for before it had been out three days. I have had many letters about it—charming ones from Mrs. Arnold and the old Baroness de Bunsen. The olive-bearing dove has gone out with healing on his wings, and all the mists are cleared off and the long-standing feuds of the Hare family healed by the book. Still the Stanleys make no sign.

In November I went north again to stay for the first time at Bretton near Wakefield, a great house in the Black Country, built by the famous 'Madam Beaumont,' who followed the example of her ancestors, in making an enormous fortune by her skilful management of her lead-mines. It is recorded that when Mr. Pitt was dining with her, and all her magnificent plate was set out, she exclaimed, with pardonable pride, 'That is all the lead-mines,' when he replied, 'Oh, really, I thought it was silver,' and would talk on, to her great annoyance, and never allow her a moment to explain. I had made friends with her grandson, Wentworth Beaumont, at Ford, when he was there with his wife Lady Margaret, whom I have always regarded as the most thoroughly pleasant specimen in existence of a really fine lady. Her powers of conversation were boundless, her gift of repartee unequalled, and her memory most extraordinary. She was the daughter of Lady Clanricarde, celebrated for her conversational talents, and whom I remember Lady Carnarvon describing as 'the most agreeable woman in England, because she was not only massive, but lively.' Lady Margaret was like a little queen amongst her guests, entertaining with the simplicity of real kindness and thoughtfulness for others, whilst her

[1] *The Memorials of a Quiet Life* : see introduction to *The Years With Mother.—Ed.*

manner was equally agreeable to all, and she never usurped attention, but rather exerted herself to draw others out and to show the best side of them. She could be alarming as an enemy, but she was a most faithful friend, and would exert herself to take definite trouble for her friends, never deserting them unless they were proved to be really unworthy. She was not exactly pretty, but her animation was more charming than mere beauty. Dress with her was not a mere adjunct, but was made as much a thing of poetic beauty as a landscape or a flower. She was devoted to her husband, but theoretically she disapproved of love in a general way. Still she was only worldly in principle and not in practice, and she was ever a devoted mother to her children, seeking their real happiness rather than their advancement before the world. I have often been at Bretton since my first visit there, and always enjoyed it from the constant animation which the hostess shed around her; the excessive comfort of the house and of the thoroughly well-regulated household; the plenty of time for work and writing, and yet the constant variety afforded by the guests coming and going.

To MISS LEYCESTER.

Bretton Park, Nov. 21, 1872.—To-day we went to luncheon at Walton, an extraordinary house in the middle of a lake, which belonged to the Roman Catholic Mr. Waterton, the great ornithologist.[1] It is approached by a long drawbridge and is most curious. A Mr. Hailstone lives there now, a strange man, who spends his large fortune on antiquities, and has a wife who writes on lace, and wonderful collections.[2] Their son has never eaten anything but buttered toast, cheese, and port-wine (has never tasted meat, vegetables, or fruit), but is eight years old and very flourishing.

Lord and Lady Salisbury[3] are here. The latter can only be described by the word 'jocund,' except when she does not wish to make acquaintance or desires to snub people, when she becomes hopelessly impenetrable. There is a party of fourteen, all new to me, but I get on very well. They look upon me as an aboriginal from another hemisphere, and indeed they are that to me; but it is too new a set to feel the least shy in. There is great satisfaction in being only a *background* figure, and Lady Margaret is quite charming, the house handsome, and the park pretty. We all went to church this morning in a sort of family drawing-room in the grounds, the vulgar herd screened off by red curtains, only the clergyman in his pulpit visible above the screen.

I made a very interesting excursion with Lady Margaret and some of her guests to Haworth, the wild weird home of the Brontës on the Yorkshire fells, where the steep street with the stones placed edgeways, up

[1] Charles Waterton (1782–1865). Travelled especially in British Guiana (1804–1812) and the West Indies (1824). His most famous work is his *Wanderings* (1825).—*Ed.*

[2] Edward Hailstone (1818–1890), Bradford solicitor, whose remarkable collection of works on Yorkshire is now at the Chapter at York. He published his *Portraits of Yorkshire Worthies* in 1869. —*Ed.*

[3] The 3rd Marquis and Prime Minister. See note on p. 17.

LOUISA, MARCHIONESS OF WATERFORD

which the horses scramble like cats, leads to the wind-stricken churchyard, with its vast pavement of tombstones set close together. On one side of this is the dismal grey stone house where the three unhappy sisters lived, worked, and suffered, with the window at the side through which Patrick Brontë used to climb at night. Not a tree is to be seen in the neighbourhood except the blackened lilac before the Rectory door. Nature is her dreariest self, and offers no ameliorations. The family were buried beneath their pew in the church,[1] so that Charlotte, the last survivor, sat in church over the graves of her brothers and sisters. The people seemed half savage, most of all the Rector, who violently hurled Lady Margaret and Lady Catherine Weyland from his door when they asked to see the house, being bored, I suppose, by the pertinacity of visitors.

I went for two days from Bretton to Lord Houghton at Fryston, which has since been burnt, but which was so filled with books of every kind that the whole house was a library, each bookcase being filled with a different subject—the French Revolution, Demonology and Witchcraft, &c., &c.[2] Lady Houghton was living then, a most gentle, kind woman, a sister of Lord Crewe. Talking of the Baroness Burdett Coutts,[3] Lord Houghton said, 'Miss Coutts likes me because I never proposed to her. Almost all the young men of good family did: those who did their duty by their family *always* did. Mrs. Browne (Miss Coutts' companion) used to see it coming, and took herself out of the way for ten minutes, but she only went into the next room and left the door open, and then the proposal took place, and immediately it was done Miss Coutts coughed, and Mrs. Browne came in again.'

JOURNAL.

Dec. 13.—I arrived at Hatfield in the dark. A number of carriages from the house met the guests at the station. As I emerged from it, a little groom touched his hat and said, 'Please, sir, are you the Lord Chancellor?' I thought I must have grown in dignity of aspect. The Lord Chancellor was expected, and came later in the evening.

I found Lord and Lady Salisbury[4] in the library, lined with Burleigh books and

---

[1] This church, the most interesting memorial of the Brontë life at Haworth, was wantonly destroyed in 1880–81.

[2] Richard Monckton Milnes, 1st Baron Houghton, 1809–1885; friend of Tennyson and Hallam, parliamentary reformer, advocate of the copyright act, president of the London Library, poet, and writer on political and social questions. Also a collector of pornography. See James Pope-Hennesey's biography.—*Ed.*

[3] Angela Georgina, Baroness Burdett-Coutts, 1814–1906, daughter of Sir Francis Burdett, the reformer, and grand-daughter (through her mother) of Thomas Coutts, the banker, whose property she inherited from the Duchess of St. Albans, his second wife. She was the richest heiress in all England, took an active part in the banking business, was intimate with all the celebrities (English and foreign) of her time, and was a noted philanthropist. Married 1861, William Ashmead Bartlett. She is buried in Westminster Abbey.—*Ed.*

[4] Robert Arthur Talbot Gascoigne-Cecil (1830–1903), 3rd Marquess, lineal descendant of Robert Cecil, 1st Earl. Three times Prime Minister. Strong anti-Liberal, who regarded democracy as inimical to individual freedom. An imperialist in foreign policy. Was born and died at Hatfield.

B

MSS. Mr. Richmond[1] the artist was with them. He has the most charming voice, which, quite independently of his conversation, would make him agreeable. He talked of the enormous prices obtained for statues and pictures at the present time, while Michelangelo only got £90 and a block of marble for the great David at Florence, and Titian the same for his Assumption at Venice. He spoke of the amount of chicanery which existed amongst artists even then—how the monks, and the nuns too, would supply them with good ultra-marine for their frescoes, and how they would sell the ultramarine and use smalt. He described how Gainsborough never could sell anything but portraits: people came to him for those, but would not buy his other pictures, and his house was full of them when he died. Gainsborough gave two pictures to the carrier

HATFIELD

who brought his other pictures from Clifton to London: the carrier would take no fare, so he painted his wagon and horses and another picture and gave them to him: these two pictures have been sold lately for £18,000.

Dec. 14.—Lady Salisbury showed us the house. In the drawing-room, over the chimney-piece, is a huge statue of James I of bronze. It is not fixed, but supported by its own weight. A ball was once given in that room. In the midst of the dancing some one observed that the bronze statue was slowly nodding its head, and gave the alarm. The stampede was frightful. All the guests fled down the long gallery.

In the same room is a glorious portrait of Lord Salisbury's grandmother by Reynolds. It was this Lady Salisbury who was burnt to death in her old age. She came in from riding, and used to make her maid change her habit and dress her for dinner at

[1] George Richmond, portrait painter, 1809–1896; famous for his portraits of William Wilberforce, Hallam, Macaulay, Ruskin, Earl Granville, Sir George Scott, Keble, Faraday, etc. A man of remarkable social gifts and brilliant conversation.—*Ed.*

once, as less fatiguing. Then she rested for two or three hours with lighted candles near her, and read or nodded in her chair. One evening, from the opposite wing of the house, the late Lord Salisbury saw the windows of the rooms near hers blazing with light, and gave the alarm, but before anybody could reach his mother's rooms they were entirely burnt—so entirely, that it would have been impossible to identify her ashes for burial but for a ruby which the present Lady Salisbury wears in a ring. A little heap of diamonds was found in one place, but that proved nothing, as all her jewels were burned with her, but the ruby her maid identified as having put on her finger when she dressed her, and the ashes of that particular spot were all gathered up and buried in a small urn. Her two favourite dogs were burnt with her, and they are probably buried with her.

In *Oliver Twist*, Bill Sykes is described as having seen the fire at Hatfield as he was escaping from London.

In Lady Salisbury's own room is a picture of Miss Pine, Lord Salisbury's other grandmother, by Sir Joshua; also the Earl and Countess of Westmoreland and their child, by Vandyke; also a curious picture of a lady.

'She looks dull but good,' said Miss Palmer.

'She looks clever but bad,' said I.

'She *was* desperately wicked,' said Lady Salisbury, 'and therefore it is quite unnecessary to say that she was very religious. She endowed almshouses—"Lady Anne's Almshouses,"—they still exist, and she sent her son to Westminster with especial orders that he should be severely flogged, when he was seventeen, and so soured his temper for life and sent him to the bad entirely; and none but "a thoroughly highly-principled woman" could do such a villainous action as that. The son lived afterwards at Nuixwold, and led the most abominably wicked life there, and died a death as horrible as his life. He sold everything he could lay hands on, jewels and everything, all the old family plate except one very ugly old flat candlestick and six old sconces, which were painted over mahogany colour, and so were not known to be silver. His is the phantom coach which arrives and drives up the staircase and then disappears. Lord Salisbury heard it the other night when he was in his dressing-room, and dressed again, thinking it was visitors, and went down, but it was no one.'

Dec. 15.—My cough prevented my going out, but we had Sunday-afternoon service in the chapel, with beautiful singing. In the evening Lady Salisbury asked me to tell stories to all the party, and it was sufficiently alarming when I saw the Lord Chancellor in the first row, with the Attorney-General on one side of him and Lord Cairns on the other. The Attorney-General afterwards told us—

'There is at Clifton a Mr. Harrison, who is the second medical authority there, a man of undoubted probity and reputation. He told me this.

'At Clifton lived a Mrs. Fry with her brother-in-law and his two daughters, Elizabeth and Hephzibah. These were persons who, like many Bristol people, had large property in the West Indies. The elder daughter, Elizabeth, had been born in the West Indies, and when she fell into bad health, her father took the opportunity of taking her back to benefit by her native air, when he went to look after his West Indian property, leaving his younger daughter, Hephzibah, with Mrs. Fry.

'They had not been gone long when Hephzibah took a chill, and in a very few days she died. Mr. Harrison attended her. Some days after he called as a friend upon Mrs. Fry, when she said, "I want to tell you something which has happened to me: I have seen Elizabeth."—"Impossible," said Mr. Harrison. "No," she said, "it was so. I was sitting reading the Bible when I fell into a state which was neither sleeping nor waking, and in that state—I was not asleep—I saw Elizabeth standing by me. I spoke to her, and, forgetting what had happened in my surprise, I told her to call her sister. But she said to me that she had seen her sister already, and that she was in a box, and had a great deal of sewing about her chest. She especially used the word 'sewing': then she vanished away, and the place in the Bible where I had left off was changed: some one had turned it over." Mr. Harrison noted all this.

'Some time after came a letter from the father to Mrs. Fry, written before he had heard of Hephzibah's death. After speaking of other matters he said, "I must now tell you of a very curious circumstance which has occurred, and which is much on my mind. The other day Elizabeth, who had been much better, and who is now nearly well, surprised us by falling into a stupor, and when she came to herself she would insist upon it that she had been to Clifton, and that she had seen you and Hephzibah, and that Hephzibah was in a long box, with a great deal of sewing upon her chest: and she says so still." The dates were precisely the same.

'Hephzibah's death was so sudden that there was a post-mortem examination, though it was not considered necessary to distress Mrs. Fry by telling her of it. On this occasion Mr. Harrison was unable to be present. He went afterwards to the student of the hospital who was there, and who remembered all about it, and he said—what Mr. Harrison had not previously known—that after the examination the body was sewn up, with a great deal of sewing upon the chest.'

Dec. 16.—The Archbishop of Canterbury and Mrs. Tait arrived before afternoon-tea, at which there was much lively conversation. Apropos of Radicalism and the conversation of Bishops, Lord Salisbury mentioned Sydney Smith's saying that he would 'rather fall a victim to a democratic mob than be sweetly and blandly absorbed by a bishop.'

Dec. 17.—Mr. Richmond talked of great writer and talkers, how their art was not the creation of something new, but the telling of old things well in a new dress—the bringing up the thoughts long bedridden in the chambers of their own brain.

He talked of Carlyle—of how his peculiarities began in affectation, but that now he was simply lost in the mazes of his own vocabulary. One night, he said, he met a man at Albert Gate at 12 P.M., who asked for a light for his cigar. He did not see who it was till, as he was turning away, he recognised Carlyle, who gave a laugh which could be heard all down Piccadilly as he exclaimed, 'I thought it was just any son of Adam, and I find a friend.' It was soon after the Pope's return to Rome, and Mr. Richmond spoke of him. 'The poor old Pope,' said Carlyle, 'the po-o-r old Pope! He has a big mouth! I do not like your button-holes of mouths, like the Greek statues you are all so fond of.'

Dec. 20.—The last collection of guests have included the Duke of Wellington, the Cowleys, Lord and Lady Stanhope, and M. and Madame de Lavalette—all full of interest. Certainly Hatfield is magnificent and grandly kept up.

Dec. 27, East Sheen.—Mrs. Stuart Wortley came to luncheon. She remarked how that which was most striking in Italy was not the effect of light, but of shadow. Into the shadows of England you could not penetrate, but the shadows of Italy were transparent; the more you looked into their cavernous depths, the more you saw there, discovering marvels of beauty which existed there in repose.

She told us that the secret of 'the Haunted House in Berkeley Square' is that it belonged to a Mr. Du Pré of Wilton Park. He shut up his lunatic brother there in a cage in one of the attics, and the poor captive was so violent that he could only be fed through a hole. His groans and cries could be distinctly heard in the neighbouring houses. The house is now to be let for £100 the first year, £200 the second, £300 the third, but if the tenant leaves within that time, he is to forfeit £1,000. The house will be furnished in any style or taste the tenant chooses.

My book, *Wanderings in Spain*, came out in the autumn of 1872, and met with a more enthusiastic reception from the public than anything I have ever written. Three editions were called for in six weeks, but there the sale ended.[1] The reviews were rapturously laudatory, but I felt at the time how little reliance was to be placed upon their judgment, though for the moment it was agreeable. The unusual success which was attending my *Walks in Rome*, and the many notes which I already possessed for a similar work in the neighbourhood, made me now devote my time to *Days near Rome*, and in January I left England to make Rome a centre from whence to revive my recollection of the towns I had already visited in the Campagna and its surrounding mountains, and to examine and sketch those I had not yet seen. Altogether, *Days near Rome* is the one of my books in the preparation of which I had the greatest enjoyment, and from which I have had least disappointment since its publication.[2] I was, however, terribly ill soon after my arrival at Rome and, nearly died there.

To Miss Leycester.

Paris, Jan. 19, 1873.—I have felt most dolorous on the journey, and often repented having decided to come abroad: I so dread seeing Rome again. Still, as last year I added £252 to my income by small writings exclusive of the *Memorials*, I must look upon it as a profession, and of course as *such* it is very pleasant.

81 *Via della Croce, Rome, Jan.* 27.—I left Florence on a still, mizzly morning. How familiar all the dear places seemed on the way, and yet how changed the feeling with which one saw them—Thrasymene, Perugia, Assisi, Spoleto—all so much to *us*, so woven into *our* lives, and I was thankful for the twilight obscurity before the steep of Fidenae rose beside us, and then the towers of the beloved city crested the hill, the hill down which my darling drove so often in her little carriage to the Ponte Salario and the Ponte Nomentano, drinking in the full beauty of the historic loveliness. On Saturday I removed to these rooms in the house of Voight, a German artist, much beloved by the Bunsens, and indeed married to his old still-existing Signora from their house. I think that the rooms will answer sufficiently, though, as the Voights have never let rooms before, there is a terrible amount of talking over everything I need.

[1] This was so for a long time. Then in about ten years several more editions were called for in rapid succession. One can never anticipate how it will be with books.

[2] 1890.—This was so for many years: then the sale of *Days near Rome* suddenly and unaccountably stopped.

The whole family, of three generations, were called into council the first time I desired to have an egg for breakfast, and then it came in raw, and yesterday the scene was repeated. However, '*pazienza*.'

Feb. 1.—I have been very ill for the last three days with Roman fever, which has brought on a violent return of my cough. Perhaps the chill of these rooms has something to do with it. I feel much the absence of the sympathising help I have had here in illness before, especially of Lea's good food and attentions. . . . I am especially sorry to be shut up at this time, as there are so many pleasant people in Rome, not least the really charming Prince Arthur,[1] to whom I was presented the other day, and whom I think most engaging, and hope—if I can only get better—to see more of next week, when I have been asked, and have promised, to go with him to several sights.

The *old* interest of Rome has wonderfully passed away, not only to me, but I think also to many others. The absence of pope, cardinals, and monks; the shutting up of the convents; the loss of the ceremonies; the misery caused by the terrible taxes and conscription; the voluntary exile of the Borgheses and many other noble families; the total destruction of the glorious Villa Negroni and so much else of interest and beauty; the ugly new streets in imitation of Paris and New York, all grate against one's former Roman associations. And to set against this there is so very little—a gayer Pincio, a live wolf on the Capitol, a mere scrap of excavation in the Forum, and all is said.

Feb. 16.—Last week I felt as if life was really passing away—such was my utter exhaustion and suffering. . . . After a most kind touching note about the *Memorials*, I have had an hour's visit from Lord Chichester, and he is coming again often. I constantly see Lady Ashburton, who rains her benefits upon me. I am doing all I can to be able to go out with the Prince soon, having put him off again and again with a greater pang each time, but I wish I could feel a little less dreadfully weak.

It was on the 18th of February that I was first able to have one of my lectures for Prince Arthur. It was arranged for the Palace of the Cæsars. I had asked him if Lady Ashburton[2] and her daughter might go with us, and to this he had consented. Lady Ashburton insisted upon coming to fetch me, but, knowing her unpunctual habits, I was most unwilling she should do so. Nothing else would serve her, however, and she promised again and again to be punctual. However, the time came and she did not arrive. Having secured no other carriage I waited minute after minute in an agony, and not till after the time at which we ought to have been at the Palatine did Lady Ashburton appear on the Pincio. When we reached the Palatine, the Prince and all his suite were still in the road, unable to enter without my order. 'I have been waiting ten minutes,' he said, 'and they wouldn't let me in.' It was a terrible beginning. However, his lively pleasure and active interest in all that was to be seen soon

---

[1] Duke of Connaught, then aged 23—*Ed.*

[2] Widow of the second Baron Ashburton (William Bingham Baring), whose second wife she was. —*Ed.*

made me at home with him. If anything especial attracted his notice, he generally asked, 'Do you think my brother and sister (the Prince and Princess of Wales)[1] saw this?'

A few days after, I had another lecture for the Prince on the Cœlian. This time I refused altogether to go with Lady Ashburton, and when I arrived ten minutes before the time at the steps of S. Gregorio, found that

VIEW FROM THE TEMPIETTO, ROME

she had already been there half an hour, walking up and down in the dew! This time the Prince was even pleasanter than before. Generally he begged that his name might not be mentioned, but this was necessary to get into the garden of SS. Giovanni e Paolo, which at that time was always closed. While we were in the church, a monk came up to me and said that the General of the Passionists was coming to pay his respects to the Prince.

Prince Edward and Princess Alexandra.—*Ed.*

I said, 'Sir, the General of the Passionists is coming to have the honour of being presented to you.' The Prince began to say, 'No, no, no,' but at that moment the white robes of the abbot appeared in the doorway, followed by a whole train of monks. The Prince immediately did the right thing, receiving them and speaking to them on the steps of the tribune, and I have often thought what a picture the scene would have made. In the shadow of royalty, Lady Ashburton was the first woman allowed to visit the Passionist garden, but to the Prince's great annoyance, three Americans (probably not knowing who it was) got in too, by pretending to belong to our party. They followed us afterwards to the Villa Mattei. The Prince then asked Lady Ashburton to sit down near the entrance, and we raced up and down the walks, with the Americans cantering after us, and eventually slipped under one of the high box hedges, returned by the concealed way, snapped up Lady Ashburton, and escaped from the Villa, the gates of which were locked behind us; and how those Americans got out I have never known.

At one of my lectures at the Palace of the Cæsars a curious thing happened. We were about forty in number, and I had taken my company all over the palace, explaining and telling the story of the different rooms as we went. Finally, as was my habit, I assembled them on the slope towards the Forum for a sort of recapitulation and final discourse on all we had seen. I had observed a stranger who had attached himself to our party looking more and more angry every minute, but the 'why' I could not understand. When I had concluded, the stranger stepped forward, and in a very loud voice addressed the whole party—'Gentlemen and ladies, it is not my habit to push myself forward, and it is excessively painful to me to do it on the present occasion; but there are some things which no gentleman ought to pass unnoticed. All that this *person* has been telling you about the Palace of the Cæsars, he has had the effrontery to relate to you as if it were his own. You will be astounded, gentlemen and ladies, to hear that it is taken, word for word—word for *word*, without the slightest acknowledgment, from Mr. Hare's *Walks in Rome*!'

I only said, 'Oh, I am *so* much obliged to you. I did not know there was anybody in the world who would defend my interests so kindly. I am Augustus Hare.'

To MISS LEYCESTER.

Il Tempietto, Rome, March 9, 1873.—I think a Republic here will soon follow that of Spain.[1] Victor Emmanuel is so hated, and the profligacy of the Court, and the cruel

[1] Victor Emmanuel II died in 1878, but was succeeded by his son Humbert. Contrary to what Hare says, Victor Emmanuel was by no means unpopular and he was very devoted to his duties as a constitutional monarch. His weakness for women and his several mistresses—apart from a general dislike of the Sardinian government—may have prejudiced Hare against him.—*Ed.*

taxes are hastening the end. People already shout '*Viva la Republica*' and bawl Garibaldian hymns all night. I wonder whether you would think the freedom of religious worship a compensation for the moral changes here—the shops always open on Sundays, which were formerly so strictly closed, the churches deserted, stalls for infidel books in the streets, and an ostentatious immorality which was formerly unknown. In the Carnival, in insulting reference to the Pope, a pasteboard dome of St. Peter's was made to travel up and down the Corso in a car, with a parrot imprisoned in a cage on the top, '*pappagallo*' being Italian for a parrot, and 'Papa Gallo' a nickname given to Pio Nono during the French occupation. The parrot struggled and fluttered through the first day, but it died of sea-sickness in the evening, and afterwards it appeared stuffed. The Pope has felt bitterly the confiscation of the convents and other religious institutions which the Sardinian Government, when it first entered Rome, promised so strictly to respect; and *triduos* have been held at St. Peter's and at S. Ignazio to implore that the spoliation may be averted, or that a judgment may follow the spoiler. In St. Peter's twenty thousand persons were collected on Sunday afternoon to join with one voice in this supplication. Pius IX took no part in the manifestation: on Sunday afternoon he is quietly occupied as a bishop in the Sala Regia, in explaining the Epistle and Gospel for the day, and praying with the people of the different Roman parishes, who come to him in turn, attended by their priests. Amongst the nuns who have suffered most are the Poor Clares of S. Lorenzo Panisperna, who, when they were driven out of the greater part of their convent in February 1872, were allowed to retain and fit up a few small rooms, from which they are now forcibly ejected altogether. The nuns of S. Antonio on the Esquiline, who plaited all the palms used in the processions at St. Peter's, were driven out more than a year ago, though their convent has never hitherto been used for anything else. The nuns of S. Giacomo alla Lungara are reduced to absolute beggary. The Carmelites of S. Maria Vittoria have been driven out, and their Superior died of a broken heart on the day of their ejection. The nuns of S. Teresa, when driven out of their convent, were permitted to take refuge in that of Regina Cœli, where they were allowed to fit up a corridor with canvas partitions: now they are driven out again, in spite of solemn promises, and without any compensation. If the dowries of all these ladies, given to them by their parents exactly as marriage portions are given, were restored, comparatively little could be said, but their fortunes are all confiscated by the Government.

The heads of the clerical schools have inquired from Pius IX whether their pupils were to salute Queen Margaret when she passed them. 'Certainly,' answered the Pope; 'is she not a member of the royal house of Savoy?'

There is a stall for Bibles now opposite S. Carlo. A great dog manages it, such a fine beast. He cannot be expected to do all the business, so he just receives the customers, and, when any one wants a Bible, he puts his feet up and barks.

March 17.—Yesterday I drove with Lady Ashburton to Castel Fusano; Miss Wright, Miss Howard, and Walter Jekyll going in another carriage, and we picnicked under the grand old pine-trees, and had a delicious day, wandering through the labyrinths of sweet daphne and rosemary, and over carpets of cyclamen in fullest bloom.

Albano, April 6.—Yesterday, after dining with Mrs. Lockwood, I went to meet Princess Alice[1] at the S. Arpinos'. They have a beautiful suite of rooms in the Bona-

---

[1] Princess Alice, 3rd child of Queen Victoria, born 1843; married Prince Louis of Hesse (afterwards Grand Duke); died 1878.

parte Palace, the same in which 'Madame Mère' died. Many ambassadors and Roman princes and princesses were there, but only five English. I was presented at once to Prince Louis, who is very German and speaks very broken English, but is much better-looking than his photographs. He talked for a long time about Rome and my book. Later in the evening I was presented to the Princess. She said at once, 'Oh, I know your face, I have seen you before,' and with royal memory recollected all about coming to see my Mother, &c. She is grown much fatter and prettier, and was very simply dressed in high slate-coloured silk with a pearl necklace. We all stayed till she left at 11 P.M., and then made an avenue down the recep.ion rooms, through which she passed, saying a little separate word to each lady.

On Wednesday I met Miss Wright and Miss Howard at Albano, and we had an interesting afternoon amongst the huge Cyclopean remains of Alatri, driving on in the beautiful gloaming to Ferentino, where we slept at a primitive but clean Italian tavern. The next day we reached Segni, a Pelasgic city on the very highest peak of the Volscian mountains. On Friday I joined Lady Howard de Walden and her two daughters, and with them revisited the glorious old Papal citadel of Anagni, where Boniface VIII was imprisoned, and where there are many relics of him.

Subiaco, April 16.—We spent Good Friday on the seashore at Porto d'Anzio, a delightful place, overgrown with gorgeous pink mesembryanthemum, and with huge remains of Nero's palace projecting far into the sea. For Easter we were at Velletri, and on Monday drove through the blooming country to Cori, where, after seeing the beautiful temple, we rode along the edge of stupendous precipices to Norba, and the man-deserted flower-possessed fairy-like town of Ninfa, returning by the light of the stars. Tuesday we went to Palestrina, an extraordinary place with a perfectly savage population; and Wednesday we came hither through Olevano, which is a paradise of beauty. This place seems quite as grandly beautiful as we thought it fifteen years ago.

A few days later I left Rome again with Mr. and Mrs. Arbuthnot Feilden and the Misses Crawford (daughters of Mrs. Terry, and sisters of Marion Crawford) for a tour in the Ciminian Hills, which always come back to me as a dream of transcendent loveliness. We left the railway at Civita Castellana, an unspeakably beautiful place, which I drew in the early dewy morning, sitting on the edge of its tremendous rocky gorge, above which Soracte, steeped in violet shadows, rises out of the tender green of the plain. On May-day we ascended Soracte, queen of lovely mountains, mounting gradually from the rich lower slopes into the excelsior of olives, and thence to steeps of bare grey rock, crowned—in the most sublime position—by the ruined monastery of S. Silvestro. It is the most exquisite drive from Civita Castellana, by Nepi, with a great machicolated castle overhanging a foaming waterfall, and Sutri—'the key of Etruria'—with its solemn Roman amphitheatre surrounded by some of the grandest ilexes in the world, to Ronciglione. Hence we visited Caprarola, and I will insert a little extract from *Days near Rome* about this expedition, it reminds me of so wondrously beautiful and delightful a day.

From the little deep-blue lake of Vico it is a long ascent. . . . The road is generally a dusty hollow in the tufa, which, as we pass, is fringed with broom in full flower, and all the little children we meet have made themselves wreaths and gathered long branches of it, and wave them like golden sceptres. Along the brown ridges of thymy tufa by the wayside, flocks of goats are scrambling, chiefly white, but a few black and dun-coloured creatures are mingled with them, mothers with their little dancing elf-like kids, and old bearded patriarchs who love to clamber to the very end of the most inaccessible places, and to stand there embossed against the clear sky, in triumphant quietude. The handsome shepherd dressed in white linen lets them have their own way, and the great rough white dogs only keep a lazy eye upon them as they themselves lie panting and luxuriating in the sunshine. Deep down below us, it seems as if all Italy

S. ORESTE, FROM SORACTE

were opening out, as the mists roll stealthily away, and range after range of delicate mountain distance is discovered. . . . As we emerge from our rocky way, the wonderful position of the place [Caprarola] bursts upon us at once. The grand tremendous palace stands backed by chestnut woods, which fade into rocky hills, and it looks down from a high-terraced platform upon the little golden-roofed town beneath, and then out upon the whole glorious rainbow-tinted view, in which, as everywhere we have been, lion-like Soracte, couching over the plain, is the most conspicuous feature. The buildings are so vast in themselves, and every line so noble, every architectural idea so stupendous, that one is carried back almost with awe to the recollections of the great-souled Farnese who originated the design, and the grand architect who carried it out. S. Carlo Borromeo, the great patron of idle almsgiving, came hither to see it when it was completed, and complained that so much money had not been given to the poor instead. 'I have let them have it all little by little,' said Alessandro Farnese, 'but I have made them earn it by the sweat of their brows.' . . . How we pity the poor

King and Queen of Naples, the actual possessors, but who can never come here now.
The whole place is like a dream which you wish may never end, and as one gazes
through the stony crowd across the green glades to the rosy-hued mountains, one
dreads the return to a world where Fauns and Dryads are still supposed to be mythical,
and which has never known Caprarola.

We spent several days at Viterbo—'the city of beautiful fountains'—
which has never been half appreciated by travellers, and made many
curious excursions into Etruria, which are all described in my book; and
then proceeded to Orvieto—all-glorious Orvieto. Once more I will
quote *Days near Rome*.

On turning the crest of the hills which shelter Bolsena, one looks down into a
wide valley filled with the richest vegetation—peach-trees and almonds and figs, with
vines leaping from tree to tree and chaining them together, and beneath, an unequalled
luxuriance of corn and peas and melons, every tiniest space occupied. Mountains of the
most graceful forms girdle in this paradise, and, from the height whence we first gaze
upon it, endless distances are seen, blue and roseate and snowy, melting into infinity
of space; while, from the valley itself, rises, island-like, a mass of orange-coloured
rock, crowned with old walls and houses and churches, from the centre of which is
uplifted a vast cathedral, with delicate spray-like pinnacles, and a golden and jewelled
front—and this is Orvieto. . . .

Unlike Viterbo, gaiety and brightness seem to have deserted its narrow streets of
dark houses, interspersed with huge tall square towers of the Middle Ages, and themselves, in the less frequented parts, built of rich brown stone, with sculptured cornices
to their massive doors and windows, and resting on huge buttresses. From one of the
narrowest and darkest of these streets we come suddenly upon the cathedral, a blaze
of light and colour, the most aërial gothic structure in the world, every line a line of
beauty. There is something in the feeling that no artists worked at this glorious temple
but the greatest architects, the greatest sculptors of their time, that no material was used
but that which was most precious, most costly, and which would produce the most
glorious effect, which carries one far away from all comparisons with other earthly
buildings—to the description in the Revelation of the New Jerusalem. The very
platform on which the cathedral stands is of purple Apennine marble; the loveliest
jaspers and *pietre dure* are worked into its pinnacles and buttresses; the main foundation
of its pictured front is gold. A hundred and fifty-two sculptors, of whom Arnolfo
and Giovanni da Pisa are the greatest names handed down to us, worked upon the
ornamentation near the base: sixty-eight painters and ninety workers in mosaic gave
life to the glorious pictures of its upper stories. . . .

No passing traveller, no stayer for one night, can realise Orvieto. Hours must be
passed on those old stone benches, hours in reading the wondrous lessons of art, of
truth, of beauty and of holiness which this temple of temples can unfold. For Orvieto
is not merely a vast sculpture-gallery and a noble building, but its every stone has a
story to tell or a mystery to explain.

My companions returned to Rome from Orvieto and I went on to
Florence, where I found two old friends of my childhood—Ann-Emilia

and Kate Malcolm, the latter of whom has always been one of the most agreeable and charming women I have ever known.[1] I remember her telling me, on this occasion, of a friend of hers who was one day sitting at the end of her terrace at a retired watering-place, and heard a bride and bridegroom talking together beneath. 'My dear,' said the bridegroom, 'I think it would not be unpleasant if a friend were to turn up this evening.' —'My dear,' retorted the bride, 'I should be thankful to see even *an enemy.*' With the Malcolms I saw much of Sir James Lacaita. He was very full of convents and their abuses. He told me that he had personally

PIAZZA MAGGIORE, BERGAMO

known a nun who was forced into a convent to prevent her from marrying the man she loved; but he made a silken ladder, and, by bribing the gardener, got it fixed to her window. The nun escaped, but was in such a hurry to descend, that she slid down the cords, cut open both her hands, and bore the marks all her life. Her lover was rich, had relays of horses, and they escaped to Sicily, were married at once, and had eleven children.[2]

---

[1] Daughters of Sir John Malcolm.—*Ed.*

[2] Sir James Lacaita, 1813–95, was born and educated in Italy. Through employment in the British legation at Naples he came into contact with distinguished British travellers, including Mr. Gladstone, his disclosures to whom, concerning the Bourbon régime, obliged him to leave Italy. From 1853 till 1856 he was Professor of Italian in London and from 1857 until his return to Italy was secretary to Lansdown and to Gladstone's mission to the Ionian Islands. After the expulsion of the Bourbons he returned to Italy, though he spent much time each year in England.—*Ed.*

From Florence I went to Cremona and Bergamo, lingering at them and seeing them thoroughly in glorious weather, which made one observe that, though the Southern Italian skies are the opal ones, the Northern are the blue.

I spent June (1873) in London. At luncheon at Lady Marion Alford's I met Mr. Carlyle, who was full of the *Memorials*. He said, 'I do not often cry and am not much given to weeping, but your book is most profoundly touching.' He talked of Lady Ashburton[1]—'Ah! yes, Lady Ashburton is just a bonnie Highland lassie, a free-spoken and open-hearted creature as ever was; and Hattie Hosmer, she is a fanciful kind of a being, who does not know yet that art is dead.' Finally he went off into one of his characteristic speeches. 'That which the warld torments me in most is the awful confusion of noise. It is the devil's own infernal din all the blessed day long, confounding God's warks and His creatures—a truly awfu' hell-like combination, and the warst of a' is a railway whistle, like the screech of ten thousand cats, and ivery car of them all as big as a cathédral.'

JOURNAL.

July, 3.—The most extraordinary thing the Shah has done has been offering to buy Lady Margaret Beaumont (to carry off to Persia) for £500,000!

July 26.—I reached Chevening about 6 P.M. Between the house and the lake is the loveliest of flower-gardens, a wilderness of old-fashioned flowers, most perfectly charming. Here Lady Stanhope was sitting out with Lord and Lady Carnarvon and Lord and Lady Mahon. Lord Carnarvon is agreeable and his wife most lovely and piquant. Lady Mahon, very prettily dressed *en bergère*, looked like a flower herself as she moved in her bright blue dress through the living labyrinth of colour.

Chevening, July 29.—I walked with Mahon in the gardens and up the hill, crushing the wild thyme and sweet marjory, and then drove with Lord Stanhope,[2] a long charming drive up the Brasted hill, by poor Vine's Gate and Chartwell, both of many associations. He stopped the carriage to have some foxgloves gathered, and said how the name pleased him, for the plant was the fairies' own special flower, and the name came from folk's love. He would only have one great stem of each foxglove gathered, the rest must be left for the fairies. Lord Stanhope told me that when he took Macaulay up that hill he looked long at the view and then said, 'How evident it is that there has never been, can never have been, an invasion here: no other country could supply this view.'

---

[1] Carlyle refers to the second Lady Ashburton, Caroline Mackenzie, but it will be remembered that he was greatly attached also to the first, Lady Harriet Montagu, and how Mrs. Carlyle resented it.—*Ed.*

[2] Philip Henry Stanhope, fifth earl, 1805–75; until 1852 was active in politics and took an active part in the amendment of copyright law in 1841–2. He is better known, however, as an historian and for his founding of the National Portrait Gallery. His most important writing was a Life of Pitt in 4 vols., but his other works were numerous.—*Ed.*

To MISS WRIGHT.

Holmhurst, Sept. 10, 1873.—The little Hospice[1] has been full all summer. The present inmates are most romantic in title as well as dress—'Sister Georgina Mary, Sister Mildred, and Sister Lilian.' They come from St. Albans', Holborn, so you may imagine that Charlotte Leycester has already had some passages at arms with them. But they are truly excellent as well as pleasant guests, and I console Charlotte by telling her that if she likes to supply me with any suffering Methodists when they are gone, I shall be equally glad to see them.

JOURNAL.

Sept. 30.—I came to Binstead Wyck[2] from Thornhill. It is a charming family home on the edge of a deep declivity, with wide views into the purple hollows between the beech-trees. From the windows we could see Blackmoor, whither we went the next day—the great modern mediæval house of the Lord Chancellor Selborne,[3] set down, as it were, anywhere in an utterly inexpressive part of his large low-lying property, but with pleasant Scotchified views of heath and fir plantations. The Chancellor, pleasant and beaming, was kind, Lady Selborne very nice, and the four daughters charming. The next day we went to 'White's Selborne,' through bowery lanes, where the hedges are all bound together by clematis. It is a beautiful village, just under a wooded hill called 'the Hanger.' The old house of Gilbert White is now inhabited by a striking old man, Mr. Bell, a retired dentist, the beneficence, the 'Bon Dieu,' of the neighbourhood. He showed us his lovely sunny lawn, with curious trees and shrubs, sloping up to the rich wooded hillside, and, in the house the stick, barometer, and spectacles of Gilbert White.

Oct. 4–10.—A charming visit at Shavington, the great desolate brick house of Lord Kilmorey. . . . Lady Fanny Higginson talked much of their old neighbours the Corbets of Adderley: how, when Lady Corbet was a child, she squinted very much, and how Dr. Johnson, when she was introduced to him, said, 'Come here, you little Squintifinko'—which gave her the greatest horror of him. When the family doctor called at Adderley, it was generally just before dinner, and Lady Corbet used to ask him to stay for it, and he found this so pleasant that he came very often in this way, merely for the sake of the dinner; but when his bill came in, she found all these visits charged like the others. She returned it to him with his visits divided into two columns, one headed 'Official' and the other 'Officious,' and she always afterwards spoke of him as 'the officious official.'

Ford Castle, Oct. 17.—'Do you know,' said Lady Waterford to-day,' that Jane Ellice has got one convert to her teetotalism; and do you know who that is? That is *me.* I have not touched wine for six months. I think it is good for the household. They used to say, if they saw me as strong as a horse, "Ah! there, look at my lady; it is true she is as strong as a horse, but then she always has all the wine she wants," but now they say, "My lady has no wine at all, and yet you see she is as strong as a horse." '

[1] In the grounds of 'Holmhurst', which Hare made available (with supplies of groceries) to impoverished gentlewomen.—*Ed.*

[2] The house of William Wickham, who married my cousin Sophia Lefevre.

[3] Sir Roundell Palmer, first Earl of Selborne, entered parliament as a Conservative but gradually passed over to the Liberals; Solicitor-General in Palmerston's Ministry, 1861; Attorney-General in Lord Russell's ministry 1863–6; Lord Chancellor, 1872; also served under Gladstone.—*Ed.*

Miss Fairholme was tired. 'Now do rest,' Lady Waterford said—'there is the sofa close by you—*qui vous tend les bras*'; and then she talked to us of old Lady Balcarres, 'the mother of Grandmama Hardwicke'—the severe mother, who, when one of her little boys disobeyed her, ordered the servants to fling him into the pond in front of the house. He managed to scramble out again; she bade them throw him in a second time, and a second time he got out, and, when she ordered it a third time, he exclaimed in his broad Scotch accent, 'Woman, wad ye droun yer ain son?'

Oct. 18.—This morning Lady Waterford wished that the Misses Lindsay had been dressed alike even in details. 'It is a law of nature, I think, that sisters should dress

FORD CASTLE, THE TERRACE

alike. A covey of partridges are all alike; they do not want to have feathers of different colours; and why not children of the same family?'

We had a charming walk to Etal in the afternoon. Lady W. talked of the beauty of the sedges and of their great variety—of the difficult law, or rather no law, of reflections. Then of marriages—of the number of widows being so much greater than that of widowers, and of the change which the loss of a husband made in all the smallest details of life: of the supreme desolation of Lady Charlotte Denison,[2] 'after a honeymoon of forty-three years.' Old Lady Tankerville was of another nature.

[1] See *The Years With Mother*, pp. 224–5.

[2] Lady Charlotte Bentinck married John Evelyn Denison, speaker of the Commons from 1857–72, in 1827. He died in 1873, so Hare is a few years out. Lady Charlotte survived her husband for many years and latterly changed her name to Scott.

She was urging a widowed friend to do something. 'Oh, but my cap, my cap!' groaned the friend. '*Comment*,' exclaimed Lady Tankerville, '*c'est le vrai bonnet de la liberté.*'

Speaking of complexions—'My grandmother used to say,' said Mrs. Fairholme, 'that beauty "went out" with open carriages. "Why, you are just like men, my dear," she said, "with your brown necks, and your rough skins, and your red noses. In our days it was different; young ladies never walked, ate nothing but white meat, and never washed their faces. They covered their faces with powder, and then put cold cream on, and wiped it off with a flannel: that was the way to have a good complexion." '

'I think it was Henri III,' said Lady Waterford, 'who used to go to sleep with raw veal chops on his cheeks, and to cover his hands with pomade, and have them tied up to the top of the bed by silk cords, that they might be white in the morning.'

Oct. 23.—Lady Waterford talked of 'Grandmama Hardwicke'—how terrified she was of robbers: that one day, when she was going to cross a wide heathy common, she said, 'If any one comes up to the carriage, I shall give up all I have at once: I shall give him no chance of being violent.' Soon after, a man rode up. 'Oh, take my money, but spare my life,' exclaimed Lady Hardwicke, and threw her purse at him. 'My good woman, I don't want your purse,' said the man, who was a harmless traveller.[1]

Oct. 24.—Lord Houghton arrived. He is rather crusty, but most amusing. His conversation is always interesting, even when no one else can speak, and he seems to be saying, with Sydney Smith, to the art circle here—'My dears, it's all right; you keep with the dilettanti: I go with the talkettanti.'

Lord Houghton talked of the Bonapartes, and of the graves of Josephine and Hortense at Rueil, and of Madame Mère. 'I had a very narrow miss of seeing Madame Mère, and I am very sorry I did not do it, for it would only have cost a scudo. She was a very long time dying, it was a kind of lying in state, and for a scudo the porter used to let people in behind a screen which there was at the foot of the bed, and they looked at her through the joinings. I was only a boy then, and I thought there was plenty of time, and put it off; but one day she died.'

Lord Houghton also said: 'One of the prettiest ghost stories I ever heard is that of General Radowitz. He was made Governor of Frankfort, and not being able to go himself, and having servants who had lived with him a long time and knew all his tastes, he sent them on before him to secure a suitable house and get everything ready. They chose an excellent house, with a large garden full of lilacs and laburnums, over-looking the glacis. When General and Madame Radowitz arrived some time after, they found everything as they wished, and began to question their old servants as to how they had got on, and especially as to the neighbours. The servants said that the next villa was inhabited by a person who was quite remarkable—a lady who was always known in Frankfort as the "*weisse Frau* [white lady],"—a very sweet, gentle person, who was full of charity and kindness, and greatly beloved. She had, however, quite lost her memory as to the past since the death, very long ago, of her lover in battle: she had even forgotten his name, and answered to all questions about him or her own past, "*Ich weiss nicht! ich weiss nicht!* [I don't know]" but always with a sweet sad smile. And she had lived in the place so long, that, every one belonging to her having passed away, no one really knew her history. Yet, while her mind was gone as to the past,

---

[1] For more about Grandma Hardwicke see *The Years With Mother*. She was the daughter of the 5th Earl of Balcarres: she married the Earl of Hardwicke and was the mother of Lady Stuart de Rothesay and therefore Lady Waterford's grandmother.

as to the practical present she was quite herself, went to market and transacted her own affairs.

'Gradually the confidential maid of Madame Radowitz made friends with the servants of the *weisse Frau*—for the gardens of the two houses joined—and from servants' gossip the Radowitz family learnt a good deal about her, and from all around they heard of her as greatly respected, but always the same, sad and sweet, always dressed in white, never remembering anything.

'One day the *weisse Frau*, who had taken a great fancy to the maid of Madame Radowitz, invited her to come to her at twelve o'clock the next day: she said she expected some one; indeed, she pressed the maid to come without fail. The maid told her mistress, who said certainly she had better go; she should on no account wish so excellent a person as the "weisse Frau" to be disappointed.

RABY CASTLE

'When the maid went, she found the little salon of the *weisse Frau* in gala decoration, the table laid and bright with flowers, and places set for three. The Frau was not in her usual white dress, but in a curious old costume of rich brocade, which was said to have been intended for her wedding-dress. She still said she expected some one, but when asked who it was, looked distressed and bewildered, and only said, "*Ich weiss nicht!*"

'As it drew near twelve o'clock she became greatly agitated—she said *he* was coming. At length she threw the windows wide open, and gazing out into the street, looked back and said, "*Er kommt! er kommt!* [He is coming!]" She had a radiant expression no one remembered to have seen before; her eyes sparkled, every feature became animated—and as the clock struck twelve, she went out upon the landing, appeared to enfold some one invisible in her arms, and then walking very slowly back into the room, exclaimed "Hoffmann," and sank down dead!

'In the supreme moment of life she had remembered the long-forgotten name.'

Oct. 25.—Last night Lord Houghton talked much about Mrs. Harcourt's diaries, which he had edited (she was lady in waiting to Queen Charlotte), but the royal family had cut out so much as to make them not worth publishing. When the poor Princesses heard of another German prince marrying, they used to say in a despairing tone, 'Another chance lost.'

At Weymouth, Mrs. Harcourt described going to see the royal family in the evening. 'I ventured,' she said, 'to express my regret that the Queen should have had so unfavourable a morning for her water expedition,' whereat Prince William somewhat coarsely replied, 'I only wish the accursed bitch would have spewed her soul up, and then we should have had some peace in the house.'

The Duke of York was the only one of his sons the King really cared for, and he said that the Duke's faults were the cause of his madness.

Raby Castle, Nov. 1.—The first morning I was here, as I was walking on the terraced platform of the castle with Lady Chesham, she talked of the silent Cavendishes, and said it was supposed to be the result of their ancestor's marriage with Rachel, Lady Russell's daughter; that after her father's death she had always been silent and sad, and that her descendants had been silent and sad ever since. 'Lord Carlisle and his brother were also silent. Once they travelled abroad together, and at an inn in Germany slept in the same room, in which there was also a third bed with the curtains drawn round it. Two days after, one brother said to the other, 'Did you see what was in that bed in our room the other night?' and the other answered, 'Yes.' This was all that passed, but they had both seen a dead body in the bed.'

The Duchess [of Cleveland] expects every one to devote themselves to *petits jeux* in the evening, and many of the guests do not like it. There is also a book in which every one is expected to write something when they go away. There is one column for complaints: you are intended to complain that your happy visit has come to an end, or something of that kind. There is another column of 'Why you came'—to which the natural answer seems to be 'Because I was asked.'

One evening I told a story, unfortunately; for if I ever afterwards escaped to my room, after five o'clock, there came a tap and a servant—'Their Graces want you to come down again'—always from their insatiable love of stories.[1]

To Miss Wright.

Highclere Castle, Nov. 12, 1873.—This is a beautiful park, with every variety of scenery, hill, valley, woods, with an undergrowth of rhododendron, a poetical lake! and is so immense—thirteen miles round—that one never goes out of it, and rather feels the isolation of the great house in the centre, which, though very handsome, is not equal to the place. Lady Carnarvon[2] is very lovely and winning, and boundlessly

---

[1] William Harry Vane, the first Duke of Cleveland of the second creation, married twice: first Katherine Powlett, his maternal cousin, co-heiress of the Duke of Bolton, by whom he had eight children, including three sons, all of whom took the title in succession, though all died without male issue. His second wife was Elizabeth Russell, daughter of a market gardener, discarded mistress of the Duke of Bedford (see p. 149). His first son, Henry (died 1864) married Sophia Powlett (died 1859); the second, William (also died 1864) married Lady Caroline Paulet (died 1883), but he took the name of Powlett under the terms of the Duchess of Bolton's will and reverted to Vane on his succession; the third son, Harry (died 1891), married Catherine, daughter of Lord Stanhope, widow of Lord Dalmeny, and he too took the name of Powlett, for the same reason as his brother. The Duke and Duchess referred to in this book after 1864, are, of course, Harry and Catherine, the widow of William being referred to as the Dowager Duchess or as the Duchess Caroline.—*Ed.*

[2] Lady Evelyn Stanhope, wife of Henry Howard Molyneux Herbert, fourth Earl of Carnarvon, statesman. She died in January, 1875.—*Ed.*

interesting to listen to: one understands Mr. Delane saying that he believed that there could be no successor to Lady Palmerston till he saw Lady Carnarvon. She says that she has hitherto been too exclusive; that henceforth she shall wish to fill her house more with people of every shade—'for Carnarvon's sake.'

JOURNAL.

Highclere, Nov. 13.—Mr. Herman Merivale[1] told us—

A captain was crossing to America in his ship, with very few sailors on board. One day one of them came up to him on the deck and said that there was a strange man in his cabin—that he could not see the man's face, but that he was sitting with his back to the door at the table writing. The captain said it was impossible there could be any one in his cabin, and desired the sailor to go and look again. When he came up, he said the man was gone, but on the table was the paper on which he had written, with the ink still wet, the words—"Steer due south." The captain said that, as he was not pressed for time, he would act on the mysterious warning. He steered due south, and met with a ship which had been long disabled and whose crew were in the last extremity.

The captain of the disabled ship said that one of his men was a very strange character. He had himself picked him up from a deserted ship, and since then he had fallen into a cataleptic trance, in which, when he recovered, he declared that he had been in another ship, begging its captain to come to their assistance. When the man who had been sent to the cabin saw the cataleptic sailor, he recognised him at once as the man he had seen writing.

Mr. Merivale said that a case of the same kind had happened to himself.

He was staying at Harrow, and very late at night was summoned to London. Exactly as the clock struck twelve he passed the headmaster's door in a fly. Both he and the friend who was with him were at that moment attracted by seeing a hackney-coach at the door—a most unusual sight at that time of night, and a male figure wrapped in black, descend from it and glide into the house, without, apparently, ringing, or any door being opened. He spoke of it to his friend, and they both agreed that it was equally mysterious and inexplicable. The next day, the circumstance so dwelt on Mr. Merivale's mind, that he returned to Harrow, and going to the house, asked if the headmaster, Dr. Butler, was at home. 'No,' said the servant. Then he asked who had come at twelve o'clock the night before. No one had come, no one had been heard of, no carriage had been seen; but Dr. Butler's father had died just at that moment in a distant county.

Sir Charles Russell told us—

When the 34th Regiment was quartered at Gibraltar, it had the stupidest and dullest set of officers that can possibly be imagined; they not only knew nothing, but they preferred to know nothing; and especially were they averse to learning anything of Spanish, which was certainly very short-sighted of them, as it cut them off from so many social pleasures. But nevertheless they all very much admired a beautiful young Spanish señorita who was living at Gibraltar, and pretended that they were not otherwise than in her good graces, which of course was simply bombast, as none of them knew a word of Spanish and scarcely a word of French, so that not one of them had ever spoken to her.

[1] Herman Merivale, 1806–1874; barrister, professor of Political Economy at Oxford (1837), Under-Secretary for India.—*Ed.*

One day, while the regiment was at Gibraltar, a young ensign came to join, who had never been abroad before, and who knew even less of any foreign language than his comrades. Nevertheless, in a short time he had taken cue by them, and pretended more than all the others to be in the good graces of the young lady, and was well laughed at accordingly.

One evening at mess one of the officers mentioned that the señorita was going to Cadiz. 'No, she is not,' said the young ensign. 'Oh, you young jackanapes,' said his fellow-officers, 'what can you know about it? You know nothing about her.'—'Yes,' he said sharply, 'I do. She is not going to Cadiz; and what is more, I beg that her name may not be brought forward in this way at mess any more: I am engaged to be married to her.'

There was a universal roar, and an outcry of 'You don't suppose we are going to believe that?' But the ensign said, 'I give you my word of honour as an officer and a gentleman that I *am* engaged to be married to her.'

Then the Colonel, who was present, said, 'Well, as he represents it in this way, we are bound to believe him.' And then, turning to the young ensign, said, 'Now my dear fellow, as we do accept what you say, I think you need not leave us up in the clouds like this. Will you not tell us how it came about? You cannot wonder that we should be a little surprised, when we know that you do not speak a word of Spanish and only two or three words of French, that you should be engaged to be married to this young lady.'

'Well,' said the ensign, 'since you accept what I say, yes, I do not wonder that you are a little surprised. I do not mind telling you all about it. It is quite true I do not understand a word of Spanish, and only three or four words of French, but that does not matter. After the ball at the Convent the other day (the house of the Governor of Gibraltar is called 'the Convent') we went out upon the balcony, and we watched the moonlight shimmering on the waves of the sea, and I looked up into her eyes, and I said, "*Voulez vous?*" and she said, "*Quoi?*"—and I said, "*Moi*"; and she said, "*Oui*"—and it was quite enough.'

Ascot Wood, Jan. 5, 1874.—I came to London three weeks ago in a thick fog, such as Charles Lamb would have said was meat, drink, and clothing. One day I went with Lady Ashburton to visit Mr. Carlyle. It was most interesting—the quaint simple old-fashioned brick house in Cheyne Row; the faded furniture; the table where he toiled so long and fruitlessly at the deification of Frederick the Great; the workbox and other little occupatory articles of the long dead wife, always left untouched; the living niece, jealous of all visitors, thinking that even Lady Ashburton must have either testamentary or matrimonial intentions; and the great man himself in a long grey garment, half coat, half dressing-gown, which buttoned to the throat and fell in straight folds to the feet or below them, like one of the figures in Noah's Ark, and with the addition, when he went out with us, of an extraordinary tall broad-brimmed felt hat, which can only be procured at a single village in Bavaria, and which gave him the air of an old magician.

He talked of Holman Hunt's picture of the Home at Nazareth, 'the most unnatural thing that ever was painted, and the most unnatural thing in it the idea that the Virgin should be keeping her "preciosities" in the carpenter's shop.'

He talked of Landor, of the grandeur and unworldliness of his nature, and of how it was a lasting disgrace to England that the vile calumnies of an insolent slanderer had been suffered to blight him in the eyes of so many, and to send him out an exile from England in his old age.[1]

He complained much of his health, fretting and fidgeting about himself, and said he could form no worse wish for the devil than that he might be able to give him his stomach to digest with through all eternity.

We walked out with him in the street, one on each side. I saw the cab-drivers pointing and laughing at the extraordinary figure, and indeed it was no wonder.

Colonel and Mrs. Henderson (of the Police Force) were at dinner [at Mrs. Thornton's]. He said his father had been executor to old Lord Bridport, who had a box which no one was ever allowed to open, and of the contents of which even Lady Bridport was ignorant. After Lord Bridport's death, the widow sent for Colonel Henderson to look into things, and then said, 'I wish you would open that box; one ought to know about it.' Colonel Henderson did not like doing it, but took the box into the library and sat down before it, with candles by his side. Immediately he heard a movement on the other side of the table, and, looking up, saw old Lord Bridport as clearly as he had ever seen him in his life, scowling down upon him with a furious expression. He went back at once to Lady Bridport and positively refused to open the box, which was then destroyed unopened. He said, 'I shall never to my dying day forget the face of Lord Bridport as I saw him after he was dead.'[2]

In Wilton Crescent I saw Mrs. Leycester, who was just come from Cheshire. She said:—

A brother of Sir Philip Egerton has lately been given a living in Devonshire, and went to take possession of it. He had not been long in his rectory before, coming one day into his study, he found an old lady seated there in an arm-chair by the fire. Knowing no old lady could really be there, and thinking the appearance must be the result of an indigestion, he summoned all his courage and boldly sat down upon the old lady, who disappeared. The next day he met the old lady in the passage, rushed up against her, and she vanished. But he met her a third time, and then, feeling that it could not always be indigestion, he wrote to his sister in Cheshire, begging her to call upon the Misses Athelstan, sisters of the clergyman who had held his living before, and say what he had seen. When they heard it, the Misses Athelstan looked inexpressibly distressed and said, 'That was our mother: we hoped it was only to us she would appear. When we were there she appeared constantly, but when we left, we hoped she would be at rest.'

About 'ghost-stories' I always recollect what Dr. Johnson used to say—'The beginning and end of ghost-stories is this, all argument is against them, all belief is for them.'

I have had a charming visit here at Ascot to the Lefevres. Sir John Lefevre described a place in Essex belonging to a Mr. (now Sir William) and Mrs. Stephenson. When they first went there, the housekeeper said there was one room which it was never the custom to use. For a long time it continued to be unoccupied, but one day,

[1] In 1857 Landor got himself involved in a quarrel between two ladies he knew. To one of them he passed on a legacy he had received. The recipient passed on half of the sum to the other lady. After a quarrel between the two ladies, the second accused the first of having got the money from Landor for discreditable reasons! As a result Landor twice indulged in libel, for one of which he apologised; but in the second case there was nothing for it but to leave the country. The case went against him and at the age of 84 he found himself entirely dependent on his family. He did not return to this country, but died in 1864 at Florence.—*Ed.*

[2] Alexander Hood, Viscount Bridport, admiral and brother of Admiral Lord Hood; admiral of the blue, 1794; vice-admiral of England, 1796. Portrait by Reynolds at Greenwich.—*Ed.*

when the house was very full and an unexpected arrival announced, Mrs. S. said she should open and air it, and sent for the key. All the people staying in the house, full of curiosity, went with her when she visited the room for the first time. It was a large panelled room containing a bed like a catafalque, with heavy stuff curtains drawn all round. They drew aside the curtains, and there was the mark of a bloody hand upon the pillow! The room was shut up again from that time forward.

JOURNAL.

Jan. 25, 1874.—My books have made me almost well known after a fashion, and people are very kind, for, with what Shakespeare calls 'the excellent foppery of the world,' many who used to snub me now almost 'make up to me,' and all kinds of so-called 'great people' invite me to their houses. Sometimes this is very pleasant, and I always enjoy being liked. I do not think it is likely to set me up; I have too strong a feeling of my own real inferiority to the opinion formed of me. Intellectually, I am so ill grounded that I really know nothing well or accurately; and if I am what is called 'generous,' certainly that is no virtue, for it pleases myself as well as others. I think it is still with me as George Sand says of herself, '*Je n'ai pa de bonheur dans la vie, mais j'ai beaucoup de bonheurs* [I have no happiness in life, but I have many happinesses].'

II

LITERARY WORK AT HOME AND ABROAD

1874–75

꙳

THE success of *Walks in Rome*, and the great pleasure which I had derived from the preparation of my *Days near Rome*, made me undertake, in the spring of 1874, the more ambitious work of *Cities of Northern and Central Italy*, in preparation for which I left England at the end of January.

JOURNAL.

Villa La Cava, Cannes, Jan. 30, 1874.—What a view I look upon here from my beautiful room!—a pure blue sky all around, fading into the softest most delicate golden hues where it meets the waveless expanse of sea, upon which the islands seem asleep in the sunshine; on one side the old town of Cannes, with its pier and shipping and the white sails of its boats; on the other, the endless villas, and Mougins, and the mountains—all rising from a wealth of orange and cypress groves; and, close at hand, masses of geraniums and roses and the 'sunshine tree' (golden mimosa) in full blossom, —and thus, they say, it has been all winter.

I left in the evening for my four-and-twenty hours' journey [from Paris]. The train was crowded, every place full, but, in spite of my seven companions and their twenty-eight handbags, which obliged me to sit bolt upright the whole way, I rather enjoyed it. There is something so interesting in the rapid transitions: the plains of Central France: the rolling hills of Burgundy in the white moonlight: the great towns, Dijon and Lyons, deep down below, and mapped out by their lamps: the dawn over the Rhone valley: the change to blue sky melting into delicate amber: the first stunted olives: the white roads leading, dust-surrounded, to the white cities, Avignon and Tarascon and Arles: the desolate stone-laden Crau: the still blue Mediterranean, and Marseilles with its shipping, and then the granite phase of southern Provence and its growth of heath and lavender and pines.

To MISS LEYCESTER.

Parma, Feb. 12, 1874.—I had an interesting railway journey on Monday with Madame Franzoni, who lives in the house at Taggia described in *Dr. Antonio*. She was Swiss. Her husband, of an old Swiss-Italian family, was disinherited on becoming Protestant, and was obliged to become an engineer. His father, still living, has been prevented by his priests from speaking to him for five-and-twenty years, though devotedly fond of him. She took her two little children and made them sing a hymn beneath the tree in which their grandfather was sitting. Tears streamed down the old man's cheeks, but he would not look at them; he said it must be a lesson to his other children. The mother offered her whole fortune if her son would consent to hear one mass; she believed that one mass would reconvert him. Since then the Protestant part of the family have been dreadfully poor, whilst the rest are immensely rich. Madame Franzoni said that the priests of Taggia were very kind to them privately, but would not recognise them in public.

I enjoyed Genoa, and my work there, and made several pleasant Italian acquaintances, the Genoese are so hospitable. The Marchese Spinola showed me all the treasures and pictures of his old palace himself. I suppose I must take this as a great compliment, for I was amused the other day by an anecdote of the Marchesa Spinola, who made herself most agreeable to an Englishman she met at the Baths of Monte Catini. On taking leave, he politely expressed a hope that, as they were both going to Rome in the winter, they might meet there. '*Mais non, Monsieur,*' she replied;

CAGNES

'*à Monte Catini je suis charmée de vous voir, mais à Rome c'est toute autre chose* [No, Sir, at Monte Catini I am charmed to meet you, but at Rome that is quite another matter].' Yesterday I spent in correcting my account of Piacenza—bitterly cold, children sliding all over the streets, which were one mass of ice.

59 *B. Mario de' Fiori, Rome, Feb.* 22.—Rome is fearfully modernised, such quantities of new houses built, such quantities of old buildings swept away—the old shell fountain in the Felice, the lion of the Apostoli, the Vintner's fountain at Palazzo Simonetti, the ruins of the Ponte Salara, and . . . all the shrines in the Coliseum, even the famous cross on the wall. The last nearly caused a Revolution. On the Pincio a Swiss cottage is put up, strangely out of place amongst the old statues, and a clock which goes by water. Even the most ardent Protestants too are a little shocked that the famous Quirinal Chapel, so redolent of Church history, should be turned into a cloak-room for balls, and the cloak-tickets kept in the holy water basins. The poverty and suffering amongst the Romans is dreadful, the great influx of Torinese taking the bread out of their mouths.

You would be amused with the economy of my servants Ambrogio and Maria. They think it most extravagant if I have both vegetables and a pudding, and quite sinful to have soup the same day; and the first day after I had seen the kitchen fire blazing away all afternoon, and '*Il Signorino è servito*' was announced very magnificently, behold the dinner was—three larks! But what a pleasure it is to hear again from servants—'*Felicissima notte,*'—that sweetest bidding of repose, as Palgrave calls it.

March, 1.—The spoliation of Rome continues every day. Its picturesque beauty is *gone*. Nothing can exceed the tastelessness of all that is being done—the Coliseum, Baths of Caracalla, and the temples are scraped quite clean, and look like sham ruins built yesterday: all the pretty trees are cut down: the outsides of the mediæval churches (Prassede, Pudentiana, &c.) are washed yellow or painted over: the old fountains are stripped of their ferns and polished: the Via Crucis and other processions are forbidden: and the Government has even sent out the *pompieri* [firemen] to cut down all the ivy from the aqueducts. I have, however, got back one thing—the Lion of the Apostoli! I went round to a number of people living in that neighbourhood, and engaged them to go in the morning to the Senators in the Capitol and demand its restoration: and a message was sent that the lion should be restored at once. So the little hideous beast goes back this week to his little vacant sofa, where he has sat for more than six hundred years.[1]

The cardinals have been dying off a good deal lately, and a curious relic of old times was the lying in state of Cardinal Bernabo in the Propaganda Fide—the chapel hung with black, the catafalque with cloth of gold, a chain of old abbots and cardinals standing and kneeling round with tapers, and all the students singing.

Tivoli, March 22.—I have been greatly enjoying a little mountain tour with Lady Castletown and Mrs. Lewis Wingfield. On Wednesday we spent the day in the villas Aldobrandini and Mondragone at Frascati, and the next morning had the most charming drive by Monte Porzio and Monte Compatri, chiefly through the desolate chestnut forests, to Palestrina. It was the fair of Genazzano, and the whole road was most animated, such crowds of peasants in their gayest costumes and prettiest ornaments. At beautiful Olevano we had just time to go to the little inn and visit my friend of last year, Peppina Baldi. It was a tiring journey thence to Subiaco after such a long day, and we only passed the worst precipices by daylight, so it was quite dark when we

---

[1] The following is an extract from Hare's *Walks in Rome* concerning the tidying up of the city: 'Twelve years of Sardinian rule—1870–82—have done more for the destruction of Rome . . . than all the invasions of the Goths and Vandals. The whole aspect of the city has changed . . . The glorious gardens of the Villa Negroni and Villa Ludovisi have been annihilated; many precious street memorials of medieval history have been swept away; ancient convents have been levelled to the ground or turned into barracks; historic churches have been yellow-washed or modernised; the cloisters of Michelangelo have been walled up; the pagan ruins have been denuded of all that gave them picturesqueness or beauty; and several of the finest fountains have been pulled down or bereaved of half their waters. The palace of the Cæsars is stripped of all the flowers and shrubs which formerly adorned it. The glorious view from the Pincio has been destroyed by the hideous barracks built between the Tiber and St. Peter's. The Tiber itself has been diverted from its exquisitely picturesque course, to the destruction, amongst other interesting memorials, of the lovely Farnesina gardens, and the fatal injury of the inestimable frescoes in the Palace. The Baths of Caracalla, which, till 1870, were one of the most beautiful spots in the world, are now scarcely more attractive than the ruins of a London warehouse. Many of the most interesting temples have been dwarfed by the vulgarest and tallest of modern buildings. Even the Colosseum . . . has been deprived not only of its shrines, but of its marvellous flora, though in dragging out the roots of its shrubs more of the building was destroyed than would have fallen naturally in five centuries. . . .'—*Ed.*

reached Subiaco, where we found rooms with difficulty, as, quite unwittingly, we had arrived on the eve of the great festa of S. Benedetto. Most delighted we were, however, of course, and most picturesque and beautiful was the early pilgrimage, with bands of music and singing, up the stony mountain paths. Lady Castletown travels with a second carriage for her maids, so prices naturally rise at first sight of so grand a princess. . . . On the way here we diverged to the farm of Horace in the Licenza valley, all marvellously unaltered—the brook, the meadows, the vines, the surrounding hills and villages, still just as he described them eighteen hundred years ago.

I have seldom enjoyed Tivoli more than in this spring of 1874. It was then that, sitting in the scene I describe, I wrote the paragraph of *Days near Rome* which I insert here.

Nothing can exceed the loveliness of the views from the road which leads from Tivoli by the chapel of S. Antonio to the Madonna di Quintiliolo. On the opposite height rises the town with its temples, its old houses and churches clinging to the edge

GENAZZANO

of the cliffs, which are overhung with such a wealth of luxuriant vegetation as is almost indescribable; and beyond, beneath the huge pile of building known as the Villa of Maecenas, the thousand noisy cataracts of the Cascatelle leap forth beneath the old masonry, and sparkle and dance and foam through the green—and all this is only the foreground to vast distances of dreamy campagna, seen through the gnarled hoary stems of grand old olive-trees—rainbow-hued with every delicate tint of emerald and amethyst, and melting into sapphire, where the solitary dome of St. Peter's rises, invincible by distance, over the level line of the horizon.

And the beauty is not confined to the views alone. Each turn of the winding road is a picture; deep ravines of solemn dark-green olives which waken into silver light as the wind shakes their leaves—old convents and chapels buried in the shady nooks on the mountain-side—thickets of laurustinus, roses, genista, and jessamine—banks of lilies and hyacinths, anemones and violets—grand masses of grey rock, up which white-bearded goats are scrambling to nibble the myrtle and rosemary, and knocking down showers of the red tufa on their way;—and a road, with stone seats and parapets, twisting along the edge of the hill through a constant diorama of loveliness, and peopled by groups of peasants in their gay dresses returning from their work, singing in parts wild canzonetti which echo amid the silent hills, or by women washing at the wayside fountains, or returning with brazen *conche* poised upon their heads, like stately statues of water-goddesses wakened into life.

Great was the difficulty of securing any companion for the desolate excursion to the Abruzzi, but at length I found a clever artist, Mr. Donne, who agreed to go with me.

To Miss Leycester.

Sora in the Marsica, April 2.—Mr. Donne and I left the train at Terni, taking diligence to Rieti, the capital of the Sabina. Next day we had a long dreary drive to Aquila, a dismal place, but full of curious remains, surrounded by tremendous snow mountains. Thence we crossed a fearful pass in ghastly barren mountains to Solmona, a wonderful

SUBIACO

mediæval city seldom visited. On Sunday we clambered up the mountains above the town to the hermitage of Pietro Murrone, afterwards Cœlestine V., and then, as the snow was too deep to make it possible to cross the mountain, returned by night to Aquila. On Tuesday our journey of a whole day was through perfectly Lapland scenery, the road a mere track in the deep snow, which covered hedges and fields alike. Fortunately the weather was lovely, but it was a relief to come down again to even partial civilisation at Avezzano, on the borders of what was once the Lago Fucino, now dried up and spoilt by Prince Torlonia.

Easter Sunday, 1874.—We have been spending to-day in the monastery of Monte Cassino, gloriously beautiful always, with its palatial buildings on a mountain-top and all around billows of purple hill tipped with snow. An introduction from the Duke of Sermoneta caused the gentle-looking Abbot to receive us, and then the great bent figure of the great Tosti came forward, his deep-set eyes excessively striking. After the service in the church they entertained us to an excellent dinner, finishing with delicious Aleatico wine.

April 7.—In the second-class carriage of the train on our way to Velletri sat a venerable and beautiful old man, to whom we talked of Aquino, the birthplace of St. Thomas Aquinas, where we spent yesterday. Gradually we found out that he was the Abbot of Monte Vergine, and he told us much that was interesting about that wonderful place—of the intense love and veneration of the Neapolitan people for the sanctuary, which is connected with the different events of their domestic life; that no betrothal or marriage or birth was considered entirely consecrated without receiving a benediction at the sanctuary; that peasant women had it entered in their marriage contracts that they should be allowed to make the pilgrimage from time to time, and after the birth of each child; that because, on account of the suppression, two miles of the road to the sanctuary still remained unfinished, the peasants voluntarily undertook to finish it themselves, 30,000 persons subscribing one soldo apiece; that when, at the same time, he, the Abbot, was obliged to give up keeping a carriage, five Neapolitan families insisted upon undertaking to keep one for him, one paying the horses, another the coachman, &c. The Abbot gave us his benediction on taking leave, and invited us to Monte Vergine.[1]

April 14.—I met Mademoiselle von Raasloff at Mrs. Terry's. She narrated to me some facts which had been told to her by the well-known Dr. Pereira.

An acquaintance of his, a lady, was travelling with some friends in an out-of-the-way part of Poland. Suddenly, late at night, their carriage broke down and they were obliged to get out, and as they knew of no shelter near, they were in great difficulties. At this juncture a gentleman appeared, who said to the lady that if she would take the trouble to walk a few steps farther, she would come to the gate of his house; that he was unable to accompany her, but that if she would mention his name she would be received, and would find all she required. She thanked him and followed his directions. The servant to whom she spoke at the house seemed very much surprised, but seeing her plight, brought her in, left her in a library, and went to get some refreshment. When she was alone, a door in the panelling opened and the unknown master of the house came in and sat down by her. As he said nothing, she felt rather awkward, and more so when the servant, coming in with a tray, seemed to brush up close to him in a very odd way as he set it down. When the servant left the room, the unknown said, '*Ne vous étonnez pas, Mademoiselle, c'est que je suis mort* [Don't be surprised, Mademoiselle; but I am dead];' and he proceeded to say that he was most thankful she had come, and that he wished her to make him a solemn promise; that the people who were now in possession of the property were not the rightful heirs, but that he had left a will, deposited with a certain lawyer in a certain place, the name of which he made her write down. She listened as in a trance, but did as she was bid. The servant, coming in again about this time, walked straight *through* the unknown. Presently the carriage, being mended, was announced to be at the door, upon which the unknown walked with her to the porch, bowed, and disappeared.

When the lady got to Warsaw, she had an *attaque des nerfs*, was very ill, and sent for Dr. Pereira. She told him all she had seen, and also gave him the paper with the directions she had written down. Dr. Pereira, finding that the person and place mentioned really existed, inquired into the matter, and the result was that the will was

---

[1] This excellent old Abbot was afterwards cruelly murdered at Rome.

found, the wrongful possessors ejected, and the rightful owners set up in their place.

One evening at the Palazzo Odescalchi, when everybody had been telling stories, and nothing very interesting, Mademoiselle von Raasloff suddenly astonished us by saying, 'Now I will tell you something.' Then she said—

'There was a young lady in Denmark, whose family, from circumstances, had lived very much before the Danish world, and with whom, in so small a society as that of Copenhagen, almost every one was acquainted. Consequently it was a subject of interest, almost of universal interest, at Copenhagen, when it became known that this young lady, with the full approval of her parents and joyful consent of every one concerned, had become engaged to a young Danish officer of good family and position.

'Now in Danish society a betrothal is considered to be almost the same thing as a marriage: new relationships date from that time, and if either the affianced bride or bridegroom die, the family of the other side mourn as for a son or brother, as if the marriage had actually taken place.

'While this young lady of whom I have spoken was only engaged, her betrothed husband was summoned to join his regiment in a war which was going on; and very soon to the house of his betrothed came the terrible news that he was dead, that he was killed in battle. And the way in which the news came was this. A soldier of his regiment was wounded and was taken prisoner; and as he was lying in his cot in the hospital, he said to his companion who was in the next bed, "I saw the young Colonel —I saw the young Colonel on his white horse, and he rode into the ranks of the enemy and he never came back again." And the man who said that died, but the man to whom he said it recovered, and, in process of time, he was ransomed, and came back to Copenhagen and told his story with additions. "My comrade, who is dead, said that he saw the young Colonel on his white horse, and that he saw him ride into the ranks of the enemy and the soldiers of the enemy drag him from his horse and kill him, so that he never came back again." This was the form in which the story reached the family of the affianced wife of the young Colonel, and they mourned him most truly; for they loved him much, and they put on all the outward signs of deepest grief. There was only one person who would not put on the outward signs of mourning, and that was his affianced bride herself. She said, and persisted in saying, that she *could* not believe that, where two persons had been as entirely united as she and her betrothed had been, one could pass entirely out of life without the other knowing it. That her lover was sick, in prison, in trouble, she could believe, but that he was dead —*never*, without her having an inner conviction of it; and she would not put on the outward signs of mourning, which to her sense implied an impression of ill omen. Her parents urged her greatly, not only because their own reality of grief was very great, but because, according to the feeling of things in Copenhagen, it cast a very great slur upon their daughter that she should appear without the usual signs of grief. They urged her ceaselessly, and the tension of mind in which she lived, and the perpetual struggle with her own family, added to her own deep grief, had a very serious effect upon her.

'It was while things were in this state that one day she dreamt—she dreamt that she received a letter from her betrothed, and in her dream she felt that it was of the most vital importance that she should see the date of that letter; and she struggled and laboured to see it, but she could not make it out; and she laboured on with the utmost intensity of effort, but she could not decipher it; and it seemed to her the most wearisome night she had ever spent, so incessant was her effort, but she could not read it:

still she would not give it up, and at last, just as the dawn was breaking, she saw the date of the letter, and it was May the 10th. The effort was so great that she woke; but the date remained with her still—it was May the 10th.

'Now she knew that if such a letter had been really written on the 10th of May, by the 1st of June she must receive that letter.

'The next morning, when her father came in to see her before she was up, as he had always done since their great sorrow, he was surprised to find her not only calm and serene, but almost radiant. She said, "You have often blamed me for not wearing the outward signs of mourning for my betrothed: grant me now only till the 1st of June, and *then*, if I receive no letter from him, I will promise to resign myself to believe the worst, and I will do as you desire." Three weeks of terrible tension ensued, and the 1st of June arrived. She said then that she felt as if her whole future life hung upon the postman's knock. It came—and there was the letter! Her lover had been taken prisoner, communication with him had been cut off—in fact, till then it was impossible she should hear. Soon afterwards he was exchanged, came home, and they were married.

'Now,' said Mademoiselle von Raasloff, as she finished her narrative, 'that is no story which I have heard. The young lady was my dear mother; she is here to testify to it: the young officer was my dear father, General von Raasloff; he is here to confirm it.' And they were both present.

To MISS LEYCESTER.

Assisi, April 26.—I had a proposal from the Miss Seymours and Miss Ellis that if I would wait at Rome till Saturday the 18th, they would set off with me in search of the lost monastery of Farfa, which was, of all places, the one I wanted most to see, and from which fear of brigands had previously caused all my companions to fail at the last moment. If you have read any old histories of Italy, you will remember how all-important Farfa was in the Middle Ages, and will wonder that no one, not even the best Roman antiquarians, knew anything about its present state, or even where it is. We could only judge by old maps and chronicles. However, the excursion completely answered, and, after divers little adventures, we not only arrived at Farfa, but found the Father-General of the Benedictines accidentally there to receive us. Greatly astonished he was at our arrival, but said that one enterprising stranger had reached the place three years before—I need hardly add, an English lady. Really Farfa is one of the most radiant spots in Italy, and the sheets of wild-flowers, and the songs of nightingales and cuckoos enhanced its charms.

JOURNAL.

May 4, *Florence.*—Mademoiselle von Raasloff told me that Count Piper, an ancestor of the present Count Piper, was a very determined gambler. Being once at one of his desolate country estates, he was in perfect despair for some one to play with him, but he was alone. At last, in a fit of desperation, he said, 'If the devil himself were to come to play with me, I should be grateful.' Soon a tremendous storm began to rage, during which a servant came in and said that a gentleman overtaken by night was travelling past, and implored shelter. Count Piper was quite enchanted, and a very gentleman-like man was shown in. Supper was served, and then Count Piper proposed a game of cards, in which the stranger at once acquiesced. Count Piper won so enormously, that he felt quite ashamed, and at last he proposed their retiring. As they were leaving the room, the stranger said, 'I am very much concerned that I have not sufficient money with me to pay all my debt now; however, I shall beg you to take my ring as a guarantee, which is really of greater value than the money, and which has very peculiar properties, one of which is that as long as you wear it, all you possess is safe from fire.' The Count took the ring, and escorting the stranger to his room, wished him good night. The next morning he sent to inquire after him: he was not there, his bed had not been slept in, and he never was heard of again. Count Piper wore the ring, but after some time, as it was very heavy and old-fashioned, he took it off and put it away. The next morning came the news that one of his finest farm-houses had been burnt down. And so it always is in that family. The descendants of Count Piper always have to wear the ring, and if ever they leave it off for a single day, one of their houses on one of their great estates is burnt.

VIEW FROM THE BOBOLI GARDENS, FLORENCE

Florence, May 10.—Ten days here in the radiant spring-tide have been very delight-ful. I have seen a great deal of Mrs. Ross, Lady Duff Gordon's[1] beautiful daughter, who is now writing the story of her mother's life. She has a noble head, which is almost more full of expression than that of any one I know, and I am sure that her character is noble too, with all the smallnesses of life, which make a thoroughly anglicised character ignoble, washed out, and its higher qualities remaining to be mingled with the Italian frankness and kindly simplicity which *English*-English do

[1] Lady Lucie Duff-Gordon, 1821–1869; daughter of John Austin the jurist; author and translator. She married Sir A. C. Duff-Gordon, Bart. and their home at Queen Square, Westminster, was the centre of a remarkably wide circle of celebrities, British and foreign, including Dickens, Thackeray, Kinglake, Tennyson, etc. She spent her last years in Egypt and in *Letters from Egypt* produced a valuable record of Eastern life and customs at that time.—*Ed.*

FRANCES BARONESS BUNSEN

in 1874

not possess, and consequently cannot understand. Her singing to a guitar is capital—chiefly of Italian *stornelli*, rendered with all the *verve* which a *contadina* [peasant-woman] herself could give them. It is no wonder that Italians adore her. Each summer she and her husband spend at Castagnuolo with the Marchese Lotteria della Stufa, the great friend of her father, who died in his arms. This is 'Il Marchese' *par excellence* with the Florentines, to whom he is public property. When a child accidentally shot him with a pistol through the crown of his hat, thousands of people thronged the street before his house to inquire, and in all the villages round his native valley of Signa the price of wax went up for a fortnight, so many candles were burnt to the Madonna as thank-offerings for his escape.

I have been out with Mrs. Ross to the Stufa villa of Castagnuolo, seven miles off, near the Badia di' Settimo, in a tiny *baroccino* [two-wheeled pony-cart], drawn by Tocco, the smallest of spirited ponies. As we turned up from the highroad to the villa on the hills through the rich luxuriant vineyards, the warmest welcome met us from all the peasants. In a house in the grounds the whole family of inmates thronged round her with '*Vi piglierò un consiglio, Signora* [We want your advice, Signora],' about a sick child. We wandered up the woods, gathering lovely wild orchids, and then went to the farm, where the creatures, like the people, seemed to regard Mrs. Ross as one of themselves: the cows came and licked her, the sheep came and rubbed against her, the pigeons perched, and even the wild boars were gentleness itself. She was first able to make her way at Castagnuolo by nursing day and night an old *contadino* who died in her arms. She described comically, though pathetically, the frank grief which ensued: how the son, Antonio, tried to drown himself, and was pulled out of the water by his breeches: how the whole family insisted upon being bled: how a married daughter, a niece, and a cousin came and had strong convulsions; and how when she ventured to leave them for a little to go to her dinner, the *fattore* [factor] rushed after her with—'*Ma Signora, tutte le donne son svenute* [All the women have fainted]'; how eventually she locked up each separately for the night with a basin of soup, having made them a little speech, &c. Whenever any of the *contadini* have burns, they are cured by poultices of arum-leaves.

I spent the rest of the summer in London. It was during this year that I became a member of the Athenæum Club—an incalculable advantage. . . . I have since spent every London morning in steady work at the Athenæum, less disturbed there than even at Holmhurst. The difficulties which the club rules throw in the way of receiving visitors are a great advantage to students, and my life at the Athenæum has been as regular as clockwork. At breakfast I have always occupied the same table,—behind the door leading to the kitchen, the one which, I believe, was always formerly used by Wilberforce. In the afternoons, when all the old gentlemen arrive, to poke up huge fires in winter and close all the windows in summer, I have never returned to the club.

Captain Fisher, who is engaged to be married to Victoria Liddell, told me that—

'When Mr. Macpherson of Glen Truim was dying, his wife had gone to rest in a room looking out over the park, and sat near the window. Suddenly she saw lights

c

as of a carriage coming in at the distant lodge-gate, and calling to one of the servants, said, 'Do go down; some one is coming who does not know of all this grief.' But the servant remained near her at the window, and as the carriage came near the house, they saw it was a hearse drawn by four horses and covered with figures. As it stopped at the porch door, the figures looked up at her, and their eyes glared with light; then they scrambled down and seemed to disappear into the house. Soon they reappeared and seemed to lift some heavy weight into the hearse, which then drove off at full speed, causing all the stones and gravel to fly up at the windows. Mrs. Macpherson and the butler had not rallied from their horror and astonishment, when the nurse watching in the next room came in to tell her that the Colonel was dead.

Captain Fisher also told us this really extraordinary story connected with his own family:—

Fisher may sound a very plebeian name, but this family is of very ancient lineage, and for many hundreds of years they have possessed a very curious old place in Cumberland, which bears the weird name of Croglin Grange. The great characteristic of the house is that never at any period of its very long existence has it been more than one story high, but it has a terrace from which large grounds sweep away towards the church in the hollow, and a fine distant view.

When, in lapse of years, the Fishers outgrew Croglin Grange in family and fortune, they were wise enough not to destroy the long-standing characteristic of the place by adding another story to the house, but they went away to the south, to reside at Thorncombe near Guildford, and they let Croglin Grange.

They were extremely fortunate in their tenants, two brothers and a sister. They heard their praises from all quarters. To their poorer neighbours they were all that is most kind and beneficent, and their neighbours of a higher class spoke of them as a most welcome addition to the little society of the neighbourhood. On their part the tenants were greatly delighted with their new residence. The arrangement of the house, which would have been a trial to many, was not so to them. In every respect Croglin Grange was exactly suited to them.

The winter was spent most happily by the new inmates of Croglin Grange, who shared in all the little social pleasures of the district, and made themselves very popular. In the following summer, there was one day which was dreadfully, annihilatingly hot. The brothers lay under the trees with their books, for it was too hot for any active occupation. The sister sat in the verandah and worked, or tried to work, for, in the intense sultriness of that summer day, work was next to impossible. They dined early, and after dinner they still sat out in the verandah, enjoying the cool air which came with evening, and they watched the sun set, and the moon rise over the belt of trees which separated the grounds from the churchyard, seeing it mount the heavens till the whole lawn was bathed in silver light, across which the long shadows from the shrubbery fell as if embossed, so vivid and distinct were they.

When they separated for the night, all retiring to their rooms on the ground-floor (for, as I said, there was no upstairs in that house), the sister felt that the heat was still so great that she could not sleep, and having fastened her window, she did not close the shutters—in that very quiet place it was not necessary—and, propped against the pillows, she still watched the wonderful, the marvellous beauty of that summer night. Gradually she became aware of two lights, two lights which flickered in and out in the belt of trees which separated the lawn from the churchyard, and as her gaze became fixed upon them, she saw them emerge, fixed in a dark substance, a definite ghastly *something*, which seemed every moment to become nearer, increasing in size and substance as it approached. Every now and then it was lost for a moment in the long shadows which stretched across the lawn from the trees, and then it emerged larger than ever, and still coming on—on. As she watched it, the most uncontrollable horror seized her. She longed to get away, but the door was close to the window and the door was locked on the inside, and while she was unlocking it, she must be for an instant nearer to *it*. She longed to scream, but her voice seemed paralysed, her tongue glued to the roof of her mouth.

Suddenly, she never could explain why afterwards, the terrible object seemed to turn to one side, seemed to be going round the house, not to be coming to her at all, and immediately she jumped out of bed and rushed to the door, but as she was unlocking it, she heard scratch, scratch, scratch upon the window, and saw a hideous brown face with flaming eyes glaring in at her. She rushed back to the bed, but the creature continued to scratch, scratch, scratch upon the window. She felt a sort of mental comfort in the knowledge that the window was securely fastened on the inside. Suddenly the scratching sound ceased. and a kind of pecking sound took its place. Then, in her agony, she became aware that the creature was unpicking the lead! The noise continued, and a diamond pane of glass fell into the room. Then a long bony finger of the creature came in and turned the handle of the window, and the window opened, and the creature came in; and it came across the room, and her terror was so great that she could not scream, and it came up to the bed and it twisted its long bony fingers into her hair, and it dragged her head over the side of the bed, and—it bit her violently in the throat.

As it bit her, her voice was released, and she screamed with all her might and main. Her brothers rushed out of their rooms, but the door was locked on the inside. A moment was lost while they got a poker and broke it open. Then the creature had already escaped through the window, and the sister, bleeding violently from a wound in the throat, was lying unconscious over the side of the bed. One brother pursued the creature, which fled before him through the moonlight with gigantic strides, and eventually seemed to disappear over the wall into the churchyard. Then he rejoined his brother by the sister's bedside. She was dreadfully hurt and her wound was a very definite one, but she was of strong disposition, not given either to romance or superstition, and when she came to herself she said, 'What has happened is most extraordinary and I am very much hurt. It seems inexplicable, but of course there *is* an explanation, and we must wait for it. It will turn out that a lunatic has escaped from some asylum and found his way here.' The wound healed and she appeared to get well, but the doctor who was sent for to her would not believe that she could bear so terrible a shock so easily, and insisted that she must have change, mental and physical; so her brothers took her to Switzerland.

Being a sensible girl, when she went abroad, she threw herself at once into the interests of the country she was in. She dried plants, she made sketches, she went up mountains, and, as autumn came on, she was the person who urged that they should return to Croglin Grange. 'We have taken it,' she said, 'for seven years, and we have only been there one; and we shall always find it difficult to let a house which is only one story high, so we had better return there; lunatics do not escape every day.' As she urged it, her brothers wished nothing better, and the family returned to Cumberland. From there being no upstairs in the house, it was impossible to make any great change in their arrangements. The sister occupied the same room, but it is unnecessary to say she always closed her shutters, which, however, as in many old houses, always left one top pane of the window uncovered. The brothers moved, and occupied a room together exactly opposite that of their sister, and they always kept loaded pistols in their room.

The winter passed most peacefully and happily. In the following March the sister was suddenly awakened by a sound she remembered only too well—scratch, scratch, scratch upon the window, and looking up, she saw, climbed up to the topmost pane of the window, the same hideous brown shrivelled face, with glaring eyes, looking in at her. This time she screamed as loud as she could. Her brothers rushed out of their room with pistols, and out of the front door. The creature was already scudding away across the lawn. One of the brothers fired and hit it in the leg, but still with the other leg it continued to make way, scrambled over the wall into the churchyard, and seemed to disappear into a vault which belonged to a family long extinct.

The next day the brothers summoned all the tenants of Croglin Grange, and in their presence the vault was opened. A horrible scene revealed itself. The vault was full of coffins; they had been broken open, and their contents, horribly mangled and distorted, were scattered over the floor. One coffin alone remained intact. Of that the lid had been lifted, but still lay loose upon the coffin. They raised it, and there, brown, withered, shrivelled, mummified, but quite entire, was the same hideous figure which had looked in at the windows of Croglin Grange, with the marks of a recent pistol-shot in the leg; and they did the only thing that can lay a vampire—they burnt it.

JOURNAL.

Highcliffe, June 30, 1874.—It is delightful to be here again. I came on Friday with Everard Primrose,[1] a friend who always especially interests me, in spite of the intense melancholy which always makes him say that he longs for an early death.

This place, so spiritually near the gates of heaven, is a great rest—quite a halt in life—after London, which, though I thought it filled with all great and beautiful things, packs in too much, so that one loses breath mentally. Here all is still, and the touching past and earnestly hopeful future lend a wonderful charm to the quiet life of the present.

The dear lady of the castle [Lady Waterford] is not looking well. I believe it is owing to her conversion to Lady Jane Ellice's teetotalism; but she says it is not that. Lady Jane herself is a perpetual sunshine, which radiates on all around her and is quite enchanting. Miss Lindsay is the only other guest. In the evening Lady Jane sings and Miss Lindsay recites—most wonderfully—out of Shakespeare, with great power and pathos.

June 30.—Mrs. Hamilton Hamilton came last night. She was a daughter of Sir G. Robinson. Her father's aide-de-camp, Captain Campbell, a poor man, wanted to marry her, and she was attached to him; but it was not allowed, and they were separated. She was married to Mr. Hamilton Hamilton, but Captain Campbell never ceased to think of her, and he was ambitious for her sake, and became Sir Colin Campbell and Lord Clyde. Afterwards, when she was free, it was thought he would marry her. He sent her an Indian shawl, and he wrote to her, and he came to see her, but he never proposed; and she waited and expected, and at last she heard he had said, 'No, it could not be;

[1] Hon. E. Primrose, second son of the Duchess of Cleveland by her first marriage with Lord Dalmeny.

people would say it was absurd.' But it would not have been absurd at all, and she would have like it very much.[1]

July 1.—A delightful morning in the library, fitful sunlight gleaming through the stained windows and upon the orange datura flowers in the conservatory, Lady Waterford painting at her table, Lady Jane and Miss Lindsay and Lady Mary Lambart[2] (a noble-looking girl like a picture by Bronzino) working around.

July 3.—Lady Waterford spoke of the picture of Miss Jane Warburton near her bedroom door; how she was appointed maid of honour to Queen Caroline at a time when maids of honour were rather fast, and how, at dinner, when the maids proposed toasts, and one gave the Archbishop of Canterbury, another the Dean of St. Paul's, or some other old man, she alone had the courage to give the smartest and handsomest man of the day, the Duke of Argyll.[3] She was so laughed at by her companions that it made her cry, and at the drawing-room somebody said to the Duke of Argyll, 'That is a young lady who has been crying for you,' and told him the story. He was much touched, but unfortunately he was married. Afterwards, however, when his Duchess died, he married Miss Warburton, and, though she was very ugly, he thought her absolute perfection. In the midst of the most interesting conversation he would break off to 'listen to his Jane'; and he had the most absolute faith in her, till once he discovered that she had deceived him in something about a marriage for one of her daughters with an Earl of Dalkeith, which was not quite straightforward; and it broke his heart, and he died.

July 5.—I came up to London with Lady Waterford on Friday, and as usual I find what Carlyle calls 'the immeasurable, soul-confusing uproar of a London life' rather delightful than otherwise. To-day I have been with Mary Lefevre to Marylebone, to hear Mr. Haweis preach. He is like a Dominican preacher in Italy, begins without a text, acts, crouches, springs, walks about in the pulpit—which is fortunately large enough, and every now and then spreads out vast black wings like a bat, and looks as if he was about to descend upon his appalled congregation. Part of his sermon was very solemn, but in part preacher and audience alike giggled.[4]

I went afterwards to luncheon at Lady Castletown's; she was not come in from church, but I went up into the drawing-room. A good-looking very smart young lady was sitting there, with her back to the window, evidently waiting also. After a pause, I made some stupid remark to her about heat or cold, &c. She looked and me, and said, 'That is a very commonplace remark. I'll make a remark. If a woman does not marry, she is nobody at all, nothing at all in the world; but if a man ever marries at all, he is an absolute fool.' I said, 'I know who you are; no one but Miss Rhoda Broughton would have said that.' And it was she.[5]

[1] Sir Colin Campbell, Baron Clyde, son of a Glasgow carpenter, born 1792. Served in the Peninsula (1810–13), in the West Indies and in China. He commanded the first division in Crimea; became Commander-in-Chief in India, 1852; suppressed the Indian Mutiny; created Field-Marshal, 1862; died and was buried in Westminster Abbey, 1863.—*Ed.*

[2] Daughter of the 8th Earl of Cavan, afterwards Baroness von Essen.

[3] John Campbell, second Duke of Argyll, 1678–1743. Immortalised by Pope. Took a leading part in proclaiming George I in 1714 and suppressed Mar's insurrection 1715.—*Ed.*

[4] Hugh Reginald Haweis, 1838–1901, incumbent of St. James, Marylebone, from 1866–1901. His sensational methods of preaching filled his church. Was something of a musician, and wrote considerably on that subject, as well as on theological questions. His wife was an artist and the daughter of Joy, the painter.—*Ed.*

[5] Rhoda Broughton, 1840–1920, was a popular novelist in her day, and amongst her books were *Not Wisely but too Well, Belinda, A Waif's Progress.*—*Ed.*

Mr. Browning came and sat on the other side of her at luncheon. She said something of novels without love: I said something of black dose as a cure for love. Mr. Browning said that Aristophanes spoke of 'the black-dose-loving Egyptians.' Miss Broughton said, 'How do you know the word means black dose?'—'Because there is a similar passage in Herodotus which throws light upon the subject, with details on which it would not be delicate to dwell.'

July 11.—Luncheon with Lady Morley, meeting Miss Flora Macdonald, who has still a reminiscence of the great beauty which brought such a surprise to the old Duchess of Gloucester when she asked Victor Emmanuel what he admired most in England, and he answered so promptly, 'Miss Flora Macdonald.' Lady Katherine Parker described—'because, alas! it was discovered that we date just a little farther

GATEWAY, LAMBETH PALACE

back than the Leicesters,' having to sit near ——, the most airified man in London. She was congratulated afterwards upon his having condescended to speak to her, but said he wouldn't, only his neighbour on the other side was even more insignificant than herself, and to her he did not speak at all. He said, apropos of a dinner at Dorchester House, 'Pray who *are* these Holfords?'—'Oh,' said Lady Katherine, 'I believe they are the people who have got a little shake-down somewhere in Park Lane.'

I was at the 'shake-down' in the evening—something quite beautiful. The staircase is that of an old Genoese palace, and was one blaze of colour, and the broad landings behind the alabaster balustrades were filled with people, sitting or leaning over, as in old Venetian pictures. The dress of the time entirely lends itself to these effects. I sat in one of the arcades with Lady Sarah Lindsay and her daughters, then with Lady Carnarvon. We watched the amusing contrasts of the people coming upstairs—the shrinking of some, the *dégagée* manner of others, the dignity of a very few—in this, no one to be compared with Princess Mary. The Prince and Princess of Wales were close by (he very merry, talking with much action, like a foreigner), also the Prince and Princess of Prussia.[1] Lady Somers looked glorious in a black dress thickly sprinkled with green beetles' wings and a head-dress of the same.

July 12.—Yesterday there was a great party at Hatfield. I drove with the Woods to King's Cross for the special train at 4 P.M., but was separated from them at the station, and joined Lady Darnley and Raglan Somerset. A tremendous storm was brewing over London, but we left it behind at first. Quantities of carriages from the house were in waiting at the Hatfield station. The street was lined with wreaths and flowers, and a succession of triumphal arches made the steep hill look like a long flowery bower. In the park, the grand old limes were in full blossom in front of the stately brick house. On the terrace on the other side the mass of guests was assembling. I went off with Lady Braybrooke to the labyrinth, then with Lady Darnley and the E. de Bunsens over the house. The storm now broke with tremendous lightning and loud peals of thunder, and in the Golden Gallery it was almost dark. Just as it began, the royal party drove up, the Prince and Princess of Wales, Prince and Princess of Prussia, Prince Arthur, the Tecks, the Duchess of Manchester, and a great quantity of suite—a very pretty procession, vehemently cheered by the people. When the storm cleared, we went out upon the terraces; the royal party went to the labyrinth. As it returned, I was standing with the Leghs of Lyme at the head of the steps, when Prince Arthur came up to me, was very cordial, and talked for some time about Rome, &c. I asked him if the Queen drew still. 'Oh, yes,' he said, 'she is quite devoted to it: and I am very fond of it too, but then *I* have so little time.'

Owing to the rain, the dinner for eight hundred had to be moved into the Armoury. The royal guests and a few others dined in the Marble Hall; the Princess of Prussia was forgotten as they were going in, and had to be hunted for. Afterwards the terraces and house were beautifully illuminated with coloured lights, in which, through what looked like a sea of fire and blood, the cascades of white roses frothed up. Every one walked out. The royalties seemed to spring up everywhere; one was always running against them by mistake. There was a pretty procession as they went away, and immediately afterwards I returned with Miss Thackeray, her sister, and the Master of Napier.

To Miss Wright.

Holmhurst, July 19, 1874.—I know half my friends wonder how I can like the change from the intellectual interests and luxurious life of London to the society of the bumble-bees and butterflies in this little hermitage; but I am sure the absolute quietude is very good for one, and I rush into my work at once, and get through no end of it. I came away from London, however, rather pining to stay for the party at Holland House, because I thought it was a duty to Lea and Miss Leycester, and I experienced the bathos, which so often comes when one is rather conceited about a little piece of self-sacrifice, of finding they would both much rather I had gone to the party, that they might have heard all about it!

Journal.

July 29.—I have been in London again for two days. On Tuesday Sir Howard Elphinstone, the Lefèvres, and I went to Holland House, where Lady Castletown and Mrs. Wingfield joined us. We drew in the Arcade, and then Miss Coventry came out in her Spanish hat and called us in to Lady Holland. She was in the west room, sitting

---

[1] Frederick and Princess Victoria (Queen Victoria's eldest child).—*Ed.*

in the wide window, and, like a queen, she sat on, moving for nobody. She was, however, very kind, and pleased with our drawings.

Wednesday was Victoria Liddell's wedding-day. All Fulham turned out, and Walham Green was a succession of triumphal arches, garlands, and mottoes. I went with Victor Williamson, and they mistook us for the bridegroom and best man. They told us to go up and wait near the altar, and the Wedding March struck up, but stopped abruptly as we went into a pew.

THE ROCK WALK, HOLMHURST

July 30.—Yesterday I dined at Lord Castletown's, and met, as usual, an interesting party. Lord Castletown talked of his youth at Holland House, when he was brought up there as the ward of Lord Holland.

'Once I escaped from Eton, and Lord Holland caught me—found me in the streets of London. He made me get into his carriage at once, and told the man to drive to the White Horse Cellar, whence the coach started for Eton. Unfortunately for me, there was one starting at once, and he made me get in. I remonstrated, saying that I had not got my things. "They shall be sent after you," he said. "But I shall be flogged, sir,"—"Serve you right, too; I hope you will be flogged," he said. I looked very piteous, and as I got into the coach he said, "Well, good-bye, John; I hope you'll be flogged," and he shook hands with me, and in my hand I found a five-pound note. He was always doing those kind things.'

At Holland House I saw everybody most worth seeing in Europe. All that was best flowed in to Lord Holland, and he was equally hospitable to all. The Whigs, not only of England, but of all the world, came to him.

Chevening, August 10, *Sunday.*—This afternoon I drove with Lord Stanhope in the long grassy glades of the park, the highest and prettiest of which gave a name to the place—Chevening, 'the Nook in the Hill.' We drove afterwards from one fine young Wellingtonia which he had planted to another, examining them all, and came back by the Spottiswoodes'. It is a fine old place, intended as an imitation of the Villa Doria at Rome, and though in nowise like Villa Doria, it has a look of Italy in its groves of ilexes and its cypresses. Lady Frederick Campbell[1] lived here. Her first husband was the Lord Ferres who was hanged, and some evidence which she gave was instrumental in bringing about his condemnation. Lord Ferres cursed her, saying that her death would be even more painful than his; and so in fact it was, for in 1807 she was burnt in one of the towers of the house, from spontaneous combustion it is said. Nothing was found of her but her thumb, she was so completely consumed, and ever since it is said that the ghost of Lady Frederick Campbell wanders in the grounds at night, brandishing her thumbless hand, and looking for her lost thumb. The place lends itself to this form its wonderful green glades lined with cedars and guarded by huge grey stone vases.

Coomb Bank was afterwards bought by the Claytons, who spent all they had in the purchase and had nothing left for keeping it up, so eventually they sold it to Mr. Spottiswoode, the King's Printer, to whom the monopoly of printing Bibles and Prayer-books has been the source of a large fortune. Mr. Spottiswoode himself is a most remarkable man, who, for hours before his daily walk to the City, is occupied with the highest mathematical speculations, and returns to spend his evenings in studies of the most abstract nature. It is said that the present generation is more indebted to him than to any other person for its improved powers of analysis.

Powderham Castle, Oct. 4.—A week here has been most delightful. I had not felt certain how much I might like it, how much my dear friend of old days might be changed by lapse of time and new relations. I can only say that, if he is changed, it is in being more entirely and perfectly delightful than ever. . . .

I arrived about half-past five. Powderham has a low park, rising into high ground as it approaches the castle, which has a gateway and courtyard. Here Charlie [Wood][2] was walking about amongst orange-trees in large boxes like those at the Tuileries. The bedrooms are dilapidated and falling into decay: Lord Devon will not restore them, nor will he set any of his estates free by selling the rest, but he goes on planting quantities of Wellingtonias in his park and making expensive fences round them. In himself he is charming, with a perfect and entirely courteous manner.[3]

With Charlie and Lady Agnes I have been completely at home and perfectly happy. But yesterday was quite charming; I had much wished to go to Lady Morley at

---

[1] Daughter of Amos Meredith, Esq. She married, secondly, a son of the 4th Duke of Argyll.

[2] Later, Lord Halifax.—*Ed.*

[3] William Reginald Courteney, 11th Earl of Devon, politician and philanthropist; president of the poor law board; chancellor of the Duchy of Lancaster. Charles Wood married Agnes, Courteney's daughter.—*Ed.*

C*

Whiteway, and after luncheon we set off—Charlie, Lady Agnes, and I. When the narrow lanes grew too steep for the pony-carriage, we left it under a hedge, and putting a saddle on Jack the pony, rode and walked by turns up the hill and across the wild heath of the open moor: Charlie rode pick-a-back behind Lady Agnes. In the woods we met Morley, greatly surprised to see us arrive thus. The others were out, but Morley showed all the curiosities of the house, which were many in a small way. Just as we were setting off, Lady Morley and Lady Katherine returned, and, after many pro's and con's, we stayed to a most amusing dinner, and only set off again at 10 P.M. with lanthorns in pitch darkness. Morley and Lady Katherine walked with us the first three miles over the wild moor with *their* lanthorn, and then we dived down into the eerie lanes closely overhung with green and fringed with ferns, and most lovely were the effects as the lanthorn revealed one gleam of glistening foliage after another out of the darkness.

Stone Hall, Plymouth, Oct. 13.—Another pleasant family home! I came on Monday to the George Edgcumbes. I had known Mrs. Edgcumbe well before at Rome, but had never seen her 'dear old man,' her 'bird,' &c., as she calls her kind old husband.[1] We went to 'the Winter Villa,' a luxurious sun-palace with a great conservatory, backed by natural rock. The late Lord Mount Edgcumbe lived here for many years, quite helpless from rheumatic gout. It was his mother[2] who was buried alive and lived for many years afterwards. It was known that she had been put into her coffin with a very valuable ring upon her finger, and the sexton went in after the funeral, when the coffin was put into the vault, to get it off. He opened the coffin, but the ring was hard to move, and he had to rub the dead finger up and down. This brought Lady Mount Edgcumbe to life, and she sat up. The sexton fled, leaving the doors of the vault and church open. Lady Mount Edgcumbe walked home in her shroud, and appeared in front of the windows. Those within thought it was a ghost. Then she walked in at the front door. When she saw her husband, she fainted away in his arms. This gave her family time to decide what should be done, and they settled to persuade her it had been a terrible delirium. When she recovered from her faint, she was in her own bed, and she ever believed it had been a dream.

Ford Castle, Oct. 29.—I came here yesterday after a weary journey from Devonshire to Northumberland. . . . This morning we had most interesting visitors. Two women were seen coming in under the gateway, one in a red cloak, the other carrying a bundle. It was Her Majesty Queen Esther Faa and the Princess Ellin of the Gipsies! When she had had her breakfast, the Queen came up into the library. She has a grand and beautiful old face, and she was full of natural refinement and eloquence. She said how she would not change places with any one, 'not even with the Queen upon the throne,' for 'God was so good to her;' that she 'loved to wander,' and that she wanted nothing since she 'always drove her own pair,' meaning her legs.

She spoke very simply of her accession—that she was the last of the Faas; that she succeeded her uncle King William; that before him came her great-uncle, of whom we 'must have read in history, Jocky Faa'; that as for her subjects, she 'couldna allude to them,' for they were such a set that she kept herself clear of them; that she had had fourteen children, but they were none of them Faas. She spoke of her daughter as

---

[1] George, second son of the 2nd Earl of Mount Edgcumbe, married Fanny Lucy, eldest daughter of Sir John Shelley.

[2] Sophia, daughter of the 2nd Earl of Buckinghamshire.

'the Princess that I have left downstairs,' but all she said was quite simple and without any assumption. She sang to us a sort of paraphase of Old Testament history. Lady Waterford asked her if there was anything she would like to have. She said she cared for nothing but rings—all her family liked them; that her daughter, Princess Ellin, had wished to have the ring Lady Waterford gave her when she last came to Ford, but that she had told her she 'never meant to take off her petticoats till she went to bed;' that next to rings, she liked 'a good nate pair of shoes,' for she 'didna like to gang confused about the feet.'

When she went away she blessed us. She said to Alick, 'You *are* a bonnie lad, and one can see that you belong to the Board of Health.' She said to me that she loved Lady Waterford, so that, 'if it wouldna be too bould,' she should 'like to take her in her arms and kiss her and cuddle her to her old bosom.'

Oct. 31.—Lady Waterford said, 'Now I must tell you a story. Somers[1] came to Highcliffe this year. I like having Somers for a cousin, he is always so kind and pleasant, and tells me so many things that are interesting. I felt it particularly this year, for he was suffering so much from a piece of the railroad that had got into his eye and he was in great pain, but he was just as pleasant as ever. "Oh, love has sore eyes," he said, but he *would* talk. The next day he insisted on going off to Lymington to see Lord Warwick,[2] who was there, and who had been ill; and it was an immense drive, and when he came back, he did not come down, and Pattinson said, "Lord Somers is come back, but he is suffering so much pain from his eyes that he will not be able to have any dinner." So I went up to sit with him. He was suffering great pain, and I wanted him not to talk, but he said, "Oh, no; I have got a story quite on my mind, and I really must tell it you." And he said that when he got to Lymington, he found Lord Warwick ill in bed, and he said, "I am so glad to see you, for I want to tell you such an odd thing that has happened to me. Last night I was in bed and the room was quite dark (this old-fashioned room of the inn at Lymington which you now see). Suddenly at the foot of the bed there appeared a great light, and in the midst of the light the figure of Death just as it is seen in the Dance of Death and other old pictures—a ghastly skeleton with a scythe and a dart: and Death balanced the dart, and it flew past me, just above my shoulder, close to my head, and it seemed to go into the wall; and then the light went out and the figure vanished. I was as wide awake then as I am now, for I pinched myself hard to see, and I lay awake for a long time, but at last I fell asleep. When my servant came to call me in the morning, he had a very scared expression of face, and he said, 'A dreadful thing has happened in the night, and the whole household of the inn is in the greatest confusion and grief, for the landlady's daughter, who slept in the next room, and the head of whose bed is against the wall against which your head now rests, has been found dead in her bed.'

Nov. 1, *Sunday.*—Lady Waterford talked much of her mother's [Lady Stuart's] life in Paris as ambassadress, and of her own birth there at the Embassy. 'I went many years after with Mama to Spa, and there was a very agreeable old gentleman there, to whom we talked at the *table-d'hôte*. He found out that we knew Paris and the people there, and then he talked, not knowing who we were, of the different ambassadresses. "The ambassadress I preferred to all others," he said, "was Lady Granville." [Fr.] He saw somehow that he had not said quite the right thing, and next day he wanted to

[1] Charles, 3rd Earl of Somers.
[2] George Guy Greville, 4th Earl of Warwick.

make the *amende*, and he talked of the Embassy again before all the people, of this room and that room, and then he said, "Was it in this room, Milady, that you were brought to bed with Milady Waterford?"[Fr.] He was a M. de Langy, and was a very interesting person. His family belonged to the *petite noblesse*, and at the time of the flight to Varennes, after the royal family was captured, theirs was one of the houses to which they were brought to rest and refresh on the way,—for it was the custom then, when there were so few inns. M. de Langy's mother was a staunch royalist, and when she knew that the King and Queen were coming, she prepared a beautiful little supper, everything as nice as she could, and waited upon them herself. When they were going away, the Queen, who had found it all most comfortable, said, "Where is the mistress of the house? I have been so happy here, that I would like to thank her before I go." Madame de Langy, who was waiting, said simple, "I was the mistress of this house before your Majesty entered it." ' [Fr.]

In the evening she [Lady Waterford] talked much of her first visit to Italy, her only visit to Rome. 'Char. was just married then, and I was just come out: we went *pour un passe-temps*. We travelled in our own carriage, and the floods had carried away the bridges, and it was very difficult to get on. It was the year of the cholera, and we had to pass quarantine. My father knew a great many of the people in authority, and we hoped to get leave to pass it in one of the larger towns. Mantua was decided upon, but was eventually given up because of the unhealthiness, and we had to pass ten days at Rovigo. We arrived at last at Bologna. The people were greatly astonished at the inn when we asked if the Cardinal Legate was at home: it was as if we had asked for the Pope: and they were more astonished still the next day when he came to call upon us. We went to a party at his palace. He was Cardinal Macchi. I shall never forget that party or the very odd people we met—I see them now. The Cardinal was in despair because the theatres were closed—"I would have lent you my box, and I would have provided ices!" The next day Rossini came to see us—"I am an extinct volcano," [Fr.] he said. Afterwards we went to Rome and stayed four months there. I liked the society part best—the balls at the Borgheses' and those at the Austrian Embassy: they were great fun.'

Nov. 7.—Yesterday, Lady Waterford, Miss Lindsay, and I had a delightful long walk across the moor and through charming relics of forest. When we reached home, we found the Bloomfields arrived.[1] In the evening Lady Bloomfield told a curious story.

'I was very intimate at Vienna with the Princess Reuss, whose first husband was Prince of Anhalt. She was a niece of Queen Teresa of Bavaria. She told me that her aunt was at Aschaffenberg with the intention of going next day to Munich. In the evening the lady-in-waiting came in and asked the Queen if she was intending to give an audience. The Queen said, "Certainly not," and that "she could not see any one." The lady then said that there was a lady sitting in the ante-chamber who would not go away. Queen Teresa then desired her brother to go out and find out who it was. He came back much agitated, and said it was *sehr unheimlich* (very uncanny), for it was the Black Lady, and that when he came up to her she disappeared; for the Bavarian royal family have a Black Lady who appears to them before a death, just as the White Lady appears to the Prussian royal family. The next day the Queen left Aschaffenberg, but being a very kind-hearted woman, she sent back her secretary to fetch some

[1] My mother's first cousin, Georgina Liddell, had married Lord Bloomfield, formerly ambassador at Berlin and Vienna. [John Arthur Douglas Bloomfield, the second baron, 1802–1879.—*Ed.*]

petitions which had been presented, but which she had not attended to, and when the secretary came into her room, he found the Black Lady standing by the table where the papers were, but she vanished on his approach. That night, when the old castellan of Aschaffenberg and his wife were in bed, the great bell of the castle began to toll, and they remembered that it could toll by no human agency, as they had the key of the bell-tower.

'At that moment Queen Teresa died at Munich. She arrived at three: at five she was seized with cholera: at eleven she was dead.'

Nov. 10.—Last night Mr. Fyler [the Vicar of Cornhill] told his famous story of 'the nun.' It is briefly this:—

A son of Sir J. Stuart of Allanbank, on the Blackadder, where Lady Boswell lives now, was in Rome, where he fell in love with a novice in one of the convents. When his father heard of it, he was furious, and summoned him home. Young Stuart told the nun he must leave Rome, and she implored him to marry her first; but he would do nothing of the kind, and, as he left, she flung herself under his carriage; the wheels went over her, and she was killed. The first thing the faithless lover saw on his return to Scotland was the nun, who met him in the bridal attire she was to have worn, and she has often appeared since, and has become known in the neighbourhood as 'Pearlin Jean.' On one occasion seven ministers were called in to lay her, but with no effect.

Raby Castle, Nov. 20.—A week here with a large party, which I began to think delightful as soon as I could cure myself of the uncomfortable sensation of being so much behind my kind, all the other people knowing each other better, and being more in possession of their tongues and faculties than myself. 'Be insignificant, and you will make no enemies,' is, however, a very good piece of advice I once received. Interesting members of the circle have been the Fitzwilliams from Wentworth, and the Quaker family of Pease,[1] of whom the mother is one of the sweetest, most charming people I ever saw, like a lovely picture by Gainsborough, and with the expression of one of Perugino's angels. But the great feature of the visit has been the Butes, and I have been absorbed by them. I never expected to make much acquaintance, but from the first Lord Bute[2] annexed himself to me, perhaps because he thought I was shy, and because of other people he felt very shy himself. He has great sweetness and gentleness of manner, and a good-looking, refined face.

Lady Bute says the happiest time in her life was the winter they spent in Majorca, because then she got away, not only from all the fine people, but from all the people who wanted to know what they thought must be the fine people; but that it was such a bore even there bearing a name for which the natives *would* raise their prices. Next winter they mean to spend at Nazareth, where they will hire the Bishop's house; 'no one can get at us there.'

I walked with Lord Bute each day. It was like reading *Lothair* in the original, and most interesting at first, but became somewhat monotonous, as he talks incessantly —winding into his subject like a serpent, as Johnson said of Burke—of altars, ritual, liturgical differences; and he often almost loses himself, and certainly quite lost me, in sentences about 'the Unity of the Kosmos,' &c.

[1] See page 113.

[2] John Patrick Crichton-Stuart, 3rd Marquis of Bute, 1847—1900, in 1868 abandoned the presbyterian church for the Roman Catholic, a situation which probably suggested the plot of Disraeli's novel *Lothair* (Hare seems to have seen this fact, having regard to his remarks in a later paragraph). A benefactor of Scottish universities.—*Ed.*

He spoke much of Antichrist—the mark 666, the question if it had been Nero, or if Nero was only a type, and the real Antichrist still to come; and of the other theory that the reason why no ten thousand were sealed of Dan was that Antichrist was to come from that tribe, the dying words of Jacob tending to this belief.

He talked much of fasting; that he had often fasted for twenty-four hours, and that he preferred fasting as the practice existed 'before the folly of collations.' I asked if it did not make him ill. He said, 'No,' for if the hunger became too great he took a cigar, which allayed it, and that he went out and 'ate the air' while taking plenty of exercise; that poor people seldom became thin in Lent, because what they did eat was bread and potatoes. I said I thought it must make him dreadfully ill-tempered to be so hungry, and thus conduce rather to vice than virtue. He said he did not think

WARKWORTH, FROM THE COQUET

it made him vicious; but he agreed with me that persons naturally inclined to be ill-tempered had better fast *alone*.

From what he said it was evident that he would like to give up all his goods to the poor, and that the Island of Bute stands a chance of becoming a vast monastery.

Ravensworth, Nov. 29.—Lord Ravensworth[1] welcomed me with such cordial kindness, and has been so genial and good to me ever since, that I quite feel as if in him I had found the ideal uncle I have always longed for, but never before enjoyed. He is certainly the essence of an agreeable and accomplished scholar, with a faultless memory and apt classical quotations for every possible variety of subject. He told me, and made me write down, the following story:—

It is going back a long time ago—to the time of Marie Antoinette. It will be remembered that the most faithful, the most entirely devoted of all the gallant adherents of

[1] My mother's first cousin, Henry Thomas Liddell, 1st Earl of Ravensworth.

Marie Antoinette was the Comte de Fersen. The Comte de Fersen was ready to lay down his life for the Queen, to go through fire and water for her sake; and, on her side, if Marie Antoinette had a corner in her heart for any one except the King, it was for the Comte de Fersen.[1] When the royal family escaped to Varennes, it was the Comte de Fersen who dressed up as coachman and drove the carriage; and when the flight to Varennes failed, and when, one after another, he had seen all his dearest friends perish upon the scaffold, the Comte de Fersen felt as if the whole world was cut away from under his feet, as if life had nothing whatever left to offer, and he sunk into a state of apathy, mental and physical, from which nothing whatever seemed to rouse him; there was nothing whatever left which could be of any interest to *him*.

The physicians who were called in said that the Comte de Fersen must have absolute change; that he must travel for an unlimited time; that he must leave France; at any rate, that he must never see again that Paris which was so terrible to him, which was stained for ever with the blood of the Queen and Madame Elizabeth. And he was quite willing; all places were the same to him now that his life was left desolate: he did not care where he went.

He went to Italy, and one afternoon in November he drove up to what was then, as it is still, the most desolate, weird, ghastly inn in Italy—the wind-stricken, storm-beaten, lava-seated inn of Radicofani. And he came there not to stay; he only wanted post-horses to go on as fast as he could, for he was always restless to be moving—to go farther on. But the landlord said, 'No, it was too late at night; there was going to be a storm; he could not let his horses cross the pass of Radicofani till the next morning.'— 'But you are not aware,' said the traveller, 'that I am the Comte de Fersen.'—'I do not care in the least who you are,' said the landlord; 'I make my rules, and my rules hold good for one as well as for another.'—'But you do not understand probably that money is no object to me, and that time is a very great object indeed. I am quite willing to pay whatever you demand, but I must have the horses at once, for I must arrive at Rome on a particular day.'—'Well, you will not have the horses,' said the landlord; 'at least to-morrow you may have them, but to-night you will not; and if you are too fine a gentleman to come into my poor hotel, you may sleep in the carriage, but to-night you will certainly not have the horses.'

Then the Comte de Fersen made the best of what he saw was the inevitable. He had the carriage put into the coach-house, and he himself came into the hotel, and he found it, as many hundreds of travellers have done since, not half so bad as he expected. It is a bare, dismal, whitewashed barracky place, but the rooms are large and tolerably clean. So he got some eggs or something that there was for supper, and he had a fire made up in the best of the rooms, and he went to bed. But he took two precautions; he drew a little round table that was there to the head of the bed and he put two loaded pistols upon it; and, according to the custom of that time, he made the courier sleep across the door on the outside.

He went to bed, and he fell asleep, and in the middle of the night he awoke with the indescribable sensation that people have, that he was not alone in the room, and he raised himself against the pillow and looked out. From a small latticed window high in the opposite whitewashed wall the moonlight was pouring into the room, and making a white silvery pool in the middle of the rough boarded oak floor. In the middle of this pool of light, dressed in a white cap and jacket and trousers, such as

---

[1] John Axel Fersen, making the tour of France at nineteen, was presented to the Dauphine, herself nineteen, in 1774. Throughout his friendship with her, the perfect reserve of a great gentleman and great lady was never broken.

masons wear, stood the figure of a man looking at him. The Comte de Fersen stretched
out his hand over the side of the bed to take one of his pistols, and the man said, 'Don't
fire: you could do no harm to me, you could do a great deal of harm to yourself: I
am come to tell you something.' And the Comte de Fersen looked at him: he did not
come any nearer; he remained just where he was, standing in the pool of white moonlight, half way between the bed and the wall; and he said, 'Say on: tell me what you
have come for.' And the figure said, 'I am *dead*, and my body is underneath your bed.
I was a mason of Radicofani, and, as a mason, I wore the white dress in which you
now see me. My wife wished to marry somebody else: she wished to marry the landlord
of this hotel, and they beguiled me into the inn, and they made me drunk, and they
murdered me, and my body is buried beneath where your bed now stands. Now I
died with the word *vendetta* upon my lips, and the longing, the thirst that I have for
revenge will not let me rest, and I never shall rest, I never can have *any* rest, till I
have had my revenge. Now I know that you are going to Rome; when you get to
Rome, go to the Cardinal Commissary of Police, and tell him what you have seen,
and he will send men down here to examine the place, and my body will be found, and
I shall have my revenge.' And Comte de Fersen said, 'I will.' But the spirit laughed
and said, 'You don't suppose that I'm going to believe *that*? You don't imagine that
you are the only person I've come to like this? I have come to dozens, and they have
all said, "I will," and afterwards what they have seen has seemed like a hallucination,
a dream, a chimæra, and before they have reached Rome the impression has vanished
altogether, and nothing has been done. Give me your hand.' The Comte de Fersen
was a little staggered at this; however, he was a brave man, and he stretched out his
hand over the foot of the bed, and he felt something or other happen to one of his
fingers; and he looked, and there was no figure, only the moonlight streaming in
through the little latticed window, and the old cracked looking-glass on the wall and
the old rickety furniture just distinguishable in the half light; there was no mason there,
but the loud regular sound of the snoring of the courier was heard outside the bedroom door. And the Comte de Fersen could not sleep; he watched the white moonlight fade into dawn, and the pale dawn brighten into day, and it seemed to him as
if the objects in that room would be branded into his brain, so familiar did they become—the old cracked looking-glass, and the shabby washing-stand, and the rush-
bottomed chairs, and he also began to think that what had passed in the earlier part
of the night was a hallucination—a mere dream. Then he got up, and he began to wash
his hands; and on one of his fingers he found a very curious old iron ring, which was
certainly not there before—and then he *knew*.

And the Comte de Fersen went to Rome, and when he arrived at Rome he went
to the Swedish Minister that then was, a certain Count Löwenjelm,[1] and the Count
Löwenjelm was very much impressed with the story, but a person who was much more
impressed was the Minister's younger brother, the Count Carl Löwenjelm, for he had
a very curious and valuable collection of peasant's jewelry, and when he saw the ring
he said, 'That is a very remarkable ring, for it is a kind of ring which is only made and
worn in one place, and that place is in the mountains near Radicofani.'

And the two Counts Löwenjelm went with the Comte de Fersen to the Cardinal
Commissary of Police, and the Cardinal also was very much struck, and he said,
'It is a very extraordinary story, a very extraordinary story indeed, and I am quite

---

[1] In 1879 I told this story to the Crown Prince of Sweden and Norway, who took the trouble
to verify facts and dates as to the Löwenjelms, &c., and found everything coincide.

inclined to believe that it means something. But, as you know, I am in a great position of trust under Government, and I could not send a body of military down to Radico-fani upon the faith of what may prove to have been a dream. At any rate (he said) I could not do it unless the Comte de Fersen proved his sense of the importance of such an action by being willing to return to Radicofani himself.' And not only was the Comte de Fersen willing to return, but the Count Carl Löwenjelm went with him. The landlord and landlady were excessively agitated when they saw them return with the soldiers who came from Rome. They moved the bed, and found that the flags beneath had been recently upturned. They took up the flags, and there—not sufficiently corrupted to be irrecognisable—was the body of the mason, dressed in the white cap and jacket and trousers, as he had appeared to the Comte de Fersen. Then the landlord and landlady, in true Italian fashion, felt that Providence was against them, and they confessed everything. They were taken to Rome, where they were tried and con-demned to death, and they were beheaded at the Bocca della Verità.

The Count Carl Löwenjelm was present at the execution of that man and woman, and he was the person who told the Marquis de Lavalette, who told Lord Ravensworth, who told me. The by-play of the story is also curious. Those two Counts Löwenjelm were the natural sons of the Duke of Sudomania, who was one of the aspirants for the crown of Sweden in the political crisis which preceded the election of Bernadotte. He was, in fact, elected, but he had many enemies, and on the night on which he arrived to take possession of the throne he was poisoned. The Comte de Fersen himself came to a tragical end in those days. He was very unpopular in Stockholm, and during the public procession in which he took part at the funeral of Charles Augustus (1810) he was murdered, being (though it is terrible to say so of the gallant adherent of Marie Antoinette) beaten to death with umbrellas. And that it was with no view to robbery and from purely political feeling is proved by the fact that though he was *en grande tenue*, nothing was taken away.

Wentworth Wodehouse, Dec. 3.—This house has a very stately effect as you approach it, with a truly majestic portico. On the first floor is an immense hall like those in the great Roman houses, and on either side diverge the reception rooms, hung with pictures. The rooms themselves want colour and effect. Sixty guests can stay in the house, and a hundred and twenty can dine without any crowd, but the place needs great parties of this kind, for smaller ones are lost in these vast suites of too lofty rooms. Lord Fitzwilliam[1] is the very type of a high-bred nobleman, and Lady Fitzwilliam[2] has a sweet and gentle manner; but Lady F. is calm and placid, her two daughters calmer and placider, and Lord F. calmest and placidest.

Dec. 4,—Lady Albreda drove us about the park and to the 'Mausoleum,' a com-memorative monument raised to the Minister Lord Rockingham[3] by his son. It is copied from the Roman monument at S. Remy near Arles, and contains, in a kind of Pantheon, a statue by Nollekens of Lord Rockingham surrounded by his friends. The face is from a mask taken after death, and the figure is full of power and expression, with a deprecatory 'Oh, pray don't say such a thing as that.'

Temple Newsam, Dec. 6.—This great house is four miles from Leeds, by a road passing through a squalid suburb of grimy houses and muddy lanes, with rotten

[1] The 6th Earl of Fitzwilliam.
[2] Lady Frances Douglas, daughter of the 18th Earl of Morton.
[3] Charles Watson-Wentworth, the second Marquis; Whig and twice Prime Minister (1765 and 1782); supported the independence of American colonies and partial Catholic emancipation.—*Ed.*

palings and broken paving-stones, making blackened pools of stagnant water: then black fields succeed, with withered hedges, stag-headed trees, and here and there a mountain of coal refuse breaking the dismal distances. It was almost dark as I drove up the steep park to the house.[1]

In an immense gallery, hung with red and covered with pictures, like the gallery at Chesney Wold in Bleak House, I found Mrs. Meynell Ingram and Freddie Wood[2] sitting. It was like arriving at a bivouac in the desert; the light from the fire and the lamps gleamed on a little tea-table and a few chairs round it, all beyond was lost in the dark immensity.

Dec. 7.—Deep snow all to-day and a furious wind. But yesterday we reached Leeds for the assize sermon from the Sheriff's chaplain.

This house, where Lord Darnley was born, and whence Lord Strafford issued his summons to the Cavaliers to meet in defence of the King, is very curious. In point of amusement, the Judge is the principal feature of the present party, and how he does trample on his High Sheriff! He coolly said to him yesterday that he considered a High Sheriff as 'dust under his feet'; and he narrated before him a story of one of his brother judges, who, when his High Sheriff had left his hat in court, not only would not let him go to fetch it, but would not wait while his servants fetched it, and ordered him instantly to take him back to his lodgings without his hat! In court, Judge Denman was annoyed by some stone-breakers outside the window, and was told it would cost a matter of £40 to have them stopped. 'Stop the noise instantly,' he said; and the Mayor had to pay for it out of his own pocket. Yesterday, when the snow was so deep, the High Sheriff timidly suggested that they might be snowed up. 'That is impossible,' said the Judge; 'whatever the difficulties, Mr. High Sheriff, you are bound to see me conveyed to Leeds by the opening of the court, if the whole of Leeds is summoned out to cut a way for me.'[3]

Ripley Castle, Dec. 12.—I found here Count and Countess Bathyany, people I was very glad to see. They retain their old castle in Hungary, where they are magnates of the first rank, but for some years they have lived chiefly in England, at Eaglehurst on the Solent, and receive there during the yachting season. The Countess has remains of great beauty and is wonderfully agreeable. As I sat by her at dinner, she talked much of Lady William Russell,[4] and told me the story of Lord Moira's appearance, which she had heard from her own lips.

Lady William was at Brighton, where her friend Lady Betty —— was also staying. One day when Lady Betty went to her, she found her excessively upset and discomposed, and she said it was on account of a dream that she had had of her uncle, who, as Lord Moira, had brought her up, and who was then Governor of Malta. She said that she had seen a very long hall, and at the end of the hall a couch with a number of female figures in different attitudes of grief and despair bending over it, as if they were holding up or attending to some sick person. On the couch she saw no one, but immediately afterwards she seemed to meet her Uncle Moira and embraced him, but said, with a start, 'Uncle, how terribly cold you are!' He replied, 'Bessie, did you not

---

[1] Temple Newsam became the property of the City of Leeds in 1922. The park now contains golf courses and playing-fields.—*Ed.*

[2] Eldest daughter and youngest son of Viscount Halifax.—*Ed.*

[3] George Denman, judge, 1819–1896; son of the Lord Chief Justice, Thomas Denman, first Baron; judge of the high court, Queen's Bench division.—*Ed.*

[4] Mother of the 9th Duke of Bedford, a most charming and hospitable person.

know that I am dead?' She recollected herself instantly and said, 'Oh, Uncle, how does it look on the other side?'—'Quite different from what we have imagined, and far, far more beautiful,' he replied with a radiant smile, and she awoke. Her dream occurred just when Lord Hastings[1] (formerly Lord Moira) died on a couch in a hall at Malta; but she told the circumstances to Lady Betty long before the news came.

Another story which Countess Bathyany told from personal knowledge was that of Sir Samuel Romilly.

Lord Grey[2] and his son-in-law, Sir Charles Wood, were walking on the ramparts of Carlisle. The rampart is there still. It is very narrow, and there is only one exit; so if you walk there, you must return as you came. While they were walking, a man passed them, returned, passed them again, and then disappeared in front of them over the parapet, where there was really no means of exit. There was a red scarf round his throat. 'How very extraordinary! and how exactly like Sir Samuel Romilly!' they both exclaimed. At that moment Sir Samuel Romilly had cut his throat in a distant part of England.[3]

We have tea in the evening in the oak room in the tower, where Miss Ingilby has often had much to say that is interesting, especially this story.

A regiment was lately passing through Derbyshire on its way to fresh quarters in the North. The Colonel, as they stayed for the night in one of the country towns, was invited to dine at a country-house in the neighbourhood, and to bring any one he liked with him. Consequently he took with him a young ensign for whom he had taken a great fancy. They arrived, and it was a large party, but the lady of the house did not appear till just as they were going in to dinner, and, when she appeared, was so strangely *distraite* and preoccupied that she scarcely attended to anything that was said to her. At dinner, the Colonel observed that his young companion scarcely ever took his eyes off the lady of the house, staring at her in a way which seemed at once rude and unaccountable. It made him observe the lady herself, and he saw that she scarcely seemed to attend to anything said by her neighbours on either side of her, but rather seemed, in a manner quite unaccountable, to be listening to some one or something behind her. As soon as dinner was over, the young ensign came to the Colonel and said, 'Oh, do take me away: I entreat you to take me away from this place.' The Colonel said, 'Indeed your conduct is so very extraordinary and unpleasant, that I quite agree with you that the best thing we can do is to go away;' and he made the excuse of his young friend being ill, and ordered their carriage. When they had driven some distance the Colonel asked the ensign for an explanation of his conduct. He said that he could not help it: during the whole of dinner he had seen a terrible black shadowy figure standing behind the chair of the lady of the house, and it had seemed to whisper to her, and she to listen to it. He had scarcely told this, when a man on horseback rode rapidly past the carriage, and the Colonel, recognising one of the servants of the house they had just left, called out to know if anything was the matter. 'Oh, don't stop me, sir,' he shouted; 'I am going for the doctor: my lady has just cut her throat.'

[1] Lord Moira was created Marquis of Hastings 1816, and died at Malta, November 26, 1826. [Francis Rawdon Hastings, who distinguished himself in the American War of Independence; Governor-General of Bengal, 1813; established British supremacy in Central India.—*Ed.*]

[2] Charles, 2nd Earl Grey. [Whig Prime Minister who introduced the Reform Bill which was eventually passed in 1832.—*Ed.*]

[3] Sir Samuel Romilly, who effected great reforms in the criminal punishment code. He committed suicide on the death of his wife.—*Ed.*

Hickledon, Dec. 12.—I came here yesterday, cordially welcomed by Lord and Lady Halifax, and was glad to find the John Greys here. In the evening my dear Charlie and Lady Agnes came. Charlie had brought back many stories from Bedgebury. Mr. Beresford Hope told him that:—

His uncle Lord Decies, who had lived very much in Paris, met, somewhere abroad, young Lionel Ashley, a brother of Lord Shaftesbury, then about twenty-two, and living abroad, as he was, very much out at elbows. Lord Decies remarked upon a very curious iron ring which he wore, with a death's-head and cross-bones upon it. 'Oh,' said young Ashley, 'about that ring there is a very curious story. It was given to me by a famous conjuring woman, Madame le Norman, to whom I went with two friends of mine. She prophesied that we should all three die before we were twenty-three. My two friends are already dead, and next year I shall be twenty-three: but if you like I will give you the ring;' and he gave it to Lord Decies. When Lord Decies returned to Paris, Lionel Ashley came there too, and he frequently dined with him. A short time before the expiration of the year, at the end of which Ashley was again engaged to dine with him, Lord Decies was sitting in his room, when the door opened, and Lionel Ashley came in. As to what was said, Mr. Hope was not quite clear, but the circumstances were so singular, that when he was gone, Lord Decies rang the bell, and asked the servant who had let Mr. Ashley into the house. 'But, Milord, Mr. Ashley died yesterday,' said the servant.[1]

Another curious story was that—

Lord Waterford (the third Marquis) was one day standing talking to the landlord of the little inn in the village close to his place of Curraghmore, when some one rushed up looking very much agitated, and said that there had been a most dreadful murder in the neighbouring hills. 'Then it must be the little one,' exclaimed the landlord. 'What can you possibly mean?' said Lord Waterford, feeling that the landlord's knowing anything about it was at the least very suspicious. 'Well, my lord,' he said, 'I am afraid you will never believe me, but I must tell you that last night I dreamt that two men came to my inn, a tall man and a little man, and in my dream I saw the tall man murder the little man with a very curious knife, the like of which I never saw before. I told my wife when I woke, but she only laughed at me. To my horror, in the course of the morning, those very two men came to my inn, and I was so possessed by my dream, that I refused them admittance; but coming back some time after, I found that my wife had let them in when my back was turned. I could not turn them out of my house when they were once in it, but going in, some time after, with some refreshments, my horror was increased by seeing on the table between them the very knife I had seen in my dream. Then they paid for their refreshments and went away.'

The dream of the landlord and the coincidences were considered so extraordinary, that as the bridge at Carrick-on-Suir was the only bridge in that part, and so in a sort of sense divided the country, a watch was put there, and in course of time a man exactly answering to the landlord's description crossed the bridge and was arrested. In prison, he confessed that he had been in the cod-fishery trade with his companion, who had boasted to him of his great earnings. He forthwith attached himself to him, travelled with him, and watched for the opportunity of murdering him. His weapon was a knife used in the cod-fishery, quite unknown in those parts.

[1] Anthony Lionel Ashley, died Jan. 14, 1836.

Dec. 27.—I have been staying at Brighton with old Mrs. Aïdé,[1] who looks like Cinderella's godmother or some other good old fairy. It amused me exceedingly to see at Brighton an entirely new phase of society—two pleasant old ladies, daughters of Horace Smith, being its best and leading elements. Every one was full of the 'Rink,' where all the young gentlemen and all the young ladies skate all morning on dry land, come home to luncheon, and skate again all afternoon. No balls or picnics can promote the same degree of intimacy which is thus engendered, young men walking about (on wheels) all day long, holding up and assisting their partners. I heard this curious story:—

The Princess Dolgorouki had been a great heiress and was a person of great wealth and importance. One day she was driving through a village near S. Petersburg, when she heard the clear glorious voice of a young girl ringing through the upper air from a high window of one of the poor houses by the wayside. So exquisitely beautiful was the voice, that the Princess stopped her carriage to listen to it. The voice rang on and on for some time, and, when it ceased, the Princess sent into the house to inquire who the singer had been. 'Oh,' they said, 'it is one of your own serfs: it is the girl Anita'; and they brought the singer out, a sweet, simple, modest-looking girl of sixteen, and at the bidding of the Princess she sang again, quite simply, without any shyness, in the road by the side of the carriage. The Princess was greatly captivated by her, and finding that she was educated beyond most of those in her condition of life, and being at that time in want of a reader in her palace at S. Petersburg, she took her to live with her, and Anita occupied in her house a sort of intermediate position, arranging the flowers, and reading when she was wanted. Gradually the Princess became very fond of her, and gave her masters, under whom she made such astonishing progress, that she became quite a well-educated young lady, while her glorious voice formed the great attraction to all parties at the Dolgorouki Palace.

The Princess Dolgorouki never foresaw, what actually happened, that when her son returned from 'the grand tour,' which young men made then, and found a very beautiful, interesting girl domesticated with his mother, he would fall in love with her. When she saw that it was so, she said to her son that she had a great regard for the girl and could not have her affections tampered with, so that he had better go away again. The young prince answered that he had no idea whatever of tampering with the girl's affections, that he loved her and believed that she loved him, and that he meant to marry her.

On hearing this the fury of the Princess knew no bounds. She tried to reason with her son, and when she found him perfectly impracticable, she expelled him from her house and got him sent to France. She also sent for the parents of Anita, and told them that they must look out at once for a suitable person for her to marry, for that she must be married before Prince Dolgorouki returned. She said that she had no complaint to make of the girl, and that she would help her to make a good marriage by giving her a very handsome dowry; all that she required was that she should be married at once. Before leaving, however, Prince Dolgorouki had found means to be alone for a few minutes with Anita, and had said to her, 'I know my mother well, and I know that as soon as I am gone she will try to insist upon your marriage. She will not consider you, and will sacrifice you to the fulfilment of her own will. Have faith, however, in

[1] Mother of Charles Hamilton Aïdé, author and musician. Daughter of Admiral Sir George Collier, she married an American merchant, who came to England during the Regency and was killed in a duel at Paris in 1830. Mrs. Aïdé herself died in 1875. Her son's novels enjoyed a vogue in Victorian days.—*Ed.*

me, hold out, and believe that, however impossible it may seem, I shall be able at the last moment to save you.'

The bridegroom whom Anita's father found was a certain Alexis Alexandrovitch, a farmer near their village and a person in a considerably higher position than their own. He was rich, he was much esteemed, he was greatly in love with Anita, but he was vulgar, he was hideous, he was almost always drunk, and Anita hated him. He came to her father's house and proposed. She refused him, but he persisted in persecuting her with his attentions, and her own family tried to force her consent by ill-treatment, half-starved her, cut her off from all communication with others and from all her usual employments, and shut her up in a room at the top of the house.

At last, when the girl's position was becoming quite untenable and her courage was beginning to give way, Prince Dolgorouki contrived to get a note conveyed to her. He said, 'I know all you are suffering; it is impossible that you can go on like this. Pretend to accede to their wishes. Accept Alexis Alexandrovitch, but believe that I will save you at the last moment.'

So Anita said to her father and mother that she gave in to their wishes, that she would marry Alexis Alexandrovitch. And the wedding-day was fixed and the wedding-feast was prepared. And the old Princess Dolgorouki gave not only a very handsome dowry, but a very splendid set of peasant's jewellery to the bride. She did not intend to be present at the ceremony herself, but she would send her major-domo to represent her.

The wedding-day arrived, and the bride went with her family to the church, which was darkened, with candles burning everywhere. And Alexis Alexandrovitch also arrived, rather more drunk than usual. The church was thronged with people from end to end, for the place was within a drive of S. Petersburg, and it was fine weather, and hundreds of persons who remembered Anita and had admired her wonderful voice at the Dolgorouki palace drove out to see her married. According to the custom of the Greek Church, the register was brought to be signed before the ceremony. He signed his name 'Alexis Alexandrovitch,' and she signed her name 'Anita.' And the service began, and the crowd pressed thicker and thicker round the altar, and there was a constant struggle to see. And the service went on, and the crowd pressed more closely still, and somehow in the press the person who stood next to Anita was not Alexis Alexandrovitch, and the service went on, and Anita was married, and then the crowd opened to let the bridal pair pass through, and Anita walked rapidly down the church on the arm of her bridegroom, and it was not Alexis Alexandrovitch, and it was Prince Dolgorouki. And a carriage and four was waiting at the church door, and the bridal pair leapt into it and were whirled rapidly away.

The old Princess Dolgorouki sent at once to stop them at the frontier, but the flight had been so well arranged, that she was too late. Then she swore (having everything in her own power) that she would cut off her son without a penny, and that she would never see him again. Happy in each other's love, however, the young Prince and Princess Dolgorouki lived at Paris, where, though they were poor, Anita's wonderful voice could always keep them from want. There, their two children were born. Four years elapsed, and they heard nothing from their Russian home. Then the family lawyer in S. Petersburg wrote to say that the old Princess Dolgorouki was dead. Whether she had repented of disinheriting her son and had destroyed her will before her death, or whether she had put off making her unjust will till it was too late, no one ever knew. The will of disinheritance was never found, and her son was the heir of all his mother's vast estates.

The young couple set out with their children for Russia to take possession, but it was in the depth of winter, the Prince was very delicate, and the change to the fierce cold of the north made him very ill, and at some place on the frontier—Wilna, I think —he died. The unhappy widow continued her journey with her children to S. Peters-burg, but when she arrived, the heir-at-law had taken possession of everything. 'But I am here; I am the Princess Dolgorouki,' she said. 'No,' was the answer; 'you have been residing for four years with Prince Dolgorouki, but the person you married was Alexis Alexandrovitch, and the register in which you both signed your names before your marriage exists to prove it.' A great lawsuit ensued, in which the young widow lost almost all the money she had, and eventually she lost her lawsuit too, and retired in great penury to Warsaw, where she maintained herself and her children by singing and giving music lessons.

But at Warsaw, as at Paris, her beauty and gentleness, and the patience with which she bore her misfortunes, made her a general favourite. Amongst those who became devoted to her was a young lawyer, who examined into the evidence of the trial which had taken place, and then, going to her, urged her to try again. She resisted, saying that the case was hopelessly lost, and besides, that she was too poor to reopen it. The lawyer said, 'If you regain the vast Dolgorouki inheritance, you can pay me something: it will be a drop in the ocean to you; but if the lawsuit fails I shall expect no payment.' So she let him try.

Now the lawyer knew that there was no use in contending against the register, but he also felt that as—according to his view—in the eyes of God his client had been Princess Dolgorouki, there was no harm in tampering with that register if it was possible. It was no use, however, to alter it, as hundreds of witnesses existed who had seen the register as it was, and who knew that it contained the name of Alexis Alexan-drovitch as the husband of Anita, for the trial had drawn attention to it from all quarters. It was also most difficult to see the register at all, because it was now most carefully guarded. But at last there came a time when the young lawyer was not only able to see the register, but when for three minutes he was left alone with it. And he took advan-tage of those three minutes to do what?

He scratched out the name, or part of the name of Alexis Alexandrovitch, and he wrote the name of Alexis Alexandrovitch over again.

Then when people came and said, 'But here is the register—here is the name of Alexis Alexandrovitch,' he said, 'Yes, there is certainly the name of Alexis Alexandro-vitch, but if you examine, you will find that it is written over something else which has been scratched out.'

And the case was tried again, and the young widow was reinstated in the Dol-gorouki property, and she was the grandmother of the present Prince Dolgorouki.

Battle Abbey, Jan. 26, 1875.—The news of dear Lady Carnarvon's death came yesterday as a shadow over everything. Surely never was there a more open, lovable, unselfish, charming, and truly noble character. She was the one person in England capable '*tenir salon.*' to succeed—in a far more charming way—to Lady Palmerston's celebrity in that respect.

Apparently radiant with happiness, and shedding happiness on all around her, she yet had often said latterly that she 'did not feel that the compensations made up for the anxieties of life,' and that she longed to be at rest.

In the agreeable party at Battle it has been a great pleasure to find the French Ambassador and the Comtesse de Jarnac. Lord Stanhope is here,[1] and has talked pleasantly as usual. Apropos of the custom of the living always closing the eyes of the dead, he reminded us of the admirable inscription over the door of the library at Murcia, 'Here the dead *open* the eyes of the living.'

Jan. 27.—Count Nesselrode has come. He has been describing to the Duchess[2] how parents are always proposing to him for their beautiful young girls of fifteen or sixteen. He says that he answers, 'Could I think of marriage at my age?' and that they reply, 'With your name, M. le Comte, one is always young.' . . . 'and that gives me gooseflesh.'[Fr.]

There used to be a ghost at Battle Abbey. Old Lady Webster told Mr. Hussey of Scotney Castle how she saw it soon after her marriage, an old woman of most terrible aspect, who drew the curtains of her bed and looked in. Immediately after, Sir Godfrey came into the room. 'Who was that old woman?' she said. 'There could have been no old woman.' 'Oh, yes, there was, and you must have met her in the passage, for she has only just gone out of the room.' In her old age Lady Webster would describe the pattern on the old woman's dress, and say that she should recognise it anywhere.

Holmhurst, Feb. 1.—A long visit to Lord Stratford de Redcliffe[3] in Lady Jocelyn's singular house at St. Leonards, which you enter from the top storey. Lord Stratford is a grand old man with high forehead and flowing white hair. He can no longer walk, and sits in his dressing-gown, but his artistic daughters make him very picturesque, hanging his chair with a shade of purple which matches the lining and cuffs of his dressing-gown, &c. He talked of many different people he had seen, of Goethe, 'who had a very high forehead' (but 'the highest forehead known was that of the immortal Shakespeare, who had every great quality that could exist phrenologically'), and then he spoke of Mezzofanti, whom he had known personally in Italy, and who had told him the story of his life. He had been a carpenter's apprentice, and had one day been at his work outside the open window of a school where a master was teaching. Having a smattering of Greek, which he had taught himself, he felt sure that he detected the master in giving a wrong explanation. This worried him so much that he could not get it out of his head, and, after the school and his own work were both over, he rang the bell and begged to see the master. 'I was at work, sir, and I heard you speaking, and I think you gave such and such an explanation in Greek'—'Well, and what do you know about Greek?'—'Not much, sir; but, if you will forgive my saying so, I am sure you will find, if you examine, that the explanation was not the correct one.' The master found that the young carpenter was right, and it led to his obtaining friends and being educated.[4]

Lord Stratford talked much of the extraordinary change, not only in politics, but in 'the way of carrying on politics,' since he was young.

[1] Lord Stanhope died the same year as this entry.—*Ed.*
[2] Of Cleveland.—*Ed.*
[3] Stratford Canning, first Viscount Stratford de Redcliffe (1786–1880), diplomatist. Amongst multifarious activities, negotiated the Russo-Turkish Treaty of Budapest (1812), was plenipotentiary in Switzerland to settle the federal government (1814–20), with the sanction of the Congress of Vienna, was our envoy to Washington, St. Petersburg and Constantinople. He was the ambassador *par excellence.*—*Ed.*
[4] Giuseppe Caspar Mezzofanti (1774–1849), cardinal and linguist, chief keeper of the Vatican library and director of studies in the Congregation. He is said to have spoken fluently some fifty or sixty languages.—*Ed.*

Feb. 17, 1875.—Yesterday, when I was with Louisa, Lady Ashburton, at Kent House, which is being beautifully arranged, Lady Bloomfield came in and then Mr. Carlyle—weird and grim, with his long coat and tall wizard-befitting hat. He talked in volumes, with fathomless depths of adjectives, into which it was quite impossible to follow him, and in which he himself often got out of his depth. A great deal was about Garibaldi, who was the 'most absolute incarnation of zero, but the inexplicable perversity and wilfulness of the human race had taken him up, poor creature, and set him on a pedestal.' Then he went on about 'the poor old Pope, so filled with all the most horrible and detestable lies that ever were conceived or thought of.' He was like the man who asked his friends to dinner and said, 'I am going to give you a piece of the most delicious beef—the most exquisite beef that ever was eaten,' and all the while it was only a piece of stale brown bread; but the host said to his guests, 'May God damn your souls for ever and ever, if you don't believe it's beef,' so they ate it and said nothing.

Then he talked of the books of Mazzini, which were 'well worth reading,' and of Saffi, 'made professor of something at Oxford, where he used to give lectures in a moth-eaten voice.'

Feb. 11.—I have frequently seen lately, at the Lefevres', old Lord Redesdale,[1] with whom we have some distant cousinship through my Mitford great-grandmother. He is very kind, clever, old-fashioned, and always wears a tail-coat. He took us into the far-away by telling us of having heard his father, Speaker Mitford, describe having known a man in Swaledale named Rievely, whose earliest recollection was of being carried across the Swale by Henry Jenkyns (who lived to 160), who recollected having gone as a boy, with a sheaf of arrows and his elder brother on a pony, from Ellerton in Swaledale to Northallerton, to join the army before the battle of Flodden. He would tell all about the battle in a familiar way—'the King was not there; but the Duke of Suffolk was there,' &c.

Much of the conversation in certain houses is now about Moody and Sankey, the American 'revivalists,' who are supposed to 'produce great effects.' Moody preaches and Sankey sings. They are adored by some, others (including most Americans) think them 'mere religious charlatans'—and altogether they offer a famous opportunity for all the barking and biting which 'truly religious people' often delight in.

London, March 7, *Sunday.*—Breakfast at Lord Houghton's, who has adopted Rogers' custom of social breakfasts. There was a young man there whom I did not notice much at first, but I soon found that he was very remarkable, and then that he was very charming indeed. It was Lord Rosebery.[2] He has a most sweet gravity almost always, but when his expression does light up, it is more than an illumination —it is a conflagration, at which all around him take light. Quantities of good stories were told—one of a party given by George IV as Prince Regent to the Irish peer Lord Coleraine. Smoking was allowed. After supper, when Lady Jersey drank, the Regent kissed the spot upon the cup where her lips had rested: upon which the Princess took a pipe from Lord Coleraine's mouth, blew two or three whiffs, and handed it back to him. The Prince was quite furious, but it was a lesson.

[1] John Thomas Freeman-Mitford, first Earl of Redesdale, 1805–1886; he and his father were strong opponents of Catholic emancipation and, in the year of this note, he carried on a press controversy with Cardinal Manning that became notorious.—*Ed.*

[2] Archibald Philip Primrose, the fifth Earl, then aged 28, who died in 1929. His subsequent illustrious career in politics is an interesting reflection on Hare's comments at this early age.—*Ed.*

Holmhurst, March 14.—Went to see Lord Stratford de Redcliffe, who talked incessantly and most agreeably for an hour. He said how surprised he had been to read in the 'Greville Memoirs' of himself as ill-tempered; he always thought he was 'rather a good-tempered sort of fellow.' It was Madame de Lieven who said that, and she had always hated him. She prevented him having an embassy once, but they made peace afterwards through a compliment he paid her at Paris. He talked of Madame de Lieven's extraordinary influence, arising chiefly from our inherent national passion for foreigners.

The enormous circulation of the *Memorials of a Quiet Life* in the two years which had elapsed since its publication astonished those who were opposed to it; and in America the sale had been even greater than in England. Numbers of Americans had come to England entirely from the desire to visit the different scenes of my mother's quiet life, and had gone in turn to Toft, Stoke, Alton, Hurstmonceaux, Holmhurst, and some even to the distant grave of Lucy Hare at Abbots Kerswell. At Holmhurst there were frequently many sets of visitors in a day, and even if I was at home I could never bear to refuse them admittance. It was in answer to a constantly expressed desire that, in the autumn of 1874, I occupied myself with the third volume of the *Memorials*. The book was, as it were, a gift to the public. It had a large circulation, but no remuneration whatever was ever looked for or obtained. A review appeared in the *Spectator* (July 8, 1876), speaking of 'the veiled self-conceit' with which Mr. Hare had placed himself 'upon the voluminous records of his family as upon a pedestal'; that Mrs. Hare was far from being honoured by 'the capital' her adopted son had made of her, though, 'if his public likes and is willing to pay for the contents of the family album, there is nothing more to be said. . . . Here, however, let us be thankful, is, so far as anything can be predicated safely on such a subject, the last of the *Memorials*, and that is so grateful a thought as to justify tolerance of what already is.' It seemed a singular review to have been admitted by the *Spectator*, which, four years before (December 11, 1872), had written of the *Memorials* as containing 'passage after passage worthy of comment or quotation,' and as 'an interesting record of spiritual conflicts and spiritual joy, free from narrowness and fanaticism, and marked throughout by the most guileless sincerity.'

Annually, I tried to make my dearest mother's home as useful as possible to all those in whom she was most nearly interested, as well as to keep up her charities, especially at Alton. It had also been a great pleasure, with what my books produced, to fit up a cottage close to Holmhurst as a Hospice for needy persons of a better class. These I have always invited to come for a month at a time, their travelling expenses being fully paid, and firing, linen, farm and garden produce, with an outfit of grocery, being supplied to them. Many are the interesting and pleasant persons whom I have thus become acquainted with.

In the spring of 1875 I was obliged to go to Italy again, to continue collecting materials for my *Cities of Northern and Central Italy*.

To MARY LEA GIDMAN.

Rimini, April 4, 1875.—I made my first long lonely expedition from Turin, going for an hour by rail to the town of S. Ambrogio, and then walking up through the forests to the top of the high mountain of S. Michele, where there is a famous monastery in which the sovereigns of the country—Dukes of Savoy—used to be buried many hundreds of years ago. It is a wonderful place, quite on the highest peak, looking into

IL SAGRO DI S. MICHELE

the great gorges of snow. As I was sketching, the old Abbot was led by on his mule, and stopped to speak to me. I found he was a famous missionary preacher—Carlo Caccia—and had been in England, where he knew Lord Bute well, and was very glad to hear of him. So we made great friends, and as he was going to Turin for Easter, we travelled back together.

From Turin I went to Parma, where I had a great deal of work to finish. The cold there was ferocious, but I made the great excursion I went for—to Canossa, where the Emperor Henry IV performed his famous penance, though it is a most dreadfully fatiguing walk, either in snow above the knees, or in the furrows of streams from the melted snow. At Bologna I never saw anything like the snow—as high as the top of the omnibus, and darkening the lower windows, with a way cut through it down the middle of the street.

Journal.

Forli, April 2.—In one of the old churches here is the tomb of Barbara Ordelaffi, wife of the Lord of Forli, who was one of the most intensely wicked women of her own or any other age. But her tomb is indescribably lovely, her figure, that of quite a young girl, lying upon its marble sarcophagus with a look of innocence and simplicity which can scarcely be equalled.[1]

The tomb is in a side-chapel, separated by a heavy railing from the church. Inside this railing, in an arm-chair, with his eyes constantly fixed upon the marble figure, sat this morning a very old gentleman, paralysed and unable to move, wrapped in a fur cloak. As I looked in at the rails, he said, 'And you also are come to see Barbara; how beautiful she is, is she not?' I acquiesced, and he said, 'For sixty years I have come constantly to see her. It is everything to me to be here. It is the love and the story of my life. No one I have ever known is half so beautiful as Barbara Ordelaffi.

VICENZA

You have not looked at her yet long enough, but gradually you will learn this. Every one must love Barbara. I am carried here now; I cannot walk, but I cannot live without seeing her. My servants bring me; they put me here; I can gaze at her figure, then I am happy. At eleven o'clock my servants will come, and I shall be taken home, but they will bring me again to see Barbara in the afternoon.'

I remained in the church. At eleven o'clock the servants came. They took up the old gentleman and carried him up to the monument to bid it farewell, and then out to his carriage; but in the afternoon, said the Sacristan, they would come again, for he always spent most of the day with Barbara Ordelaffi; when he was alone with the marble figure, he was quite quiet and happy, and as they always locked him into the chapel, he could never come to any harm.

[1] There have been wickeder women. Barbara (by birth a Menfredi) was the wife of Piero Ordelaffi, 15th century Lord of Faenza, to whom she was betrothed at seven years. She conspired with her father to induce Piero to imprison his own brother, the lord of Forli, and so become master of that city. But feeling insecure with the brother still alive, she attempted but failed to poison him. So she had him killed by hired assassins. Finally, she herself died of poison, said to have been administered by her own husband.—*Ed.*

To Miss Wright.

Florence, May 2, 1875.—No words can express the fatigue or discomfort of my Tuscan tour. The food, in the mountain convents especially, was disgusting—little but coarse bread with oil and garlic; the inns were filthy and the beds damp; and the travelling, in carts or on horseback, most fatiguing, often sixteen hours a day. And yet—and yet how thrilling is the interest of Monte Oliveto, S. Gemignano, Volterra, La Vernia, Camaldoli!

Journal.

Castagnuolo, May 3.—I am writing from the old country palace of the Marchese Lotteria Lotharingo della Stufa. It is reached by driving from Florence through the low envineyarded country for five miles. Then, on the left, under the hills, one sees what looks like a great old barrack, grimy, mossy, and deserted. This is the villa. All outside is decay, but when you enter, there are charming old halls, and chambers, connected by open arches, and filled with pictures, china, books, and beautiful old carved furniture. A terrace, lined with immense vases of lilies and tulips, opens on a garden with vine-shaded pergolas and huge orange-trees in tubs; and beyond are the wooded hills.

The presiding genius of the place is Mrs. Ross (Janet Duff Gordon), who has redeemed lands, planted vineyards, introduced new plans for pressing the grapes—whose whole heart and soul are in the work here.

Herrenalb, in the Black Forest, June 14.—The semi-mountain air of this lovely place is as refreshing to the body as the pure high-minded Bunsen character is to the soul. Herrenalb itself takes its name from the abbey on the little river Alb, while a monastery for women on the same stream a few miles off gives its name to 'Frauenalb.' The former is Protestant now, the latter is still Catholic, but in the valley of Herrenalb are the immense buildings of the abbey, its great granaries with wooden pillars, and the ruins of its Norman church.

Frances de Bunsen and one of her Sternberg nieces met me in the valley, and we were soon joined by the dear old Frau von Bunsen in her donkey-chair. At eighty-six her wonderful power of mind and charm of intellect and conversation are quite unimpaired.[1]

To this happy visit at Herrenalb, and to the long conversations I used to have with my dear old friend, walking beside her donkey-chair in the forest, I owe the power of having been able to write her Memoirs two years afterwards. It was my last sight of this old friend of my childhood.[1]

Journal.

June 26.—A great party at Lambeth Palace, the lawn and its many groups of people very charming. Going in to tea with Miss Elliot down a narrow passage, I came suddenly upon Arthur Stanley. In that moment I am sure we both tried hard to recollect what had so entirely separated us for five years, but we could not, and shook hands. The Spanish Lady Stanley seeing this, threw up her hands—'*Gratias a Deo! O gratias a Deo! una reconciliatiōn!*'

---

[1] Frances de Bunsen, 1791–1876, co-heiress with Lady Llanover to the fortune of their father Benjamin Waddington. She married Baron Christian Bunsen at Rome in 1817, who was later (1841–54) German Ambassador in London. From 1855 until her death she lived in Germany.—*Ed.*

In the evening there was an immense party at Lady Salisbury's to meet the Sultan of Zanzibar. He had a cold, so sent to say he could not have the windows opened; the consequence of which was, that with thousands of wax-lights and crowds of people, the heat was awful, positively his native climate. The Sultan has a good, sensible, clever, amused face, but cannot speak a word of any language except Arabic, of which Lady Salisbury said that she had learnt some sentences by the end of the evening, from hearing them repeated so often through the interpreter, and at last ventured to air her new acquirements herself. When the Sultan went away, the suite followed two and two—a picturesque procession. Lord Salisbury walked first, leading the Sultan, or rather holding his right hand in his own left, which it seems is the right thing to do. The Sultan was immensely struck by Lady Caithness, and no wonder, for her crown of three gigantic rows of diamonds, and then huge diamonds and emeralds, had the effect of a sunlit wave in the Mediterranean.

June 27, Sunday.—To Holland House. Lady Holland sat at the end window, looking on the garden, with a group round her. I went out with Lord Halifax,[1] then with Everard Primrose, who appeared as usual from the library, and a third time with Lord Stanhope, who took me afterwards in his carriage to Airlie Lodge. There the garden was in great beauty, and we met Lady Airlie sauntering through its green walks with the Duke of Teck.[2] We went to sit in a tent, where we found Mr. Doyle, Mr. Cheney, and a young lady who greeted me with, 'Now, Mr. Hare, may I ask if you never *can* remember me, or if you always intend to cut me on purpose?' It was Miss Rhoda Broughton.

Lady Airlie talked of the death of Madame Rossetti. Her husband[3] felt so completely that all his living interests were buried with his wife, that he laid his unpublished poems under her dead head, and they were buried with her. But, after a year had passed, his feeling about his wife was calmed, while the longing for his poems grew daily, and people urged him that he was forcing a loss upon the world. And the coffin of the poor lady was taken up and opened to get at the poems, and behold her beautiful golden hair had grown and grown till the whole coffin was filled with it—filled with it and rippling over.[4] Lady Airlie had the account from an eye-witness. For one moment Madame Rosetti was visible in all her radiant loveliness, as if she were asleep, then she sank into dust. She was buried with her Testament under her pillow on one side and her husband's poems on the other.

The Duke of Teck looked very handsome and was most pleasant and amiable. He said that an old lady in Germany, an ancestress of his, had the most glorious pearl necklace in the world, and when she died, she desired that the pearl necklace might be buried with her. And the family were very sorry to part with their aged relative, but they were still more sorry to part with the family jewels; and in time their grief for the old lady was assuaged, but their grief for the pearl necklace was never assuaged at all, and at last there came a moment when they dug up the coffin, and took the pearl necklace from the aged neck. But behold the pearls were quite spoilt and had lost all their lustre and beauty. Then pearl-doctors were summoned, men who were learned in such things, and they said that the only thing which would restore the beauty of

[1] Charles Wood's father, the first Viscount Halifax.—*Ed.*

[2] The father of H.M. Queen Mary.—*Ed.*

[3] Dante Gabriel Rossetti. [Mrs. Rossetti, Elizabeth Eleanor Siddel, died in 1862.—*Ed.*]

[4] Professor Forster has since assured me that this was impossible, for that hair will only continue to grow for a few hours after death.

the pearls would be if three beautiful young ladies would wear them constantly, and let the pearls drink in all their youth and beauty. So the eldest daughter of the house took them and wore them constantly, and all the beauty and brilliancy of her loveliness flowed into the pearls, which grew brighter and better every day. And as her beauty faded, another daughter of the house took them, and so three beautiful young ladies took them and wore them in three generations, till, when sixty years were passed, the pearls were so beautiful and glorious, so filled with youth and radiancy, that there is no such pearl necklace in the whole world.

June 29.—With the Archbishop of Dublin, Miss Trench, and Lady Charles Clinton to Strawberry Hill, the 'little plaything house' of Horace Walpole. It had been so wet that one had almost to wade from the station to the house, and the beautiful breakfast was sopping in a tent on the mossy lawn, so little being left in the house that the Princess of Wales[1] had to drink her tea out of a tumbler in a corner. Still the interior of the house was full of interest—the historic pictures, especially those of the three beautiful Waldegrave sisters, and of Maria, Duchess of Gloucester; and then in the gallery are, by Sant and Bucknor, all the especial friends of the house—all the beautiful persons who have stayed there.

Lady Waldegrave[2] (assisted by art) looked twenty-five years younger than she did twenty-five years ago. The Princess of Wales, in a pink dress under black lace and a little hat to match, copied as a whole from pictures of Anne Boleyn, looked lovely.

In the evening I went to Lady Salisbury's reception. At the latter was the Sultan of Zanzibar. Suddenly, in the midst of the party, he said to Lady Salisbury, 'Now, please, it is my time to say my prayers: I should like to go into your room, and to be alone for ten minutes.' And he did, and he does it four times a day, and never allows anything whatever to interfere with it. The Archbishop of Dublin, when presented, said, 'I am glad to have the honour of being presented to a man who has made a promise and *kept* it.' The Sultan answered, 'It can only be your goodness which makes you say that.'

JOURNAL.

June 30.—In the evening I went to Lady Margaret Beaumont's to meet the Queen of the Netherlands, '*La Reine Rouge* [The Red Queen],' as she is often called from her revolutionary tendencies.[3] She sat at the end of the room, a pleasant natural woman, with fuzzy hair done very wide in curls, and a quaint little diamond crown as an ornament at the back. She was most agreeable in conversation, and, as Prosper Merimée says in one of his letters to Panizzi, 'would have been quite perfection, if she had not wished to appear a Frenchwoman, having had the misfortune to be born in Würtemburg.'

[1] Later Queen Alexandra.—*Ed.*

[2] Frances Elizabeth Anne, Countess Waldegrave, then aged 54, was the daughter of John Braham, the famous English tenor who first appeared at Covent Garden in 1787 and was closely associated with Drury Lane for many years. The seventh Earl Waldegrave was her second husband and she inherited his estate in 1846. A year later she married George Harcourt and became a leader of society, with mainly Liberal associations. Her fourth husband was Baron Carlingford. She did much to restore Strawberry Hill.—*Ed.*

[3] This was Sophia, the daughter of William I of Würtemburg, wife of William III of Holland. A woman of great intelligence and accomplishments, she was from the first at complete variance with her husband, whose private life was something of a scandal. She died in 1877, and the king later married Emma, the mother of Queen Wilhelmina.—*Ed.*

July 1.—Luncheon at Lord Stanhope's to meet Miss Rhoda Broughton. Lord Stanhope aired one of his pet hobbies—the virtues of the novel *Anastasius*. Mrs. Hussey says that his father used to say of him, 'My son is often very prosy, but then he has been *vaccinated*'; for the fourth Earl Stanhope had a familiar of whom he always spoke as 'Tesco,' and Tesco had inveighed against vaccination to him, and had told him that to be vaccinated had always the effect of making the recipient prosy.

Mrs. Hussey mentioned this at a dinner to Mr. John Abel Smith, who exclaimed, 'Oh, that accounts for what has always hitherto been a mystery to me. I went with that Lord Stanhope to hear a man named Belloni lecture on "the Tuscan Language," and we sat behind him on the platform. He was most terribly lengthy. Suddenly, Lord Stanhope caught him by the coat, and, arresting the whole performance, said, "Pray, sir, have you ever been vaccinated?"—"Certainly, my Lord," said the astonished lecturer. "Oh, that is quite enough; pray continue," said Lord Stanhope, and the lecture proceeded, and Lord Stanhope composed himself to sleep.'

July 2.—I dined with the Ralph Duttons and sat by Lady Barker, who was full of Moody and Sankey, to whom she has been often with the Duchess of Sutherland, who insists upon going every day. She says the mixture of religious fervour with the most intense toadyism of the Duchess was horribly disgusting; that the very gift of fluency in the preachers contaminated and spoilt their work. Sometimes they would use the most excellent and powerful simile, and then spoilt it by something quite blasphemous. Speaking of the abounding grace of God, Moody compared Him to a banker who scolded the man who only drew for a penny, when he might draw for a pound and come again as often as he liked. So far the sermon was admirable, and all understood it; but then he went on to call it the 'Great I Am Bank,' and to cut all sorts of jokes, whilst the audience roared with laughter; that when a man presented his cheque, however large—'Here ye are, says I Am,' &c.

Went on to the ball at Dorchester House, which was beautiful; the Prince and Princess of Wales and the Tecks were there. The great charm of the house is in the immensely broad galleries, which are so effective when filled with beautiful women, relieved, like Greek pictures, against a gold background. Miss Violet Lindsay, in a long white dress embroidered with gold and a wreath of gold oak-leaves, was quite exquisitely lovely.

July 3.—Breakfast with Sir James Lacaita to meet Mr. Gladstone, Lord Napier and Ettrick,[1] and the Marchese Vitelleschi. The great topic was Manning. About him and Roman Catholicism in general, Gladstone seems to have lost all temperance, but he told much that was curious. He described the deathbed of Count Streletski and Manning's attempts to get in. Lacaita said that there was a lady still living to whom Manning had been engaged and that he had jilted her to marry one of two heiress sisters: now, whenever she hears of any especial act of his, she says, 'As ever, fickle and false.'

'False,' said Gladstone, 'always, but never fickle.'

Gladstone said he knew that the Pope (Pius IX.) had determined against declaring the doctrine of *personal* infallibility, till Manning had fallen at his feet, and so urged and implored him to do so, that at length he had consented. He (Gladstone) upheld that there was no going back from this, and that even in case of the Pope's death, the condition of the Roman Church was absolutely hopeless. Vitelleschi agreed

[1] Sir Francis Napier, ninth Baron Napier, first Baron Eltrick; Ambassador at St. Petersburg and at Berlin; Governor of Madras and later temporary Governor-General of India. Died in 1898 aged 80.

so far, that if a foreign Pope were chosen, for which an effort would be made, there was no chance for the Church; but if an Italian were elected—for instance, Patrizi or Bilio, who had especially opposed the doctrine of personal infallibility—the sense of the doctrine would be so far modified that it would practically fade into nothingness, and that every advantage would be taken of the Council not being yet closed to make every possible modification.

Lord Napier every now and then insisted on attention, and delivered himself of some ponderous paragraph, on which occasions Gladstone persistently and defiantly ate strawberries.

Highcliffe, July 18.—The usual party are here. . . . Lady Jane Ellice is full of a theory that she is an Israelite, that we are all members of the lost tribes of Israel, that our royal family are the direct descendants of Tepha, the beautiful daughter of Zedekiah, who was brought to Ireland by Jeremiah, and married to its king.

Heckfield Place, August 13.—I went with Lord Selborne and Miss Palmer to Strathfieldsaye. The Duke (of Wellington),[1] dressed like a poor pensioner, received us in his uncomfortable room, where Lord Selborne, who has a numismatical mania, was glad to stay for two hours examining coins. Meanwhile the Duke, finding we were really interested, took Miss Palmer and me upstairs, and showed us all his relics. It was touching to see the old man, who for the greater part of his lifetime existed in unloving awe of a father he had always feared and been little noticed by, now, in the evening of life, treasuring up every reminiscence of him and considering every memorial as sacred. In his close stuffy little room were the last pheasants the great Duke had shot, the miniatures of his mother and aunt and of himself and his brother as children, his grandfather's portrait, a good one of Marshal Saxe, and the picture of the horse Copenhagen. Most of the bedrooms were completely covered with prints pasted on the walls. It was the great Duke's fancy.

Deanery, Salisbury, August 15.—There is here in Salisbury the usual familiar society of a cathedral close—the Canon in residence and the other inhabitants meeting and going in and out of each others' houses at all hours. With Canon Douglas Gordon I have been to the Palace, where we found the Bishop in his garden, which is quite lovely, the rich green and brilliant flowers sweeping up into and mingling with the grey arcades and rich chapels of the cathedral; and from all points the tall heaven-soaring spire is sublime, especially in the purple shadows of evening, with birds circling ceaselessly round it.

The Palace has a grand dull room full of portraits of deceased bishops, where we had tea. Bishop Moberly, who is still rather schoolmasterish, has no end of daughters, all so excellent that it has been observed that whenever a colonist sends home for a commendable wife, you may, with the most perfect confidence, despatch a Miss Moberly.[2]

Oct. 4.—A most charming visit to Lady Mary Egerton at Mountfield Court. Mr. Charles Newton[3] of the British Museum is here, who is always charming, with ripple of pleasantest anecdote and kindly, genial manners.

---

[1] The second duke.

[2] George Moberley, 1803–1885, headmaster of Winchester (1835–66), canon of Chester (1868), bishop of Salisbury (1869).—*Ed.*

[3] Afterwards Sir Charles Newton, 1816–94, vice-consul at Mytilene (1852), consul at Rhodes (1853), consul at Rome (1860). Superintended excavations at Calymnos, etc. Keeper of Greek and Roman antiquities at the British Museum; Professor of Archaeology, London.—*Ed.*

D

'The origin of the Torlonia family,' said Mr. Newton, 'is very curious. When Pius VII wished to excommunicate Napoleon I, he could not find any one who was bold enough to affix the *scomunica* [excommunication] to the doors of the Lateran. At length an old man who sold matches was found who ran the risk and did it. On the return of the Pope in triumph, the old man was offered any favour he liked, and he chose the monopoly of tobacco. From that time every speculation that the Torlonias entered upon was sure to answer.'

The late Prince of Torlonia, being at Naples, went into the room where the public appointments were sold by auction. He left his umbrella there, and went back to get it while the sale was going on. The bidders, chiefly Neapolitan nobles, were aghast to see the great Torlonia reappear, and at last, after some consultation, one of them came up to him and said they would give him 60,000 francs if he would leave. Instead of showing the intense astonishment he felt at this most unexpected proposal, Torlonia only shrugged his shoulders and said, '*È póco* [It is small],' and they gave him 100,000.

III

LONDON WALKS AND SOCIETY

1876–77

ᔓᔕ

My three thick volumes of the *Cities of Northern and Central Italy* appeared in the autumn of 1875, a very large edition (3,000 copies) being printed at once. They were immediately the object of a most violent attack from Mr. Murray, who saw in them rivals to his well-known red handbook. A most virulent and abusive article appeared upon my work in the *Athenæum*, accusing me, amongst other things, of having copied from Murray's Handbooks without acknowledgment, and quoting, as proof, passages relating to Verona in both books, which have the same singular mistake. It was certainly a curious accident which made me receive the proof-sheets of Verona when away from home on a visit at Tunbridge Wells, where the only book of reference accessible was Murray's *Handbook of Northern Italy*, which I found in the house, so that the mistakes in my account of Verona *were* actually copied from Murray's Handbook, to which I was indebted for nothing else whatever, as (though much delighted with them when they first appeared) I had for years found Murray's Handbooks so inefficient, that I had never bought or made any use of them, preferring the accurate and intelligent Handbooks of the German *Gsel-fels*. Mr. Murray further took legal proceedings against me, because in one of my volumes I had mentioned that the Italian Lakes were included in his Swiss rather than his Italian Handbooks: this having been altered in recent years, but having been the case in the only volumes of his Handbooks I had ever possessed. On all occasions, any little literary success I met with excited bitter animosity from Mr. Murray.

Another curious attack was made upon me by the eccentric Mr. Freeman, the historian of the Norman Conquest. He had published in the *Saturday Review* a series of short articles on the Italian cities, which I always felt had never received the attention they deserved, their real interest having been overlooked owing to the unpopularity of the dogmatic and verbose style in which they were written. Therefore, really with the idea of doing Mr. Freeman a good turn, I had rather gone out of my way to introduce extracts from his articles where I could, that notice might thus be attracted to them—an attention for which I had already been thanked by other little-read authors, as, whatever may be the many faults of my books, they have always had a large circulation. But in the case of Mr. Freeman, knowing the singular character of the man, I begged a common friend to write to his daughter and amanuensis to mention my intention, and ask her, if her father had no objection to my quoting from his articles, to send me a list of them (as they were unsigned), in order that I might not confuse them with those of any other person. By return of post I received, without comment, from Miss Free-

FOUNTAIN COURT, TEMPLE

man, a list of her father's articles, and I naturally considered this as equivalent to his full permission to quote from them. I was therefore greatly surprised, when Mr. Freeman's articles appeared soon afterwards in a small volume, to find it introduced with a preface, the whole object of which was, in the most violent manner, to accuse me of theft. I immediately published a full statement of the circumstances under which I had quoted from Mr. Freeman in sixteen different newspapers. Mr. Freeman answered in the *Times* by repeating his accusation, and in the *Guardian* he added, 'Though Mr. Hare's conduct was barefaced and wholesale robbery, I shall take no further notice of him till he has stolen something else.' Mr Freeman made himself many enemies, but he did not make me one; he was too odd.[1]

But in spite of these little catastrophes attending its publication, I am certain that *Cities of Northern and Central Italy*, which cost me far more pains and labour, and which is more entirely original, than all my earlier books put together, was by far the best of my writings, up to that time. Before the book was out, I was already devoted to a new work, suggested by the great delight I had long found in London, and by the desire of awakening others to an enjoyment of its little-known treasures. A set of lectures delivered at Sir John Shaw-Lefevre's house in Seymour Street laid the foundation for my *Walks in London*.

JOURNAL.

Monk's Orchard, Jan. 23.—This is a fine big house, be-pictured, be-statued, with a terraced garden, a lake, and a great flat park. A Mr. and Mrs. Rodd are here with their son Rennell, a pleasant-looking boy, wonderfully precocious and clever, though, as every one listens to him, he has—not unnaturally—a very good opinion of himself: still one feels at once that he is the sort of boy who will be heard of again some day.[2]

Our host, Mr. Lewis Loyd, is in some ways one of the most absent men in the world. One day, meeting a friend, he said, 'Hallo! what a long time it is since I've seen you! How's your father?'—'Oh, my father's dead.'—'God bless me! I'm very sorry,' &c. The next year he met the same man again, and had forgotten all about it, so began with, 'Hallo! what a long time since I've seen you! How's your father?'— 'Oh, *my father's dead still!*'

Feb. 8.—The opening of Parliament. I went to Lord Overstone's. At a quarter to two the procession passed beneath—the fine old carriages and gorgeous footmen, one stream of gold and red, pouring through the black crowd and leafless trees. We all counted the carriages differently—eight, twelve, fifteen; and there were only six! All one saw of royalty was the waving of a white cap-string, as the Queen, sitting well back in the carriage, bowed to the people.

Feb. 13.—Dined at the Dowager Lady Barrington's—the great topic being dinner past, present, and prospective. George, Lord Barrington, said that he had dined at the Brazilian Minister's, and he was sure the cookery was good and also the wine, for he had eaten of every dish and drunk fourteen kinds of wine, and had passed a perfectly good night and been quite well the next morning. He also dined with Mr. Brand the Speaker, and complimented Mrs. Brand upon the dinner. She told her cook. He said, 'We are three, Lord Granville's, Mr. Russell Sturgis's, and myself; there are only three cooks in London.' When Lord Barrington afterwards saw Mrs. Brand, she told

[1] Edward Augustus Freeman, 1823–92, honorary fellow of Trinity College, Oxford, and, from 1884–92, Regius Professor of Modern History at Oxford. Amongst his writings were a *History of Norman Conquest, History of the Conquest of the Saracens*, and a *History of Sicily.—Ed.*

[2] The son became Sir James Rennell Rodd, diplomatist and author, who served as attaché in Berlin, Athens, Roman, Paris and Cairo; was envoy extraordinary to Sweden, ambassador to Italy from 1908–1919, British delegate to the League of Nations, etc., and author of several volumes of verse, memoirs and history. Hare's prophecy was accurately fulfilled.—*Ed.*

him the cook has asked who praised him, and 'when he heard,' continued Mrs. Brand, 'he also gave you his little meed of praise.' 'Ah, M. Barrington,' he said, '*c'est une bonne fourchette* [he's a good trencherman].'

Feb. 14.—Dined at Lord Halifax's to meet Lord and Lady Cardwell.[1] They are most pleasant, interesting, interested company, and it was altogether one of the happiest dinners I remember. The conversation was chiefly about the changes in spelling and their connection with changes in English history and customs.

Lord Cardwell was in the habit of using the Church prayers at family prayers. One day his valet came to him and said, 'I must leave your lordship's service at once.' —'Why, what have you to complain of?'—'Nothing personally, but your lordship *will* repeat every morning—"We have done those things which we ought not to have done, and have left undone those things which we ought to have done":—now I freely admit that I have often done things I ought not, but that I have left undone things that I ought to have done, I utterly deny: and I will not stay here to hear it said.'

If any one has ever the patience to read this memoir through, they will have been struck by the way in which, for many years before the time I am writing of, the persons with whom I lived were quite different from those amongst whom my childhood was spent. Arthur Stanley had never got over the publication of the *Memorials of a Quiet Life*, though he was always at a loss to say what he objected to in it, and Mary Stanley I never saw at all. From Lady Augusta alone I continued to receive frequent and affectionate messages.

In 1874 Lady Augusta represented the Queen at the marriage of the Duke of Edinburgh,[2] and she never really recovered the effects of the cold which she then endured in Russia. In the summer of 1875 she was alarmingly ill in Paris, was brought home with difficulty, and from that time there was little hope of her recovery. She expired early in March 1876.

JOURNAL.

Holmhurst, March 12.—I have been again up to London for dear Augusta Stanley's funeral on the 9th. It was a beautiful day. All the approaches to Westminster were filled with people in mourning.

It seemed most strange thus to go to the Deanery again—that the doors closed for six years were opened wide by death. Red cloth showed that royalty was coming, and I went at once to the library, where an immense crowd of cousins were assembled. As I went down the little staircase with Kate Vaughan, four ladies in deep mourning passed to the dining-room, carrying immense wreaths of lovely white flowers: they were the Queen and three of her daughters. The Queen seemed in a perfect anguish of grief. She remained for a short time alone with the coffin, I believe knelt by it, and was then taken to the gallery overhanging the Abbey.

Soon the immense procession set out by the cloisters, and on entering the church, turned so as to pass beneath the Queen and then up the nave from the west end. The

---

[1] Edward Cardwell, first Viscount Cardwell, 1813–1886, statesman, Secretary for War in Gladstone's ministry of 1868–74. Served also under Aberdeen, Palmerston and Russell.—*Ed.*

[2] H.R.H. Prince Alfred, fourth child of Queen Victoria, who married Marie Alexandrovna, only daughter of Tsar Alexander II in January, 1874.—*Ed.*

church was full of people: I felt as if I only saw the wind lifting the long garlands of white flowers as the coffin moved slowly on, and Arthur's pathetic face of childlike bewilderment.

The procession of mourners went round the Abbey from the choir by a longer way to the chapel on account of the people. As it passed the corner of the transept, the strange little figure of Mr. Carlyle slipped out. He had been very fond of Augusta, was full of feeling for Arthur, and seemed quite unconscious of who and where he was. He ran along, before the chief mourners, by the side of the coffin, and in the chapel itself he stood at the head of the grave, making the strangest ejaculations at intervals through the service.

RAHERE'S TOMB, ST. BARTHOLOMEW'S, SMITHFIELD

May 6.—In London again, which is full of interest as ever, and now especially beautiful from its trees just bursting into leaf with indescribable wealth of lovely young green. It is certainly a most delightful time. People think I ought to feel dreadfully depressed by a most spiteful paragraph upon *Cities of Italy* in the *Saturday*, and a more spiteful review in the *Athenæum*, but I do not a bit: they are most disagreeable doses to take, but I believe they are most wholesome medicine for one's morals and capital teachers of humility.

May 7.—An amusing tea at the Duchess of Cleveland's. The Duchess talked of Pimlico, the bought property of Lord Grosvenor, formerly called 'The Five Fields.'

The Court wished to buy it because it was so close to Buckingham Palace, but though the sum asked was too much. Lord Grosvenor gave £30,000 for it. Lord Cowper had wished to buy it, and sent his agent for the purpose, but he came back without having done so, and when Lord Cowper upbraided him, said, 'Really, my lord, I could not find it in my heart to give £200 more for it than it was worth.' Cubbitt afterwards offered a ground-rent of £60,000.

May 8.—Dined with Mrs. Thellusson to meet Lady Waterford. Whistler the artist was there. He has a milk-white tuft growing out of his black hair, a peculiarity which he declares to be hereditary in his family, as in that of the Caëtani.

May 11.—A lovely day. My 'Excursion' to the Tower. Forty-six people met me there. All the curious chambers and vaults were open to us in turn. In the White Tower we saw the prisons of Little Ease. I had given my little explanation and returned into the sunshine with the greater number of the party, when Mrs. Maxwell Lyte, who had arrived late, went in. Being told that the cell of Sir Thomas More was to be seen, and seeing a railing by the flickering torchlight, she thought that marked the place, and went underneath it, and stepped out into—nothing! With a piercing shriek she fell into a black abyss by a precipice of fourteen feet. Every one thought she was killed, but after a minute her voice came out of the depths—'I am not seriously hurt.' It was a tremendous relief.

We went on to the Queen's Head Restaurant, Emily Lefevre and I running before to order luncheon. When we arrived, we found volleys of smoke issuing from the house and the kitchen-chimney on fire. However, we waited, the party bore the smell, and eventually we had our luncheon. Tom Brassey wanted to order wine, &c., but Emily stopped him with, 'Remember, Mr. Brassey, we are limited to fourpence a head.'

The Prince of Wales arrived (from India) at 7 P.M. I waited two hours at the Spottiswoodes' house in Grosvenor Place to see him, and saw nothing but the flash of light on his bald head. It was a pleasant party, but how seldom in London society does one hear anything one can carry away.

May 12.—Trouble with Murray the publisher, who insists on believing that because some points in my *Cities of Italy* resemble his Handbooks, they must be taken from them, which they most assuredly are not. I had no Handbooks with me when I was writing, but where there is only one thing to say about places, two people sometimes say it.

May 31.—An evening party at Lord Houghton's, an omnium-gatherum, but very amusing. It recalled Carlyle's speech, who, when some ecclesiastic gloomily inquired in his presence 'What would happen if Jesus Christ returned to earth *now*?' retorted—'*Happen!* why Dickie Milnes would ask him to dinner, to be sure, and would ask Pontius Pilate to meet him.'

It took half an hour to get up the staircase. Miss Rhoda Broughton was there, beautifully dressed, pressed upon by bishops and clergy: Salvini and Irving were affectionately greeting Lady Stanley of Alderley,[1] under a perfect stack of diamonds, was declaiming very loud in her unknown tongue to an astonished and bewildered audience; and through all the groups upstairs the young King of the Belgians[2] was smiling and bowing a retreat to his escape by a back-staircase.

[1] Henrietta Maria Stanley, 1807–95, married the second Baron Stanley of Alderley. Friend of Carlyle and Jowett.—*Ed.*
[2] Leopold II.—*Ed.*

Powderham, June 9.—I found the door open last night and walked straight into the hall. Charlie Wood and Lady Agnes were there at tea, and people kept dropping in—a very pleasant party. . . . Lord Devon[1] is the kindest of hosts, full of small courtesies; but he is a great deal away, flying up to London after dinner and returning next day: they say he performs the circumference of the globe every year, and chiefly on his own lines of railway.

Lord Devon's only son, Lord Courtenay, is seldom here, but when he is, amuses every one. One evening 'Mademoiselle Bekker' arrived late at Powderham, coming in the hope to obtain a chairman for a meeting which was going to be held at Exeter in favour of the Rights of Women. There was a very distinguished party in the house—the Bishop of Winchester, Lord Halifax, the American Minister (Motley), &c., and they each, while refusing, made a speech in answer to hers, which was most eloquent. Eventually Mademoiselle Bekker declared herself so indignant as to be led to unsex herself: she was Lord Courtenay.

Charlton Hall. June 17.—I spent several hours in Bath on my way here. It was an exquisite day, and everything was in great beauty. I felt age in the way in which every-thing looked so small in proportion to my recollection. At Chippenham a dogcart from Lord Suffolk's was waiting for me, and we rolled away down the dull lanes to Malmesbury. It was curious in one day to revisit, as it were, six years out of my former life.

Charlton is a magnificent old house of yellow-grey stone, Jacobean, open on all sides, a perfect quadrangle. Inside, there was once a courtyard, but a former Lord Suffolk closed it in. It remained for many years a mere gravelled space: lately Lady Suffolk has had it paved, and to a certain extent furnished. The rooms are handsome in stucco ornaments, but not picturesque. The pictures are glorious. There is one of the noblest known works of Leonardo da Vinci—'The Virgin of the Rocks,' the figures all with the peculiar Leonardo type of face, grouped in a rocky valley—strange, wild, and fantastic.[2] There is a glorious old gallery with a noble ceiling, full of portraits and of old and interesting books. In the 'rose parlour' are more pictures, and a ceiling the design of which is repeated in the flower-garden. Many of the pictures belonged to James II. When he fled, he sent them to be taken care of by Colonel Graham, who had married the Earl of Berkshire's daughter, and William III afterwards allowed them to remain.

June 29.—Went to Holland House. The deep shade of its lofty avenue is enchanting as one turns in from the baking street of Kensington. Lady Holland sat in the inner room, with her sweet face encircled by the prettiest of old-fashioned caps. Beau Atkin-son was with her, with a lovely little Skye dog in his arms, and Lady Lilford with her two fine boys. After talking some time, we wandered into the gardens under the old cedars. When we came in, old Mr. Cheney was leaning over Lady Holland's chair, chuckling to himself over the dogmatic self-assertion of Mr. Hayward,[3] who was talking to her of books, the value of which he considered to be quite decided by his opinion of them. Especially he talked of Ticknor's Memoirs, so remarkable because,

[1] See note on p. 57. Charlie Wood had married Lord Devon's daughter.

[2] This picture was sold to the National Gallery in 1880 for £9,000, and is probably the cheapest purchase the Gallery ever made.

[3] Mr. Abraham Hayward, critic and essayist, who had been articled in early life to an obscure country attorney, always seemed to consider it the *summum-bonum* of life to dwell amongst the aristocracy as a man of letters: and in this he succeeded admirably, and was always witty and well informed, usually satirical, and often very coarse. [He died in 1884.]

D*

though he was an American of the most lowly origin, it is evident that when he came to Europe he not only saw the best society of every country he visited, but saw it intimately—which could only have been due to his own personal charm.

L. was full of a dinner she had been to at Count Beust's. The Prince Imperial[1] was there who had always hitherto been regarded as only a pleasant boy, but who electrified them on this occasion by a remarkable flash of wit. It had been impossible to avoid asking the French Ambassador, but Count Beust had taken especial pains to make it as little offensive as possible. He took in the Princess [Alexandra] of Wales to supper and placed her at the same table with the Prince Imperial. The Comte and Comtesse d'Harcourt were at another table with the Prince of Wales. Suddenly an offensive pushing man, first secretary to the French embassy, brought Mademoiselle d'Harcourt to the Prince Imperial's table and sat down. The Prince was very much annoyed. Looking up at a picture of the Emperor of Austria, he asked if it resembled him—'I do not remember him, I was so very young when I saw him,' and then in a louder tone, 'I wonder how the French Ambassador represents the Republic of France on the walls of his rooms.'

June 29.—Dined with Lady Head, and we went on together to Baroness Burdett Coutts', where Irving read *Macbeth* to an immense company, chiefly bishops and archbishops and their belongings. The reading was stilted and quite ineffective.

June 30.—A most pleasant party at Lord Ducie's—Mr. and Miss Froude, Sir James Lacaita, Miss Grant the sculptress, Lord Aberdeen and Lady Katherine, Lord Northbrook and Lady Emma Baring, Lord Camperdown, Mr., Mrs., and Miss Gladstone, Lord Vernon, George and Lady Constance Shaw-Lefevre, &c. There was very agreeable conversation, chiefly about Macaulay's Life—of his wonderful memory and the great power it gave him. Gladstone said the most astonishing thing about him was that he could remember not only the things worth knowing, but the most extraordinary amount of trash. He described another man he knew who, after once reading over the advertisement sheet of the *Times*, could repeat it straight through.

In the evening I was asked to tell a story, and did, feeling that if Irving amused people for about three hundred nights of the year, it was rather hard if I declined to amuse him on one of the remaining sixty-five. He enjoyed it more than any one else, and lingering behind, when all were gone but Mrs. Gladstone and one or two others, said, 'Now that we are such a very small party, do tell us another.'

July 7.—Went by water with Mrs. Mostyn, Miss Monk, and Miss Milnes to Fulham. Afterwards, I was at a beautiful and charming party at Holland House. A number of grown-up royalties and a whole bevy of royal children sat under the trees watching Punch and Judy. The Prince Imperial, with charming natural manners, walked about and talked to every one he knew. Towards the end, Lady Wynford said the Princess Amelie of Schleswig desired that I might be presented to her, as she had read my books, &c.

July 13.—Luncheon with Sir C. Trevelyan,[2] who showed me Macaulay's library, and then drove me to see the remnant of the house of Villiers, Duke of Buckingham, in Villiers Street. Peter the Great lived there when in London, and David Copperfield is made to lodge there by Dickens.

Dined at Lord Cardwell's, where I sat by George Otto Trevelyan, the author of

---

[1] Prince Eugène, heir to Napoleon III.—*Ed.*

[2] Sir Charles Edward Trevelyan (1807–1886), governor of Madras 1859, and finance minister in India after 1862, married Hannah Moore, Macaulay's sister.—*Ed.*

Lord Macaulay's Life. At Lord Sherborne's in the evening I found Irving, with all the three hundred nights of his *Hamlet* written on his face.

July 14.—In the afternoon I drove down with Lady Sherborne, Miss Dutton, and Miss Elliot to see Lord Russell[1] at Pembroke Lodge. It is a beautiful place; not merely a bit of Richmond Park, but a bit of old forest enclosed, with grand old oaks and fern. The Queen gives it to Lord Russell, who, at eighty-four, was seated in a bath-chair in the garden, on a sort of bowling-green, watching his grandsons play at tennis. Though he no longer comprehends present events, he is said to be perfectly clear about a far-away past, and will converse at any length about Napoleon, the escape from Elba, &c. When I was presented to him, by way of something to say, I spoke of having seen the historical mound in his garden, and asked what it was that Henry VIII watched for from thence as a death-signal, 'was it a rocket or a black flag?'—'It was a rocket.'—'Then that would imply that the execution was at night, for he would hardly have seen a rocket by day.—'No, it was not at night; it was very early in the morning. She was a very much maligned woman was that Anne Boleyn.'

We all sat by a fountain under the oak-trees, and then went into the house to a sort of five-o'clock tea on a large scale.

Highcliffe, July 25.—Lady Waterford has talked much of marriages—how even indifferent marriages tone down into a degree of comfort which is better for most women than desolation.

Lady Waterford has been speaking of sympathy for others; that there is nothing more distressing than to see another person *mortified*. 'Mama could never bear to see any one mortified. Once at Paris, at a ball they had there, was a poor lady, and not only her chignon, but the whole edifice of hair she had, fell off in the dance. And Mama was so sorry for her, and, when all the ladies tittered, as she was Madame l'Ambassadrice and a person of some influence, I don't think it was wrong of her to apply the verse, and she said, "Let the woman among us who has no false hair be the first to throw a stone at her." '

July 31.—Lady Waterford has been telling of Ruskin 'like a little wizened rat.' 'He likes to be adored, but then Somers and I did adore him, and he likes to lash his disciples with rods of iron. I do not mind that: it is his jokes I cannot bear; they make me so sorry and miserable for him.'

Ampthill Park, August 29, 1876.—At St. Pancras Station I saw a very ancient lady in a yellow wig step into a railway carriage by herself, and her footman guard the door till the train started, and I felt sure it was the Dowager Duchess of Cleveland.[2] At Ampthill Station the Lowther carriage was waiting for both of us, and we drove off together. She talked the whole way, but the carriage rumbled so that I could hardly hear a word she said, except that when I remarked 'What a fine tree!' as we entered the park, she answered rather sharply 'That *was* a fine tree.' She spoke too of the Lowther boys—'They are having their vacancies. I like that word vacancies,' she said.

It is a fine wild park, with most unexpected ups and downs and a great deal of grand old timber, on a ridge rising high above the blue Bedfordshire plain, in the

[1] Lord John Russell, first Earl Russell and third son of the sixth Duke of Bedford. Statesman and leading whig. Was active in public life from 1813–66; served in various capacities under Melbourne, Peel, Palmerston and Aberdeen, and once himself Prime Minister. Introduced the Reform Bill of 1832 for its second and third times; accompanied Queen Victoria to Germany in 1860.—*Ed.*

[2] The Duchess Caroline, who was a Lowther.

midst of which a spire rising out of a little drift of smoke indicates the town of Bedford. On one of the highest points of the ridge a cross raised on steps marks the site of the royal residence where Katherine of Aragon lived for most of her semi-widowhood, and where Anne Boleyn shot stags in a green velvet train. The later house, approached on the garden side by a narrow downhill avenue half a mile long, is in the old French style, with posts and chains, broad steps widening at the top, and a *perron.* . . .

Yesterday I drove with James, Mildred, and Cecil Lowther to Wrest. It is a most stately place, one of the stateliest I have ever seen. The gardens were all laid out by Le Notre, and the house was of that period. Lord De Grey pulled down the house, and found it rested on no foundations whatever, but on the bare ground. It was so thin, that when the still-room maid complained that her room was rather dark, the footman took out his penknife and cut her a square hole for a window in the plaster wall. Capability Brown was employed to rearrange the gardens, which were thought hideous at one time; but though he spoilt so many other places, he had sense to admire the work of Le Notre so much here, that he made no alterations, except throwing a number of round and oblong tanks into one long canal, which, on the whole, is rather an improvement. The modern house is magnificent, and like what Chantilly must have been.

On the vast flagged terrace in front of the windows we found Lady Cowper[1] sitting in an old-fashioned black silk dress and tight white bonnet. She has a most sweet face, and was very kind and charming in her manner. She told the whole story of the place, and took me to see all the finest points of view and the great collection of fine orange-trees brought from Versailles. She greatly lamented the prudishness of her great-aunt (Lady De Grey), through whom her grandmother had derived the place, who thought most of the old French statues—which, according to the custom of that day, were made of lead—to be insufficently dressed, and so sold them for the value of the metal, at the same time that she sold an incomparable collection of old plate, for the same reason, for its weight in silver. She showed one of the statues, backed by a yew hedge some centuries old. 'That poor lady, you see, was saved when all the others were sent away, because she had got a few clothes on.'

August 30.—After luncheon, I walked with the old Duchess [of Cleveland] in the avenue. She described being couched. 'Did you take chloroform?'—'Oh, certainly not: no such thing: I should not have thought of it. Don't *you* know that couching is a very dangerous operation? the very slightest movement might be fatal to it. I did not know what might happen under chloroform, but I knew that *I* should never flinch if I had my senses, and I never did: and in three weeks, though I was still bandaged up, I was out walking.'

In the evening I drove with Mr. Lowther to Haynes, till lately written Hawnes, the fine old place of Lord John Thynne, which he inherited from his uncle Lord Carteret. We met the old man riding in his park, and so much taken up with a sick cow that he almost ignored us. But when we had walked round by the charming old-fashioned gardens, we found him waiting for us on the garden doorstep, all courtesy and kindness. Several sons and daughters-in-law dropped in to tea in a kind of passage-room, but Lord John took me to see all the curiosities of the house himself, and warmed up over them greatly. There is a most noble staircase and a very fine collection of family portraits. In the drawing-room is that of Lady Ann Carteret in a white satin

[1] Anne-Florence, Baroness Lucas, Dowager Countess Cowper, elder daughter and co-heir of Thomas Philip, Earl De Grey. She died in 1880.—*Ed.*

dress, which she always wore, and is always remembered still as 'The White Lady.' Her husband was Jack Spencer, of whom there is also a fine picture. His grandmother, Sarah, Duchess of Marlborough, one day said to him suddenly, 'Jack, you must marry, and I will give you a list of the ladies you may propose to.'—'Very well, grannie,' he said, and he proposed to the first on the list. When he came back with his wife from their wedding tour they went to pay their respects to the old lady. 'Well, now,' she said, 'I am the root and you are only the branches, and therefore you must always pay me a great deal of deference.'—'That is all very well,' said Jack impertinently, 'but I think the branches would flourish a great deal better if the root was under ground.'

To-day the Duchess (Dowager of Cleveland) has been talking much of the wicked Duchess of Gordon,[1] her ancestress. She married all her daughters to drunken Dukes. One of them had been intended to marry Lord Brome, but his father, Lord Cornwallis, objected on account of the insanity in the Gordon family. The Duchess sent for him. 'I understand that you object to my daughter marrying your son on account of the insanity in the Gordon family: now I can solemnly assure you that there is not a single drop of Gordon blood in her veins.'

The Duchess of Cleveland went out walking this morning in beating rain and bitter wind—blind, broken-kneed, and eighty-four as she is. 'Well, you *are* a brave woman, Duchess,' some one said as she came in. 'You need not take the trouble to tell me that: I know that I *am* a brave woman,' she answered.

At dinner the Duchess vehemently inveighed against the deterioration of the times. 'Was there ever *anything* so ridiculous and uncalled-for as a school-feast?'—'But it is such a pleasure to the children.'—'Pleasure to them! In my days people were not always thinking how children were to be amused. Children were able to amuse themselves in my day. It is not only with the lower classes: all classes are the same—the same utterly demoralising system of indulgence everywhere. Why are not the children kept at home to learn to wash and sew and do their duty?'

'Formerly, too, people knew how to live like gentlemen and ladies. When they built houses, they built houses fit to live in, not things in which the walls were too thin to allow of the windows having any shutters. . . . Why, now people do not even know how to keep a great house. A great house ought to be open always. The master and mistress never ought to feel it a burthen, and if it was properly managed, they never would. There should always be a foundation of guests in the house, a few relations or intimate friends, who would be quite at home there, and who would be civil and go out to walk or drive, or do whatever might be necessary to amuse the others. There ought to be no *gêne* of any kind, and there ought to be plenty of *equipages*—that should be quite indispensable.'

The conversation fell upon Rogers the poet.[2] 'Mr. Rogers came here once,' said Lady Wensleydale, 'and I did not like him; I thought him so ill-bred. He came with the Duchess of Bedford of that time, who was the most good-natured woman in the world, and when he went out into the park and came in quite late for luncheon, she said he must have some, and went into the dining-room herself to see that he had it properly, and while he was eating cold beef, mixed him herself a kind of salad of oil and vinegar, which she brought to him. He waited a moment, then took up a piece

[1] Jane Gordon, 1749–1812, wife of Alexander, the fourth Duke.—*Ed.*
[2] Samuel Rogers, 1763–1855, began his career in his father's bank, but soon took to writing, and his wealth enabled him to mix with people of rank and eminence. He was offered the Laureateship in 1850 but declined it.—*Ed.*

of the beef in his fingers, rolled it in the sauce, and, walking round the table, popped it into the Duchess's mouth.

'Rogers met Lord Dudley at one of the foreign watering-places, and began in his vain way, "What a terrible thing it is how one's fame pursues one, and that one can never get away from one's own identity! Now I sat by a lady the other night, and she began, 'I feel sure you must be Mr. Rogers.'"—"And *were* you?" said Lord Dudley, looking up into his face quite innocently. It was the greatest snub the poet ever had.'

Holmhurst, Sept. 1.—I had rather dreaded the *tête-à-tête* journey with the Duchess to-day, and truly it was a long one, for we had an hour to wait at Ampthill Station, and then missed the express at Bletchley. When we first got into the carriage the Duchess said, 'Well, now, I am going to be quiet and rest my eyes,' which I thought

HOLMHURST

was a hint that I was to take my book; but very soon she got bored and said, 'I can't see, and am obliged to go on asking the names of the stations for want of being amused;' so then I was obliged to talk to her all the rest of the way.

At the stations, the Duchess was perfectly furious at the bonnets she saw. 'If any respectable persons had gone to sleep twenty years ago and woke up now, they would think it was Bedlam let loose.'

Conington, Oct. 1.—This is one of the clockwork houses, with a monotonous routine of life suited to the flat featureless country. To-day, after church, the male part of the family set off to walk a certain six miles, which they always walk after church, and, when we reached a certain bridge, the female part said, 'Here we turn back; this is the place where we turn every Sunday through the year: we always go as far as this, and we never go any farther.'

Sarsden House, Chipping Norton, Oct. 4.—I came here on Monday. At Paddington Station I met Lady Darnley and Lady Kathleen Bligh, and a procession of carriages in waiting showed that a large party was expected by the same train. It came dropping in round the five-o'clock tea-table—Lord and Lady Denbigh; Lord and Lady Aberdare and a daughter; Mr. and Mrs. J. A. Symonds; two young Plunketts; George, Lady Constance, and Madeleine Shaw-Lefevre; Lord Morton. . . .

In the evening Lord Denbigh told us:

'Dr. Playfair, physician at Florence, went to the garden of a villa to see some friends of his. Sitting on a seat in the garden, he saw two ladies he knew; between them was a third lady dressed in grey, of very peculiar appearance. Walking round the seat, Dr. Playfair found it very difficult to see her features. In a farther part of the garden he met another man he knew. He stayed behind the seat and asked his friend to walk round and see if he could make out who the odd-looking lady was. When he came back he said, "Of course I could not make her out, because when I came in front of her, her face was turned towards you." Dr. Playfair then walked up to the ladies, and as he did so, the central figure disappeared. The others expressed surprise that Dr. Playfair, having seen them, had not joined them sooner. He asked who the lady was who had been sitting between them. They assured him that there had never been any such person.

'The next morning, Dr. Playfair went early to see the old gardener of the villa, and asked him if there was any tradition about the place. He said, "Yes, there is a story of a lady dressed in grey, who appears once in every twenty-five years, and the singular part is that she has no face." Dr. Playfair asked when she had appeared last. "Well, I remember perfectly; it was twenty-five years ago, and the time is about coming round for her to appear again." '

A delightful old Mrs. Stewart has arrived from Scotland. I sat by her at dinner. She talked much of Mrs. Grote. She described an interview Mrs. Grote had with Madame George Sand. She said to Madame Sand that it was a pity she did not employ her great powers for the leavening and mellowing of mankind, as Miss Austen had done. 'Madame,' said Madame Sand, 'I am not a philosopher, I am not a moralist, I am a novelist.'

Sarsden, Oct. 5.—Last night Mrs. Stewart talked much of Hanover and her life there. Her daughter was lady-in-waiting to the Queen. She described how all the royal family might have their property back at once, but the King would make no concession—'God has given me my crown; I will only give it back to Him.'

Mrs. Stewart was with the Queen and Princess for five months at Herrenhausen after the King left for Langensalza, when 'like a knight, he desired to be placed in the front of his army, where all his soldiers could see him, and where he was not satisfied till he felt the bullets all whizzing around him.' The people in Hanover said he had run away. When the Queen heard that, she and Princess Marie went down to the place and walked about there, and, when the people pressed round her, said, 'The King is gone with his army to fight for his people; but I am here to stay with you—to stay with you till he comes back.' But alas! she did not know![1]

[1] This was George V of Hanover, who was blind. On the outbreak of the Austro-Prussian War he brought Hanover in on the Austrian side and, although Prussia demanded Hanover's neutrality, George refused and his country was overrun. At the battle of Langensalza, however (27th June, 1866), he was victorious, but the Prussians brought in fresh troops and Hanover capitulated two days later. The king was exiled and the whole state eventually annexed.—*Ed.*

All that time in Herrenhausen they were alone: only Mrs. Stewart and her daughter went out occasionally to bring in the news; the others never went out. At last the confinement became most irksome to the Princesses. They entreated Mrs. Stewart to persuade mama to let them go out. 'So,' said Mrs. Stewart, 'at last the Queen saw that it was well, and she consented. She said, "We will not take one of our own carriages, that would attract too much attention, but we will take my daughter's." And when they had gone some way up the hills, the pony fretted under the new traces and broke them, and, before they knew where they were, it was away over the hedges and fields, and they were left in the lane with the broken carriage. Two Prussian officers rode up—for the Prussians were already in Hanover—and seeing two ladies in that forlorn state, they dismounted, and offered their assistance. The Queen said, "Oh, thank you; our coachman has gone after the pony, which has run away, and no doubt he will soon come back, so we will just wait his return." But the coachman did not come back, and the gentlemen were so polite, they would not go away, so at last the Queen and Princess had to set out to return home; and the officers walked with them, never having an idea who they were, and never left them till they reached the gates of Herrenhausen. So the Queen came in and said, "You see what has happened, my dear; you see what a dreadful thing has befallen us: we will none of us ever try going out again," and we never did.

'We used to go and walk at night in those great gardens of Herrenhausen, in which the Electress Sophia died. We often did not come in till the morning, for the Queen could not sleep. But, even in our great sorrow and misery, Nature would assert herself, and when we came in, we ate up everything there was.

'One night the Queen made an aide-de-camp take the key, and we went to the mausoleum in the grounds. I shall never forget that awful walk, Harty carrying a single lanthorn before us, or the stillness when we reached the mausoleum, or the white light shining upon it and the clanging of the door as it opened. And we all went in, and we knelt and prayed by each of the coffins in turn. And then we went up to the upper floor where the statues are. And there lay the beautiful Queen, the Princess of Solms, in her still loveliness, and there lay the old King, the Duke of Cumberland,[1] with the moonlight shining on him, wrapped in his military cloak. And when the Queen saw him, she, who had been so calm before, sobbed violently and hid herself against me and said in a voice of pathos which I can never forget, "Oh, he was so cruel to me, so very, very cruel to me."

'The Queen was always longing to go away to her own house at Marienberg, and at last she went. She never came back; for, as soon as she was gone, the Prussians, who had left her alone whilst she was there, stepped in and took possession of everything.

'The Queen is a noble, loving woman, but she is more admirable as a woman than a queen. I *have* known her queenly, however. When Count von Walchenstein, the Prussian commandant, arrived, he desired an interview with her Majesty. He behaved very properly, but as he was going away—it was partly from gaucherie, I suppose—he said, "I shall take care that your Majesty is not interfered with in any way." Then our Queen rose, and in queenly simplicity she said, "I never expected it." He looked

[1] Ernest Augustus, fifth son of George III; field-marshal in the British Army, 1813; opponent of Reform and of all relaxation of Catholic penal laws; on William IV's death he became King Ernest I of Hanover in 1837; made himself an absolute monarch, but created a democratic constitution in 1840. Died in 1851.—*Ed.*

so abashed, but she never flinched; only, when he was gone out of the room, she fainted dead away upon the floor.'[1]

Mrs. Stewart told the story of Miss Geneviève Ward, the actress. In early life she was travelling with her mother, when they fell in with a handsome young Russian, Count Constant Guerra. He proposed to her, and as the mother urged it, thinking it a good match, she married him then and there in her mother's presence, without witnesses, he solemnly promising to make her his wife publicly as soon as he could. When he could, he refused to fulfil his promise; but the mother was an energetic woman, and she appealed to the Czar, who forced Guerra to keep his word. He said he would do what the Czar bade him, but that his wife should suffer for it all her life. To his amazement, when the day for the marriage arrived, the bride appeared with her mother, led to the altar in a long crape veil as to a funeral. Her brothers stood by her with loaded pistols, and at the door of the church was a carriage into which she stepped as soon as the cremony was over, and he never saw her again. She is Madame Constant Guerra, and has acted as 'Guerrabella.'

Prestbury, Oct. 6.—Mrs. Stewart again talked much of the Hanoverian Court, of the Guelph love of doubtful stories; how she saved up any story she heard for the blind King. One day she was telling him a story 'about Margaret Bremer's father' as they were driving. Suddenly the horses started, and the carriage was evidently going to be upset. 'Why don't you go on?' said the King. 'Because, sir, we are just going to upset.'—'That is the coachman's affair,' said the King; 'do you go on with your story.'

Donington Rectory, Oct. 13.—On arriving, I went on at once to Boscobel, and saw the oak which grew from an acorn of the tree that sheltered Charles II, and in the ancient half-timbered house, the hiding-place under the floor at the top of the turret-stairs, where the Prince is said to have crouched for forty-eight hours, with his trap-door concealed by cheeses. Well smothered he must have been, if Staffordshire cheeses smelt then as they do now.

We went on to Tong—a glorious church, quite a church of the dead, so full of noble tombs of Stanleys and Vernons. Near it, in low-lying lands with water, is Tong Castle, the old house of the Durants. The last Mr. Durant brought in another lady to live with his wife, which she resented, and she left him. There was a long divorce suit, which they both attended every day in coaches and six. Owing to some legal quibble, he gained his suit, though the facts against him were well known, and he was so delighted at the triumph over his wife that he erected a monument in honour of his victory on the hill above the castle. The sons all took part with their mother, and when Mr. Durant was lying in his last illness, they set barrels of gunpowder surreptitiously under the monument, and had a match and train ready. They bribed a groom at the house to ride post-haste with the news as soon as the breath was out of their father's body; and the news of his death first became known to the county by the monument being blown into shivers.

Brancepeth Castle, Nov. 8.—I reached this great castle in pitch darkness. It is a magnificent place—a huge courtyard and enormous fabric girdled in by tremendous towers of Henry III.[2] The staircase is modern, but most of the rooms have still the

---

[1] The Queen of Hanover, Alexandrina Mary, daughter of the Duke of Saxe-Altenburg, died in 1878.—*Ed.*

[2] Brancepeth Castle, about four miles from Durham, has since been used as a barracks.—*Ed.*

vaulted ceilings of Henry III's time, though the arms of the Nevilles, with which they were once painted, are gone now. The beer and wine cellars, with some cells called dungeons, are very curious. The butler pointed out with pride the *black* cobwebs which hung in festoons and cover much of the wine, a great deal of which was in the huge bottles called 'cocks' and 'hens.' The white cobwebs he had less opinion of: they are less healthy. Lady Boyne is a most pretty and winning hostess. In the evenings the whole party dance 'Durham reels' in the great hall.

Edinburgh, Nov. 19.—I have been four days at Winton with dear old Lady Ruthven. She is now blind as well as deaf, and very helpless, but she is still a loving centre of beautiful and unstinted beneficence. She says, 'It is a great trial, a very great trial, neither to see nor hear, but it is astonishing the amount of time it gives one for good thoughts. I just know fifty chapters of the Bible by heart, and when I say them to myself in the night, it soothes and quiets me, however great the pain and restlessness. It is often a little trial to me—the unsatisfied longing I have to know just a little more, just *something* of the beyond. If I could only find out if my husband and my sister knew about me.'

Lady Ruthven can repeat whole cantos of Milton and other poets, and her peculiar voice does not spoil them; rather, when one remembers her great age and goodness, it adds an indescribable pathos. She likes to be read to down her trumpet, which is not easy; and the person she hears best thus is George the under-footman; but, as she says, she 'has formidable rivals in lamps.'

Edinburgh, Nov. 20.—A visit to the Robert Shaw Stewarts has given me a pleasant glimpse of Edinburgh society. Certainly Edinburgh is gloriously beautiful, but never was there a city so richly endowed by Nature contaminated by such abject and ludicrous public monuments!

Ravensworth Castle, Nov. 26.—I have been much enjoying a visit here, and the cordial affection which abounds in my dear Liddell cousins. Old General Stanhope[1] is here, and told us—

'Lady Andover, who was the daughter of Lord Leicester, was with her husband[2] at Holkham, and when one day all the other men were going out shooting, she piteously implored him not to go, saying that she had dreamt vividly that he would be shot if he went out. She was so terribly eager about it, that he acceded to her wishes, and remained with her in her painting-room, for she painted beautifully in oils, and was copying a picture of the "Misers" which was at Holkham. But the afternoon was excessively beautiful, and Lady Andover's strong impression, which had been so vivid in the morning, then seemed to wear off, till at last she said, "Well, really, perhaps I have been selfish in keeping you from what you like so much because of my own impressions; so now, if you care about going out, don't let me keep you in any longer." And he said, "Well, if *you* don't mind, I should certainly like to go," and he went.

'He had not been gone long before Lady Andover's impression returned just as vividly as ever, and she rushed upstairs and put on her bonnet and pursued him. But, as she crossed the park, she met her husband's own servant riding furiously without his coat. "Don't tell me," she said at once; "I know what has happened,"

[1] General Philip Stanhope, fifth son of Walter Spencer Stanhope of Cannon Hall, celebrated for his kindly nature and pleasant conversation. Died 1879.—*Ed.*

[2] Charles Nevison, Viscount Andover, son of the 15th Earl of Suffolk, died January 11, 1800.

and she went back, and locked herself into her room. His servant was handing him a gun through a hedge, it went off, and he was killed upon the spot.'

Apropos of second sight, General Stanhope said: 'Did you ever hear of a man they used to call Houghy White? When I was young, I went with him down to Richmond on a water-party, which was given by Sir George Warrender. Houghy was then engaged to be married to a niece of Beau Brummel, as he was called, and when he returned from Richmond, we went to spend the evening at her mother's house, and there Houghy told this story.

'He was aide-de-camp to the old Duke of Cambridge when he was in Hanover, and was required by the Duke to go with him on a shooting-party into the Hartz Mountains. He, and indeed two of the Duke's other aides-de-camp, were then, I am sorry to say, very much in love with the wife of a fourth—a very beautiful young lady—and they were all much occupied by thoughts of her. At the place in the Hartz to which they went, there was not much accommodation, but there was one good room with an alcove in it and four beds. The two German equerries slept in the alcove, and the two English aides-de-camp in two beds outside it. In the night White distinctly saw the lady they all so much admired come into the room. She came up to both of the beds outside the alcove and looked into them; then she passed into the alcove. He immediately heard the equerry on the right cry out "What have you seen?" and the other—the husband—say, "Ach Gott! I have seen my wife!"

'White was terribly impressed, and the next day entreated to excuse himself from going out shooting with the Duke. The Duke insisted on knowing his reason, upon which he told what he had seen, and expressed his conviction that his friend was dead. The Duke was very much annoyed, and said, "You are really, as a matter of fact, so much occupied with this lady that you neglect your duties to me: I brought you here to shoot with me, and now, on account of whimsical fancies, you refuse to go: but I insist upon your going." However, White continued to say, "I must most humbly beg your Royal Highness to excuse me, but I cannot and will not go out shooting to-day," and at last he was left at home. That evening, the mail came in while they were at dinner, and the letters were handed to the Duke. He opened them, and beckoned White to him. "You were quite right," he said; "the lady died last night." '

Kinmel, Nov. 30.—I left Ravensworth early on Monday to go to Ridley Hall. In a few minutes after arriving, White the butler came to say that Cousin Susan would see me. She was in her little sitting-room, half sitting up on her sofa before an immense fire. At above eighty, her face and figure have still the look of youth which they had at thirty-five, and that quite unaided by art, though not by dress. She has now quite lost the use of her feet, and is cut off from all her usual employments, her garden, her walks, her china, and, if it were not that she is so long inured to solitary habits, her life would be indeed most desolate.

Yesterday I came here [from Ridley Hall]. A beautiful ascent through woods leads from the seaboard to this house, magnificent in the style of a Louis XIV château externally, with Morris paper and colour inside. There is a man party here—Lord Colville, Sir Dudley Marjoribanks, Lord de Lisle, Hedworth Williamson, Lord Delamere.

Dec. 1.—To-day being a hunting day, most of the men breakfasted in pink in the hall. We drove with the Barringtons to the old Shipley house of Bodryddan, where young Mrs. Conwy received us. The fine old house has been altered by Nesfield—

'restored' they call it—but, though well done in its way, the quaint old peculiar character is gone. This generation, too, has sent its predecessors into absolute oblivion. Only the pictures keep the past alive at all, and they very little.

Dec. 6.—Yesterday we drove to Wythenshawe. It is a most engaging old house, very well restored, all the historical points retained—the low narrow door inside the other, through which the defenders forced the conquerors to pass as their condition of surrender after their siege by the Commonwealth, when the family was heavily. fined: the ghost-room, where a soldier shot in the siege still appears: the difference in the panelling of the oak drawing-room, where the panels were smashed in by a cannon-ball. There is another ghost—a ghastly face of a lady, who draws the curtains and looks in upon a bride on the first night she sleeps in the house after her marriage: the late Mrs. Tatton saw it.

Sherborne Park, Dec. 12.—At Bourton-on-the-Water were many people waiting. In the dark I recognised Lord and Lady Denbigh, and then a young lady came up with her husband and spoke to me. 'I cannot see in the least who you are.'—'Oh, then I shall leave you to guess, and you will find out by-and-by.' It was Sir Garnet[1] and Lady Wolseley. With him and Lord Powerscourt, and a fat old gentleman much muffled up, whom I took for Sir Hastings Doyle, and who turned out to be Mr. Alfred Denison, I travelled in a carriage to Sherborne. I had a pleasant dinner, seated by Mr. Denison, who told me much about his curious collection of books on angling, of which he has some of the early part of the fifteenth century, and about 500 editions of Izaak Walton. He has even a Latin treatise on the Devil's fishery for souls. He was just come from Chatsworth, and had seen there a volume for which £12,000 had been refused, the original of Claude's *Liber Veritatis.*

Lord Sherborne is both very fond and very proud of his wife, but her music he pretends to detest, though her singing is quite lovely—not much voice, but intense pathos and expression.

Osterley, Dec. 16.—I came here about tea-time to what Horace Walpole calls 'the Palace of Palaces.' Sir Thomas Gresham was the original builder, and entertained Queen Elizabeth here. Then it passed through various hands till it fell to the Childs, for whom it was partially rebuilt and splendidly fitted up by the brothers Adam. An immense flight of steps leads through an open portico to a three-sided court, beneath which is the basement storey, and from which open the hall and the principal rooms. There is a gallery like that at Temple Newsam, but much longer and finer, and in this case it is broken and partitioned by bookcases into pleasant corners—almost separate rooms. The walls and ceilings are ornamented with paintings (let in) by Zucchi and Angelica Kauffmann, but the great charm lies in the marvellous variety, delicacy, and simplicity of the wood carvings, each shutter and cornice a different design, but a single piece. In one room are exquisite pink Gobelins, the chairs quite lovely: one of them represents a little girl crying over the empty cage of her lost bird; on its companion a little boy has caught the bird and is rushing to restore it to her. There is a fine picture of Lady Westmoreland, Robert Child's daughter. When Lord Westmoreland, whom he considered a hopeless ne'er-do-weel, asked for her hand, he had firmly refused it; but when Lord Westmoreland some time after took him unawares with the question, 'Now, if you were in love with a beautiful girl, and her father would

---

[1] Afterwards Viscount Wolseley, field-marshal, 1833–1913. Served in the Crimean War, Indian Mutiny, China War, Zulu War, Nile Campaign, etc. Commander-in-Chief of the British Army.—*Ed.*

not consent to your marrying her, what would you do?' answered, 'Run away with her, to be sure.' Lord Westmoreland took him at his word, and eloped with Miss Child in a coach-and-four from Berkeley Square; and when, near Gretna Green, he saw that the horses of his father-in-law, in hot pursuit, were gaining upon him, he stood up in the carriage and shot the leader dead, and so gained his bride.[1]

The Duchess Caroline (of Cleveland) was often here with Lady Jersey, and, when she sold her own place of Downham, determined to rent Osterley. Since then, though only a tenant, she had cared for it far more than its owner, Lord Jersey, and has done much to beautify and keep it up.

Dec. 17.—The Duchess is a most interesting remnant of bygone times. She is so easily put out by any one doing too much, that every one at luncheon was afraid to get up and ring the bell for her, till she was close to the bell herself, when a nervous young man jumped up and rang it before she could reach it. 'Sir, officiousness is not politeness,' she said very slowly and forcibly.

Feb. 14.—Luncheon at Miss Davenport Bromley's to meet Mr. Portal. Lord Houghton and his son and daughter were there. Mr. Portal has a scheme for educating the unfortunate Americans of gentle birth who have fallen from wealth to poverty owing to the changes on the cessation of the slave trade in South Carolina, and he has been eminently successful. He described the South Carolina reverses of fortune as most extraordinary. One of his friends died in his house who had once possessed an estate worth £300,000; yet, when his will was opened, it only contained these words—'I leave to the old and tried friend of my youth, the Rev. —— Portal, my only son!' He had nothing else whatever to leave except £9 towards his funeral expenses. Mr. Portal described how the 'darkies' had been 'done' since the change by those who had too much of the theory of religion to have any power left for the practice of it. Being at a place on the border, where some of the greatest battles were, he asked some of the 'darkies' why, when they saw the Northerners gaining the upper hand, they did not join them. A 'darkie' said, 'Mossieu, did you ever see two dogs fighting for a bone?'—'Yes, very often.'—'But, Mossieu, did you ever see the bone fight?'

The conversation fell on Philadelphia, 'the most conservative place in America, with its narrow streets and narrow notions.' Lord Houghton said that his son Robin had been shocked by the non-observance of Sunday in the native city of Moody and Sankey. Mr. Portal said that Moody and Sankey were utterly unknown, entirely without influence in their own country; that it could only be the most enormous amount of American cheek which had enabled them to come over to England, 'exactly as if it was a heathen country, to bring the light of the Gospel to the English'; that America had heard with amazement and *shock* how they were run after; that they owed their success partly to their cheek, and partly to their music.

Mr. Portal described his feeling of desolation when he first arrived in England— 'not one soul he knew amongst all these millions'; that the next day a lady asked him to conduct her and her child to a pantomime. He consented, without understanding that a pantomime meant Drury Lane Theatre, and his horror was intense when he

---

[1] John Fane, tenth Earl of Westmoreland, 1759–1841, Lord Lieutenant of Ireland, 1789–95, eloped with Miss Child in 1782. The bulk of her banker father's fortune was left to the eldest daughter of this marriage, Lady Sarah Fane, who married the fifth Earl of Jersey (George Villiers, who assumed the additional name of Child). By Lady (Sarah) Jersey he had eight children, and his eldest son, the sixth earl, married Julia, the elder daughter of Sir Robert Peel, who is the Lady (Julia) Jersey of Hare's visits to Osterley, etc.—*Ed.*

'found himself, a clergyman of forty years' standing,' in such a place. This, however, was nothing to what he felt 'when a troop of half-naked women rushed in and began to throw up their legs into the air'; he 'could have sunk into the ground for shame.' 'Was not the mother of our Lord a woman? was not my mother a woman? is not my wife a woman? are not my daughters women? and what are these?'

Mr. Knowles, the ex-editor of the *Contemporary Review*,[1] who was at luncheon, said that he had taken Alfred Tennyson to see a ballet with just the same effect. When the ballet-girls trooped in wearing *'une robe qui ne commence qu'à peine, et qui finit tout de suite* [a dress which scarcely begins and ends at once],' Tennyson had rushed at once out of the box, walked up and down in an agony over the degradation of the nineteenth century, and nothing would induce him to go in again.

March 4.—Breakfast with Lord Houghton—a pleasant male party—Dr. Ralston,[2] Henry James the American novelist, Sir Samuel Baker,[3] and three others. Harriet Martineau's Memoirs had just arrived, and were a great topic. Lord Houghton, who had known her well, said how often he had been sent for to take leave of Miss Martineau when she had been supposed to be dying, and had gone at great personal inconvenience; but she had lived for thirty years after the first time. Her fatal illness (dropsy) had set in before she went to America. Her friends tried strongly to dissuade her from going, suggesting that she would be very ill received in consequence of her opinions. 'Why, Harriet,' said Sydney Smith, 'you know, if you go, they will tar and feather you, and then they will turn you loose in the woods, and the wild turkeys will come and say, "Why, what strange bird are you?" ' [4]

Of course, much of politics was talked, especially about the Turkish atrocities. Sir S. Baker said that at the old Duchess of Cleveland's he had met Lord Winchester, now quite an old man. He said that he had ridden from Constantinople to the Danube in 1832, and had passed thirty impaled persons on the way. He himself (Sir Samuel) had seen the impaling machine on the Nile—a stake tapered like a pencil, over which a wheel was let down to a certain height, and when the man was impaled, he was let down on the wheel and rested there; he often lived for three of four days; if the machine was in the market-places of the country towns, the relations of the victims gave them coffee. 'It is not worse,' said Lord Houghton, 'than the stories we are told every Sunday: "he destroyed them all, he left not one of them alive"; especially of the cruelties of David, who made his enemies pass under the harrow, a punishment much worse than impalement. How grateful David would have been for a steam-roller! What a number of people he would have been able to despatch at once!'

March 8.—Luncheon at charming old Mrs. Thellusson's, where I met Madame Taglioni, the famous *danseuse*. She is now an old lady, with pretty refined features, perfect grace of movement, and a most attractive manner. She has begun in her old age to give lessons again for the benefit of her family, though she is, at the same time,

---

[1] See note on p. 111.

[2] Russian scholar, of the British Museum Library.

[3] Traveller and explorer, 1821–1893. Travelled in Asia Minor, explored the Abyssinian tributaries of the Nile, discovered and named the Albert Nyanza Lake, accompanied the Prince of Wales to Egypt and the Nile, was for four years governor of the equatorial Nile with the rank of Pasha, was major-general in the Ottoman Army.—*Ed.*

[4] Harriet Martineau (1802–76), published books and pamphlets on history, political economy and social problems, travel in America and the Near East, the Poor Law, and novels. She is credited with over 1600 "leaders" in the *Daily News*. She was one of the leading intellects of her day. Her health was always poor and she was deaf. Her brother James was a Unitarian Minister and a Professor of Moral Philosophy and Political Economy.—*Ed.*

presenting her princess grand-daughter—the Princess Marguerite Trubetskoi, a simple natural girl. Madame Taglioni spoke of her dancing as '*un don de Dieu*,' just as she would of music or any other art. We asked her if she would like to be young again. 'Oh, yes, indeed,' she said; 'how I *should* dance!' She said her father, a ballet-master, made her practise nine hours a day; 'however great a talent you may have, you never can bring it to perfection without that amount of practice.'

Sir Baldwin Leighton made himself so pleasant, that when he asked me to go to their box at the Lyceum in the evening, I promised to go, though I never like seeing any, even the very best plays, twice. However, the nearness of the box to the stage enabled me to see many details unobserved before. Richard III will always, I should think, be Irving's best part, for he looks the incarnation of the person. In Shakespeare, Richard III is most anxious to become king, and perfectly determined to remain king when he has become so; but Irving carries out far more than this. Irving's Richard is perfectly determined that vice shall triumph over virtue, and utterly enraptured when it does triumph, in a way which is quite diabolical. The night before Bosworth Field is most striking and beautiful. You are with the king in his tent. He draws the curtain and looks out. On the distant wind-stricken heath the camp-fires are alight, and the lights in the tents blaze out one by one, eclipsing the stars overhead. Richard says little for a time; your whole mind is allowed the repose of the beauty. The king, who has been through the last acts trying (you feel him striving against his personal disadvantages) to be kingly, is all-kingly on that night, in the immediate face of the great future on which everything hangs. He gives his orders—simply, briefly, royally. He lies down on the couch, folding himself in the royal velvet robe, which, like Creusa's cloak, is associated with all his crimes. He falls asleep. Then, out of almost darkness, just visible as outlines but no more, rise the phantoms; and, like a whiffling wind, the voice of Clarence floats across the stage. As each spirit delivers its message in the same faint spiritual harmonious monotone, the sleeping figure shudders and groans, moans more sadly.

Then there is a powerfully human touch in the way in which he, so coldly royal as he lay down, turns human-like for sympathy in his great horror and anguish to the first person he sees, the soldier who wakens him.

IV

WHILST WRITING THE BUNSEN MEMOIRS

1877–78

ᔕᗒᔕ

I T was soon after the death of my dear and honoured old friend, the
Baroness Bunsen, that her daughters, Frances and Emilia, wrote to
consult me about a Memoir of her beautiful and helpful life. I promised all the help I could give, but did not understand, till several months
later, that they wished me to undertake the whole biography myself.
This, however, I rejoiced to do. The work which I had undertaken
began at this time to bring me into constant and intimate connection with
all branches of the Bunsen family, especially with Lady Llanover,[1] the
sister of my dear old friend.

Llanover, March 18, 1877.—Yesterday I came here by the ferry over the Severn.
Lady Llanover's old ramshackle carriage met me at the Nantyderry Station, and brought
me to Llanover, I had received endless solemn warnings about what I was to say and
not to say here, what to do and not to do; but with a person of whom one is not likely
to see much in after life, one never feels any alarm. Lady Llanover is very small and
has been very pretty. Of the Bunsen family she talked from 4 till 10.30 P.M. 'You see
I have still the full use of my lungs,' she said.

At eight we had tea. There is no dinner, which I like, but every one would not.
After tea she gathered up all the lumps of sugar which remained and emptied them
with a great clatter into a box, which she locked up. With £20,000 a year, the same
economy pervades everything. Her great idea is Wales—that she lives in Wales,
and that the people must be kept Welsh, and she has Welsh schools, Welsh services,
a Welsh harper, always talks Welsh to her servants, and wears a Welsh costume at
church.

JOURNAL.

April 6, 1877.—I began by disregarding *all* advice, and taking Lady Llanover as
if I had never heard a word about her, and I am sure that it was the best way. I listened
to all she had to say, and received part of it to profit by. I found her difficult to deal
with certainly, but chiefly because, with endless power of talking and a vocabulary
absolutely inexhaustible, it is next to impossible to keep her in the straight conversational path along which she ought to be travelling. Thus, though on an average
we talked for six hours a day, not more than one of those hours could be utilised.

---

[1] Augusta Waddington, daughter and co-heiress of Benjamin Waddington of Llanover; married
Benjamin Hall in 1823, who was created baronet in 1838 and Baron Llanover in 1859.—*Ed.*

There is a great deal to admire in Lady Llanover: her pertinacity in what she *thinks* right, whether she *is* right or not: her insistence on carrying out her sovereign will in all things; but chiefly her touching devotion to the memory of the mother from whom she, the youngest and favourite daughter, was scarcely ever separated. The whitewashed 'Upper House' in the park is kept fresh and bright and aired, as if the long-lost mother were constantly expected. In her sitting-room a bright fire burns in winter, and fresh flowers are daily placed on the little table by her old-fashioned sofa. The plants she loved are tended and blooming in the little garden; the pictures and books are unremoved from the walls; the peacocks she used to feed, or their descendants, still spread their bright tails in the sun under her windows.

It is in the kitchen of the 'Upper House' that Lady Llanover's Welsh chaplain performs service on Sundays, for to the church she and her people will not go, as the clergyman is—undesirable. Lady Llanover on Sundays is even more Welsh than on week-days. She wears a regular man's tall hat and short petticoats like her people, and very becoming the dress is to her, and very touching the earnestness of the whole congregation in their national costume, joining so fervently—like one person—in the services, especially in the singing, which is exquisitely beautiful.

We had more of the Welsh music in the evening. We went and sat in the armchairs in the hall, and the household filed in above, and filled the music-gallery, and sang most gloriously, especially the burial-hymn 'It is finished,' which was sung in parts all the way from the house to the churchyard at the funerals of Mrs. Waddington and Lord Llanover and his son. At other times, the blind harper attached to the house came in and harped to us, and four little boys sat in a circle on the floor and sang.

At Llanover, in the weird house of dead associations, it was a relief when pleasant, handsome young Arthur Herbert came the last day. Almost the only other guest was Miss Geraldine Jewsbury,[1] the intimate and faithful friend of Mrs. Caryle. I found it difficult to trace in the ancient spinster the gifted brilliancy I had heard described, though of her strong will there was abundant evidence. During an illness of Mrs. Carlyle there was a comic instance of this. Miss Jewsbury had unlimited faith in black currant jelly for a cold. Now Mrs. Carlyle's throat was very bad, and Miss Jewsbury took some of her jelly to her. 'But I will not take it; I will not take it, Geraldine,' said Mrs. Carlyle, with her strong inflexion on the 'ine.' So Miss Jewsbury sat by the head of the bed and kept her black currant jelly well out of sight. But a moment came when Mrs. Carlyle fell fast asleep, and—if the truth must be told—opened her mouth very wide. It was Miss Jewsbury's opportunity, and she filled a spoon full of jelly, and popped it into the open mouth. 'Good God! Geraldine, what was that?' exclaimed Mrs. Carlyle, waking up. '*That* was black currant jelly.'—'Good God, Geraldine! I thought it was a leech gone the wrong way.'[1]

April 15.—Dined with Mrs. Rogerson, daughter of my dear Mrs. Duncan Stewart. Irving was there. I ventured to tell him how I thought his play was spoilt by the changes he had recently made, and *why*, and he was quite simple, as he always is, not the least offended, and in the end agreed with me, and said he should alter the changes as I suggested, and send me a box that I might come and see the improvement. He said how, ever since he heard me tell a story at Lord Ducie's, he had wished I should do something in public. He 'did not know if I wanted money, but thought I could make any sum I liked.' He 'believed he could guarantee' my making £8,000 a year! He advised my doing what he had intended doing himself when he had been 'making a

---

[1] Geraldine Jewsbury (1812–80) had some reputation as a novelist.—*Ed.*

mere nothing of ten guineas a week, and felt *that* could not go on.' He intended to have got Wilkie Collins to write him a story, and to take a room at the Egyptian Hall, fit it up in an old-fashioned way, sit down by the fire, and then take the audience, as it were, at once into his room and confidence. 'But in your case,' he said, 'you need not apply to Wilkie Collins.'

April 16.—Miss Northcote's[1] wedding in Westminster Abbey. I had a capital place in a stall just behind Princess Louise and Princess Mary[2] of Teck. The church was crowded, and though it was a bitter wind outside, it was quite glorious within, all the forest of arches tinted with golden sunlight. Arthur gave the blessing *magnificently*, as he always does. There were 350 people at the breakfast afterwards, which was at Lord Beaconsfield's house in Downing Street.

May 2.—A pleasant party at Lady Leslie's beautiful house to meet the Tecks. She looked more amenable than ever, yet the Princess all over.

May 12.—Dined at Mrs. Rogerson's, where I took down the Countess Bremer, who has always lived at the Hanoverian Court. She is that 'Margaret Bremer' who is celebrated for her answer to the blind King, who loved to shock her by his improper stories. 'What do you think of that, Margaret?' he asked, after telling her one of his worst. 'I think that your Majesty has a very clean way of telling a very dirty story,' she replied.

May 17.—A party at Lord Houghton's; every one there, from Princess Louise to Mrs. Anthony Trollope, a beautiful old lady with snow-white hair turned back. These crowded parties remind me of Madame de Staël's description—'*Une société aux coups de poing.*'

May 30.—On Saturday I was at a pleasant party at Lord Houghton's, meeting scarcely any one but authors, and a very odd collection—Black, Yates, and James the novelist,[3] Sir Francis Doyle[4] and Swinburne the poets; Mrs. Singleton the erotic poetess (Violet Fane), brilliant with diamonds[5]; Mallock,[6] who has suddenly become a lion from having written a clever squib called 'The New Republic,' and Mrs. Julia Ward Howe with her daughter. I was introduced to Mrs. Howe, having asked Lord Houghton who was the charming, simply-dressed woman with the sensible face, and then found she was sister of my Roman friend Mrs. Terry. She wrote the hymn, singing which the troops took Pittsburg. We asked her about it. She said she could not help feeling the little annoyance so many felt on similar occasions—that she should be only known as the authoress of one thing, one little waif out of all her work, and that people should treat her as if she had *only* written that.

[1] Daughter of Sir Stafford Henry Northcote, Chancellor of the Exchequer, 1874–1880, later created Earl of Iddesleigh.—*Ed.*

[2] Presumably Princess Marie Adelaide, wife of Francis, Duke of Teck, and mother of H.M. Queen Mary. Third child of the Duke of Cambridge.—*Ed.*

[3] William Black (d. 1898) author of *A Princess of Thule*, etc.; Edmund Yates (d. 1894), son of Frederick Yates the actor, dramatic critic, playwright, civil servant, author of *The Black Sheep*, etc.; and Henry James (d. 1916), author of *The Wings of a Dove, The Ambassadors, Portrait of a Lady*, etc.—*Ed.*

[4] Sir Francis Doyle (d. 1888), Professor of Poetry at Oxford and Civil Servant. Wrote several volumes of verse now largely neglected.—*Ed.*

[5] Mary Singleton, afterwards Baroness Currie. She figures in Mallock's *The New Republic* under the disguise of 'Mrs. Sinclair.' Her husband was Ambassador at Constantinople and Rome.—*Ed.*

[6] William Mallock (d. 1923) was a nephew of Froude and the author of satires, novels and social studies.—*Ed.*

June 4.—Dined at Lord Egerton of Tatton's. Old Mrs. Mildmay told a rather improper story there, which was received with shouts of merriment. She was at a country-house where there was a very pleasant man named Jones, and there was also a lady who had a maid called Jones: the people in the house knew this, because there was a confusion about letters. The lady's husband went away for the day, and, as she was going to walk to the station in the evening to meet him, the mistress of the house asked Mr. Jones to walk with her. When the train came in, the husband was not there, but just then a telegram was brought in. 'Oh,' said the lady, 'Oh-o-o, I'm sure my husband is dead: I can't open it.'—'Nonsense!' said Mr. Jones; 'if he is dead, he cannot have sent you a telegram.'—'Well, I can't open it; I know it's something dreadful—I can't, I can't, I can't.' So at last, Mr. Jones opened it for her and read it aloud, not seeing at once what it contained. It was—'I am all right, unavoidably detained. If you are at all nervous, *get Jones to sleep with you!*'

June 7.—Dined with George Lefevre. Mr. Bright was there, said to be the man who reviewed me so unmercifully in the *Athenæum*, and I was very glad to see the kind of man he is. He talked incessantly, never allowing a word to any one else; still after a time one found out he was interesting.[1]

June 28.—After a party at Lowther Lodge, I went to Lady Marian Alford, whom I found with a very ancient aunt, Lady Elizabeth Dickens. Lady Marian showed me her drawings. There was one glorious sketch of a Roman model, yet most unlike a model. 'She is,' said Lady Marian, 'the model who is so hated by the other models because of her stateliness. "She walks down the Corso as if it belonged to her," they say. She had two beautiful children—a boy and a girl. Last time I went to Rome, I saw her alone. "Where is your boy?" I asked.—"Oh dead," she answered.—"And the girl?"—"Oh, dead, *dead* too," she replied, pressing her hands to her forehead. And I pitied her, and I asked her about it, and she said, "I will tell you how it was." And she told me how she was coming downstairs with her boy in her arms and the girl behind her, and that just as she reached the house-door, a church-bell began to toll. "*E un giustiziáto* [it's an execution]!' said one of the neighbours. And then, she could not tell how it was somehow borne in upon her that her boy—her son—might, if he grew up, also some day fall into sin, also some day, perhaps, even be *giustiziáto* [executed]; and she turned round to the Madonna on the wall, and prayed that, if it were to be so, that she would take her son *then*, from the evil to come. And her husband, who heard her, said angrily, "*Che sono queste stragonfiáte* [what's all this butchery]"; and he beat her; but the Madonna had heard her, and that night her boy was taken ill, and in twenty-four hours he was dead.

'And then she said, "That night I went again to the Madonna, and I said, 'You have taken my boy, and, oh! if I may ever have *arrossire* [to blush] for my girl, take the girl also, take her away in her innocence;' *e la Madonna mi ha fatto anche questa caritá* [and the Madonna has done me this favour also], and I, I am alone, but my children are safe." '

A very interesting dinner at Miss Davenport Bromley's. Signor Francheschi described his life in Corsica, especially the weird women, who come like the Fates,

---

[1] John Bright, 1811–89, statesman and orator, friend of Cobden, opponent of capital punishment and of the Corn Laws, active in parliament for over forty years; served in Gladstone's ministries. Like Cobden he represents the maufacturing classes that came into political importance with the first Reform Act.—*Ed.*

as hired mourners, to bewail the dead, yet throw themselves so completely into their profession that they become quite absorbed in grief, and torrents of tears flow down their cheeks. One night he had to travel. In a desolate road he saw two strange ghastly horsemen approaching, with men walking on either side of their horses and holding them. The moonlight glared upon their fixed and horrid countenances. As they came near he heard the footmen talking to them. 'We must hasten; they are waiting for you; they are even now lamenting you.' Then he saw that the riders were dead. They were murdered men found by the highway, and had been set on horseback to be brought home. In Corsica it is the custom never to cease speaking to the dead.

July 7.—A capital party at Lowther Lodge to meet Princess Louise and Lord Lorne.[1] The garden was illuminated with magnesium light, and looked both beautiful and—boundless!

July 15.—Luncheon at Lady Combermere's, where Lord Houghton described his experience of executions. He had been to numbers of those in Newgate. Up to the time of George III the sign-manual was necessary for every execution, and it was an odd thing that George III, usually a humane man, used to hang every one. He would sit at the council-board and ask each of the ministers in turn whether a man was to suffer death. They would bow their heads in assent. Lord Melbourne was especially ready to do this when he was sitting at the council-board. One day, however, there was a case of a man who had murdered his wife under most brutal circumstances. The evidence was quite incontrovertible, and all were surprised that Lord Melbourne, usually so ready, shrugged his shoulders and seemed to have the greatest difficulty in making up his mind to give an assent to the death-warrant. One of the ministers, in going out, asked why it was. 'Why, poor man, those women are so damned provoking,' said Lord Melbourne.

Mr. Browning said he recollected seeing as many as twenty-one persons sitting together on the condemned bench in Newgate Chapel, many only for stealing a handkerchief. One day in chapel he was jostled by some one pushing in past him, and turned round annoyed. 'I beg your pardon, sir, but I am going to *suffer*,' said the man.

July 12.—Monday was a most beautiful day for the party at Chiswick, for its beautiful Italian gardens with glorious cedars. All London was there, including the Prince of Wales, with his little boy George, and the Tecks.

July 29.—On the 18th, I had an interesting visit to Apsley House, for which the Duke had sent me the following order: 'Admit Mr. Hare to see Apsley House on any day *on which the street outside is dry*.' The street was quite dry, and, moreover, I went in a cab and arrived perfectly spick and span; but the servant laughed as he produced a pair of huge list slippers to go on over my boots, before I was allowed to go into any of the rooms. 'His Grace left these himself, and desired you should wear them when you came.' Yet the floors of Apsley House are not even polished.

On the 19th I went to Lady Ducie's, to see the Macdonald family act the Pilgrim's Progress. They go through the whole of the second part, George Macdonald,[2] his wife, his twelve children, and two adopted children. Christiana (the eldest daughter)

---

[1] H.R.H. Princess Louise, in 1871 married the Marquess of Lorne, afterwards the 9th Duke of Argyll. She died in December 1939. She was the sixth child of Queen Victoria.—*Ed.*

[2] George Macdonald, 1824–1905, poet and novelist and writer of children's stories; friend of the Maurices of Hare's youth, also of Carlyle, Ruskin, Morris, etc. Spent much time on the Riviera. Amongst his works are three volumes of 'unspoken sermons,' *Fairy Tales*, *Letters from Hell*, several novels, and volumes of verse and essays.—*Ed.*

was the only one who acted well. Nevertheless, the whole effect was touching, and the audience cried most sympathetically as Christiana embraced her children to go over the great river.

On the 21st there was a delightful party at Holland House to meet the Prince of Wales, and on Wednesday I was thankful to come home.

To Miss Wright.

August 19.—I have had a pleasant visit of three days to Cobham, and felt much inclined to accede to Lord and Lady Darnley's wish at the end, that I would consider my visit just begun, and stay another three days. It is indeed a glorious old place externally, and the gardens and immense variety of walks under grand old trees, are enchanting in hot weather. I had many happy 'sittings out' and talks with Lady Darnley, and could not sufficiently admire, though I always observe it, how her perfectly serene nature enables her to carry out endless people-seeing, boundless literary pursuit, and inexhaustible good works, without ever fussing herself or any one else, leaving also time to enter into all the minute difficulties of her friends in the varied gyrations of their lives. . . . I was taken to see Cowling Castle, a romantic old place, just on the edge of those marshes of the Thames which Dickens describes so vividly. We also saw his house, close to Dover road.

Journal.

Walton Heath, Oct. 6.—I have come here to Miss Davenport Bromley at a quaint cottage, partly built out of a church, in a corner of the vast Walton Heath, but full of artistic comfort and brightness within. We drove on Thursday to Box Hill, which is most beautiful, the high steep chalky ground covered with such a luxuriance of natural wood, box grown into trees and billows of pink and blue distance so wonderfully luxuriant and wooded. The time of year is quite beautiful, and all the last festival of nature in the clematis wreaths and the bryony with its red berries dancing from tree to tree.

I have much enjoyed learning to know Miss Bromley better. She is the kindest of women, wonderfully clever and full of insight into every minutest beauty of nature. Her devotion to animals, especially pugs, is a passion. Another pleasure has been finding Mrs. Henry de Bunsen here. She told me—

'There was, and there is still, living in Cadogan Place, a lady of middle age, who is clever, charming, amiable, even handsome, but who has the misfortune of having —a wooden leg. Daily, for many years, she was accustomed to amble every morning on her wooden leg down Cadogan Place, and to take the air in the Park. It was her principal enjoyment.

'One day she discovered that in these walks she was constantly followed by a gentleman. When she turned, he turned: where she went, he went: it was most disagreeable. She determined to put an end to it by staying at home, and for some days she did not go out at all. But she missed her walks in the Park very much, and after a time she thought her follower must have forgotten all about her, and she went out as before. The same gentleman was waiting, he followed her, and at length suddenly came up to her in the Park and presented her with a letter. He said that, as a stranger, he must apologise for speaking to her, but that he must implore her to take the letter, and read it when she got home: it was of great importance. She took the letter, and when she got home she read it, and found that it contained a violent declaration of love and a proposal of marriage. She was perfectly furious. She desired her lawyer to enclose the letter to the writer, and say that she could not find words to describe her sense of his ungentlemanly conduct, especially cruel to one afflicted as she was with a wooden leg.

'Several years elapsed, and the lady was paying a visit to some friends in the country, when the conversation frequently turned upon a friend of the house who was described as one of the most charming, generous, and beneficent of mankind. So delightful was the description, that the lady was quite anxious to see the original, and was enchanted when she heard that he was likely to come to the house. But when he arrived, she recognised with consternation her admirer of the Park. He did not, however, recur to their former meeting, and after a time, when she knew him well, she grew to esteem him exceedingly, and at last, when he renewed his proposal after an intimate acquaintance, she accepted him and married him.

'He took her to his country-house, and for six weeks they were entirely, uncloudedly happy. Then there came a day upon which he announced that he was obliged to go up to London on business. His wife could not go with him because the house in Cadogan Place was dismantled for the summer. "I should regret this more," he said, "but that where two lives are so completely, so entirely united as ours are, there ought to be the most absolute confidence on either side. Therefore, while I am away, I shall leave you my keys. Open my desk, read all my letters and journals, make yourself mistress of my whole life. Above all," he said, "there is one cupboard in my dressing-room which contains certain memorials of my past peculiarly sacred to me, which I should like you to make yourself acquainted with." The wife heard with concern of her husband's intended absence, but she was considerably buoyed up under the idea of the three days in which they were to be separated by the thought of the very interesting time she would have. She saw her husband off from the door, and as soon as she heard the wheels of his carriage die away in the distance, she clattered away as fast as she could upon her wooden leg to the dressing-room, and in a minute she was down on all fours before the cupboard he had described.

'She unlocked the cupboard. It contained two shelves. On each shelf was a long narrow parcel sewn up in canvas. She felt a tremor of horror as she looked at them, she did not know why. She lifted down the first parcel, and it had a label on the outside. She trembled so she could scarcely read it. It was inscribed—"In memory of my dear wife Elizabeth Anne, who died on the 24th of August, 1864." With quivering fingers she sought for a pair of scissors and ripped open the canvas, and it contained— a wooden leg!

'With indescribable horror she lifted down the other parcel, of the same form and size. It also bore a label—"In memory of my dearest wife Wilhelmine, who died on the 6th of March 1869," and she opened it, and it contained—another wooden leg!

'Instantly she rose from her knees. "It is evident," she said, "that I am married to a Blue Beard—a monster who *collects* wooden legs. This is not the time for sentiment, this is the time for action," and she swept her jewels and some miniatures that she had into a handbag and she clattered away on her own wooden leg by the back shrubberies to the highroad—and there she saw the butcher's cart passing, and she hailed it, and was driven by the butcher to the nearest station, where she just caught the next train to London, intending to make good her escape that night to France and to leave no trace behind her.

'But she had not consulted Bradshaw, and she found she had some hours to wait in London before the tidal train started. Then she could not resist employing them in going to reproach the people at whose house she had met her husband, and she told them what she had found. To her amazement they were not the least surprised. "Yes," they said, "yes, we thought he ought to have told you: we do not wonder you were astonished. Yes, indeed, we knew dear Elizabeth Anne very well; she was indeed a most delightful person, the most perfect of women and of wives, and when she was taken away, the whole light seemed blotted out of Arthur's life, the change was so very terrible. We thought he would never rally his spirits again; but then, after two years, he met dearest Wilhelmine, to whom he was first attracted by her having the same affliction which was characteristic of her predecessor. And Wilhelmine was perhaps even more a charming person than Elizabeth Anne, and made her husband's life uncloudedly happy. But she too was, alas! early snatched away, and then it was as if the whole world was cut from under Arthur's feet, until at last he met you, with the same peculiarity which was endeared to him by two lost and loved ones, and we believe that with you he has been even more entirely, more uncloudedly happy than he was either with Wilhelmine or Elizabeth Anne.

'And the wife was so charmed by what she heard, that it gave quite a new aspect to affairs. She went home by the next train. She was there when her husband returned; and ever since they have lived perfectly happily between his house in the country and hers in Cadogan Place.'

Mrs. De Bunsen said that a cousin of hers was repeating this story when dining at the Balfours'. Suddenly he saw that his host and hostess were both telegraphing frantic signals to him, and by a great effort he turned it off. The lady of the wooden leg and her husband were both amongst the guests.

Milford Cottage, Oct. 8.—I came here with Miss Bromley on Saturday to visit Mrs. Greville and her most engaging mother, Mrs. Thellusson.

This afternoon I have been with Mrs. Greville to Mr. Tennyson at Haslemere. It is a wild, high, brown heath, with ragged edges of birch, and an almost limitless view of blue Sussex distances. Jammed into a hollow is the house, a gothic house, built by Mr. Knowles,[1] the editor of the *Nineteenth Century*—'that young bricklayer fellow that Alfred is so fond of,' as Mr. Carlyle calls him. Though the place is a bleak, wind-stricken height, where the flowers in the garden can never sit still, the house is pleasant inside and well and simply furnished, but is without any library whatever. Tennyson is older looking than I expected, so that his *unkempt* appearance signifies less. He has an abrupt, bearish manner, and seems thoroughly hard and *un*poetical: one would think of him as a man in whom the direst prose of life was absolutely ingrained. Mrs. Greville kissed his hand as he came in, which he received without any protest. He asked if I would like to go out, and we walked round the gardens. By way of breaking the silence I said, 'How fine your arbūtus is.'—'Well, I would say arbŭtus,' he answered, 'otherwise you are as bad as the gardeners, who say Clemātis.' When we returned to the house, Hallam Tennyson brought in his mother very tenderly and put her on a sofa. She is a very sweet-looking woman, with 'the glittering blue eyes' which fascinated Carlyle, and a lady-abbess look from her head-dress—a kind of veil. Mrs. Greville revealed that she had broken her promise of not repeating an unpublished poem of Tennyson's by reciting it to Mr. Carlyle, who said, 'But did Alfred give you leave to say it?' and Tennyson said, 'You are the wickedest old woman I ever met

---

[1] Afterwards Sir James Thomas Knowles (1831–1908); practised for thirty years as an architect. It was his book *The Story of King Arthur* which in 1862 attracted Tennyson's attention. He edited the *Contemporary Review* from 1870–77 and in the latter year founded *The Nineteenth Century.—Ed.*

with: it is most *profligate* conduct'—and he half meant it too. Tennyson then insisted that I should tell him some stories. I did not like it, but found it was no use to resist; I should have to do it in the end. I told him the stories of Mademoiselle von Raasloff and of Croglin Grange. He was atrociously bad audience, and constantly interrupted with questions.

On the whole, the wayward poet leaves a favourable impression. He could scarcely be less egotistic with all the flattery he has, and I am glad to have seen him so quietly. The maid who opened the door was Mrs. Cameron's beautiful model, and there were pictures of her by Mrs. Cameron all about the house.[1]

For the poet's bearish manners the Tennyson family are to blame, in making him think of himself a demigod. One day, on arriving at Mrs. Greville's, he said at once, 'Give me a pipe; I want to smoke.' She at once went off by herself down the village to the shop, and returning with two pipes, offered them to him with all becoming subservience. He never looked at her or thanked her, but, as he took them, growled out, 'Where are the matches? I suppose now you've forgotten the matches!'—'Oh dear! I never thought of those.'

Mrs. Greville has a note of Tennyson's framed. It is a very pretty note; but it begins 'Dear Mad-woman.'

Oct. 15.—Mrs. [Bridgeman] Simpson's very charming Polish sister-in-law, Mrs. Drummond Baring, recounted yesterday evening a curious story of the reminiscences of her childhood, of which her husband from knowledge confirmed every fact. Her father, Count Potocka, lived in Martinique. His wife had been married before, and her beautiful daughter, Minetta, idolised by her second husband, had made a happy marriage with the Marquis de San Luz, and resided at Port Royal about five miles from her parents. The father was a great naturalist, and had the greatest interest in introducing and naturalising all kinds of plants in the West Indies. Amongst other plants, he was most anxious to introduce strawberries. Every one said he would fail, and the neighbouring gardeners especially said so much about it that it was a positive annoyance to them when his plants all seemed to succeed, and he had a large bed of strawberries in flower. His step-daughter, Minetta, came to see them, and he always said to her that, when the strawberries were ripe, she should have the first fruit.

A ball was given at Port Royal by the Governor, and there her parents saw Minetta, beautiful and radiant as ever; but she left the ball early, for her child was not well. As she went away, she said to her stepfather, 'Remember my strawberries.'

Her parents returned home in the early morning, and a day and a night succeeded. Towards dawn on the second morning, when night was just breaking into the first grey daylight, the mother felt an irresistible restlessness, and getting up and going to the window, she looked out. A figure in white was moving to and fro amongst the strawberries, carefully examining each plant and looking under the leaves. She awoke her husband, who said at once, 'It is one of the gardeners, who are so jealous that they have come to destroy my plants;' and jumping up, he put on his *gola*—a sort of dressing-gown wrapper worn in Martinique—and, taking his gun, rushed out. On first going out, he saw the figure in white moving before him, but as he came up to the strawberry beds it seemed to have disappeared. He was surprised, and turning round towards the house, saw his wife making agonised signs to him to come back.

---

[1] Julia Cameron, 1815–79, one of the earliest and greatest of photographers. She was born in Calcutta, took up photography in England in 1865, and went to Ceylon in 1875, where she died. She made portraits of many of the great men of her day.—*Ed.*

AUGUSTUS IN 1888

AUGUSTUS IN 1871

Such was her livid aspect, that he threw down his gun upon the ground and ran in to her. He found her in a dead faint upon the floor. When she recovered, she said that she had watched him from the window as he went out, and that, as he reached the strawberry beds, the figure seemed to turn round, and she saw—like a person seen through a veil and through the glass of a window, and, though perfectly distinct, transparent—her daughter Minetta. Soon after describing this, she was seized with violent convulsions. Her husband was greatly alarmed about her, and was just sending off for the doctor, who lived at some distance, when a rider on a little Porto Rico pony came clattering into the court. They thought it was the doctor, but it was not; it was a messenger from Port Royal to say that Minetta was dead. She had been seized with a chill on returning from the ball, and it had turned to fatal diphtheria. In her last hours, when her throat was so swelled and hot, she had constantly said, 'Oh, my throat is so hot! Oh, if I had only some of those strawberries!'

Glamis Castle, Oct. 26.—I had a delightful visit to the salt of the earth at Hutton, where Mr. and Mrs. Pease were entertaining a large party, chiefly of semi-Quaker relations. Mrs. Pease is as delightful as she is beautiful, and the place is an oasis of good works of every kind. Thence I came here. As we drove up to the haunted castle at night, its many turrets looked most eerie and weird against the moonlit sky, and its windows blazed with red light. The abundance of young life inside takes off the solemn effect—the number of charming children, the handsome cordial boys, the winning gracious mistress; only Lord Strathmore himself has an ever sad look. The Bishop of Brechin, who was a great friend of the house, felt this strange sadness so deeply that he went to Lord Strathmore, and, after imploring him in the most touching manner to forgive the intrusion into his private affairs, said how, having heard of the strange secret which oppressed him, he could not help entreating him to make use of his services as an ecclesiastic, if he could in any way, by any means, be of use to him. Lord Strathmore was deeply moved, though he said that he thanked him, but that in his most unfortunate position *no one* could ever help him. He has built a wing to the castle, in which all the children and all the servants sleep. The servants will not sleep in the house, and the children are not allowed to do so.

There is much of interest in the life here—the huge clock telling the hours; the gathering in early morning for prayers by the chaplain in the chapel, through a painted panel of which some think that the secret chamber is concealed, though others maintain that it is entered through Lord Strathmore's study, and occupies the space above 'the crypt'—an armour-hung hall where we all meet for dinner, at which the old Lion of Lyon—gold, for holding a whole bottle of claret, which the old lords used to toss off at a draught—is produced. There are lions everywhere. Huge gilt lions stand on either side in front of the drawing-room fireplace, lions are nut-crackers, a lion sits on the letter-box, the very door-scraper is guarded by two lions.

Oct. 29.—Yesterday was Sunday, and we had three services in the chapel, which is painted all over with figures of saints by the same man who executed the bad paintings of the Scottish kings at Holyrood. The sermons from Mr. Beck, the chaplain, head of 'the Holy Cross' in Scotland, were most curious: the first—apropos of All Saints—being a mere catalogue of saints, S. Etheldreda, S. Kenneth, S. Ninian, &c., and their virtues; and describing All Saints' festival as 'the Mart of Holiness': the second—apropos of All Souls—speaking of prayers for the dead as a duty inculcated by the Church in all ages, and taking the words of Judas Maccabeus as a text.

E

Gorhambury, Nov. 20.—It was dark when I reached the St. Albans Station yesterday. Lord Verulam's carriage was in waiting for guests: I got into it with three others. 'Lord Beaconsfield was with us in the train,' said the young lady of the party, 'and I am sure he is going to Gorhambury, and oh! I *am* so glad he has taken a fly.' We drove up to the great porticoed house in the dark, and a small winding staircase took us to a great lofty hall, furnished as a sitting-room. Other guests appeared at dinner—the sallow basilisk face of Lord Beaconsfield: his most amusing secretary, Montagu Corry[1]: Lord Exeter, with long black hair[2]: Lady Exeter, tall, very graceful and refined-looking, but with the coldest manner in the world: a young Lord Mount-Charles: Scudamore Stanhope, remarkably pleasant: Charlie Duncombe, very pleasant too: Lady Mary Cecil: Dowager Lady Craven, always most agreeable.

Lord Verulam is permanently lame and on two crutches, but most agreeable and kindly. This morning I sat to draw the ruin of Lord Bacon's house. The place is full of relics of him, his observatory in the park: the 'Kissing Oak,' beneath which Queen Elizabeth embraced him: the 'Queen's Ride,' used when she came to visit him: curious painted terracotta busts of his father and mother and of himself as a child, in the library: and in the dining-room, a large portrait of his brother, which he (the brother) painted himself, the most prominent feature being his legs, of which he was evidently exceedingly proud.

Nov. 21.—At dinner last night and all day Lord Beaconsfield seemed absorbed, scarcely noticed any one, barely answered his hostess when spoken to. Montagu Corry said that his chief declared that the greatest pleasure in life was writing a book, because 'in that way alone man could become a creator:' that his habit was to make marionettes, and then to live with them for some months before he put them into action. Lately he had made some marionettes; now he was living with them, and their society occupied him entirely.

Nov. 25.—On Friday I drove with Lord Verulam in his victoria to Wrothampstead. The old house there is one of the long many-gabled houses, vine-covered, with windows and chimneys of moulded brick, standing, backed by fine trees, in a brilliant garden. It belongs to a Mr. Lawes,[3] who for a long time was supposed to be wasting all his time and most of his money in chemistry, but at length by his chemistry he discovered a cheap way of making a valuable manure, and 'Lawes's manure' has made him a millionaire.

Yesterday we went to Tittenhanger, already familiar to me from Lady Waterford's descriptions. It is a charming old house, utterly Cromwellian, most attractive and engaging, depending for its effect upon its high overhanging roofs, and the simple, admirable brick ornaments of its windows.

It was amusing *seeing* Lord Beaconsfield at Gorhambury: *hear* him I never did, except when he feebly bleated out some brief and ghastly utterance. His is an extraordinary life. He told Lord Houghton that the whole secret of his success was his power

---

[1] Montagu Corry, Lord Rowton, attended Disraeli at the Congress of Berlin, 1878; built the first Rowton House, the 'poor man's hotel' in 1892, after which others were built in various parts of London. Died 1903.—*Ed.*

[2] See p. 115.

[3] Afterwards Sir John Bennett Lawes, 1814–1900, the founder of the Rothamsted agricultural experimental station (1843); patented the manufacture of superphosphate as manure in 1843. A Gold Medalist of the Royal Society, 1854.—*Ed.*

of never dwelling upon a failure; he 'had failed often, *constantly* at first, yet had never dwelt on it, but always gone on to something else.'

Burghley, Nov. 29.—I have been glad to come to the place which is often called 'the finest house in England'[1]—a dictum in which I by no means agree. The guests are a row of elderly baronets of only hunting and Midland-county fame. I took a Miss Fowke in to dinner, and complained to her of the number of old baronets. 'Yes,' she said, 'they are old and they are numerous, and the central one is my father.'

The house is immense, but has little internal beauty. There is a series of stately rooms, dull and oppressive, with fine tapestry and china, and a multitude of pictures with very fine names, almost all misnamed.[2]

TITTENHANGER

Lord Exeter, with his lank black hair and his wrinkled yellow jack-boots high above the knee, looks like a soldier of Cromwell. In the evening he and the whole family dance incessantly to the music of a barrel-organ, which they take it in turn to wind.[3]

The great idol of family adoration is 'Telemachus'—the memory of Telemachus, or rather a whole dynasty of Telemachi, for they are now arrived at Telemachus X. The bull Telemachus I gained more that £1,000 at small county cattle-shows. His head is stuffed in the hall; his statue in silver stands in the dining-room (where there are also silver statues of Telemachus II and III), and his portrait hangs on the wall.

Holmhurst, Dec. 16.—I have been intensely busy. The life of Madame de Bunsen *unfolds* itself in her letters more than any life I have ever heard of. I long for the time to come when I may begin to unite my links, but at present I have only been making

[1] Burghley House, Stamford, seat of the Marquis of Exeter. Built 1553–87.—*Ed.*

[2] All the best pictures at Burghley have since been sold at Christie's.

[3] The same amusement was in vogue during the parties of the second Empire at Compiègne, where the worst of the many bad organ-grinders was the Emperor himself.

extracts—such extracts! Her power of expression is astonishing. I discover so much that I fancy I have felt myself, and never been able to put into words. I see in the vast piles of MS. the means of building a very perfect memorial to her.

Ampthill, Christmas Day, 1877.—I came here yesterday from Holmhurst. . . . It was a great pleasure to find charming old Sir Francis Doyle[1] here with his son and daughter. Sir Francis talks incessantly and most agreeably, and makes the mornings as interesting as the evenings. He has just been saying, apropos of how little one knows the true characters of those one meets:—

'H. told me a curious thing one day. He went to dine with a cabinet minister (I suppress the name), and there came down a lady, the governess, cherished by the family—"a perfect treasure." He recognised her at once as a lady he had known very well, very intimately indeed. She sank after that, sank into the lowest depth of that class of life. "I used to help her with money," he said, "as long as I could, but at last she sank too low even for that, quite out of my sphere of possibilities altogether, and here I found her reinstated. As I was questioning what I ought to do, she passed near me and said only, 'I have sown my wild oats.' I never told of her: I had nothing to do with placing her where she was." '

His stories of old times and people are endless. He said—

'I always keep a reminiscence of poor Lady Davy[2] to laugh at. It was one of those great days at Stafford House, one of their very great gala days, and Lady Davy was in the hall in the greatest anxiety about her carriage; and she, little woman, walked up to one of those very magnificent flunkeys, six feet high at least and in resplendent livery, and besought him to look after her carriage. I never saw any one *so* civil as that man was. "I have called your Ladyship's carriage three times," he said, "and it has not answered, but if your Ladyship wishes, I will try again."

'I saw the second act of that little drama. I went through the door, beyond the awning, just when the footman was stalking haughtily and carelessly among the linkboys and saying disdainfully, "Just give old Davy another call." '

At dinner the conversation turned on Lord and Lady Lytton. She was a Miss Doyle, a distant cousin of Sir Francis, and shortened his father's life by her vagaries and furies.[3] After his father's death Sir Francis left her alone for many years; then it was represented to him that she had no other relations, and that it was his duty to look after her interests, and he consented to see her, and, at her request, to ask Sir E. Bulwer to give her another hundred a year. This Sir Edward said he was most willing to do, but that she must first give a written retractation of some of the horrible accusations she had brought against him. When Lady Bulwer heard that this retractation was demanded of her, she turned upon Sir Francis with the utmost fury, and abused him with every vile epithet she could think of. She afterwards wrote to him, and directed to 'Sir Francis Hastings Doyle, Receiver of her Majesty's Customs (however infamous), Thames Street, London.' 'But,' said Sir Francis, 'I also had my day. I was asked as to her character. I answered, "From *your* point of view I believe her character to be quite immaculate, for I consider her to be so perfectly filled with envy, hatred,

[1] See note on p. 106.

[2] Presumably Lady Jane Davy, the wife of Sir Humphrey, the scientist. She was well known in the society of London and Rome.—*Ed.*

[3] She was, in fact, a Miss Rosina Wheeler, though related, as stated by Hare, to the Doyles, Lytton married her against his mother's wishes. They were legally separated after nine years, but she devoted herself thereafter to making various public attacks on her husband, making him the villain of her novel, *Cheveley,* and on one occasion denouncing him from an election platform.—*Ed.*

malice, and all uncharitableness, as to have no possible room left for the exercise of any tenderer passion." ' Lady Bulwer appeared on the hustings against her husband. His son told Sir Edward, 'Do you know my Lady is here?'—'What, Henry's wife!' —'No, *yours*.' She said, 'He ought to have gone to the colonies long ago, and at the Queen's expense.'

Dec. 27.—I had a charming drive to-day with Lady Ashburton to Woburn, the rest having preceded us. There is a long winding double avenue in the park. The stables are so enormous that we mistook them for the house, and were surprised when we turned the other way. However, the door of the real house was most dilapidated and unducal. Long passages, surrounding an open court, and filled with portraits, led to a large sitting-room, where we found most of our own party and the guests of the house. The Duchess [of Bedford] was kind and cordial. We all went to luncheon in the Canaletti room, enlivened by endless views of Venice, which, regardless of their artistic merits, are most pleasing to the eye through their delicate green-grey tints. Afterwards we went through the rooms, full of portraits, one of Lucy Harington in a ruff, very fine. In one corner is a set of interesting Tudor portraits, including a large one of Jane Seymour; hideous I thought, though Froude, when he saw it, said he did not wonder Henry VIII cut Anne Boleyn's head off to marry so bewitching a creature. A great portrait of the famous Lord Essex in a white dress has a mean feeble face and stubby red beard. The Duke offered to take us to the church. Lady Ashburton, Lady Howard of Glossop, and I drove there with him. We passed 'the Abbot's Oak,' where the last abbot was hung. Froude says he went up to London and was swallowed up by his fate. The Duke asked what this meant. It did mean that he was hung, drawn, and quartered, 'but Froude was very angry at the question; historians never like being asked for details.' The Duke said, 'Would you like to see what is going to be done with me when I am dead?' and he showed us the hole in the floor where he was to be let through 'to the sound of solemn music,' and then he took us down into the vaults beneath to see the trestles on which his coffin was to repose![1]

Crewe Hall, Jan. 6.—The number of hats in the hall told me on arriving here that there was a large party in the house, but I find no remarkable elements except Lord Houghton.

Lord Crewe welcomed me very cordially, and made himself so pleasant that I thought his eccentricities had been exaggerated, till suddenly, at dinner, he began a long half-whispered conversation with himself, talking, answering, *acting*, and nothing afterwards seemed able to rouse him back to ordinary life. During the fire which destroyed the interior of Crewe some years ago, Lord Crewe bore all with perfect equanimity, and said not a word till the fire-engines came and were at work. Then he turned to his sister, Lady Houghton, who was present, and said, 'I think I had better send for my goloshes.'[2]

This afternoon Lord Houghton told an interesting story which he heard from Mrs. Robert Gladstone:—

'She went to stay in Scotland with the Maxwells of Glenlee. Arriving early in the afternoon, she went to her room to rest. It was a lovely day. Mrs. Maxwell lay upon

[1] Francis Charles, ninth Duke of Bedford, succeeded his cousin William, the eighth Duke. He was President of the Royal Agricultural Society and carried out costly experiments in fertilisers on his estates. In later life he became a hypochondriac and in 1891 he committed suicide while suffering from pneumonia.—*Ed.*

[2] Hungerford Crewe, Lord Crewe, died Jan. 1894.—*Ed.*

the sofa at the foot of her bed. Soon it seemed to her as if the part of the room opposite to her was filled with mist. She thought it came from the fireplace, but there was no fire and no smoke. She looked to see if it came from the window; all without was bright clear sunshine. She felt herself *frisonner*. Gradually the mist seemed to assume form, till it became a grey figure watching the clock. She could not take her eyes from it, and she was so terrified that she could not scream. At length, with terror and cold, her senses seemed going. She became unconscious. When she came to herself the figure was gone. Her husband came in soon after, and she told him. He took her down to five o'clock tea. Then some one said, "You are in the haunted room," and she told what had happened. They changed her room, but the next morning she went away.

'Soon afterwards Mrs. Stamford Raffles went to stay at Glenlee. It was then winter. She awoke in the night, and by the bright firelight burning in her room saw the same effect of mist, collecting gradually and forming a leaning figure looking at the clock. The same intense cold was experienced, followed by the same unconsciousness, after a vain endeavour to awaken her husband, for her limbs seemed paralysed.

'The Maxwells soon afterwards became so annoyed that they gave up Glenlee.'

Jan. 26.—Dined with old Lady Lyndhurst,[1] who has all the clever vivacity acquired by her early life in France. Speaking of bullying at public schools, she said, 'I discovered that my Lord had been a bully when he was a boy, and I can assure you I thumped him well at eighty for what he had done at fourteen.'

Battle Abbey, March 10, 1878.—I came here yesterday, finding Lady Marian Alford, and to-day Lord Houghton came. Lord Houghton's vanity is amusingly natural. Something was said of one of Theodore Hook's[2] criticisms. 'You know even *I* never said anything as good as that,' said Lord Houghton, and quite seriously.

March 12.—Yesterday Lord Houghton and I sat very long after breakfast with the Duke [of Cleveland], who talked of his diplomatic life. He was appointed from St. Petersburg to Paris, and the revolution which enthroned Louis Philippe occurring just then, he hurried his journey. When he reached Frankfort, Chad, who was minister there, assured him that he would not be allowed to enter France, but, provided with a courier passport, he pushed on, and crossed the frontier without difficulty. At Paris the barricades were still up. The town was in the hands of the Orleanists (they bore the name then). On the evening of his arrival the Duke was introduced to Lafayette, 'quite a grand seigneur in manner.' Lafayette asked him if he did not know Lord and Lady Holland, and on his answering in the affirmative, begged that he would write to assure Lord Holland that he meant to save the lives of the late ministers, because he was accused of intending to have them executed.

The Duke talked much of the wonderful gallantry of the Emperor Nicholas— how when the rebel troops were drawn out opposite his own in the square at St. Petersburg, he stalked out fearless between them, though the Governor of St. Petersburg was shot dead at his feet. The rebel troops were only waiting to fire till they saw a rocket, the signal from Prince Troubetskoi, whose courage failed him at the last. Troubetskoi was sent to Siberia, whither his wife insisted upon following. He was

[1] Widow of John Singleton Copley, Baron Lyndhurst, 1772–1863, son of John Singleton Copley the painter; born in America, but brought to England as an infant; lawyer. Three times Lord Chancellor, but refused a fourth term.—*Ed.*

[2] Theodore Hook, novelist and wit, son of the organist at Vauxhall Gardens; famous practical joker; was one of the Prince of Wales's set. Wrote many novels and edited *John Bull*. He is the Mr. Wagg of Thackeray's *Vanity Fair.*—*Ed.*

sentenced for life, so was legally dead, and she might, had she preferred it, have married any one else.

April 3.—On Monday, March 25, as I was breakfasting at the Athenæum, I glanced into the paper, and the first thing which met my eyes was the news of the total loss of the *Eurydice*, with dear good Marcus Hare and more than three hundred men. It was a terrible shock, and seemed to carry away a whole mass of one's life in recollections from childhood. . . . It is many days ago now, and the dreadful fact has seemed ever since to be hammering itself into one's brain with ceaselessly increasing horror. How small now seem the failings in Marcus's unselfish and loving character, how great the many virtues.

April 14.—I have little to tell of London beyond the ordinary experiences. Of the many dinner-parties I have attended, I cannot recollect anything except that some one—I cannot remember who—spoke of D'Israeli as 'that old Jew gentleman who is sitting on the top of chaos.'

Last Sunday I went to luncheon at Mrs. Cavendish Bentinck's. I arrived at two, having been requested to be punctual. No hostess was there, and the many guests sat round the room like patients in a dentist's anteroom, or, as a young Italian present said, when I made his acquaintance—'like lumps of ice.' Lady Waterford came in and Mr. Bentinck, and we went in to luncheon. There was a table for about forty, who sat where they liked. Mrs. Bentinck came in when all were seated, greeting nobody in particular. The lady next me, a perfect stranger, suddenly said, 'I want you to tell me what I must do to get good. I do not feel good at all, and I want to be better: what must I do?'

'That depends on your peculiar form of badness,' I replied.

'Well, I live where I have a church on each side of me, and a church on the top of the hill under which my house is situated. But they do me no good. Now I wonder if that is owing to the inefficiency of the churches, or to the depravity of my own heart?'

'Probably half to one and half to the other,' I said.

I asked afterwards who the lady was, but neither her hostess nor anyone else had an idea.

Yesterday I dined with the Pole-Carews. Mrs. Carew told me that Dr. Benson, Bishop of Truro,[1] told her:—

'At my table were two young men, one of them a Mr. Akroyd. He began to talk of a place he knew in one of the Midland counties, and how a particular adventure always befell him at a certain gate there.

'Yes,' said the other young man, 'your horse always shies and turns down a particular lane.'

'Yes,' exclaimed Mr. Akroyd, 'but how do you know anything about it?'

'Oh, because I know the place very well, and the same thing always happens to me.'

'And then I come to a gateway, 'said Mr. Akroyd.

'Yes, exactly so,' said the other young man.

'And then on one occasion I drove through it and came to a house.'

'Ah! well, *there* I do not follow you,' said the other young man.

'It was very long ago,' continued Mr. Akroyd, 'and I was a boy with my father. When we drove down that lane it was very late, quite dark, and we lost our way. When we reached the gateway, we saw within a great house standing on one side

---

[1] Edward White Benson, afterwards Archbishop of Canterbury.—*Ed.*

of a courtyard, brilliantly lighted up. There was evidently a banquet inside, and through the large windows, we saw figures moving to and fro, but all were in mediæval dress: we thought it was a masquerade.

'We drove up to the house to inquire our way, and the owner came out to speak to us. He was in a mediæval dress. He said he was entertaining his friends, and he entreated us, as chance had brought us there that night, to come in and partake of his hospitality. We pleaded that we were obliged to go on, and that to stay was impossible. He was excessively civil, and said that if we must really go on, we must allow him to send a footman to guide us back into the right road. My father gave the footman half a crown. When we had gone some distance I said, "Father, did you see what happened to that half-crown?"—"Yes, my boy, I *did*," said my father. It had fallen *through* the footman's hand on to the snow.'

'The gateway really exists in the lane. There is no house, but there was one once, inhabited by very wicked people who were guilty of horrible blasphemies—a brother and sister, who danced upon the altar in the chapel, &c.'

V

ROYAL DUTIES AND INTERESTS

1878–79

꾹

BEING at Lowther Lodge on the 21st of May, I was sent for by the Crown Princess of Germany, who was most kind and gracious.[1] 'I have read all your books. I always buy them as soon as ever they come out and I have so much wished to see you.' When my little audience of about ten minutes was over, she said with great sweetness, 'I am afraid I am keeping you much too long from all your other friends.' She pressed me to come to stay with her at Potsdam.

As spring advanced my Life of the Baroness Bunsen was so far completed as to be ready for the inspection of her children. I therefore decided to take it to them in Germany. I turned first towards the Rhineland to visit the Dowager Princess of Wied, and profit by her recollections of one who had ever been one of the most valued of her friends.

On the last day of May I reached Cologne, and found there a succession of telegrams from the Princess of Wied desiring me to come to her. It is a long ascent of an hour and a half from Neuwied through orchards and meadows radiant with wild-flowers to Segenhaus, standing on the crest of the mountain, which is literally 'the House of Blessing' to all around it. The beautiful spacious rooms, full of books and pictures, look down over a steep declivity upon an immense view of the Rhineland. The Princess came in immediately with a most warm welcome— a noble, beautiful woman in a black dress, with snow-white hair drawn back under a long black veil. After a few minutes spent in explaining the towns in the vast maplike view below us, she said, 'There is a lady here who is anxious to make your acquaintance, and who was delighted to hear that you were coming: it is the Queen of Sweden.' At that moment the doors were thrown open, and the Queen entered—of middle age, with a beautiful expression, and possessing, with the utmost regal dignity, the most perfect simplicity and even cordiality of manner. She desired me to sit by the Princess upon a divan facing her. She said that I must

---

[1] H.R.H. Princess Victoria, eldest child of Queen Victoria, born 1840, who married Prince Frederick of Germany, afterwards Crown Prince and, for three months, Emperor.—*Ed.*

E*

consider her at once as a friend; that, in a life of great troubles, the *Memorials* had been her greatest comfort; that she never went anywhere without them; that my mother had been for several years the intimate friend to whom she always had recourse, and in whose written thoughts she could always find something which answered to her own feeling and the difficulty of the moment.

After tea the Queen ordered her donkey, which was brought round by a handsome Swedish chasseur. We went out into the forest. The Queen rode: the Princess led the donkey: I walked by the side, and only the chasseur followed. We actually went on thus for three hours, through beautiful forest glades with exquisite sylvan views. The Queen never ceased talking or asking. She wished to know the whole story of my mother's trances at Pau, of Madame de Trafford, of Prince Joseph Bonaparte—'a sort of cousin of my husband's.' She talked much and most touchingly of her own life and its anxieties. 'What I feel most,' she said, 'is the impossibility of ever being alone. I have much happiness, much to be thankful for, but I feel that what one has really to look forward to must come after death, and I do not wish to live.' When alone with her sister at the Segenhaus in the quiet forest-life, she finds most happiness, and they live in a higher world, mentally as well as physically. As we went down a steep bank the donkey stumbled, and the Queen cried out. 'Pardon me that I have seemed to be afraid,' she said; 'I have been so very ill, that my nerves are quite shattered'; and in fact a severe illness, long supposed to be mortal, had at this time obliged her for several years to leave Sweden in the winter, to be under a great doctor at Heidelberg. She asked me to come to Norway to visit her. 'You must also know my husband,' she said, 'and my four sons, my four blessings of God.' She repeatedly expressed her wish that I should be at Rome in the winter with the Prince Royal. 'I am sending him out to learn his world.'

We walked on and on through the vast woods. At the top of a high declivity the Princess unlocked a small gate. Within, in a little circular grove of lime-trees, were two marble crosses over the grave of the Prince of Wied and his martyr-like son Otto. 'And here,' said the Princess very simply, 'is my grave also.'

Behind the palace of the Princess is the great white château of Monrepos, where her son lives with his wife, who is Princess Royal of the Netherlands. Above the lower range of windows is a line of huge stags' heads, trophies of the chase of some former prince in the forest. The House of Wied are *ehenwürdig*, and so may always marry royalty. We went in, and I was shown to a room, whence I came down to that in which the court ladies were assembled. It was rather formidable, but the

Countess Ebba von Rosen, dame du palais of the Queen, talked pleasantly in English. Doors were thrown open, and the Queen and Princess entered and we went in to supper. The Queen made me sit by her: the four court ladies sat opposite: the Princess, on the other side of the Queen, made tea. Thick slices of bread and butter, like those of English school-feasts, and mutton-chops were handed round. When we went into the other room, I wrote down some names of books as desired, and then at 9.30 took leave. The Princess most cordially invited me to return, and the Queen again pressed me to visit her in her own country.

JOURNAL *and* LETTERS *to* MISS LEYCESTER *and* MISS WRIGHT.

June 15.—I have had a charming week at Herrenalb, whither Charles and Theodore de Bunsen accompanied me. It was a real pleasure to be again with the dear Frances and Emilia de Bunsen, who are so like sisters to me, and the kind pleasant Sternbergs. We were occupied almost entirely with my book, the sisters taking it in turn to talk over all the different parts, but there were also delightful intervals of forest rambles, and sittings out under the old apple-trees with Emilia.

A terrible sensation has been created by the attack on the Emperor,[1] and still more by the first false report of his death. Men and women were alike in tears, and the national disgrace is intensely felt. I hope, if the Emperor is better, that I may see the Crown Princess again at Berlin.

I spent four hours at Heidelberg, and revisited all our old haunts, the gardens most lovely in their luxuriance of green. Thence I had intended to go to Weimar to visit the Grand Duchess, but at Eisenach received a telegram from her lady-in-waiting, the Countess Kalkreuth, to put off my visit, as they were gone off to Berlin, the Empress Augusta being sister of the Duke of Weimar. A wet morning at the Wartburg and an afternoon at Erfurth brought me to Jena. There my cousin Alexander Paul met me at the station, a pleasant, fat, frank Prussian officer, with a face very like that of the first Napoleon.

Yesterday we went a fatiguing excursion to Schwartzberg, the palace of the Prince of Rudolstadt, by which we saw the finest parts of Thuringia. A railway took us to Schwarza, where, in a ball on the top of the church steeple, is a dart thrown by a Cossack as the Russian army passed through Germany. Thence we took an omnibus to the little Chrysopraz Hotel at Blankenberg, where, after beer and brown bread and butter under the trees, we walked up the Schwarzthal to Oppelei, where a Swiss cottage has been built by the Prince to indemnify a forester, whose daughter he had made his mistress! Hence, by a steep path, we ascended the Treppstein, whence there is a lovely view over the hollow in the forest-clad mountains, in the midst of which the great castle of the Prince of Rudolstadt rises above the little town. The Prince is not unpopular, though his life has an Eastern license. On the day when he succeeded to his tiny sovereignty he happened to be at Berlin. 'Bonjour, souverain,' said the Emperor when he met him, and, when he took off his hat—'Pray put on your crown.'

We dined at the charming little inn, where thousands of wild stags often assemble under the windows in the evenings, when the place is comparatively empty, but take flight into the woods before the summer guests.

[1] Emperor Wilhelm I.—*Ed.*

Berlin, June 27.—On Monday George de Bunsen met me and brought me through the Thier-Garten, like a bit of wild forest, to the charming airy Villa Bunsen, standing in its own garden on the extreme outskirts of the town. Here I have a most luxurious room, filled with royal portraits, and every possible luxury. We dined *al fresco* on the broad terrace amid the flowers. On the next evening there was a party of about fifty people—tea, and the garden and terrace lighted up, a very pretty effect; the ladies in bright dresses, the men with uniforms and orders, moving and sitting amongst the shrubs and flowers, amid which endless little supper-tables were laid at a late hour. Many were the historic names of those to whom I was introduced—Falk of the Falk laws, Mommsen the historian, Austin the poet,[1] Mohl, and many ministers and generals. I found also Arthur Balfour,[2] and many waifs and strays of old acquaintance. The 'Congress' is going on, but excites little or no general interest, and is scarcely mentioned here, German affairs being far too important.

June 30.—The day after I last wrote, I went with the Bunsens and Mr. Waddington, the French Minister (come for the Congress of Berlin) to Charlottenburg. The palace there is charming—the large gardens, the groves of orange-trees in tubs, the great lawns sweeping away into woods, and above all the mausoleum in one of the thick groves, with the tombs of Queen Louisa and her husband. Hither the old Emperor and all the royal family come still once a year, on the anniversary of her death, to look upon the beautiful form of his young mother, snatched away in the very zenith of beauty and popularity, not living to see the re-establishment of the kingdom in whose cause she sacrificed her life. Exquisitely, perfectly beautiful is the intense repose of her lovely countenance, in what I must ever feel to be the most beautiful and impressive statue in the world. The statue of the King is very fine too, but in her angelic presence he is forgotten.[3]

The next day I went to Potsdam—quite a place by itself in the world, with its endless great ultra-German palaces and stiff gardens, arid and dusty, though surrounded by many waters. Without Carlyle's *Frederick the Great*, they would be mere dead walls enclosing a number of costly objects; illuminated by the book, each room, each garden walk, thrills with human interest.

When I returned to the station, I was surprised to find the Bunsen's servant, sent on with my evening clothes, that I might accept an invitation (by telegram) to dine with the Crown Princess [Victoria]. I had only eight minutes before the royal train came up, and it was an awful scramble to wash and dress in a room the servant had taken at the station. However, when the royal train set off, I was in it. The palace-station of Wildpark was a pretty sight, red cloth laid down everywhere, and sixteen royal carriages waiting for the immense multitude of guests—quantities of ladies in evening dress (all black for the King of Hanover) and veils, splendid-looking officers, an Armenian archbishop and bishop in quaint black hoods and splendid diamond crosses. I went in a carriage with the Greek minister, and we whirled away through the green avenues to the great Neue Palais, with the sun striking warm on the old red and grey front. Count Eulenborg, Master of the Household, stood on the steps

---

[1] Alfred Austin, created Poet Laureate in 1896.—*Ed.*

[2] Arthur James Balfour, first Earl Balfour, 1848–1930, nephew of the third Marquis of Salisbury, Prime Minister, and himself Prime Minister from 1902–05. Was influential in British politics for over fifty years.—*Ed.*

[3] Louise, Queen of Prussia, 1776–1810, wife of Frederick William III, won the respect and admiration of her people by her dignity and courage during the Napoleonic wars. Napoleon tried hard to destroy her reputation but failed.—*Ed.*

to receive us, and we passed into an immense hall, like a huge grotto, decorated with shells and fountains, where several of the court ladies were.

At the end of the hall were some folding-doors closely watched by two aides-de-camp, till the rapping of a silver stick was heard from a distant pavement, when the doors were flung open, and Count Eulenborg came out, preceding the Prince and Princess. She immediately went up to Mrs. Grant (General Grant's wife) and several other ladies, and then began to go the round of the guests. I had more than my fair share of her kindly presence. 'Oh, Mr. Hare, I am so glad to see you again so soon. How little I expected it, and how sad the causes which have brought it about!' And she went on to speak of how, at our last meeting, the Duchess of Argyll had been sitting with her at tea, and how three days after she died. 'And for me it was only the opening act of a tragedy,' she said. She talked of the shock which the news of the attack upon the Emperor was to her, coming to her in the picture-gallery at Panshanger, and of her hurried journey to him. The Crown Prince came up then, and led her away to dinner. Mrs. Grant was on his other side (General Grant, a very vulgar officious man, was also there). I had been directed to a place near the Archbishop and Bishop of Armenia, but as they only spoke Armenian, I was glad that a very handsome, agreeable aide-de-camp eventually took his place between me and them.

After dinner we all went out on the terraces, and there the Crown Princess had the goodness to come again to me. She talked of all I had seen at Berlin, and of Sweden and Queen Sophie. She talked also of Queen Louisa, her husband's grandmother, preferring her statue at Potsdam even to that at Charlottenburg, and wished to have sent an aide-de-camp with me to see it. She was so good as to desire that I should return to Potsdam, and when I showed her that I could not, said, 'Oh, but you will now find your way again to Berlin to see me.' The scene on the terraces was very pretty, looking upon the bright flowers beneath in the subdued light of a fine evening in this transparent atmosphere, the whole air scented with lime-flowers.

At a quarter to nine all the carriages came again to take us away: Count Eulenborg announced them. In the ante-chamber I found the Crown Princess again. I kissed her hand, and she shook mine with many kind words, and sent affectionate messages to the Queen of Sweden.

How we whirled away through the green avenues to Potsdam, where all the people turned out to see the cavalcade! I travelled back to Berlin with the young and very handsome Prince Friedrich of Hohenzollern (brother of the Prince of Roumania and the Comtesse de Flandres), who was saved in the annihilation of his regiment of guards in the second battle of Metz by being sent back with the standard.

July 5.—I spent Sunday at beautiful old Lübeck, full of colour and rich architecture, rising spire upon spire above the limpid river. In the streets and market-place are the quaintest towers, turrets, tourelles, but all end in spires. A great fat constable went about on Sunday morning, keeping everybody from following any avocation whatever during church-time: when the services were over, they might do what they liked.

Then came the long weary journey across West Holstein—peat flats varied by marshy swamps—and a night at Schleswig, a white, colourless old town moored as if upon a raft in the marshes, where the Princess of Wales' [Alexandra's] grandmother and other royal potentates lie in exposed coffins upon the floor of the ugly rugged old cathedral, which has a belfry like a dovecot. Everywhere roses grew in the streets on the house-walls. The children were hurrying along, *carrying* the shoes they were to wear in school.

Stockholm, July 13.—Stockholm has deeply interested us, and there is an odd feeling in being at a place and knowing that it is for once and once only in a lifetime. It is a modern city of ugly streets, but in a situation quite exquisite.

Alas! we have been here a week, and, except one day, it has rained almost incessantly. One pities the poor Swedes in losing their short summer, for there are only about three months without snow, and every day is precious. The streets are sopping, but we have managed several excursions in the covered gondolas to quiet damp old palaces on the banks of lonely fiords. On our one fine day we went to Upsala by rail, and saw the cathedral where Gustavus Wasa lies aloft on a great tomb between his two pretty little wives, and we drove on to Old Upsala, where Odin, Thor, and Freya reigned as human beings and were buried as gods. In the tomb of Thor—a grassy mound—the Government still gives the mead of ancient times to foreign visitors. It is a very delightful place, like a dip in the Sussex downs, the quaint church, of immemorial antiquity, probably once a pagan temple, nestling behind the mounds of the heroes.

Yesterday we heard a hundred Upsala students, the best singers in the world, sing the best national music in the Caterina Church. The King was there, a noble royal figure. He is *the* sovereign of the age, artist, poet, equally at home in all modern languages and several ancient ones, profoundly versed in all his duties and nobly performing them. The Crown Prince was with him, a fine young fellow, spoilt in appearance by his mother's Nassau mouth, and the Prince Imperial, who is here with his cousins on a visit. The Queen is still away.

Throndtjem, July 28.—Surely this old cradle of Northern Christianity is one of the most beautiful places in the world. . . . So exquisite in the soft silvery morning lights on the fiords and purple mountain ranges, and the nearer hills covered with bilberries and breaking into steep cliffs, that one remains in a state of transport, which is at a climax when all is engraven upon an opal sunset sky, and when ships and buildings meet their double in the still transparent water. Each old wide street of curious wooden houses displays a new vista of sea, of rocky promontories, of woods dipping into the water, and at the end of the chief street is the grey massive cathedral.

But I must go back to Kristiania, which was steaming in intensity of heat when we reached it, the wet of Stockholm having cleared in Norway into cloudless sunshine which had hatched all the mosquitoes. There is no beauty in the mean little town, which was built by Christian IV. We went by rail to Kongsberg where we were annoyed by the ludicrously consequential advent of General Grant and Co. Here we hired a carriage and carriole for a five days' excursion in Tellemarken. What a drive!—by silent lakes or through deep, beautiful, ever-varying woods of noble pine-trees, rising from thickets of juniper, bilberries, and cranberries. The loveliest mountain flowers grow in these woods. But what a road, or rather what a want of one!—hills of glassy rock, up which our horses scrambled like cats, abysses where they gathered up their legs and flung themselves down headlong with the carriages on the top of them, till at the bottom we were all buried in dust, and picked ourselves up, gasping and gulping, and wondering we were alive, to begin the same pantomime over again.

We arrived at the little châlet of Tinoset on the wrong day for the steamer down its lake, and had to engage a private boat. The little lake was lashed by the wind into furious purple billows, and the voyage was most wretched. A horrid male creature from Middlesbrough, whom we surnamed the 'Bumble Bee,' accompanied us. I was brutal enough to make him over to Miss Holland, by saying, 'This lady will be deeply interested to hear all you have to say,' and to her he buzzed on perpetually.

As we returned to Kongsberg, we stopped to see Hitterdal, the date-forgotten old wooden church so familiar from picture-books. Here we were told by our landlady that she would not give us any dinner—'Nei, nei, nothing would induce her; perhaps the woman at the house with the flag would give us some.' So, hungry and faint, Miss Holland and I sallied out as *avant-couriers* to the house with the flag. All was silent and deserted except for a dog, who received us furiously. Having pacified him, and finding the front door locked, we made good our entrance at the back, examined the kitchen, pried into all the cupboards, lifted the lids of all the saucepans, and not till we had searched everything for food ineffectually, were met by the lady of the house, a pleasant young lady, speaking English perfectly, who informed us, with no small surprise at our conduct, that we had been committing a raid upon her private

BOLKESJO

residence. Afterwards we found a lonely farmhouse, where also there had once been a flag, where they gave us a very good dinner.

On the 25th we started from Kristiania for Throndtjem, the whole journey of three hundred and sixty miles very comfortable and only costing thirty francs.

August 8.—To the last the unspeakable beauty of Throndtjem grew upon us. It is not at first sight of its wide streets of low timber houses, or even of its fiord with purple mountain background, or of its glorious cathedral in the wide-spreading church-yard, which is the town-garden as well as the centre of all its sympathies, that you learn to admire it, but after many sunsets have turned the fiord into rippling gold, and sent an amethystine glow over the mountains, and after many rambles along the shores to rocky points and bosky hillocks.

After much indecision, we determined to return from Throndtjem by road, and engaged two carriages at Storen, with a pleasant boy named Johann as a driver. At every 'station' we changed horses, which were sent back by a boy who perched on the luggage behind. It was a very wild interesting life, and there was a great charm in going on and on into the unknown, meeting no one, dining on trout and pancakes at a station at midday, sleeping in odd, primitive, but always clean rooms, and setting off again at 5.30 or 6 A.M. There are bears and wolves in the forest, but we never saw any. Their skins, shot during the winter, are hanging up in almost all our sleeping-places. The prices are extraordinarily low, and the homely, cordial people kissed our hands all round on receiving the smallest gratuity, twopence halfpenny being a source of ecstatic bliss. But the journeys were tremendous, as we were sometimes called at four, and did not get in till twelve at night.

There was for a long time nothing especially fine in the scenery, except one gorge of old weird pine-trees in a rift of purple mountain, and the high moorland above Jerkinn, where the great ranges of white Sneehatten rise above the yellow grey of the Dovre Fyeld, hoary with reindeer moss. From Dombaas, we turned aside down the Romsdal, which soon became beautiful, as the road wound above a chrysopraz river, broken by many rocky islets, and swirling into many waterfalls, but always equally

IN THE ROMSDAL

radiant, equally transparent, till its colour is washed out by the melting snows in a ghastly narrow valley which we called the 'Valley of Death.'

Orkeröd near Moss, on the Kristiania Fiord, August 9.—On reaching Kristiania last night, I found a most gracious telegram from the Queen, through Countess Rosen, desiring that I would spend my last days in Norway with her. So I came this morning by the early steamer. Most beautiful were the long changing reaches of the fiord, with the rocks covered with foliage, already waving towards autumn, the rich russet and golden tints of the trees repeating themselves in the water. At Moss (to the intense astonishment of a very vulgar American family on board, who had given themselves indescribable airs to me) a royal carriage with two chasseurs in cocked hats and plumes was in waiting, and the King's chamberlain was standing on the pier to receive me. We drove swiftly up a rocky forest road to the large villa which a merchant of Kristiania has lent to the Queen for the benefit to her health from the pine air. As we drove up through the garden, a tall figure in a wide-awake hat emerged from one of the windows upon the terrace.[1] '*Sa Majesté le Roi!*' said the chamberlain;

[1] Oskar II.—*Ed.*

so I jumped out of the carriage, and he came forward at once with 'Is it Mr. Hare? The Queen has spoken of you so much, that you are not like a stranger. The Queen will be delighted to see you, and so am I. We were so glad to hear that you would come to see us in our quiet country life. You will find nearly the whole family, only my second son, Oscar, has left us to-day. I am especially glad that you will see the Prince Royal, my eldest son, Gustaf.[1] Come now and take a walk with me in the garden.' So we walked and he talked, chiefly about Rome. Then he took me to the Prince Royal, who was sitting under the trees with the Countess Rosen, two maids of honour, and Baron Holtermann, the marshal of the palace. There we sat some time and talked till the Queen emerged from the house. I went towards her, and met her amongst the flower-beds. She looks wonderfully well, far better than at Segenhaus. Nothing could be more cordial or kind than her reception of me. We walked on the terrace for some time, and she talked of the great event since we parted, the attack on the Emperor, and of the Crown Princess.

Soon the beautiful donkey of our Segenhaus walk was brought round, with its crimson trappings, and the Queen mounted, and went off through the forest to the King's house. I went in a kind of large open car with the Countess Rosen, the maids of honour, and the chamberlain. We reached the King's villa before the Queen, and all drew up in two lines in the porch to receive her. The King gave his arm to the Queen and we all went to luncheon in a garden pavilion. Here the two youngest Princes came in,—Carl, a very handsome boy of seventeen, and Eugène, of twelve. The King called me to come up to a tiny round table at the end of the room on a daîs, where he and the Queen were alone, and made me sit with them on their divan. I had had no food since six o'clock in the morning and was almost fainting with hunger, so, in spite of the honour of sitting with the King and Queen, I greatly envied the court at their good luncheon below, as their Majesties (and consequently I) had only coffee cups for their soup, and a tiny slice of bread and cheese apiece.

Then the Queen mounted her donkey again, the King lifting her up, while the young Princes, climbing the pillars of the verandah behind their mother, made a pleasant family group. Then the King and Princes started to walk, and I for a long drive with the Countess Rosen and some of the court.

August 10.—At four o'clock yesterday the whole court met in the drawing-room, so many gentlemen turning up from hidden corners, that it made twenty-four persons in all. The Prince Imperial recognised me immediately when he came in, and was exceedingly cordial and friendly. He is as nice as he can be, but as to appearance, his photographs flatter him, as he has such a bad complexion and his legs are too short. He is, however, quite delightfully frank and winning. He took the Queen, the King took Countess Rosen, and we all followed to dinner. I was desired to sit by the Prince Royal. He talks no English and atrocious French, and was difficult to get on with at first. I tried to talk of Rome, but whenever a maid of honour on the other side claimed his attention, was glad to subside into conversation with an old chamberlain. The King drank healths at dinner, the Prince Imperial's, mine, Count Murat's. The Prince Royal asked me to clink glasses with him. 'Do you like that custom?' he said. A Swedish noble, appointed to wait on the Prince Imperial, stood up when the King drank his health. Then I saw the other side of the King—in very cold stern rebuke. 'In good society gentlemen do not stand up when their healths are drunk,' and that

[1] Later Gustaf V of Sweden, then aged twenty, who acceded in 1907 and died in 1950.—*Ed.*

in the severest tones. The Queen looked surprised, and a momentary chill fell upon the whole party.

When the princes were gone to their fishing, the Queen made me come and sit by her. She returned at once to the subject of the Prince Royal and her great anxiety that I should be much with him abroad. 'He must *learn* his world,' she said, 'he knows so little of it. He is thoroughly good, but what he wants is enthusiasm, he wants to be incited to knowledge, to learning his future out of the past, and oh! you can help him so much, and if you will, I shall always be so grateful to you: but remember, and I know it will always help you to be kind to my boy if you do remember, what my boy's future must in all probability be. Oh, Mr. Hare, do when there is a chance, sow some little seeds of good in my son's young heart, and remember that what you do is not only done for the Prince Royal, not even for his mother, who entirely trusts you, but for the thousands upon thousands of people whom he may one day be called upon to influence. Whatever happens, if you will only interest yourself for my boy, you will believe in his mother's gratitude.'

The Queen continued to talk long in this manner with the utmost animation, till the Countess Rosen, suddenly seeing some sign of illness unobserved by us, ran round and said, 'Dear Majesty, you must not now speak any more,' and led her away with a charming mixture of motherly affection and playful deference.

When Countess Rosen returned, she said, 'The King desired that as soon as the Queen had ceased speaking to you, you should go to him: he especially wishes to talk to you alone.' I found the King under a tree in the garden, reading a book (the 'Odes of Horace,' I think), and, fearing to disturb him, I pretended to occupy myself with the flowers, but he perceived me at once, closed the book, and coming to me, took my arm, and walked up and down on the terrace. 'The Queen has been speaking to you of our son,' he said; 'I know what the Queen has been saying, and I wish to continue her conversation. He is a good boy, but he has not been tried; he has no idea what the world is like, nor of the many temptations which lie in wait for a young man, above all for a prince. Now the Queen and I are quite agreed that it is our wish that you should be as much to our son as possible, and I wished to see you alone that you might believe that all that his mother wishes, his father wishes also.' The King then talked in detail of the Prince's probable life in Rome, of the places and people he must see.

While we were talking, the court ladies were playing at croquet on the lawn. The King afterwards joined them, and I took a short walk with Baron Holtermann, marshal of the palace, and then went in and sat down to read in the drawing-room. Presently the King put in his head from the Queen's room—'Yes, he is here,' he said, and then he called me to come in to the Queen. They then both of them took my hands and spoke to me in a most touching manner about the Prince Royal. The Queen also spoke of the uncertainty of her life, and of renewed meetings in distant Norway, and of her hope of seeing me in another world.

The Prince Imperial and the Swedish princes now returned from fishing, singing at the pitch of their voices through the woods, and we all went upstairs to supper. Their Majesties and the whole court had—Swedish fashion—each a great bowl of sour milk, with a great hunch of bread and two preserved peaches in a glass. The Prince Royal, by whom I again sat, fortunately asked for sweet milk, so I was able to do so also.

At 8 A.M. Baron Holtermann fetched me to walk through the woods to the King's house to breakfast, after which I walked with the King to the pier at the end of the garden. There the younger princes kissed their father, and the Prince Imperial (who was going away at the same time and whom the King would accompany to Kristiania) took leave of the court. It was an intensely hot day, the town of Moss and the shore of the fiord seeming to steam with hot mist and the flowers all drooping. A little steam-pinnace took us all to the luxurious steamer, where there was boundless space for sitting or walking or whatever we liked. The voyage was very long—five hours.

Half-way down the fiord, the Prince Imperial insisted that he must bathe. At first the King said it was impossible, that the moment of his arrival at Kristiania was fixed, that the people were waiting to see him, that the steamer could not be delayed —in fact, that it was out of the question. But while the King was discoursing, the Prince Imperial stripped off every article of clothing he had on, and after rushing up and down the deck perfectly naked, jumped into the sea over the poop and swam like a fish. The King then was obliged to stop the steamer, as he could not leave the Prince Imperial in the middle of the fiord, and he told an aide-de-camp to undress and go to pick out the Prince. The Prince lay on the breast of the waves laughing at the King till the aide-de-camp reached him, and then he dived, disappeared for some time, and came up on the other side of the vessel. The Prince Royal then undressed and went in too, and two aides-de-camp, and they all swam and pursued each other like mermen.

We entered Kristiania in triumph—all the towers, houses, and masts of the vessels in the harbour decorated with flags, cannon firing, and crowds of people on the quays. At the station were crowds too, waiting for the royal carriages as they drove up. There was quite a procession of them. I went in the second carriage with Count Murat.

I spent the late summer of 1878 very quietly at home, busied in completing the *Life of the Baroness Bunsen.* Many guests came and went, amongst them Miss Wright, whose constant kindness and affection had been so much to me for many years. Whilst with me she was very ailing, but it was only supposed to be rheumatism, and doctors, who examined her carelessly, sent her from Holmhurst to Buxton, which was fatal to her, for her real disorder was heart-complaint. I never shall forget the bitter anguish of the shock, gently and tenderly broken as it was by Mary Lefevre, when I read that I should never see again the loving devoted friend of so many years. Years have passed away as I write, but I can scarcely bear to speak of her, even to write of her, even now. 'How holy are the holy dead!'

Throughout the autumn I had heard frequently from the Queen of Sweden. The entire confidence and noble friendship expressed in these letters made it impossible for me to hesitate, when, after the Prince Royal had spent some time in Paris, it became the strong wish of her Majesty that I should join him at Rome. It was in entire concert with the King and Queen that I drew up the scheme of a series of peripatetic lectures for the Prince, in which, by describing historic events on the places with which they were connected, I hoped to fix those events and their lessons in his recollection. It was, however, with great misgiving that I left England, feeling that I gave up my pleasant home and congenial occupations in England for the constant companionship of a young man who had not, in our short previous acquaintance, made a very favourable impression upon me, and who might resent my exertions in his behalf, and look upon me rather as a spy for his parents than as a friend to himself. When I once reached Rome, however, these fears were soon set at rest, and during the whole nine months which I passed in constant intimacy with the Prince, I never once had to reproach him with want of consideration for myself personally, but, on the contrary, always received from him marks of the utmost esteem and affection.

Upon the passage of the Mont Cenis I came in for terrible snowdrifts. Suddenly, after passing the tunnel, the walls of snow increased on each side of the train so as almost to block out the light, and, with a dull thud, the train came to a standstill near the wretched village of Oulx. An avalanche had fallen upon the luggage train which was pioneering our way, and three poor men were engulfed in it. The cold was terrific, and the suffering was increased in my case, because, having usually been much tried by the overheating of foreign trains, I had brought no carriage-rug or other wraps with me. After some time a way was cut through the snow walls to a miserable tavern, where sixteen ladies decided to sleep or cower in one wretched room and twelve gentlemen in another, but I gladly made my way back to the carriage before the passage was blocked again. It was then two in the afternoon, and wearily the day wore on into night, and still more wearily passed the night hours, with snow always falling thickly. I had a little brandy in the carriage, but no food. The suffering from cold was anguish. There were several invalid ladies in the train, for whom I felt greatly, knowing what this catastrophe would have been in times past before I was alone. Before morning two more avalanches had fallen behind us and the return to France was cut off. The telegraph wires were all broken, and the guard assured us that it was possible we might be detained days, or even weeks. At midday, cold and hunger made me try the hovel once more, but the filth and smells again drove me back to the carriage. At 4 P.M., however, on the second day, a welcome shouting announced that our deliverance was at hand. No trains arriving at Turin, our position was suspected, and the town-firemen were sent out *en masse* to cut a way for us. At 6 P.M. we were released from our twenty-eight hours' imprisonment, but the way was so dangerous, that we did not reach Turin till long after midnight.

To MISS LEYCESTER.

26 *Piazza di Spagna, Rome, Nov.* 25, 1878.—You will imagine how touching was the slow approach by rail round the walls of Rome, crossing all the little lanes *we*

knew so well in our drives, and seeing, one after another, S. Paolo, the Caius Cestius, the Porta S. Sebastiano, S. Giovanni in Olio, Porta Maggoire, the Minerva Medica, and then the vast space once occupied by the beautiful Villa Negroni, but now parcelled out for straight streets and stuccoed houses.

Yet, considering it is four years since I was here last, the changes are not great yet, the same old man with peaked hat and long beard and the same pretty girls stand waiting as models: the same old stonecutter is grinding away under the Tempietto, and Francesco threw open Miss Garden's door and announced (simply) '*Il Signorino,*' as if I had been there the day before.

On Sunday, Umberto and Margherita of Savoy made a triumphal entry into Rome, and I went to the Palazzo della Consulta to see them arrive at the Quirinal. It was an exquisitely beautiful evening—not a breath of air stirring the many flags: the obelisk and statues and the grand fountain of Pius VII were in deep shadow, but the sun was glinting through the old ilexes in the Colonna Gardens and illuminated S. Peter's and the town in the hollow. There was an immense crowd of every class, from ex-*guardia nobile* to peasants in the costumes of Sora and Aquino, and through them all the vast procession of sixty carriages moved to the palace, with flags flying, and flowers falling, and cannon thundering, and the one little bell of the royal chapel tinkling away as hard as it could, because the other churches would make no sign. '*I Sovrani,*' as all the people called them, looked very proud and happy, and Queen Margherita marvellously graceful, and pleased to see the millions of marguerites, which people were wearing in honour of her. The little Principe de Napoli is quite hideous, but they say well brought up under an English governess, and King Umberto in every way seems to wish to reform his dissolute father's court, as well as to screen his memory, having taken the whole of his enormous debts upon himself, besides paying off Victor Emmanuel's eight 'domestic establishments' out of his private purse. The King and Queen came out upon the balcony of the Quirinal, and were triumphantly received. (Next after the royal carriages had come a fourgon with the bouquets presented at the station.) Last night there was a torchlight procession, tens of thousands bearing torches, with music, banners, and gigantic marguerites, who passed through the Piazza di Spagna on their way to the Quirinal. Still, taxes are rather increasing than otherwise; the misery of the formerly prosperous Romans is extreme, and many think a revolution imminent.[1]

On arriving in Rome, I had found a tolerable little apartment for myself in 29 Piazza di Spagna, and the Prince Royal established in the charming sunny first floor of the Palazzo Rocca-Giovine in the Forum of Trajan. Thither I used daily, often twice a day, to go to the Prince. From the first he welcomed me very cordially, and I could see that he was really glad of my coming, still I was uncertain whether there would ever be more than an interchange of courtesy and duty between us. I never hoped to be able to give him the real affection I afterwards so sincerely felt. Somewhat to my consternation, I was desired by the King to fix my first lecture for the Prince for one of the very first days after

[1] Umberto was the son of Victor Emmanuel II and married his cousin, Margherita of Savoy. Their son, who was born in 1869, was Victor Emmanuel III, who was deposed after the Second World War. Umberto was scrupulously observant of constitutional principles and became generally known as "Humbert the Good." He was assassinated by an anarchist in 1900.—*Ed.*

my arrival, in order that Baron Holtermann, marshal of the palace, who
was returning to Stockholm, might take back a full account of 'how it
went' to their Majesties. The Queen added her special request that I would
say nothing except in English, in order to force the Prince Royal to
learn that language.

As being the central feature and axis of ancient Rome, I chose the
Capitoline for my first lecture. General and Mrs. Stuart and Lady Agnes
Douglas met me there at the top of the steps, and waited for the Prince,
who arrived on foot with Baron Holtermann and two other Swedish
gentlemen. I doubt at first whether they understood a word I said in
English, and the being obliged constantly to translate into French or bad
German did not add to the liveliness of the lecture. Our procession passed
from point to point in the most funereal manner. The Prince made no
observation whatever, Romulus, the Tarpeian Rock, Marcus Aurelius
passing equally unnoticed; only when we came to Palazzo Caffarelli he
said, 'Oh, that was where Mim Bunsen was born'; it had touched a chord
of human interest. I wonder what sort of account of this lecture Baron
Holtermann can have taken to the Swedish court; but we did better next
time, when, on the Palatine, the Prince's spirits quite rose over all the
murders of the emperors and empresses. In the latter part of the winter,
the lectures, which took place three times a week, were quite an enjoyment, he was so merry, so kind and pleasant to every one, so glad to
know everything.

For the most part the Prince's evenings were spent at home, the Italian
court showing him no attention, and scarcely any of the Roman princes
inviting him, except during the Carnival. Old Lady Morton was throughout exceedingly kind and helpful where the Prince was concerned, and
gave several parties for him. At these, the Prince's distant cousins, Princess
Gabrielli, Countess Primoli, and Countess Campello, the round fat
elderly daughters of Lucien Bonaparte, were always present.[1] They were
pleasant sensible women, especially Countess Primoli (Princess Charlotte Bonaparte). Having all married beneath their rank, they always
made a point of going in and out of a room in the order of their age,
which had often a funny effect.

Of all the people who welcomed me back to Rome, the most cordial
were the blind Duke and the Duchess of Sermoneta, whom I was delighted
to find established for the winter in the upper floor of the old Caëtani
Palace. I often took the Prince to the evening receptions of the Duchess,
at which, as at all the princely Roman houses, some tea and very sour
lemonade were considered quite sufficient as refreshments.

[1] Their grandmother was a Mademoiselle Clary, sister of Queen Desirée of Sweden.

To MARY LEA GIDMAN.

Dec. 11, 1878.—Last week we went for the whole day to Corneto, eating an excellent breakfast provided by the Prince's cook in the train. Professor Helbig, who had preceded us, met us at the station with a little omnibus. With this we went up into the high hills above old Tarquinii, and then descended with torches into the great sepulchres, where the dead of two thousand years ago are seen (in terra-cotta figures as large as life) sitting round at imaginary banquets, while the walls are covered with paintings of their deeds in life—hunting, fishing, dancing, &c., as fresh in colour as when they were painted. Then we went to visit a Countess Bruschi, who had a great collection of jewels and other beautiful things found in the tombs. This lady was the only person to whom we revealed who the Prince Royal was; but whilst we were at dinner the secret transpired, for there came from the Bruschi palace a bouquet of the most magnificent roses, like a sheaf, carried by two footmen, and another bouquet of camellias, arranged in a huge citron; and then the governor of the town arrived to make a little speech, to which the Prince gave a suitable answer, which I had to translate into Italian; and then all the people found out, and came to look at the Prince.

To MISS LEYCESTER.

Dec. 5, 1878—To-day my lecture for him was on the Aventine. At S. Sabina I sent in notice of their visitor to the Abbot and the Father-General of the Dominicans, and in his honour the two ladies of our party, Countess Barnekow and Lady Agnes Douglas, were allowed to penetrate the inmost recesses of the convent, and to visit the cell of S. Dominic, with his exquisitely beautiful picture, and the cell of S. Pius V. As we came out of the church, the Abbot presented the Prince with a large basket of oranges and apples, and some leaves from the sacred tree of S. Dominic.

Dec. 19, 1878.—The news of Princess Alice's death, announced in a sermon on Sunday, was quite a shock, as I had not heard of her being ill; and she was so kind to me when here, and so interested and amused in correcting *Walks in Rome*.[1]

The Queen writes through the Countess Rosen that she is delighted that I am going with the Prince to Florence, and that it was quite the Prince's own idea; but she fears I shall find him rather a dull companion there, as he has very little taste for picture-galleries.

Jan. 6, 1879.—I was very glad to part with 1878—a year of many sorrows—dear Miss Wright's death the greatest. On the last evening I went to Mrs. Terry's, where Miss Trollope sang exquisitely 'Should auld acquaintance be forgot' in the last minutes of the year.

My last lecture for the Prince was upon the last days of S. Paul, going to the pyramid of Caius Cestius, the last surviving witness of his life, to the desolate Tre Fontane, and then to the huge basilica which sprung from his martyrdom. At the Tre Fontane the Prince found a beautiful piece of old marble railing and a fine fragment of pietra-dura pavement, used to wall in a flower-bed; bought them, and he and I lugged them back to the carriage between us. He is now very happy, and (though there *are* black days) enjoys everything very much.

The Prince and I dined with Lady Morton the other day, meeting Prince and

[1] Third child of Queen Victoria, born 1843, who married Frederick of Hesse in 1862. Mother of the Marchioness of Milford Haven, the Grand Duchess Sergius, Princess Irene of Prussia, Duke Ernest of Hesse, and the Tsaritsa Alix. Grandmother of Earl Mountbatten of Burma and of the Queen of Sweden. Great-grandmother of the Duke of Edinburgh.—*Ed.*

Princess Altieri, Prince and Princess Sulmona, Countess Apponyi, &c. I was very glad that he should meet this completely 'black' party, as he has had few opportunities of meeting that phase of politics. On Thursday the Duchess Sermoneta gives another party for him, to which she has taken the fancy to ask all the 'learned' people in Rome. My poor Prince will not make much of them, but will be amused with many, especially with Donna Ursilia Lovatelli, who likes to converse in Sanscrit, and who had to be told that she must not bring with her more aides-de-camp than the Prince (four); as her 'court,' as she calls it, which likes to follow her, sometimes numbers sixty persons. Madame Minghetti[1] will also bring *her* court, which is far more Bohemian, amusing, and agreeable.

Dec. 29.—I am glad to hear of my book, which I have not seen, though it reached Stockholm long ago. It is a pleasure to have an outburst of approval from the Bunsens. Of reviews I think little, knowing how they scarcely ever have anything to do with the merits or demerits of a work, but only with the wish of an editor to advantage or injure an author: besides, the newspapers all copy one another, only changing the words.

We have had burning sun and intense scirocco here, which of course means a great deal of rain, and there have been torrents each day, but lovely effects between, such masses of cloud rolling over St. Peter's, with brilliant light falling through upon the many-domed town, and tremendous conflagrations at sunset. I spent Christmas Eve at the Palazzo Colonna, where the Duchess Marino had an immense Christmas-tree for her servants and friends, and a merry party of children. A prettier sight than the tree was the little Duchess herself, in a white silk dress, with a long lace veil looped upon her head and enveloping her figure.

With the Prince I have ever more entire satisfaction. I constantly see more of him, and have daily increasing affection for him. Of course the position is not perfect, but I expect this in everything, and am quite sure of his absolute confidence to a degree which I never expected.

One day we went to Frascati by rail, taking with us Count and Countess Barnekow and Count and Countess Lievenhaupt, Swedes, and Lady Agnes Douglas. While Lady Agnes did the honours of some of the villas, M. de Printzsköld and I got an excellent though thoroughly Roman dinner ready at the little inn, and afterwards the ladies had donkeys, the Prince a horse, and we others walked up to Tusculum. Here the Prince was very happy picking up mosaics in the long grass, and eventually insisted on excavating, and lugging back to Rome in his arms, a great mass, as big as that in the verandah at Holmhurst. We came down by the great desolate villa of Mondragone, and returned to Rome in the evening laden with fern and butcher's-broom, which, with its bright scarlet berries, is the Roman apology for holly.

JOURNAL.

Feb. 20, 1879.—One of the last evenings of the year was spent in the Palazzo Colonna with the sweet little Duchess of Marino. She is a great addition and enlivenment to the dull egotistical Roman society, and is brimming with good intentions and high aspirations, many of which she is really able to carry out. Greatly, for instance, did she astonish modern Rome, with its vulgar attempts at exclusiveness, by opening her rooms for a grand party in the noble old Roman style, in which princes and sculptors met on equal terms, and artists were as cordially received as if they were ambassadors.

---

[1] Wife of Italian Senator, one-time Prime Minister.—*Ed.*

On the 16th of January I went away with my Prince for a tour in Tuscany. I very soon found that for me the trial of the tour would be his hatred of fresh air. He never would have the carriage window opened, even on the hottest day and with steaming hot-water pans. Otherwise all was luxury, kindness, and comfort. We arrived at Perugia on the most glorious evening I ever remember: violet mists were rolling through the valleys, the snow mountains were rosy in the sunset. It was such a scene as can only be enjoyed in Italy, and in Italy can only be found in Umbria, perhaps only at Perugia. Next day we drove to Assisi, where he was far more delighted at buying a little old silver box in a side-street than with all the old churches and monasteries. He travelled under the name of the Comte de Tullgarn, and at Perugia no one found out who he was, which made him very happy. At Florence, however, he was unfortunately discovered, and we found great preparations—two smart carriages waiting at the station, twenty-six candles and three lamps burning in our rooms, with prices in proportion, and a serenade of music outside the windows.

We returned to Rome on the 25th. My regular lectures were over then, but as the Prince missed our little parties, I had some for him to the villas and galleries. At this time, as often afterwards, those who surrounded the Prince gave me the opportunity of testing the truth of Lord Chesterfield's observation, that 'courts are the best key to characters; there every passion is busy, every character analysed,' as well as the dictum of La Bruyère, that at court *'les joies sont visibles mais fausses, et les chagrins cachés mais réels* [the joys are visible but false, and the sorrows hidden but real].'

To Miss Leycester.

Feb. 13.—I have had a series of lectures for the Prince in the Vatican galleries and St. Peter's, and at the latter, by kindness of Monsignor Théodoli, had all the chapels of the crypt illuminated, and the precious plate and vestments (Charlemagne's robes, &c.) exhibited. We climbed up to the cross, but the ladies of our little party succumbed on the different roofs, except Lady Dunraven, who went with us to the ball.

On the 4th I was with the Prince at a ball at the Palazzo Caffarelli, the German embassy, which is much done up since Bunsen's days and exceedingly magnificent. The great hall was entirely surrounded with palm-trees, under one of which I stood, with the Swedish Countess Barnekow, to watch the procession come in and the state quadrille—which Queen Marguerite danced with M. de Keudel, and my Prince with Mme. de Keudel—alone on the long sides of the room, with a perfect tourbillon of ambassadors and ambassadresses at the narrow ends. A much prettier ball was that at Palazzo Caëtani. This the Prince had to open with the Queen, so we had to be there by eleven, but *because* the King and Queen were to be there, all the great nobles stayed away, so for once Palazzo Caëtani did not shine. The Queen looked lovely, but, ever since the attack on the King, has been more nervous than ever, perpetually picking at her gloves, twisting her fan, and shaking out the folds of her dress. Her beautiful hair was full of marguerites in diamonds. The King looked glaring and demoniacal, yet really is going on very well, and does all he can to sweep away the abuses and immoralities of his father's court, unpopular as it makes him with his father's sycophants. Yesterday I was with the Prince at a great ball at Prince Altieri's—the blackest of the 'black' houses—where I had the great pleasure of seeing again my sister's dear friend the Duchess Sora, who has lived in a sort of exile hitherto, ever since the Sardinian occupation of Rome.

Yesterday morning I went with the Prince to the antiquity market in the Campo de' Fiore. We left the carriage in the courtyard of the Cancelleria, and made a raid upon the old bookstalls, till our arms were quite full, and then we deposited our burthens and made another. The Prince is getting on wonderfully with his English, and will talk fluently by the time he reaches London. I see him ceaselessly. He has been twice to my lodgings to-day, and I have been out with him besides. He dances till 4 A.M. every night now (it is Carnival), but is never tired, and up at eight.

Feb. 24.—My present work is likely to end for a time on Thursday, when my dear Prince goes to Naples and Sorrento. On looking back, I have unmixed satisfaction that I came. He leaves Rome quite a different person from the Prince I found here— much strengthened, and I am sure much improved in character, as well as speaking and reading English and French (which he did not know before), and being able to take a lively animated part in a society in which he was previously a cypher.

We have been together several times in the Vatican, with Monsignor Pericoli, at the sale of Pius IX's things—quantities of things, from valuable pictures and sculptures to empty jam-pots; but touching in many ways, especially the boxes of the well-worn Papal slippers. All is obliged to be sold, as the produce is divided into three parts—one to the family, one to the cardinals-in-waiting, and the third to the Church. The Prince bought some valuable amethysts, and I have the Papal despatch-box engraved with his arms, a picture which hung in his room, and a pair of the Papal slippers.

For the last ten days we have been in all the dirt and squalor of the silly, filthy Carnival, which is more *mesquim* [paltry] and contemptible than ever, but the Prince is only twenty, and it has amused him. I have only been obliged to go with him to the Corso one day, when we went to one-o'clock luncheon with the Dutch Minister, and were astonished to find every shutter closed, chandeliers and candles lighted, ladies in white satin and diamonds, gentlemen in evening dress; in fact, midnight at midday! so that the Prince and I felt rather shy.

I saw much at this time of Madame Minghetti, the wife of the senator, still wonderfully beautiful and captivating, though a grandmother. Her rooms were draped with every possible nuance of colour which can harmonise together, great palm-trees and bananas shaded the sofas and arm-chairs, and the heavy curtains only let in witching rays of half light upon a gorgeous gloom. Here, in her receptions in the early Sunday afternoon, she would sit upon the floor and sing, break off in the middle of a line to receive or embrace some one, and, in an instant, be again in her place, singing as before and taking up the line which was left unfinished.

Another new friend was the pretty lively Princess of Salm Reifferscheid, whom, with her husband, I invited to accompany us to Tivoli, when the Prince gave me a carriage and told me to ask whom I liked. At Tivoli our party had a charming day, riding on eleven donkeys, penetrating into the depths of the cascades, having luncheon in front of the temple, and sitting in the sun opposite the cascatelle. At sunset we were at the Villa d'Este, and went down into the hollow to look up at the grand old villa, golden through the dark cypresses.

On the 3rd of March, a well-known partnership of upwards of sixty years was closed at Rome by the death, in his little apartment at 55 Via Sistina, of William Howitt the author, leaving his sweet old Mary alone with her unmarried daughter Margaret. Though never very remarkable, the many books of William and Mary Howitt were always excellent, and the writers were deeply respected. I attended Mr. Howitt's funeral on the 5th, walking with Mrs. Terry, Baron Hoffmann, and Prince George of Solms, immediately after the daughter and son-in-law. The ceremony was a very touching one, and the coffin buried in wreaths of camellias, lilies, and violets. As William Howitt was a Quaker, the service was different from ours, but hymns were beautifully sung over his coffin in the chapel and at the grave, where the American clergyman, Dr. Nevin, gave a really touching and beautiful address, as the daughter was pouring basket after basket of flowers into the open grave.[1]

I dined with the Prince on the day before that fixed for his departure to Naples. When our last moment together came, he took me into his room and parted from me there, with many most affectionate words, and gave me the Order of St. Olaf, which the King of Sweden and Norway had conferred upon me, begging me to wear it for his sake.[2] I left him with the truest affection, and with, I think, unbounded confidence and regard on both sides.

JOURNAL.

Mrs. F. Walker told me how she went out one evening at Freshwater to meet her brother-in-law and niece as they were returning from an excursion along the cliffs. On her way she saw a lady in deep mourning, with a little boy, emerge apparently from a side path to the one on which she was, and walk on before her. She noticed the lady's peculiarly light step. Mother and son stopped at a little railed-in enclosure at the top of the hill, and gazed over the railings; then they went on again in front of her. At length, beyond them, Mrs. Walker saw Mr. Palmes and his daughter coming to meet her. Between her and them she saw the lady and boy suddenly disappear— apparently go down some side path leading to the sands; but, when she came to the place, there was *no* path, the cliff was perfectly precipitous. Miss Palmes equally saw the lady and boy coming towards her, and was greatly agitated by their sudden disappearance.

---

[1] William Howitt (1792–1879) and Mary Howitt (1799–1888), were prolific writers of miscellaneous work, some written independently and some jointly. Their partnership lasted nearly sixty years, and included translations from the German, Swedish, Danish and other languages, poems, books on English and foreign life, on magic, of popular history and topography, novels and juvenile literature.—*Ed.*

[2] I have not been able to do this, as there is a prohibition in England against wearing foreign orders, dating from Elizabeth, who said, 'My dogs shall wear nothing but my own collars.'

Afterwards they found that the same sight was constantly seen there. It was the little boy's grave into which the two had gazed. He had fallen over the cliff just there and had been killed, and was buried by his mother's wish inside that little circular railing.

The Prince was in Rome for one night on his way from Naples to Munich. I went to him in the early morning, and was with him till 2 P.M., when he left, spending the time in driving about with him, chiefly to the antiquity shops, in which he always had the greatest delight. The very day after he left I fell in with other royalties, of whom at first I seemed likely to see a great deal. I was at the Princess Giustiniani Bandini's, when the Hereditary Grand Duke and Duchess of Saxe-Weimar were announced—a very simple homely pair. The lady-in-waiting, hearing my name, most cleverly recollected all about me, and I was presented, and very cordially and kindly received. A few days after, Princess Teano asked me to meet them at dinner. Only the Keudells of the German Embassy and the Minghettis dined besides the family, but an immense party came in the evening. The Hereditary Grand Duke is a weak-looking little man with a very receding forehead. The Grand Duchess (who was his cousin) is a fine big woman—'*bel pezzo di carne* [a fine piece of flesh]'—with intense enjoyment and good-humour in everything. Both talked English perfectly. They arranged then that I should show them the Palatine. But a few days afterwards I heard from the Duchess Sermoneta that the Grand Duchess had said to her that, owing to the furious jealousy of the German archaeologists, she was unable to go with me.

JOURNAL.

March 17, 1879.—I have seen much, almost daily, of Lord Hylton's young son, George Jolliffe. We went together yesterday to the Palazzo Massimo alle Colonne, where the old blackened portico was hung with bright tapestry, and the whole staircase and rooms strewn with box, because it was the day on which S. Filippo Neri raised the Massimo child from the dead. Most surprising were the masses of people—cobblers and contadini elbowing cardinals up the long staircase, washerwomen on their knees crowding princesses round the altar. Prince Massimo, in full evening dress, received in the anteroom of the chapel, and the Princess (daughter of the Duchesse de Berry) invited every one she knew to have ices and coffee.

March 20.—A young American drove me to the meet at Centocelle. It was a lovely day of soft scirocco, fleecy clouds floating over the pale pink mountain distances and the Campagna bursting into its first green, across which the long chains of aqueduct arches threw their deep shadows. Crowds of people and carriages were out, but we followed Princess Teano, who knew all the ups and downs of the ground, and drove with young Lady Clarendon so cleverly, that we were in at the death in the great ruins of Sette Basse.

March 21.—Tea with Countess Primoli (Princess Charlotte Bonaparte) in her little boudoir at the end of a long suite of quaint old-fashioned rooms. She talked very pleasantly, but with too constant reference to the Empress and Prince Imperial as 'my family.' I went afterwards to see the Favarts at Ville Lante. It is a beautiful place, and the noble face of Madame Favart is worthy of its setting. Consolo was there and played marvellously on the violin, every nerve seeming to vibrate, every hair to leap in unison with his chords.

Florence, March 27.—I left Rome on Tuesday—a lovely morning, and I looked my last at the glorious view from the Medici Terrace with a heavy heart. Now I am in the old Palazzo Mozzi at Florence, as the guest of the Sermonetas. On the side towards the Via dei Bardi the palace rises up gaunt and grim like a fortress, but at the back it looks into a beautiful garden, with terraces climbing up the steep hillside to the old city wall. The rooms are large and dreadfully cold, but the Duchess has made them very picturesque with old hangings and furniture. The Duke talks incessantly and cleverly. I asked him why his Duchess signed 'Harriet Caëtani,' not 'Sermoneta,' and he explained how all the splendour of the family arose from the fact that they were Caëtani; that many of the greatest of the old families, such as the Frangipani, had no titles at all: that even the Orsini had no title of place, and that it was only modern families, like the Braschi, who cared to air a title. The oldest title in Italy was that of Marchese, which came in with the French: Duke came with the Imperialists; but the title of Prince, for which he had the utmost contempt, was merely the result of Papal nepotism: Borghese was the first Prince created.

JOURNAL.

April 29, 1879, *London.*—I have heard again the curious story of Sir T. Watson from Mrs. T., to whom he told it himself, so will write it down.

Sir Thomas Watson, better known as Dr. Watson, was a well-known physician.[1] During the last years of his life he was in failing health, and only saw patients at his own house, but till then he went about in England wherever he was sent for. One day he was summoned to attend an urgent case at Oxenholme in Cumberland. There was only one carriage in the train which went through to Oxenholme, and in a compartment of that carriage he took his seat. He tipped the guard, and said he should be glad to be alone if he could.

The train at Euston was already in motion, when a young lady came running down the platform, with a porter laden with her handbags and cloaks. The man just contrived to open the carriage door, push the young lady in, throw in her things after her, and the train was off. The young lady, a very pretty, pleasing young lady, took the seat opposite Dr. Watson. Being a polite, gallant old gentleman, very soon Dr. Watson began to make himself agreeable: 'What beautiful effects of cloud there were. How picturesque Harrow church steeple looked through the morning haze,' &c. &c., and the young lady responded pleasantly. At last, as their acquaintance advanced, Dr. Watson said, 'And are you travelling far?' 'Oh yes,' said the young lady, 'very far, I am going to Oxenholme in Cumberland.' 'How singular,' said Dr. Watson, 'for that is just where I am going myself. I wonder if you happen to know Lady D. who lives near Oxenholme.' 'Yes,' said the young lady, 'I know Lady D. very well.' 'And

---

[1] Sir Thomas Watson (1792–1882), President of the College of Physicians, physician to Queen Victoria, President of the Pathological Society and of the Clinical Society. He was one of the doctors present at the death of the Prince Consort.—*Ed.*

Mrs. P. and her daughters?' said Dr. W. 'Oh yes I know them too.' 'And Mr. Y.?' There was a moment's pause, and then the young lady very naïvely and ingenuously said, 'Yes, I do know Mr. Y. very well; and perhaps I had better tell you something. I am going to be *married* to him to-morrow. My own parents are in India, and I am going to be married from his father's house. Since I have been engaged to him, I have made the acquaintance of many of his friends and neighbours, and that is how I know so many people near Oxenholme, though I have never been there before.'

Dr. Watson was charmed with the simple candour of the young lady. They went on talking, and they became quite friends. The train arrived at Rugby, and they both got out and had their bun in the refreshment-room. They were in the carriage again, and the train was already moving, when, in great excitement, the young lady called out: 'Oh stop, stop the train, don't you see how he's urging me to get out. There! that young man in the brown ulster, that's the young man I'm going to be married to.' Of course it was impossible to get out, and the young lady was greatly distressed, and though Dr. Watson assured her most positively that there was no one standing where she described, she would not and could not believe him.

Then Dr. Watson said, 'Now, my dear young lady, you're very young and I'm very old. I am a doctor. I am very well known, and from what you have been seeing I am quite sure, as a physician, that you are not at all well. Now, I have my medicine chest with me, and you had better let me give you a little dose.' And he did give her a little dose.

The train arrived at Stafford, and exactly the same thing occurred. 'There, there! don't you see him! *that* young man with the light beard, in the brown ulster, don't you see how he's urging me to get out.' And again Dr. Watson assured her there was no one there, and said, 'I think you had better let me give you another little dose;' and he gave her another little dose.

But Dr. Watson naturally felt that he could not go on giving her a dose at every station all the way to Oxenholme, so he decided within himself that if the same thing happened at Crewe, the young lady's state indicated one of two things: either that there was some intentional vision from Providence, with which he ought not to interfere; or that the young lady was certainly not in a state of health or brain which should allow of her being married next day. So he determined to act accordingly.

And at Crewe just the same thing happened. 'There, there! don't you see him! he's urging me more than ever to get out,' cried the young lady. 'Very well,' said Dr. Watson, 'we will get out and go after him,' and, with the young lady, he pursued the imaginary figure, and of course did not find him. But Dr. Watson had often been at Crewe station before, and he went to the hotel, which opens on the platform, and said to the matron, 'Here is this young lady, who is not at all well, and should have a very quiet room; unfortunately I am not able to remain now to look after her, but I will leave her in your care, and to-morrow I shall be returning this way and will come to see how she is.' And he slipped a five-pound note into the woman's hand to guarantee expenses.

Dr. Watson returned to the railway carriage. There was another young lady there, sitting in the place which the first young lady had occupied—a passenger who had arrived by one of the many lines which converge at Crewe. With the new young lady he did not make acquaintance, he moved his things to the other side of the carriage and devoted himself to his book.

Three stations farther on came the shock of a frightful accident. There was a collision. The train was telescoped, and many passengers were terribly hurt. The heavy case of instruments, which was in the rack above the place where Dr. Watson had first been sitting, was thrown violently to the other side of the carriage, hit the young lady upon the forehead and killed her on the spot.

It was long before the line could be sufficiently cleared for the train to pass which was sent to pick up the surviving passengers. Many hours late, in the middle of the night, Dr. Watson arrived at Oxenholme. There, waiting upon the platform, stood the young man with the light beard, in the brown ulster, exactly as he had been described. He had heard that the only young lady in the through carriage from London had been killed, and was only waiting for the worst to be confirmed. And Dr. Watson was the person who went up to him and said: 'Unfortunately it is too true that a young lady has been killed, but it is not your young lady. Your young lady is safe in the station hotel at Crewe.'

To MISS LEYCESTER.

May 13, 1879, 34 *Jermyn Street, London.*—This morning I went with Mrs. Duncan Stewart and a very large party to Whistler's studio—a huge place in Chelsea. We were invited to see his pictures, but there was only one there—'The Loves of the Lobsters.' It was supposed to represent Niagara, but looked as if the artist had upset the inkstand and left Providence to work out its own results. In the midst of the black chaos were two lobsters curvetting opposite each other and looking as if they were done with red sealing-wax. 'I wonder you did not paint the lobsters making love before they were boiled,' aptly observed a lady visitor. 'Oh, I never thought of that,' said Whistler! It was a joke, I suppose. The little man, with his plume of white hair ('the Whistler tuft,' he calls it) waving on his forehead, frisked about the room looking most strange and uncanny, and rather diverted himself over our disappointment in coming so far and finding nothing to see. People admire like sheep his pictures in the Grosvenor Gallery, following each other's lead because it is the fashion.

May 14, *Sunday.*—An immense luncheon at Mrs. Cavendish Bentinck's. I sat near Mr. Herbert, the artist of the great fresco in the House of Lords.[1] He described things over which he became almost inspired—how in the Bodleian he found an old MS. about the Magdalen which made him determine to go off at once to St. Maximin in Provence (near La Sainte Baume, the mountain hermitage where she died) to see her skull: that when he reached St. Maximin, he found that the skull was in a glass case upon the altar, where he could not really examine it, and he was told that it was never allowed even to kings and emperors: that he represented with such fervour his object in making the pilgrimage, that at last the priests of the church consented to his sending twelve miles for a *vitrier* and having the case removed: then he was allowed to place a single candle behind, and in that moment, as he described it, with glowing face and voice trembling with emotion—'I saw the outline of her profile; the Magdalen herself, that dear friend of our Blessed Lord, was revealed to me.'

Miss Leslie, who was sitting near, asked how it was known that the Magdalen came to St. Maximin. 'How can you help knowing it,' said Mr. Herbert, 'when it is all written in the Acts of the Apostles!'

---

[1] John Rogers Herbert (1810–90) who first exhibited at the Academy in 1830. Apart from the decoration of the peers' robing room, his more famous pictures include: *Sir Thomas More and his Daughter* (at the National Gallery), the fresco at Westminster *King Lear disinheriting Cordelia* and various biblical subjects.—*Ed.*

May 15.—Dined with Lord and Lady Aberdeen—a very large party, seventy-four pots of flowers upon the table. The dinner was very fine, but rather uninteresting—the after-dinner better.

May 19.—The Prince (of Sweden and Norway) has arrived with his suite at Claridge's. He received me most cordially and affectionately. We made many plans for sight-seeing and people-seeing, but in England I have no responsibility; Count Piper, the Swedish Minister, has it all.

I dined at charming Lady Wynford's, sitting near Lord Delamere, who was very full of a definition he had heard of the word 'deputation.' 'A noun of multitude, which signifies many, but not much.' It was attributed to Gladstone, who said, 'I only wish I *had* made it.' Lord Eustace Cecil produced a definition of 'Independent Member' as 'a Member on whom nobody can depend.'

There was an immense gathering at Lady Salisbury's afterwards; my Prince there and much liked. There, for the first time, I saw the Empress Augusta of Germany.

May 24.—Lady Salisbury's party at the Foreign Office, the staircase with its interlacing arches and masses of flowering shrubs, like the essence of a thousand Paul Veroneses. My Prince was there in a white uniform.

May 27.—At dinner at Sir John Lefevre's I met Mr. Bright. He has a grand old lion-like head in an aureole of white hair, and his countenance never seems to wake from its deep repose, except for some burst of enthusiasm on a subject really worth while. He spoke of Americans, 'who say an infinity of foolish things, but always do wise ones.' Mr. Bryce of *The Holy Roman Empire* was there, a bearded man with bright eyes, who talked well.[1] Afterwards there was a party at Lady Beauchamp's to meet Prince and Princess Christian. How like all the princesses are to one another.

May 29.—A dinner at Lord Carysfort's and ball at Lady Salisbury's. I presented so many relations to the Prince that he said that which astonished him more than anything else in England was 'the multitude of Mr. Hare's cousins.'

June 8.—Luncheon with the Prince. We drove afterwards to see Lady Russell. Pembroke Lodge looked enchanting with its bright green of old oaks and its carpet of bluebells—a most perfect refuge for the latter years of an aged statesman. Lady Russell was waiting for us at the entrance, with Lady Agatha and Rollo. On the lawn we found many other members of the family, with Mr. Bouverie and Mr. Froude the historian. I presented them all, and we walked in the grounds. At tea Lord Bute came in from a neighbouring villa—always most pleasant and cordial to me.

June 11.—Dined with old Lady Harrington, and left as early as I could to go to Mrs. Schuster's, where Sarah Bernhardt was to act. She appeared first in the great scene of the 'Phédre'—her face bloodless, her arms rigid, her voice monotonous and broken. Gradually, under the influence of her love, she became animated, but the animation began at the tips of her fingers, till it burst all over her in a flood of irrepressible passion. She did not seem to see her audience or to think of them. For the time being she was *only* her part, and, when it was over, she sank down utterly exhausted, almost unconscious.

[1] James Bryce, created Viscount Bryce in 1914, died in 1922 aged 84. His essay on the *Holy Roman Empire*, which gained him a world reputation, was published in 1864, when he was 26. He was Regius Professor of Civil Law at Oxford 1870–93; a Liberal M.P. from 1880–1906; ambassador at Washington from 1907–13. He wrote, among other works, *The American Commonwealth*, travelled widely and was a notable mountaineer.—*Ed.*

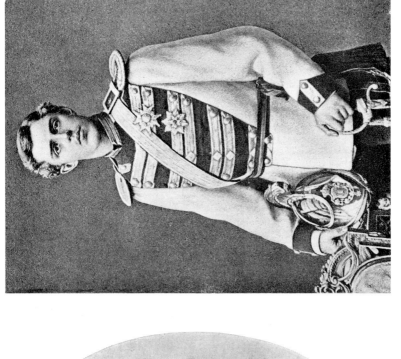

GUSTAV, CROWN PRINCE OF SWEDEN AND NORWAY

(later Gustav V of Sweden)

QUEEN SOPHIA OF SWEDEN AND NORWAY

She appeared again in a small part, in which she was a great lady turned sculptress. The part was nothing; she had little more to say than 'Let me see more of your profile; turn a little more the other way;' yet the great simplicity of her perfect acting made it deeply interesting, and, in the quarter of an hour in which the scene lasted, she had done in the clay a real medallion which was a striking likeness.[1]

June 13.—Dined at Sir Charles Trevelyan's. I took down a lady whose name seemed to be 'Mrs. Beckett.' I did not interest her, and she talked exclusively to Lord O'Hagan,[2] who was on the other side of her. Towards the close of dinner she said to me, 'We have been a very long time at dinner.'—'To me it has seemed quite endless,' I said.—'Well,' she exclaimed, 'I do not wonder that you were chosen to speak truth to Princes.'

I asked her how she knew anything about that, and she said, 'I have lived a long time in a court atmosphere myself. I was for twelve years with the late Queen of Holland.'—'Oh,' I said, *'now* I know who you are; you are Mrs. Lecky!' and it was the well-known author's wife.[3]

June 14.—Dined with Count Piper, the Swedish Minister, to meet the Prince Royal. I sat by Madame de Bülow, who is always pleasant. The only other lady unconnected with the Embassy was Mademoiselle Christine Nilsson, who sang most beautifully afterwards till Jenny Lind arrived. Then the rivalry of the two queens of song became most curious, Nilsson planting herself at the end of the pianoforte with her arms akimbo, and crying satirical bravas during Jenny's songs, and Jenny avenging herself by never allowing Nilsson to return to the pianoforte at all. The party was a very late one, and supper was served, when the Prince offered Jenny his arm to take her down. She accepted it, though with great diffidence; which so exasperated Nilsson, that with *'Je m'en vais donc,'* utterly refusing to be pacified, she swept out of the room and out of the house, though how she got away I do not know.

June 16.—Met the Prince early at Paddington, whence we had a saloon carriage to Oxford, with Sir Watkin Wynne as director to watch over us. We went a whole round of colleges and to the Bodleian, where Mr. Coxe exhibited his treasures. Then the Prince wished to see the boats, so we walked down to the river.

It was a fatiguing day, and I felt greatly the utter apathy and want of interest in all the Swedes, who scarcely noticed anything, admired nothing, and remembered nothing.

June 18.—Again to Oxford with the Prince. This time the town was in gala costume, and we drove through a street hung with flags, and through crowds of people waiting to see the Prince, to the Vice-Chancellor's Lodge at Pembroke. Here the Prince dressed, and I went on at once with his gentlemen to the Theatre, where places were reserved for us just under the Vice-Chancellor's throne. . . . Immediately after the Vice-Chancellor came my Prince, looking tall and handsome in his white uniform with the crimson robe over it, and perfectly royal. He received his degree standing

---

[1] I often saw Mademoiselle Bernhardt act afterwards, and was far less impressed by her, feeling the truth of the expression *'Une tragédienne du Boulevard.'*

[2] Lord O'Hagan, 1812–1885, Lord Chancellor of Ireland from 1868–74 and 1880–81.—*Ed.*

[3] Elizabeth van Dedem before her marriage in 1871, maid of honour to Queen Sophia of the Netherlands. William Lecky, the historian was author of a *History of European Morals* and a 12-volume *History of England in the Eighteenth Century*. He died in 1903 and his memoirs were written by his wife.—*Ed.*

F

by the Vice-Chancellor's side, and the whole body of undergraduates sang a little impromptu song, to the effect of 'He's a charming Swedish boy.'

In the evening I was with the Prince at Mrs. E. Guiness's ball, on which £6,000 are said to have been wasted. It was a perfect fairy-land, ice pillars up to the ceiling, an avenue of palms, a veil of stephanotis from the staircase, and you pushed your way through a brake of papyrus to the cloak-room.

June 20.—Oh, what a shock it has been that, while the balls last night were going on, telegrams announced the death of the dear young Prince Imperial![1] I am sure I cried for him like a nearest relation; there was something so very cordial and attaching in him, and there is something so unspeakably terrible in his death. The Prince was overwhelmed, and could not dine at Lowther Lodge, where there was a large party expressly to meet him, but he was quite right.

June 21.—We can think of nothing else but the Prince Imperial and the awful grief at Chislehurst. Immediately on hearing the telegram, Lord Dorchester wrote to M. Pietri a letter of condolence. M. Pietri was away in Corsica, and the Empress opened his letter. It begged Pietri to offer deep sympathy to the Empress in her over-whelming affliction. She felt her son was dead, and when Lord Sydney and Mr. Borth-wick arrived, they found her in tears; but when she heard the awful truth that her darling had been deserted and assegaied, she gave terrible shrieks and fainted away.

July 5.—At dinner at Sir Rutherford Alcock's[2] I heard the startling news of the death of Frances, Lady Waldegrave.[3] To me she was only a lay figure, receiving at her drawing-room door, but I remember her thus ever since I was a boy at Oxford, when she was living at Nuneham. In spite of her faults, she had many and warm friends: Lord Houghton sobbed like a child on receiving the news in the midst of a large party.

July 11.—Dined at Sir Dudley Marjoribanks'—Brook House a beautiful interior with marvellous china. There was such a procession of Earls and Countesses, that it fell to my share to take Mrs. Gladstone in to dinner. Disraeli had said to her, 'Now *do* take care of Mr. Gladstone; you know he is *so* precious.'

July 15.—Lady Ashburton had asked the Hereditary Grand Duke of Baden to dinner as well as my Prince, so I went to help her by acting Master of the Ceremonies and receiving the royalties in the hall of Kent House. While I was waiting, watching at the window, a fair young man arrived unattended and ran upstairs. I took no notice of *him*. Then I received the Prince Royal properly, escorted him as far as Lady Ash-burton's curtsies, and came back to wait for the young Grand Duke. At last Lady Ashburton sent down to tell me he was *there*, had been there the whole time: he was the young man who ran upstairs.

I had much talk with him afterwards—a tall, simple, pleasing-mannered youth, much more responsive than my Prince, and good-looking, though very German in

---

[1] The Prince Imperial, heir to Napoleon III, took part in the British expedition against the Zulus and was killed by native spears.—*Ed.*

[2] Sir Rutherford Alcock, 1809–1897, consul in China and Japan, and in 1865 British Minister at Peking. A president of the R.G.S.—*Ed.*

[3] Daughter of John Braham, the singer. She married (1) James Waldegrave, Esq.; (2) George-Edward, 7th Earl Waldegrave; (3) George Granville Harcourt, Esq., of Nuneham; (4) Chichester Fortescue, Lord Carlingford. When she was a child a gipsy foretold that she would marry first to please her parents, secondly for rank, thirdly for wealth, and fourthly to please herself.—*Ed.*

appearance. There were glees at dinner, sung in the anteroom, and a large party and concert in the evening.

July 16.—A beautiful party at Holland House. There was quite a mass of royalty on the lawn—the Prince and Princess of Wales and their little girls[1] (in pink trimmed with red), the Edinburghs, the Connaughts, the Tecks, with their little girl[2] and two nice boys in sailor's dress, the Duchess of Mecklenbourg, the Prince of Baden, and my Prince. The royal children were all in raptures over some performing dogs, which really were very funny, as a handsome Spitz looked so ecstatically delighted to ride about on the lawn on a barrel pushed by a number of other dogs.

July 19.—Went down with the special train to Hatfield, and drove up from the station to the house with old Lady Ailesbury. An immense party of Dukes and Duchesses, &c., were already collected to welcome the royalties, Lady Salisbury receiving them in a large rough straw garden-bonnet. I walked about with different friends till the royal party drove up in six carriages. They were all going to stay at Hatfield till Monday, fifty people, besides servants. I came back at eight.

July 26.—I took leave of the Prince in his bedroom before he was dressed. Our real separation must come soon; and though in many ways I shall feel wonderfully set free when my responsibility is over, my heart always yearns toward him.

Glamis Castle, August 13.—I arrived at Glamis at 9 P.M., and found an immense party in the house—Sir James[3] and Lady Ramsay, Lord and (the very charming) Lady Sydney Inverurie, Lord and Lady Northesk, and many others. Lord Strathmore has made great preparations, and the Prince would have had the most royal reception here which he has met with anywhere; but, to the great inconvenience of every one, he has put off leaving Hopetoun, where he is, being ill with toothache.

August 24.—I left Glamis on Monday, and went by Dalmally to Oban through the Brander Pass—beautiful exceedingly, the mountains so varied and encircling such varied waters.

On Thursday, at dawn, I saw all the mountains meeting their shadows in the still waters of Oban Bay, and determined to go to Staffa. It was a crowded, rolling, smelly steamer, and I was very miserable, but rather better than worse when the fresh air in the Atlantic made up for the additional rolling. At twelve we reached Iona—different from what I expected, the island larger and the ruins smaller, and without the romantic effect of those on Holy Island. An agony of Atlantic swell brought us to Staffa, but oh! how grand it is!—the grandest cathedral of nature, black with age and roofed with golden vegetation, rising out of the blue sea and lashed by the white foam. I never saw any single place which makes such an impression of natural sublimity.

How the interests and emotions of life are mingled! In the train, on leaving Glamis, I heard of the death of my dear uncle-like cousin Lord Bloomfield,[4] and while I was drawing Dunolly Sir John Lefevre[5] was passing away! Though the delicate thread

---

[1] Edward VII and Alexandra, with the Princess Louise, Victoria and Maud.—*Ed.*

[2] H.M. Queen Mary.—*Ed.*

[3] Sir James Ramsay of Barrett, tenth baronet and historian, died in 1925 aged 93.

[4] See note on p. 60.

[5] See note on p. 153 of *The Years With Mother*.

which bound his life to earth was so indescribably frail, it *had* lasted so long, that it is difficult to realise that his loving sympathy and the holy example of his beautiful, humble, and self-forgetful life are removed from us. He was the best man I have ever known and the truest friend.

Cheltenham, Sept. 15, 1879.—I do not know when, if ever, I have seen anything so beautiful as the park at Holme Lacy. All Sunday afternoon I wandered with Sir Henry Stanhope in its glorious glades, with fern nine feet high, grand old oaks, white stemmed beeches, and deep blue depths of mossy dingle. The garden too is quite a poem—such a harmony of colour backed by great yew hedges and grand old pine-trees. Seven hundred people on an average come to see it on the days it is shown, and no wonder. . . . We went to service at an old church full of tombs of the family, and afterwards to the rectory close by, where there is a wonderful old pear-tree, of which the branches always take root again when they fall off, and cover an immense extent, sometimes producing as much as 2,000 gallons of perry.

Cheltenham, Sept. 16.—Mrs. Orlando Kenyon is staying here with the Corbetts. She was a Cotton, and is a very charming person. She described going with her cousin Miss Cotton (now Dowager Marchioness of Downshire) to Peover for a ball. Just as they were setting off news arrived of the death of her cousin's grandfather, old Mr. Fulke Greville.[1] However, as the visit was settled, it was decided that it should take place, only that Miss Cotton should not go to the ball and her cousin should. They slept together at Peover. In the night Miss Cotton woke Mrs. Kenyon and said, 'I have had such an extraordinary dream. I have seen my mother moving backwards and forwards between the doors at the end of the room, not walking, but apparently moving in the air—floating with a quantity of gossamer drapery round her; and when I close my eyes, I seem to see her still.' In the morning the cousins returned to Combermere.

Just before dinner a servant called Mr. Cotton (Mrs. Kenyon's father) and said Lord Combermere wanted to speak to him. 'Oh,' said Miss Cotton, springing forward, 'then I am sure some news has come by the post,' and she tried to insist upon following her uncle, but he would not allow her. Mr. Cotton came back greatly agitated, but insisted on their all going in to dinner. It was a most wretched meal. Afterwards he told the son and daughter that their mother had died (just after her father's funeral) very suddenly, just when she had appeared at Peover.

Llanover, Sept. 20.—Yesterday I went for an hour to Caerphilly on the way here to Llanover, where I arrived at 7 P.M. The Hereditary Grand Duke of Baden had already arrived and gone up to his room. I first saw him when the party was assembled for dinner. After a very long dinner we all went into the hall, when, from the curtains at the end, all the servants tripped in, each footman leading a maid by each hand, in most picturesque Welsh costumes, made obeisance to the Prince, went backwards, and then danced the most complicated and picturesque of reels, with ever-varying figures. Lady Llanover's own maid was the great performer, and nothing could exceed her consummate grace and dignity. Then a board was brought in and placed in the centre of the floor and three candles upon it, around and between which the footmen and the harper's boys performed the wonderful candle-dance with the greatest agility.

In three carriages we went to Llanarth to luncheon. I went with the royal carriage,

[1] Charles Cavendish Fulke Greville, 1794–1865, diarist and the intimate friend of the statesmen of his time.—*Ed.*

which, with its smart scarlet postillions, certainly went slow enough; for the dear old lady, to do the Prince more honour, had engaged for the occasion not only the two horses used for the weddings at Abergavenny, but also the two used at funerals, and the steeds of death outweighed those of mirth, and kept us down to a funereal pace.

Holmhurst, Sept. 27.—On Monday, all Llanover was in motion for the Prince's departure, more scarlet cloth than ever all over the place, the Welsh harpers harping at the door, the Welsh housemaids, in high hats and bright scarlet and blue petticoats, waiting with bouquets in the park, and every guest in the house compelled to go to the station to see the Prince off. Highly comical was the scene on the platform—the yards of red cloth hurriedly thrown down by two footmen wherever the poor boyish Prince, in his brown frieze suit and wideawake hat, seemed likely to tread.

We spent Tuesday at Cliveden, a pouring day, but it did not matter. The Duchess of Westminster[1] is Ronald Gower's favourite sister, and was very pleasant and cordial to his friend. She is gloriously handsome, though so large. We talked for four hours without ceasing, and she took us into every corner of the beautiful house full of charming pictures, and then put on an ulster and hood and walked with us through the torrents of rain to the conservatories.

Osterley Park, Nov. 13.—I came here yesterday, most kindly welcomed by the good old Duchess [Caroline] of Cleveland, who is delightful. The greatness of her charm certainly lies in the absence of charm: no one ever had less of it. But what bright intelligence, what acute perceptions, what genuine kindness, what active beneficence! After dinner, the Duchess made me sit exclusively by her, saying kindly that she could not waste any of my short visit. She talked in a very interesting way of the great Duke of Wellington, and then of the present Duke. She said that when she asked the latter if the great Duke had never shown him any kindness, he said, 'No, he never even so much as patted me on the shoulder when I was a boy, but it was because he hated my mother.'

As Lady Caroline Paulet, the Duchess of Cleveland used to be very proud of her little foot. She wore an anklet, and would often sit upon a table, and let it fall down over her foot to show it. It was inscribed, '*La légèreté de Camille et la vitesse d'Atalante.*' One day Lady Isabella St. John, who was equally proud of her little foot, said, 'I wish you would let me try if I can get your anklet over my foot, Lady Caroline.' And she put it on, and, to Lady Caroline's great disgust, *kicked it off*, to show how easily her foot would go through it.

How many and amusing are the anecdotes remembered of that Duchess Elizabeth,[2] who went on receiving a pension from the Duke of Bedford, as his cast-off mistress, after she was married to the Duke of Cleveland. She had been a washerwoman. She left Newton House, where she lived as a widow, to her nephew Mr. Russell, whose grandson married a Lushington. She gave £70,000 to her niece Laura when she married Lord Mulgrave, and the marriage very nearly went off because the Normanbys stuck out for £100,000. 'Laura is not my only niece, remember that,' she said, and then they became frightened. She used to call Lord Harry Vane 'My 'Arry.' One day, with Mr. Francis Grey, the conversation turned upon Venus. 'I do not like her,' she said, 'she had a bad figure, and by no means a good character.' Her companion laughed and said, 'She mistakes her for a living person,' and so she did.

[1] Constance-Gertrude, youngest daughter of the 2nd Duke of Sutherland.
[2] See note on p. 35.

Nov. 14.—In the afternoon we went to Ham House—a most curious visit. No half-inhabited château of a ruined family in Normandy was ever half so dilapidated as this home of the enormously rich Tollemaches. Like a French château too is the entrance through a gateway to a desolate yard with old trees and a sundial, and a donkey feeding. All the members of the family whom I knew were absent, but I sent in my card to Mr. Algernon Tollemache, who received us. As the door at the head of the entrance-stair opened, its handle went through a priceless Sir Joshua of Louisa, Countess of Dysart: it always does go through it. We were taken through a half-ruined hall and a bedroom to an inner room in which Mr. Algernon Tollemache (unable to move from illness) was sitting. It presented the most unusual contrasts imaginable— a velvet bed in a recess backed by the most exquisite embroidery on Chinese silk; an uncarpeted floor of rough boards; a glorious Lely portrait of the Duchess of Lauderdale; a deal board by way of washing-stand, with a coarse white jug and basin upon it; a splendid mirror framed in massive silver on a hideous rough deal scullery table without a cover; and all Mr. Tollemache's most extraordinarily huge boots and shoes ranged round the room by way of ornament.

The vast house is like a caravansary; in one apartment lives young Lord Dysart, the real owner; in another his Roman Catholic mother, Lady Huntingtower, and her two Protestant daughters; in a third, his great-aunt, Lady Laura Grattan; in a fourth, his uncle, Mr. Frederick Tollemache, who manages the property; in a fifth, Mr. and Mrs. Algernon Tollemache, who made a great fortune in Australia.

We were sent over the house. All was of the same character, marvellous old rooms with lovely delicate silk hangings of exquisitely beautiful tints, though mouldering in rags; old Persian carpets of priceless designs worn to shreds; priceless Japanese screens perishing; beautiful pictures dropping to pieces for want of varnish; silver grates, tongs, and bellows; magnificent silver tables; black chandeliers which look like ebony and are solid silver; a library full of Caxtons, the finest collection in the world except two; a china closet with piles of old Chelsea, undusted and untouched for years; a lovely little room full of miniatures, of which the most beautiful of all was brought down for us to examine closer. 'Do you see that mark?' said Mr. Tollemache. 'Thirty years ago a spot appeared there upon the miniature, so I opened the case and wetted my finger and rubbed it: I did not know paint came off (!). Wasn't it fortunate I did not wipe my wet hand down over the whole picture: it would *all* have come off!'[1]

And the inhabitants of this palace, which looks like that of the Sleeping Beauty in the Wood, have wealth which is inexhaustible, though they have scarcely any servants, no carriage, only bread and cheese for luncheon, and never repair or restore anything.

All the family have had their peculiarities. The late Lord Huntingtower was at one time separated from his wife, and when he was persuaded that he ought in common justice to allow her to return to Ham, he assented, but he draped the gates and portico with black cloth for her reception, and he put a band of black cloth round the left leg of every animal on the estate, the cows in the field, the horses in the stable, even the dogs and the cats. *His* grandfather, Lord Huntingtower, was more extraordinary still. When he bought a very nice estate with a house near Buckminster, he bought all the contents of the house at the same time. There was a very good collection of pictures, but 'What do I want with pictures? All that rubbish shall be burnt,' he said. 'But, my

---

[1] Ham House has been greatly, perhaps too much, restored since this, by the 8th Earl of Dysart.

lord, they are very *good* pictures.' 'Well, bring them all down here and make a very great fire, and I will see them burnt.' And he did.

There is a ghost at Ham. The old butler there had a little girl, and the Ladies Tollemache kindly asked her to come on a visit: she was then six years old. In the small hours of the morning, when dawn was making things clear, the child, waking up, saw a little old woman scratching with her fingers against the wall close to the fireplace. She was not at all frightened at first, but sat up to look at her. The noise she made in doing this caused the old woman to look round, and she came to the foot of the bed, and grasping the rail with her hands, stared at the child long and fixedly. So horrible was her stare, that the child was terrified, and screamed and hid her face under the clothes. People who were in the passage ran in, and the child told what she had seen. The wall was examined where she had seen the figure scratching, and concealed in it were found papers which proved that in that room Elizabeth, Countess of Dysart, had murdered her husband to marry the Duke of Lauderdale.[1]

Holmhurst, Nov. 24.—I have heard a very eerie story from Lady Waterford:— There is a place in Scotland called Longmacfergus. Mr. and Mrs. Spottiswoode lived there, who were the father and mother of Lady John Scott, and they vouched for the story. The villagers of Longmacfergus are in the habit of going to do their marketing at the little town of Dunse, and though their nearest way home would be by crossing the burn at a point called 'the Foul Ford,' they always choose another and longer way by preference, for the Foul Ford is always looked upon as haunted. There was a farmer who lived in Longmacfergus, and who was highly respected, and very well-to-do. One night his wife was expecting him back from the market at Dunse, and he did not appear. Late and long she waited and he did not come, but at last, after midnight, when she was very seriously alarmed, he knocked violently at the door and she let him in. She was horrified to see his wild and agonised expression, and the awful change which had taken place in his whole aspect since they parted. He told her that he had come home by the Foul Ford, and that he must rue the day and the way, for he must die before morning. He begged her to send for the minister, for he must see him at once. She was terrified at his state, and implored him rather to send for the doctor, but he said, 'No, the minister—the minister was the only person who could do him any good.' However, being a wise woman, she sent for both minister and doctor. When the doctor came, he said he could do nothing for the man, the case was past his cure, but the minister spent several hours with the farmer. Before morning he died, and what he said that night to the minister never was told till many years after.

Naturally the circumstances of the farmer's death made the inhabitants of Longmacfergus regard the Foul Ford with greater terror than before, and for a few years no one attempted to use it. At last, however, there came a day when the son of the dead farmer was persuaded to linger longer than usual drinking at Dunse, and after being twitted by his comrades for cowardice, in not returning the shortest way, he determined to risk it, and set out with a brave heart. That night *his* wife sat watching in vain for his return, and she watched in vain till morning, for he never came back. In the morning the neighbours went to search for him, and he was found lying dead on the bank above the Foul Ford, and—it is a foolish fact perhaps, but it has always

---

[1] Elizabeth Murray succeeded to the title of her father, the first Earl of Dysart, and her title was confirmed by Charles II in 1670. She married Sir Lionel Tollemache in 1647, and on his death married the Duke of Lauderdale in 1672.—*Ed.*

been narrated as a fact incidental to the story, that—though there were no marks of violence upon his person, and though his coat was on, his waistcoat was off and lying by his side of his body upon the grass; his watch and his money were left intact in his pockets.

After his funeral the minister said to the assembled mourners and parishioners, that now that the second death had occurred of the son, he thought that he should be justified in revealing the substance of the strange confession which the father had made on the night he died. He said that he had crossed the wooden bridge of the Foul Ford, and was coming up the brae on the other side, when he met a procession of horsemen dressed in black, riding two and two upon black horses. As they came up, he saw amongst them, to his horror, every one he had known amongst his neighbours of Longmacfergus, and who were already dead. But the man who rode last—the last man who had died—was leading a riderless horse. As he came up, he dismounted by the farmer's side, and said that the horse was for him. The farmer refused to mount, and all his former neighbours tried to force him on to the horse. They had a deadly struggle, in which at last the farmer seemed to get the better, for the horseman rode away, leading the riderless horse, but he said, 'Never mind, you will want it before morning.' And before morning he was dead.

It was with a feeling of strangeness that, in the autumn of 1879, I felt that my royal duties were over. I did not see the Prince of Sweden again after his return from Scotland.

VI

A HALT IN LIFE

1879–81

ஜ்

I N May 1878, my publishers, Messrs. Daldy and Isbister, had astounded the literary world by becoming bankrupt. They had been personally pleasant to deal with; I had never doubted their solvency; and I was on terms of friendly intercourse with Mr. Isbister. In April 1878 he wrote to me saying that he knew I applied the interest of money derived from my books to charitable purposes, and that he would much rather bestow the large interest he was prepared to give for such purpose than any other, and he asked me to lend him £1,500. I had not the sum at the time he asked for it, but, about a week later, being advised to sell out that sum from some American securities, I lent it to him. Then, within a month, the firm declared itself bankrupt, owing me in all nearly £3,000, and the £1,500 and much more was apparently lost for ever.[1] In accepting contracts for my different books, I had always fully understood, and been given to understand, that I never parted with the copyright. I believe that most publishers would have informed an ignorant author that the very unusual forms of agreement they prepared involved the copyright, but I was allowed to suppose that I retained it in my own hands. I first discovered my mistake after their bankruptcy, when, besides owing me nearly £3,000, Messrs. Daldy and Isbister demanded a bonus of £1,500 (which I refused, offering £850 in vain) for giving me the permission to go on circulating my own books through another publisher.

As it was impossible to come to terms, my unfortunate books lapsed. In the autumn of 1879 Messrs. Daldy and Isbister offered to submit to an arbitrator the question of the amount to be paid to my so-great debtors for the liberty of continuing to publish my books. Three eminent publishing firms chose an arbitrator, but when he sent in his estimate they would not agree to it.

These circumstances made such a discouragement for any real work, that for two years I did nothing of a literary character beyond collecting the reminiscences contained in these volumes. The first year was chiefly

---

[1] Two thousand pounds and its interests for many years have (1900) never been repaid.

occupied by my duties towards the Crown Prince of Sweden and Norway. In the second year I had a comparative holiday.

In November 1879 an event occurred which would at one time have affected me very deeply—the death of the Mary Stanley who for many years ruled my adopted family by the force of her strong will, and who, after my dearest Mother was taken away from me, remorselessly used that power to expel me from the hearts and homes of those over whom she had any influence, in her fury at the publication of the *Memorials of a Quiet Life*. Yet, when her restless spirit was quieted by Death, I could only remember the kind 'Cousin Mary' of my childhood. I often wish, as regards her, I could have profited more by words of Mrs. Kemble which I read too late to apply them—'Do you not know that to mis-understand and be misunderstood is one of the inevitable conclusions, and I think one of the especial purposes, of our existence? The principal use of the affection of human beings for each other is to supply the want of perfect comprehension, which is impossible. All the faith and love which we possess are barely sufficient to bridge over the abyss of indivi-dualism which separates one human being from another; and they would not, or could not, exist, if we really understood each other.'

In December I went abroad to join the two Miss Hollands—my Norwegian companions—at Ancona, and go on with them to Sicily, a journey through deep snow and agonising cold. Our wretched journey made the first morning at Messina quite enchanting, as we climbed the heights, looking down upon the straits and to the purple peaks of Italy, their tips glistening with snow. Nespoli, daturas, and camellias grew as trees in full bloom; the gardens were a mass of salvias, trumpet-flower, and roses; heliotrope in full blossom hung over the high walls, and quantities of scarlet geraniums grew wild upon the beach.

More lovely still was Taormina, hanging like an eagle's nest on the ledge of the mountain, and looking down into the blue sea, which breaks into emerald near the snowy line of breakers. On one side is Etna, quite gigantic, with pathless fields of snow even upon the lower heights; on the other are the grand ruins of the Theatre, from which, above the broken arches and pillars, the queen of fire and snow looms unspeakably sublime. Our pleasant primitive inn was in a quiet street, where all the daily incidents were lovely—the goats coming in the early morning to be milked: the peasants riding in upon their asses: the convent bells jangling: the women returning from the fountain with vases of old Greek forms upon their heads, burnished yellow, green, or red: the singing at Ave Maria and Benediction. We spent several days at Taormina, drawing quietly in the mornings amongst the rocky beds of pinks, and snapdragon, and silene: reading aloud in the evenings—Thucydides, Gregorovius, and then a novel for relaxation.

Each morning at Syracuse we engaged little carriages (costing one shilling the hour) for the day, and took with us a well-filled luncheon basket for ourselves and our charming young drivers, and we wandered, and studied, and drew for hours. We spent a whole day on the grand heights of Epipolae, looking on one side across a luxuriant plain to snowy Etna, and on the other across the vast ruined city to the blue sea, with Ortygia gleaming upon it like a jewel. Another whole day was given to

TAORMINA

ascending the rivers Anapus and Pisma to the mystic blue fountain of Cyane: the most romantic of boating excursions, the boatmen every now and then being obliged to jump into the water and push the boat over the shallows or through the thick water-plants: the papyrus with its exquisite feathery crests almost meeting overhead, or grouped into the most glorious masses on the islets in midstream: enchanting little views opening every now and then to palms and cypresses and blue rifts in the roseate rocks of Megara; now a foreground of oleanders, then of splendid castor-oil plants. In returning, we walked up a hill to the Temple of Jupiter Olympus, through a perfect blaze of dwarf blue iris, the loveliest flowers I ever saw.

At Girgenti we found an excellent hotel, with rooms opening to delightful balconies, overhanging—at a great height—one of the noblest views in the world, billow upon billow of purple hill, crested with hoary olives, and with masses of oranges and caroubas in all the sheltered nooks, a vast expanse of glistening sea, and a range of Greek temples in desolate loveliness. The landlord, Don Gaetano de Angelis, was a stately old Sicilian, who treated us far more like honoured guests than customers, and fed us so luxuriously and magnificently that we wondered how it was possible he could repay himself. He had lately married for the second time, a pretty merry child-wife in huge gold earrings, who paid us frequent visits and was delighted with us and our drawings, and to sit for her portrait. They quite enjoyed the preparation of the luncheon basket, with

ROMAN AMPHITHEATRE, SYRACUSE

which we always set off at 9 A.M., not returning till the sunset had turned the sea rose-colour and set the mountains aflame. Each day we picnicked amongst the asphodels and lilies in the shadow of one of the Greek temples, and were glad to find a shelter from the burning sun, which blazed in a sky that only turned from turquoise to opal. We all agreed in thinking Girgenti more beautiful than any other place, and its people even more charming than the scenery, so full of kindly simplicity, from the Syndic to Pasqualuccio, the little goatherd, with coins in his earrings after the old Greek fashion, who gives each of his goats a *colazione* of acanthus leaves, set out like plates on a dinner-table, on the fallen columns in the Temple of Juno.

The second day after our arrival, as we were returning home up the hill in the still warm evening light, we turned aside to the old deserted convent of S. Niccola. A merry crowd of gentlemen and ladies and little boys and girls were shouting and singing on the terrace, and dancing the tarantella to the music of three peasants on a bagpipe, tambourine, and triangle. Like a Bacchanalian rout of old times they came rushing down to meet us, twenty-six in number, chained together with garlands, and the girls all wreathed with wild scarlet geranium. They escorted us all over the garden, gathering flowers and fruits for us, the crowd of little children gambolling and dancing in front. Then they begged us to go back with them to the terrace, and began dancing again, and were delighted when Miss Howard and Miss G. Holland danced with them. Then came invitations to a party and ball at Casa Gibilaro, the sons of the house, Cesare and Salvatore, coming to escort us up the steep street. Italian ladies sang, and so did our party, and all danced, and we taught the

TEMPLE OF CONCORD, GIRGENTI

Girgentines Sir Roger de Coverley, which greatly enchanted them. The family of twenty-six—grandmother, uncles, aunts, cousins, were all there, living in the happiest union and affection, no daughter of the house ever marrying out of the place, and all meeting constantly.

One day, Salvatore and Pasqualina dined with us, and we afterwards went again to their house, where there was another dance, at which all the professors of the university (on delightful terms of merriment with their pupils) assisted, the Professor of Theology frisking about in the tarantella, and the Professor of Philosophy leading the cotillon. We wished this time to leave early, but our hosts insisted on our waiting till the arrival of ices, an unwonted luxury with them, but ordered in our honour. We had dined before, and since coming to the dance had been obliged to eat quantities of *pasticcie*, so were aghast when we found that we were each expected to eat an ice larger than an ordinary tea-cake. We managed as well as we could, but it was dreadful. I deposited more than half mine under a table.   Miss Holland thought she was getting on pretty well with hers, when a Contessa Indelicato, on the opposite side of the room, seeing her flagging, filled a large spoon with her own ice, and rushing across, popped it into her mouth. With great promptitude Miss Howard instantly popped a spoonful of *her* ice into the mouth of a Contessina Indelicato! Great were the lamentations and embraces from this amiable family when we left Girgenti, dear little Antonio Gibilaro going with us to the station.

CLOISTERS, MONREALE

In the afternoon of January 11 we went on to Palermo. Under the later Bourbon kings Sicily was perfectly safe and brigandage utterly unknown, for the principal officials in each village and parish were made responsible for its security; but the annihilation of the rural police under the Sardinian Government taking place at the same time with the abolition of capital punishment, had introduced brigandage; and though it had become rare since the formation of railroads, it was not considered safe for us to go far from Palermo without an escort, and we were obliged to give up Segeste. When we were at Palermo, murders for *vendetta* were of constant occurrence, and only cost three hundred francs, as the punishment was so slight,—generally two years' imprisonment without labour, and with a life of much greater comfort than the culprit could have enjoyed at home. Besides, the murderers are scarcely ever given up, as the *vendetta* would then fall upon those who betrayed them. Some of our party went to visit Calatafimi, the brigand who carried off a gentleman from Cefalu, and, when he got only half the ransom required, laboriously snipped with scissors till his head came off, in a cave on Monte Pellegrino. He was found very merry, in most comfortable quarters, with quantities of fruit, newspapers, &c. When he was tired of being there, his family would bribe the gaoler, and he would get out.

The glorious weather we enjoyed in the south of the island turned to torrents of rain at Palermo, but it is said that there are only forty-two days in the year without rain there. I shall always associate the place with the ceaseless melancholy roar of the sea, the drip and splash of the rain, which fell day and night, and the monotony of the mouldy deserted walks. In the Lazaretto cemetery—a lovely little spot hedged with Barbary aloes— it was touching to see the tomb of my almost unknown father. He also hated the place and was deeply depressed there.

We went to Monreale, the grand semi-Saracenic cathedral, covered with mosaics, on the heights behind Palermo. It reminds me of a story the late Lord Clanwilliam used to tell, which I will insert here:—

A Knight of Malta, who, by the rules of his Order, was both a soldier and a priest, was once travelling in Sicily. Being at Palermo, he strolled up to Monreale; it was a lovely evening, and in the great cathedral, where the shade was so welcome after the heat of the way, the effect was exquisitely beautiful, as the sunset streamed through the long windows upon the mosaic walls. Being an artist, the knight took out his sketch-book and began to draw, first one lovely arch and then another, till the waning light warned him that night was approaching. Then he made his way to the western door, but it was closed. He turned to the side doors, to the sacristy; they were closed also. It was evident that he was locked into the cathedral, and though he shouted and kicked at the door, he could make no one hear. Spending the night alone in a church had no terrors for him; it was only on account of the discomfort that he objected to it; so he found his way to a confessional far up the church, and made himself as com- fortable there as he could with all the cushions he could collect.

Most wondrously beautiful is the cathedral of Monreale when the moon casts its magic halo over the ancient mosaics, and so it was on this night, when the artist- soldier-priest sat entranced with its unspeakable loveliness. The whole building was bathed in softest light, each avenue of arches at once a poem and a picture, when the clock struck twelve. Then from the west door a figure seemed to be approaching, a cowled figure in monastic robes, and the stranger felt with satisfaction that he had been missed and that one of the monks of the adjoining monastery was come to seek him. But, as he watched the figure, he observed its peculiar movement, rather floating than walking up the nave, enveloped in its sweeping draperies, and as it passed he heard a low musical voice like a wiffling wind which said, 'Is there no good Christian who will say a mass for my poor soul?' and the figure passed on swiftly, on behind the altar, and did not return.

Through an hour the Knight of Malta sat watching and expecting, and then, as the clock struck one, the figure again floated up the nave, and again the same sad low voice murmured, 'Is there no good Christian will say a mass for my poor soul?' Then the Knight came out of the confessional and pursued the vanishing figure, pursued it to a particular spot behind the altar, where it disappeared altogether.

When the clock struck two, the figure appeared again, and when it again uttered the words, 'Will no good Christian say a mass for my poor soul?' the priest-soldier answered, 'I will; but you must serve the mass,' for there can be no mass without a server. The holy vessels were upon the altar, and the soldier-priest began the mass. Then the monk threw back his cowl and displayed a skull, but he served the mass, which the priest courageously went through to the end: then he fell down unconscious in front of the altar.

In the morning, when the monks came into the church, the stranger was found still unconscious upon the altar steps. He was taken into the convent, and, when he came to himself, he told what had happened. Great search was made in the archives of the monastery, though nothing was found to account for it. But long after, when some repairs were being made in the cathedral, the body of a monk in his robe and cowl was found walled up, evidently for some crime, near the altar, just at the spot where the Knight had seen him vanish.

A railway took us from Palermo to Caldane, almost on the opposite coast, and there we were transferred to a wretched tumble-down diligence, which went swinging and jolting over the deep pools in the rocky road. Though there were no regular brigands on this road, the peasants, who were too idle to work, constantly formed themselves into great bands and attacked the diligences; so the Sardinian Government, too feeble to attempt managing the people themselves, sent a guard to defend us from them. Two soldiers with guns sat on the luggage, and loaded pistols peeped ominously from under the cloaks of the Sicilians within. However, late at night we reached Caltanisetta, a great poverty-stricken city, with white houses, white rocks, and no vegetation, high in the sulphur district.

On going to the station the next morning, we heard that the railway near Messina was washed away, and that the last train had narrowly escaped a Tay Bridge disaster by the breaking of the high bridge at Ali, so we telegraphed to Taormina to send a carriage to meet us at Giardini, the place nearest the scene of the disaster. We did not reach Giardini till it was pitch-dark; the sea was raging close to the railway, and the rain had been falling all day in torrents. It was such a night as one scarcely ever sees, so tempestuous, so utterly black! There was no carriage for us, and no one to meet us; the telegraph had been swept away in the storm. Blankly and grimly did the officials see the large party deposited at the desolate station surrounded by waters, and great was the consternation of my four female companions when they found that it was just going to be closed and abandoned. We got a man to wade through the marsh to

Giardini to try to get a carriage to come to us: the carriage tried, but an intercepting torrent was so swollen, it was impossible for it to cross without being swept out to sea. The man came back along the railway parapet, and told us that we must give up all hope of getting away. The officials refused to send any one with us; no one would face the furies of the night; nor could they lend us a lanthorn; they wanted it themselves. Happily I had made friends with a young man of Taorminan who happened to be at the station. He had a lanthorn, and kindly waited for us, till at last my companions consented to kilt up their dresses and venture out into the blackness. It was four miles by the road, about a mile and a half by the precipices; we chose the latter. But the path through the precipices, which we had toiled up before in burning sunshine, was now a roaring torrent. However, there was nothing for it but to plunge in absolute blackness from stone to stone of the steep ascent, holding on to the broom and asphodels. Fortunately the rain almost ceased during the ascent, and at last, by scrambling, jumping, or grovelling, we found ourselves in the street of Taormina. The people of the inn were gone to bed, but soon the great event of a large party with ladies arriving on such a terrific night caused many windows to open in the friendly primitive street, and heads and candles to appear: the hotel was roused, and we were warmly welcomed.

For three days we remained in a state of siege with the elements howling around in our rock-fortress of Taormina, sometimes seeing Etna reveal itself above the black storm-clouds, Then we crossed to Reggio, and went on by night to Taranto, where we spent the morning in drawing the curious island-town, and took the train again to Trani. My last days with my companions were spent at beautiful Amalfi, and after a few lovely days at Naples and Rome, I followed them to England.

JOURNAL.

St. James's Place, May 8.—To Mrs. Stewart's. Lord Houghton was there, very cheery and kind. I was struck the other day by hearing some one say, 'Lord Houghton is not only a friend in poverty, he is a friend in *disgrace*.' Can there be higher praise? He was very amusing apropos of my employing Henningham and Holles to leave my cards, and said that Miss Martineau at first absolutely refused to conform to the ways of the world in paying visits, it was 'such a waste of time'; but it was suggested to her that she should send out 'an inferior authoress' with her trumpet in a hackney-coach to represent her and do her work, and that if the authoress only let the trumpet appear out of the coach-window, she would do just as well as herself.

May 26.—Dined at the Thorntons'.[1] Lord Houghton was there. He said how he had discussed with George Sand the question how far it was well to know authors

[1] Most probably William Thomas Thornton, author and economist, friend of J. S. Mill. He died in 1880.—*Ed.*

whose works you admired. She had urged him never to know them, that they all put
their best into their books; whatever you find afterwards can only be inferior material.
Carlyle, Lord Houghton allowed, was just like his books; in his case you could know
the man and not be disappointed: it is the same mixture of grim humour, irony, and
pathos, of which his books are composed, which enables the man personally to
produce such an indescribable impression. Carlyle always hated having his picture
taken, but was persuaded to sit to Millais. When he went there, to the beautiful house
full of priceless art-treasures, he asked what brought them there. 'My art,' answered
Millais proudly. 'Then there are more fools in the world than I imagined,' said Carlyle.

May 30.—Sat a long time with Lady Airlie, who talked of the power of prayer and
the number of people who really believed in it. She said she prayed for everything,
but always left it to God to decide for her, making a complete act of submission, but
adding, 'I should *like* this or that best.' The mystic Mr. Laurence Oliphant[1] came in
and talked for a long time. Being asked as to his past and future, he said he could only
act 'under direction,' *i.e.*, of spirits. He said the separation from the spiritual world
was entirely dependent upon the constitution of the individual. No wonder that the
hallucinations of this brilliant and fascinating visionary wreck the comfort as well as
the practical usefulness at once of his own life and the lives of those dearest to him.

June 9.—Dined with the Haygarths. Mr. Bouverie was there, and very entertaining
with stories of the old Duke of Wellington, of whom he justly said that his character
had greatly risen through the publication of his letters, while other characters had
been lowered. 'They will knock down a great many statues,' the Duke had said in
speaking of them to Mr. Bouverie in his lifetime.

Apropos of the Duke's love of military discipline, Mr. Bouverie mentioned how,
when he was at Walmer, all the officers of the neighbouring garrison called except
Lord Douro, who thought it would be absurd, as he was seeing his father every day.
Consequently, the Duke asked all the officers to dinner except his own son, and at
dinner said to the Colonel, 'By the by, who is your Major? for he has not called on
me.'

Another example of the Duke's character as a martinet was that Lord Douro once
met him in plain clothes. The Duke took no notice of him whatever. Lord Douro,
knowing how angry his father must be, rushed in, changed his clothes for uniform,
and met his father again. 'Hallo, Douro! how are you? it is a long time since I have
seen you,' said the Duke; but he had seen him quite well a quarter of an hour before.

June 10.—Dined with the Miss Duff Gordons, meeting Tosti the singer and tall
young Carlo Orsi from one of the old *castelli* in the Tuscan valley of Signa. He was
very naïve about his coming to London, and his asking himself when he woke, 'And
can it be thou, Carlo who art here?' Mrs. Caulfield and Tosti sang exquisitely in the
evening.

[1] Laurence Oliphant (1829–88), only child of Sir Anthony Oliphant, (one-time chief Justice of
Ceylon); diplomatist, member of parliament, traveller, novelist, journalist, war-correspondent and
mystic; one of the most remarkable characters of his time; of versatile and brilliant intellect, there was
some inconsistency between his eccentric religious tendencies and his capacities as a shrewd financier,
a social favourite and a brilliant writer. Was born at the Cape; spent his early years in Ceylon; travelled in India, China, Japan, Korea, Russia, America and the Balkans; plotted with Garibaldi;
was present at the siege of Sebastapol; was secretary to Lord Elgin in America and China; was *Times*
correspondent in Circassia, etc. Hare's references to his private life concern his and his wife's associa-
tion with a 'prophet' named Harris, who ran a mystical community of whose principals one was
that marriage should be a platonic relation. See Margaret Oliphant's *Memoirs*, published in 1891.—*Ed.*

June 14.—With Mrs. Stewart to Alma Tadema's studio—a small house on the north of the Regent's Park. Inside it is a labyrinth of small rooms with gilt walls and ceilings, and doors hung with quaint draperies. A vague light fell through alabaster windows upon Madame Tadema[1] in a cloth of gold dress backed by violet draperies. The Dutch artist, her husband, thinks her red hair glorious, and introduces her in all his pictures. In his studio is a strange picture of 'The Triumph of Death' by Breughel the Devil. I was glad to meet again Madame Riaño—Doña Emilia de Guyangos—gliding through the half-dark rooms after the ubiquitous wife of Tom Hughes.[2]

June 26.—In the evening I was at the Speaker's party. His beautiful rooms were additionally illuminated by the glare from a great fire on the opposite bank of the river. The bridge, and the chain of omnibuses and cabs, with their roofs crowded with the black figures of spectators, and the background of flames, gave the whole scene the aspect of the Devil's funeral with appropriate fireworks. In a great hooded car, nodding against the flame, the Devil's widow seemed to follow. We watched from the windows for nearly two hours—inside, bright uniforms, low dresses, glistening diamonds: outside, flames and a black shimmering river. At last the fire-engines got the victory, a roof fell in, the glare began to fade, the bereaved demons returned from the ceremony, and the illuminations were extinguished. No human life was lost, only the two great bloodhounds which were the guards of the timber-yard, and which for years have gained the prize in every dog-show.

July 11.—Dined at Lord Foley's. George Russell was there. He said he had said something about Lord Salisbury's carriage to the Duchess Dowager of Cleveland. 'I did not know Lord Salisbury had a carriage,' said the old lady. 'Surely, my dear Duchess?'—'No; I have even heard it said that the present Marquis of Salisbury goes about in a vehicle called a brougham!'

Sir Robert and Lady Sheffield were going down to visit some friends near West Drayton, where a carriage was to meet them. Arriving in the dark, they found a carriage waiting and jumped into it. After driving some way, they entered a park and drove up to the door of a great house. They were shown up to a long gallery, where a little old lady was arranging some books. 'Ah! some companion,' they thought, and for a time they took no notice of her. At last they said, 'Is Lady —— not coming down soon?'— 'I am not cognisant of the movements of my Lady ——,' said the old lady very sharply, rapping her ebony stick violently on the floor; 'but you are under a misapprehension. This is Osterley Park, and I—am the Duchess of Cleveland.' And then subsiding into her most gracious manner,—'And now, whilst my carriage is getting ready to take you on to Lady ——, I hope you will allow me to have the pleasure of giving you some tea.'

July 14.—Dinner at Lady Charlemont's. Mr. Synge, who declared at once his belief in ghostly apparitions, told a pretty story of a clergyman in Somersetshire who had ridden to the bank and drawn out all the money for his poor-club, which he was taking back with him, when he became aware of another horseman riding by his side, who did not speak, and who, at a certain point of the road beyond a hollow, disappeared.

---

[1] Laura Teresa, daughter of George Napoleon Epps, homeopathic practitioner and surgeon. Sir Lawrence Alma-Tadema (1836–1912) was born in Holland but settled in London in 1870: became an R.A. in 1879, was knighted in 1899 and received the O.M. in 1907. His subjects were taken in large part from Classic Greece and Rome and mediæval Europe.—*Ed.*

[2] Author of *Tom Brown's Schooldays*. A disciple of F. D. Maurice of Hare's childhood.—*Ed.*

In that hollow highwaymen, who knew the clergyman was coming with the money, were waiting to attack him; but they refrained, 'for there are two of then,' they said. It was his guardian angel.

Lady Charlemont talked much of the Lord Chancellor Thurlow.[1] He asked for the Bishopric of Durham for his brother. George IV replied that he thought Lord Thurlow should have known that that Bishopric, being a principality, could only be given to persons of the very highest rank and connections. 'It is therefore, your Majesty,' said Lord Thurlow, 'that I have asked for it for the brother of the Lord High Chancellor of England.'

A clergyman desirous of a living went to the Bishop of London and asked him for an introduction to the Lord Chancellor Thurlow. The Bishop said, 'I should be willing to give it, but an introduction from me would defeat the very end you have in view.' However, the clergyman persisted in his request, and the introduction was given.

The Lord Chancellor received him with fury. 'So that damned scoundrel the Bishop of London has given you an introduction: as it is he who has introduced you, you will certainly not get the living.'—'Well, so the Bishop said, my lord,' replied the clergyman. 'Did the Bishop say so?' thundered Lord Thurlow: 'then he's a damned liar, and I'll prove him so: you *shall* have the living,' and the man got it.

July 16.—At Mrs. Ralph Dutton's I took Mrs. Procter in to dinner—Barry Cornwall's widow,[2] always full of interest and excellence, and of many unknown kindnesses. She talked of her early days, of the charm of Monckton Milnes [Lord Houghton] when young—his brightness and vigour: of the decadence of society now, when at least a thousand persons were invited to Grosvenor House whom our grandmothers would not consent to be in the same room with; but that society now required high seasoning, and royalty the strongest pepper of all: that in former days no guest would have continued in a house where he was received on entering by a wet sponge from ——: that the abbreviation of P. B.'s in use for 'professional beauties' was a sign of the depth to which we have fallen.

Mrs. Stewart told me a characteristic story of Mrs. Procter's wit. 'The Lionel Tennysons—dear good excellent people—asked that woman Sarah Bernhardt, the actress, to luncheon, asked her to go all the way to them in Kensington, and invited some good, quiet, simple folk to meet her, just trusting in his prestige as the laureate's son. I need hardly say that, though they waited luncheon for Sarah Bernhardt till four o'clock, she never came. She knew the company she was to meet, and she did not think it worth while. They told Mrs. Procter of it. 'Why,' she said, 'if people will invite monkeys, they must provide them with *nuts*.'

'Dear Mrs. Procter is so satirical,' says Mrs. Stewart, 'that when I go to her and find other people in the room, I always stay till the last, that she may have no one to discuss me with.'

July 17.—Two days ago I went to Lady Airlie's, where a large party was collected to hear Mr. Browning read. I never heard any one, even a child of ten, read so atrociously. It was two of his own poems—'Good News to Ghent' and 'Ivan Ivanowitch,' the latter always most horrible and unsuitable for reading aloud, but in this case rendered utterly unintelligible by the melodramatic vocal contortions of the reader.

[1] Edward Thurlow, first Baron Thurlow, 1731–1806, inflexible defender of royal prerogatives and an opponent of every kind of change. Presided at the trial of Warren Hastings. Served in the Rockingham, Shelburne and Pitt ministries.—*Ed.*

[2] See note on p. 213.

Oct. 29.—A charming visit to Broadlands, Lord Mount-Temple's[1]—the people so full of genial goodness, the house most comfortable and gardens lovely. Lady Mount-Temple—in whom, as Miss Tollemache, Ruskin saw such statuesque severity with womanly sweetness joined—a marvellous union of beauty, goodness, and intelligence. The grounds, with fountain, river, well-grouped trees, and a Palladian summerhouse, are like a beautiful Claude-Lorraine picture. The same landscape—of a river, winding amongst cedar-shadowed lawns—forms the predella to Rossetti's picture of 'The Blessed Damozel.'

Dec. 16.—Several Midland county visits afford nothing to recollect. Certainly country-house visits are a lottery. One old lady said, 'My dear, I *am* so glad to see you. It is so delightful to see any one *at all* pleasant. In London one can have any agreeable company one likes, but you know God Almighty fills one's house in the country.'

I spent the Christmas of 1880 again with the kind Lowthers at Ampt-hill, meeting, as before, Louisa, Lady Ashburton, and going, as before, to spend a day at Woburn. In January 1881 I was at Bretton with the Beaumonts, meeting Julia, Lady Jersey, and a large party.

We went to see Nostell, a very grand but little known house of the Winns, full of splendid things, glorious tapestries, china, Chippendale furniture, but, most remarkable of all, a doll's house of the last century, with miniature fairy furniture, exquisitely carved and painted, a doll's trousseau with point lace, and a Liliputian service of plate. We also went a long drive to Stainborough (Wentworth Castle), through a country which may be pretty in summer clearness, but which is hideously black in winter. The house is a great Italian palace, half Queen Anne, half older, with little temples in the grounds, the building of one of which is described by Evelyn. Lady Harriet Wentworth, who showed us everything herself, gave us the characteristic of her life when she said 'I do so hate the *thraldom* of civilisation.' Her stately rooms have no charm for her, and, though they are so immense, she declares she cannot breathe in them, and she lives entirely and has all her meals in the conservatory, with a damp, warm, marshy climate, from which she does not scruple to emerge through the bitter winds of the Yorkshire wolds (for the conservatory does not join the house) with nothing extra on.

JOURNAL.

Jan. 11, 1881.—There is a large party here (at Tortworth), but one forgets all its other elements in dear Mrs. Duncan Stewart. Last night she wanted to introduce me to Mrs. Grey, an American lady who is staying here. 'I cannot do it better,' she said, 'than in the words of Alfred d'Orsay when he brought up Landseer to me, saying,

---

[1] William Francis Cowper, first Baron Mount-Temple, 1811–1888; Lord of the Admiralty; Under-Secretary for Home Affairs; president of the Board of Health; Commissioner of Works. etc.

"Here, Mrs. Stewart, is Landseer, who can do everything better than he can paint,"
—so here, Mrs. Grey, is Mr. Hare, who can do everything better than he can write.'

To-day, at luncheon, Mrs. Stewart talked much of Paris, and of her intercourse
with a French physician there. Dr. —— spoke to her of the happy despatch, and
unhesitatingly allowed that when he saw a patient condemned to hopeless suffering,
he practised it. 'But of course you insist on the acquiescence both of the patients and
of their families,' said Mrs. Stewart. 'Never,' shouted Dr. ——. 'I should be a mean
sneak indeed if I waited for *that*.'

Mrs. Stewart talked of the great want of appreciation of Byron—of his wonderful
satire, evinced by the lines in the 'Age of Bronze' on Marie Louise and Wellington:
of his philosophy, for which she cited the lines on Don Quixote: of his marvellous
condensation and combination, for which she repeated those on the burning of
Moscow.

She also talked of Trollope's novels, and said how Trollope had told her of the circumstances which led to the death of Mrs. Proudie. He had gone up to write at the
round table in the library at the Athenaeum, and spread his things all over it. It was
early in the morning, and there is seldom any one there at that time. On this occasion,
however, two country clergymen were sitting on either side of the fire reading one
of his own books: after a time they began to talk about them. 'It is a great pity Trollope does not get some fresh characters,' said one. 'Yes,' said the other, 'one gets so
tired of meeting the same people again and again, especially of Mrs. Proudie.' Then
Trollope got up, and planting himself on the rug between them with his back to the
fire, said, 'Gentlemen, I do not think it would be honest to listen to you talking about
my books any more, without telling you that I am the victim; but I will add that I
quite agree with what you have been saying, and that I will give you my word of
honour that Mrs. Proudie shall die in the very next book I write.'

Jan. 12.—Mrs. Stewart talked of Madame Jerome Bonaparte, *née* Paterson—her
beauty, her cleverness, her father to whom she always wrote of her *succès de société*,
looking down upon him; but he could always avenge himself: he could always write
to her, 'My dear Betsy.' 'She would tell him how she had been received at this court
and at that, and then would come his answer with "My dear Betsy." Oh, it was a
terrible revenge.'

January 12.—Mrs. Stewart has been talking of the cases in which a lie is justi-
fiable. Of herself she said, 'There was once a case in which I thought I ought to tell
a lie, but I was not sure. I went to Dr. and Mrs. Bickersteth, and I asked them. They
would only answer, "We cannot advise you to tell a lie;" they would not advise it,
but they did not forbid it. So when a husband came to question me about his wife,
I equivocated. I said, "She was certainly not seduced by that man." He said to me very
sternly and fiercely, "That is no answer; is my wife innocent? I will believe you if
you say she is." And I said. "She is." I said it hesitatingly, for I knew it was false, and
he knew it was false; he knew that I had lied to him, and he did not believe me in his
heart: but he was glad to believe me outwardly, and he was grateful to me, and that
husband and wife lived together till death. I believe that was one of the cases in which
it is right to tell a lie. You will say that it might lead me to tell many others, but I
don't think it has.'

We have been to luncheon at Berkeley Castle to-day. Lady Fitzhardinge, fat to
a degree, is charming, and has the most wonderful knowledge of all the delicate

finesses of form and colour, and the application of them to furniture. Her rooms are quite beautiful, everything composing the most harmonious picture, down to a string of blue beads suspended from a yellow vase. Lord Fitzhardinge came in to luncheon with Lord Worcester, Lord Guildford, and another man—four statues! Not one of them spoke a word, I believe because not one of them had a word to say, except about racehorses, about which we none of us could say anything.

Jan. 15.—Mrs. Stewart has been talking much of her great delight in the works of Ampère, and of the intense devotion, the passionate love of the younger Ampère for Madame Recamier. She was guilty of a *trahison* to him, though. When he was at Weimar, he wrote to her a private letter, telling her particulars about all the people there, which he had better not have told, but he wrote them in strict confidence. She made that letter public. 'My dear Mr. Hare,' said Mrs. Stewart, 'I have never read any letter more exquisitely, more tenderly pathetic than that which Ampère wrote her when he heard this—a letter struggling between his old respect and admiration and the feeling that his idol had fallen, that he could not but reproach her.'

In the evening Mrs. Stewart spoke much of the Sobieski Stuarts—their gallant appearance when young, and their change into 'the mildew of age.'

Apropos of the last words of St. Evremond, *'Je vais savoir le grand puet-être,'* Mrs. Stewart mentioned Mrs. Grote having said to her at their last meeting, 'I trust dear, that you are living, as I am, in *respectful hope.'*

This led to much talk of Mrs. Grote, who had died (Dec. 29, 1878) when I was away at Rome with the Prince Royal, and Mrs. Stewart described how, when she returned from Hanover after the fall of the royal family, and was quite full of events there, she went down at once to visit the Grotes in the country. 'My dear,' said Mrs. Grote, 'I cannot enter into your feelings about all your princesses and duchesses, but as regards your king, I can enter into them fully: he has lived "as it is written."' Mrs. Stewart wrote this to the King, who knows Shakespeare to his finger-ends, and he said it did him more good than anything else anybody wrote or said to him. As long as he lived, he and Mrs. Grote exchanged stories and messages afterwards, through Mrs. Stewart.

Lady William Russell said with much truth of Mr. and Mrs. Grote, 'He is ladylike, and she is such a perfect gentleman.'

When Lady Eastlake undertook to write Mrs. Grote's life after her death, she asked Mrs. Stewart for all her 'jottings' of Mrs. Grote's conversations, but she made no use of them. She was so anxious that every one should find the book too short, that she really omitted almost everything characteristic. She wrote her regrets afterwards to Mrs. Stewart, who answered, 'You are suffering, my dear, from a granted prayer,'—for, in fact, the book was so short and dry that it passed almost unnoticed.

After being for a time with Mrs. Stewart and hearing her talk, I feel how great the decay of conversation is since my childhood, when there were many people who knew how to *converse*, not merely to *utter*. Scarcely any one now ever says what they really think, and there is an unwholesome striving after aestheticism, Louis Quatorze, blue china, &c., which another age, if it remembers it, will think most ridiculous.

London, Jan. 24.—To Miss Bromley, who had been on Saturday to take leave of Carlyle, to whom she has been the most faithful of friends for many years. He has been sinking for some time, full of power, pathos, and patience. He woke out of what was supposed to be a death stupor to recognise her, and pressed her hand to his lips.

March 1.—Met Lady Lyveden at dinner at General Higginson's. She described Mrs. Grote saying one day, 'I have to go out this morning, my dear; it's not my usual time, and in fact it's very inconvenient to me, but then you know, my dear, it's *an affliction job.*'

Mrs. Grote, to the last, was very proud of her appearance. Her hands and feet she was especially proud of. One day Lady Lyveden asked her to come in the evening to meet some pleasant people in her neighbouring house in Savile Row. She would not do it. 'I shall not come, my dear,' she said, 'because I never go out; but besides that, I *could* not come, for, if I did, I should have to put my well-formed figure into one of your abominably low arm-chairs.'

There was a charm about her primitive household. There was not one of her servants who spoke of her otherwise than 'the Missis.'

After dinner, she would leave 'the historian,' as she called him, in his study, and come up to the drawing-room, where she would talk to her guests and be most entertaining. At nine o'clock, tea would be brought up—such a tea as one never sees now, with tablecloth, muffins, cakes, &c. Then she would say to the servant, 'Bring up the historian'—and the historian was 'brought up.' He was vastly civil, of the old school, and wore a great deal of frill. He would take his place opposite the table, and immediately taking a large clean pocket-handkerchief from his pocket, spread it very deliberately over his knees, after which a dog jumped up and sat upon it. Then he would say, as to a perfect stranger, 'And now, Mrs. Grote, will you kindly favour us with a sonata?' and Mrs. Grote, who was an admirable musician, would play a very long sonata indeed; after which he would say, 'Thank you, Mrs. Grote. I am sure Lady Lyveden joins with me in being very much obliged to you for your beautiful sonata.'[1]

March 22.—The London world has been full of the *Reminiscences of Carlyle*, published with furious haste by Froude a fortnight after his death. They have dwarfed their subject from a giant into a pigmy. His journal and letters speak well of no one except his own family, and assail with the utmost vituperation all who differed from him. For his wife there is a long wail of affection, which would be touching if the devotion had not begin after her death. 'Never marry a genius,' she said to Lady Ashburton; 'I have done it, and suffered from it; but then, after my death I shall have an apotheosis'—and she has had it. Much of Carlyle's virulence arose from the state of his health: he used to say, 'I can wish the devil nothing worse than that he may have to digest with my stomach to all eternity; there will be no need of fire and brimstone then.'

March 28.—Dined at Lady Lyveden's. Sat by Lady S., who was very pleasant. She talked of Tennyson, who had been to stay with her. He desired his sons to let her know that he should like to be asked to read some of his poems in the evening. Nevertheless, when she asked him, he made a piece of work about it, and said to the other guests, 'I do it, but I only do it because Lady S. absolutely insists upon it.' He read badly and with too much emotion: over 'Maud' he sobbed passionately.

Afterwards, at Lady Ridley's party, Lord Houghton talked to me about Carlyle—of how his grimness, which was unrelieved in the *Reminiscences*, was relieved in the

---

[1] Mr. Grote was ever imperturbably placid. When Jenny Lind was asked what she thought of Mr. Grote, she said he was 'like a fine old bust in a corner which one longed to dust.' Mrs. Grote dusted him.

man by much kindly humour. He said that he and Lady Houghton were almost the only people spoken well of in the book.

Holyrood Palace, May 27.—On the evening of the 14th, at Cleveland House, first Lady Aberdeen, and then Aberdeen, asked me to come hither with them as equerry, during their residence for the Lord High Commissionership. I joined them on Friday, arriving at 9 P.M., when ninety guests were at dinner in the brilliantly lighted picture gallery, in which all the kings of Scotland were, painted to order by the same hand and from the same model. After dinner by myself in a small room, I joined the party in the reception-rooms, where I entered at once upon my duties, which, for the most part, seem to be to talk right and left to every one I see. Each evening the Synods of the different districts dine, some eighty or a hundred clergymen, and I have generally found from my clerical neighbours that they regard it as their carnival, looked forward to throughout the whole year, and giving them much to talk of when they return home.

Holyrood Palace, May 28.—On Sunday we were at St. Giles's in the morning, and in the afternoon had a long service and sermon in the picture-gallery. These Scotch services are most wearisome, and the long prayers, *informing* the Almighty upon subjects on which He is all-wise and we are utterly ignorant, are most revolting.

May 29.—Yesterday we drove out to Winton to Lady Ruthven. It was a lovely day, the sea deep blue, and the trees, especially the sycamores, in their richest foliage. We found the house just set in order after its devastation during the fire which consumed the dining-room three weeks ago, when everything was thrown out of the windows. And she bade every person on the property go to church the next day to return thanks for her preservation. She received me with the greatest affection, and bade me kiss her.

At the great dinner at Holyrood in the evening I took in a Mrs. Murray, who talked pleasantly about the old phase of Edinburgh society which she remembered. 'There were three subjects—wine, law, and contradiction: wine is extinct now as a topic, but the other two, and especially the last, are as much to the fore as ever.' She said that she had studied law herself, because it was the subject on which her husband was most interested, and she liked him to be able to discuss all his occupations with her.

London, July 10.—With Lady Paget to hear Spurgeon preach at his great Tabernacle near the Elephant and Castle. The vast congregation, the united sound of the thousands of voices in the hymn, the earnestness and zest of everything, were very striking: but far more so the strange, common, coarse preacher. . . . The rough similes just suited the congregation, and also the jokes, at which the people laughed aloud, but not irreverently.

I was suddenly called away in the middle of the season by the alarming illness of my dearest old nurse, and for several weeks was at Holmhurst with her, in the mysterious solitude of the shadow of death, in which so many of my earlier years were passed, and then I had the intense thankfulness of seeing life return into the dear old face connected with so much that no one else remembers.

VII

HOME SORROWS

1881–82

᠅

I T was on the 11th of July, after I had returned to London, that Miss
Johnes passed by, and told me that Arthur Stanley was ill. I thought
little of it at the time, as he was so often sick, and I had lately seen
him looking better and happier than he had done since his sister Mary's
death. On Thursday 14th there was a great dinner-party at the Deanery.
Catherine Vaughan dined, and as, at the last moment, Arthur was not
well enough to appear, she went in to sit with him after dinner, and finding
him very dispirited and unwell, gave up her intention of going to Llandaff next day, and moved to the Deanery instead. That day erysipelas
came on, and she was prevented seeing him till 3 A.M. on the morning
of Monday the 18th, when the doctors called her, saying that an alarming
change had come on. At 10 A.M. on Monday, I broke through the cordon
which surrounded the Deanery, and made my way up to Catherine, who
was glad to have me with her. It was the dead heat of July, not a leaf
stirring. In the afternoon, Arthur was so much better that I went away,
and even kept an engagement to dine out. But next morning came the
shock of his death. Catherine and I both took leave of the Deanery for
ever the next morning, but I went back to Westminster for the sad
services of Sunday and Monday.

On the day after his death his sister and Hugh Pearson,[1] his dearest
friend, wrote to me, asking me to undertake his biography, to which I
gladly assented. But Sir George Grove, one of his literary executors,
did not permit my undertaking it.

JOURNAL.

Kinmel, Oct. 14.—A kind invitation from Lord and Lady Penrhyn took me from
Penrhos to Penrhyn Castle, which is a very stately building outside, though the huge
stone corridors and richly decorated Norman rooms are very unsuited for home
comfort. The lady of the castle herself[2] is one of the most natural and unworldly
women in the world; and Lord Penrhyn[3] was most agreeable with his personal reminis-

[1] Canon of Windsor since 1876.
[2] Mary Louisa, Lady Penrhyn, daughter of Henry, 5th Duke of Grafton.
[3] Edward Gordon Douglas Pennant, Baron Penrhyn, who had succeeded to Penrhyn Castle
in right of his first wife, Miss Dawkins Pennant.

cences. He described the coronation of George IV, where he stood close to Queen
Caroline as she entered the carriage to drive away, and he said the expression of her
countenance was the most diabolical thing he ever looked upon. Lord Penrhyn rode
after Lord Anglesea, the Waterloo hero, when he was followed by a hooting mob
through St. James's Park. Lord Anglesea backed his horse between the trees, set his
teeth, and hissed back at the yelling people. Then he said, 'If every man of you were
a hundred men, and each of them had a hundred hands, and a bayonet in each hand,
I should still do my—*duty*!' Then the people cheered him.[1]

COURTYARD, THE DEANERY, WESTMINSTER

The life at Penrhyn Castle was most easy and agreeable, with the freedom which
only exists in very great houses, the plenty of time to oneself, and yet interesting
society.

London, Nov. 1.—Dined with Lady Lyndhurst[2] in Eaton Square. She talked of
her early life. 'I lived in Paris with my father, and I saw nobody. I never expected
to marry; why should I? I had no fortune and no attractions. The first time I saw my

[1] Sir Henry William Paget, first Marquis of Anglesey, 1768–1854, commanded the cavalry in
Spain under Sir John Moore and the cavalry and horse artillery at Waterloo, losing a leg in the battle.
Field-marshal in 1846.—*Ed.*

[2] See note on p. 118.

Lord was when he came to Paris with his first wife. He came to see my father, and we went out driving with him. He and my father sat forward, and another young lady and I sat back, and most terribly afraid I was of him, and not a word did I speak—a shy, awkward girl sitting bolt upright.

'When my Lord was a widower, he came to Paris again. I was seven-and-twenty then, and was keeping my father's house. Lord Lyndhurst came to breakfast with my father, and I gave them their coffee and whatever they wanted, and then sat there reading my *Galignani*, and not thinking a bit about them. Suddenly Lord Lyndhurst asked me if I knew of any very sunny apartment to let. "Oh, yes," I said; "there is a friend of mine who wants to let just what you wish for, and, if you will wait a minute, I will run and get the keys, and can show it you." So I got the keys, and he went with me, and the apartment was a capital one and suited him very well; and then, to my surprise, he asked me if I should be at home in the afternoon, and I thought, "What on earth can the old man want to come again for?"—and I answered him that I did not know. And, in fact, I forgot all about it, and went out driving to the Bois; and when I came in, the servant said Lord Lyndhurst had been. It gave me a sort of shock, and I went to my room, and said to myself, "What on earth can this mean?" But the next day before I was up—*before I was up*, if you please—I had a note from Lord Lyndhurst asking when I should be at home; and he came at that hour, and he came twice a day for three months, and it became quite awkward, every one talked of it—Paris is so small a world. However, at the end of that time he proposed. Afterwards I said, "Now do tell me what the dickens made you want to marry me—a woman without family, without fortune, and most decidedly without beauty?" and he said he did not know. After he had engaged me to marry him, he had to go back to England to his law-courts, and my father told me that I had better begin to get my things ready and buy my trousseau; but I said, "No, I should most certainly do nothing of the kind, for I did not believe for an instant that my Lord would ever come back again."

'But he did come back, and we were married, and I had twenty-six years of the most perfect happiness ever allotted to woman. My Lord had the most perfect temper in the world, and in all the years we were together, we never had even a difference of opinion. He never came in to breakfast, and he never took luncheon, so he never appeared in our rooms till dinner-time, but I trotted in and out of his library, and the oftener I went in, the better he was pleased.

'I had seen nothing of the world before I was married, but I saw plenty of it afterwards: indeed, a few years after, he was made Lord Chancellor, and that was the top of everything. The world was the one drawback to my happiness, for through almost the whole time of my married life I had to go out. My Lord's eldest daughter was married three years after I married my Lord, and four years after, Soph, his second girl, was married; and then very soon there was my own girl to take out. Oh, how I hated it, but I never let my Lord know what I felt. We dined with him, and afterwards there was his whist, or people came to see him, and at ten o'clock he went to bed; then I went to my daily task of dressing to take the girls out, and sometimes I fairly cried as I was dressing.

'I was always up so late at night that I breakfasted in my own room, but there was always breakfast downstairs for the girls and Auntie—for my Lord's elder sister, Miss Copley, always lived with us. Auntie was no trouble in the house, and I was very fond of her, for she perfectly adored my Lord. When I married, people wondered at my wishing to have my sister-in-law to live with me, but I said, "Bless you, have I not been brought up in France, where whole families live together, and have to accommodate themselves to each other? and it would be hard indeed if I could not get on with poor old Auntie, when she is so fond of my Lord."

'It was at the marriage of my daughter to Sir Charles Du Cane that my Lord said he had nothing left to live for, his work was done. He comforted me by telling me that he was so very old—and so he was,—and that if he lived he must become helpless, and so perhaps would be unhappy, and then perhaps even his mind might go. He said, "You will take care of Auntie?" and I said, "Of course I will," and Auntie was always with me afterwards, and I loved her dearly, and she died in this very room at ninety-three. She was always well and cheerful, but one day she asked for her cup of tea as usual, and afterwards she—fell asleep,—she was so very old.

'My dear Lord was very old too when he died, but to me he was always like a young man, he was so bright and cheerful and so kind—always the pleasantest of companions. However, I could believe it was time that he should go, because *he* told me so.

'That is the story of my life, Mr. Hare, and now I am only waiting, hoping that some day,—perhaps some day not very far off,—I may see my dear Lord again.'

Jan. 13, 1882.—With Ronald Gower and Hugh Pearson over the three great houses of London in the same morning. Grosvenor House is the pleasantest to live in, but Stafford House the most magnificent. When the Queen was being received there by the late Duchess, she said, with her happy power of expression, 'I come, my dear, from my house to your palace.'

Feb. 21.—I sat at dinner by Mrs. Duncan Stewart, who talked with her usual power. 'When I was young, I lived with my guardian and his wife at Havre de Grâce, and thence I married Mr. Duncan Stewart, who was a Baltic merchant, a prosperous and well-to-do man then, though he was ruined afterwards. We lived in Liverpool; but my husband loved hunting and fishing, and at certain times of the year he was "away after the grouse," as every Scotchman is. I stayed with my children then, but I too had my time of the year for going away, and I always went to London, where I became very intimate with Lady Blessington and all that set—a very bad set, it must be allowed.

'One day when I was sitting alone in my house in Liverpool, and my husband was away with the grouse, a note of introduction was brought in for me from Mrs. Milner Gibson, whom I had known in London, with the cards of Mr. and Mrs. Disraeli. He was a young man then, all curly and smart, and his wife, though so much older than himself, was a very handsome, imperial-looking woman. I told them that I should be delighted to show them everything in Liverpool, as Mrs. Milner Gibson asked me.[1]

'When I went to see them next day at the hotel, I asked Mrs. Disraeli how she had slept, and she said, "Not at all, for the noise was so great." Then I said, "Why not move to my house, for my house is very quiet, and I am alone, and there is plenty of room?" And they came, and a most delightful ten days I had. We shut out Liverpool and its people, and we talked, and we became great friends, and when we parted it was with very affectionate regard on both sides; and afterwards they wrote to me every week, and when I went to London, my place was always laid at their table, and if I did not appear at their dinner, they always asked me why I had not come to them.

[1] Thomas Milner-Gibson was at school with Disraeli; was a supporter of the Conservative cause to start with, but changed over to the Liberals in 1841.—*Ed.*

'After she died, we drifted apart, he and I, and though I saw him sometimes, it was never in the old intimate way. The last time I saw him though, we had a really good talk together. It was not till we were parting that I said to him, "I hope you are quite well," and I shall never forget the hollow voice in which he said to me, "*Nobody is quite well.*" After that I never saw him again.'

Mrs. Duncan Stewart described Lady Beaconsfield as originally a factory-girl. Mr. Lewis first saw her going to her factory, beautiful, and with bare feet. He educated her and married her, died, and left her very rich, and then she married Disraeli. When asked *why* she married her second husband, she would say, as if it was a feather in her cap, 'My dear, he made love to me whilst my first husband was alive, and therefore I know that he really loved me.'

On the 11th of March I again left England for Italy. I could not endure leaving Holmhurst and my dear old nurse, but it seemed necessary to go to finish collecting materials for my book on Southern Italy, as there were still so many places which I had not seen. At Rome I paid an interesting visit to the blind Duke of Sermoneta, still full of mental vigour, and of indignation at '*la stupidézza del Vaticano e l'infámia del Quirinale* [the foolishness of the Vatican and the infamy of the Quirinale].' Miss Garden had been to see him, and defended the policy of the Quirinal, saying Italy was a young country, would come round, &c. He retorted, 'If you say that from politeness, as I think you do, you are wrong; but if you really think so, you must be an idiot.' This was my last visit to the kind old Duke, for he died in the following autumn.

At Naples, returning at night from the hotels in the lower town to those on the ridge of the hill, a gentleman engaged me in conversation and strolled along by my side. Suddenly, in the most desolate part of the road, he blew a whistle, and another man leapt out of the bushes, and both rushing upon me demanded '*L'orológio e la bórsa* [Your watch and purse].' I declared that I had neither watch nor purse. They insisted on my turning out all my pockets, which contained only three francs in paper and sixteen soldi in copper. Then they demanded my ring. I refused, and said it was no use for them to try to get it; it had not been off my finger for more than thirty years: it would not come off. They struggled to get it off, but could not. Then they whispered together. I said, 'I see what you mean to do: you mean to cut off my finger and then drop me into the sea (which there—opposite the Boschetto—is deep water); but remember, I shall be missed and looked for.'—'No, we took good care to ascertain that first,' said my first acquaintance; 'you said you had only been two days in Naples (and so I had): people who have been only two days in Naples are never missed.'—'But I do know Naples well—*bisogna esaminarmi sopra Napoli* [you must ask me about Naples],' I protested.

'*Dunque chi fu la Principessa Altamonti* [Then who is the Princess Altamonti]?'—'*Fu figlia del Conte Cini di Roma, sorella della Duchessa Cirella* [She is the daughter of Count Cini of Rome and the sister of the Duchess Cirella].'—'*E chi è il Principe S. Teodoro* [And who is Prince S. Teodoro].'—'*Fu Duca di S. Arpino, se maritava con una signora Inglese, Lady Burghersh, chi sta adesso Lady Walsingham* [He is Duke of S. Arpino, who married an English lady, Lady Burghersh, who is now Lady Walsingham].' After this they decided to let me go! But the strangest part of all was that the first brigand said, 'After this scene you will not

SCILLA

be able to walk home, and a carriage from the *guardia* costs sixty centesimi; therefore that sum I shall give you back,' and they counted twelve soldi[1] from the sum they had taken. It is this fact which makes me speak of the men who attacked me at Naples as brigands, not as robbers.

I spent a few days delightfully in beautiful Capri, but most miserable were my after travels in the desolate wind-stricken plains or malaria-teeming swamps of wretched Calabria, of which I had formed a lofty estimate from Lear's almost wholly imaginary drawings. Each place I had to visit seemed uglier and more poverty-stricken than the last, but perhaps came to a climax at Cotrone, where the windowless prison-van (being the only vehicle in the town) was sent to meet us, arriving by the

---

[1] Twelve soldi = about sixpence at that time. 100 centisimi = 20 soldi = 1 lira.

night-train at the distant desolate station, and where the stairs of the hotel were crowded with beggars, who had nowhere else to sleep, lying in heaps, and swarming with vermin.

I see that I wrote to Miss Leycester—'Calabria was indescribably horrible, its poisonous swamps and arid plains too hideous for words: nothing whatever but dry bread to eat: the so-called inns the filthiest of hovels: the people ruffians: the remains of the Greek cities a few stones apiece.' I pushed on to Reggio and Scilla. But soon I became so ill that I fled to Venice, where I was fit for nothing but to float in a gondola on the breast of ocean till I grew better.

JOURNAL.

Venice, April 25, 1882.—It was by a happy accident that I found myself here on St. Mark's Day. Madame von Usedom[1] called for me in her gondola, and we went together to S. Marco at 10 A.M. Most glorious it looked, glints of sunlight falling here and there on the golden walls, and waving peacock-hued pavement, and violet shadows resting on all the inner recesses of arcades and cupolas, through which the grand mosaic forms of the saints were dimly visible. Crowds of people were present, yet in that vast space many thousands can move with ease. It is only a few days since the Patriarch, newly elected and a cardinal, entered Venice in triumph, followed by three hundred gondolas, standing at the prow of his barge, in his new scarlet robes, blessing the people. He is a young man, but is greatly beloved, and every eye followed him as the grand procession swept chaunting round the church, and he was almost borne along by his huge golden robes, held up by the white-mitred attendant bishops of Chioggia and Torcello.

In the afternoon the Comtesse de Lützow took me to see Besarel, a very remarkable self-taught genius, and a very good simple man and sculptor in wood and marble: and then we floated peacefully for hours through the labyrinthine streets of this wonderful water-city. In the evening, as I was sitting with the Lützows and Lady Augusta Cadogan at one of the tables in the piazza in front of Florian's caffè, a table near was occupied by a party in which the conspicuous figures were a lady, not old, but with snow-white hair, and a very beautiful young woman, sipping *graniti* and listening to the music: they were Queen Mary and Princess Mary of Hanover.

I returned to England by way of Nüremberg, which seemed to me strangely smaller and less interesting than when I saw it as a boy, and was more thankful than ever before to find myself again, on the 10th of May, at Holmhurst, where my dear old Lea's most sweet and beautiful old face welcomed me with a brighter smile than ever.

At Venice a great sorrow had come to me—another blank in the narrowing circle of my beloved ones. It was the sort of sorrow from which "all at once one awakes and finds a whole wing of one's palace has fallen," as Emerson says. Dearest Hugh Pearson was dead. He has left the most undimmed memory it is possible for man to leave. To none of those

---

[1] Olympia, Countess von Usedom, eldest daughter of Sir John Malcolm.

who knew him is it possible that there can be even a breath upon the mirror of his perfectly beautiful and lovable life.

London, June 22.—Tea with Mrs. Duncan Stewart, who, talking of her youth, recounted how Washington Irving had taken her eleven nights consecutively to see Talma act, and of the acting of Madame Rachel; how, in the 'Cinna' of Corneille, she sat quietly in a chair whilst all the people were raging round her, and of the wonderful power with which she hissed out—

> 'Je recevrois de lui la place de Livie,
> Comme un moyen plus sur d'attenter à sa vie.'

Mr. and Mrs. Kendal were there,[1] a pleasant handsome pair; and Madame Modjeska came in, and taking a live chameleon, which was clinging to the breast of Miss Thompson, her pet, posed with it perched on her finger, though it looked the very incarnation of devildom.

In the beginning of September, my friend Harry Lee came to Holmhurst as usual for his autumn holidays, and, with the wish of giving him change and pleasure, I took him with me for a fortnight to Holland. We saw the whole of that little country, and enjoyed several of the places very much, especially the so-thoroughly Dutch Dort; quiet Alkmaar, with its charming old weigh-house; and Zwolle, with its fine old gateway. But the tour is not one which leaves much interest behind it. There is such a disadvantage in not being able to understand what people say, and all the Dutch we had anything to do with were so unaccommodating, so excessively grasping and avaricious. Besides, all my luggage, registered through to Brussels, disappeared and could not be traced, so that I had the odd experience of traversing a whole country with nothing more than a comb and a tooth-brush. Two months afterwards the luggage arrived quite safe at Holmhurst, covered with labels, quite intact, having made a long tour by itself quite in a different direction from the one we took, and without any explanation or any expense.

JOURNAL.

Babworth Hall, Notts, Oct. 7, 1882.—Yesterday we went by appointment to Welbeck, arriving by the darksome tunnel, more than two miles long, upon which the late Duke[2] spent £60,000, and £60,000 more apiece upon banking up (and spoiling) his sheet of water with brick walls and building a gigantic riding-school. The house itself stands well, considering the ugliness of the park, and is rather handsome. We were shown through a long suite of rooms containing a good many treasures, the most interesting being a glorious old chest of metal, in which the Bentincks, who came over with William III, brought over their jewels. In the last room we found Lady Bolsover, the Duke's stepmother.

---

[1] William Hunter Kendal and Margaret Robertson, actors.

[2] William John Cavendish Bentinck-Scott, fifth Duke of Portland, 1800–1879, A staunch Tory but did not distinguish himself either in the Commons or the Lords. The race-course and his estates occupied most of his time. He was a bachelor and a recluse, but he gave an immense amount of money to charity.—*Ed.*

G

The house, vast as it is, has no staircase worth speaking of. The late Duke lived almost entirely in a small suite of rooms in the old part of the house. He inherited the peculiarity of his mother, who would see no one, and he always hid himself. If he gave permission to any one to visit Welbeck, he always added, 'But Mr. So-and-so will be good enough not to *see* me' (if they chanced to meet). He drove out, but in a black coach like a hearse, drawn by four black horses, and with all the blinds down; and he walked out, but at night, with a woman, who was never to speak to him, and always to walk exactly forty yards in front carrying a lanthorn. When he went to London, it was in a closed brougham, which was put on a railway truck, and which deposited him at his own house at Cavendish Square, his servants all being ordered out of the way: no one ever saw him go or arrive. When he needed a doctor, the doctor only came to the door, and asked questions through it of the valet, who was allowed to feel his pulse.

The Duke's mania for a hidden life made him build immense suites of rooms underground, only approachable by a common flight of steps leading to a long tunnel, down which the dinner is conveyed from the far-distant kitchen on a tramway. From a great library one enters a billiard-room capable of holding half-a-dozen billiard-tables. A third large room leads to an enormous ball-room, which can contain 2000 people. The approach to this from above is by means of a gigantic hydraulic drop, in which a carriage can be placed, or twenty persons can be accommodated—the guests being thus let down to the ball-room itself. A staircase through the ceiling of one of the rooms, which is drawn up by a windlass, leads hence to the old riding-school, which is lighted by 1000 jets of gas. Hence a tunnel, 200 yards long, leads to a quadrangle piece of ground, unbuilt upon, but excavated in preparation for a large range of bachelor's rooms, smoking rooms, and nurseries, to cover four acres of ground. Another tunnel, three-quarters of a mile long, leads thence to the stables, cow-houses, and dairies, like a large village. At the Duke's death there were ninety-four horses in the stables, only trained for exercise or feeding. Beyond the stables is a large riding-school, in which there are 8000 jets of gas, an exercising ground under glass, with a gallop on straw and sawdust for a quarter of a mile. Close by is an enormous garden, of which six acres are used for strawberry beds, every alternate row being glazed for forcing the plants. Alongside of this is a glazed wall a quarter of a mile long. The garden is about thirty acres in extent, and requires fifty-three men. In the late Duke's time there were forty-five grooms and helpers in the stables. The cow-houses are palaces, with a covered strawyard attached, and are surrounded by hydraulic screens, which are let down or raised according to the wind. There were eighty keepers and underkeepers.

All is vast, splendid, and utterly comfortless: one could imagine no more awful and ghastly fate than waking up one day and finding oneself Duke of Portland and master of Welbeck.

Alas! whilst I was enjoying this Babworth visit, the greatest sorrow which still remained possible for me was preparing, and a few days later it fell. It would be difficult for any one who had not shared our life to understand how much my dearest old nurse, Mary Lea, was to me, or the many causes which, with each succeeding year, had drawn closer and closer the tender tie, as of mother and son, which existed between us.

JOURNAL.

Oct. 11, 1882.—Yesterday two terrible telegrams met me when I went to my breakfast at the Athenæum, telling me that my dearest Lea was dangerously ill, and bidding me return at once. In half-an-hour I was in the train. I found the carriage at St. Leonards, having been waiting five hours, with a perfectly hopeless account.

Thursday, Oct. 12.—Last night she slept quietly, and her two nurses by her. I went in and out continuously, and she scarcely moved. In the morning she was better, and able to sit in the arm-chair near her bed. It was the day on which we always used to try to leave for Rome, and she spoke of it, and this drew her into many pleasant recollections, such as the dear Mother had on her last day here; of the anemones in the Villa Doria at Rome, and the especial corners in which the best were to be found; of the daisies in the Parco S. Gregorio, and of many happy hours spent in other favourite places.

Oct. 15.—Last night was better, but all to-day she has been terribly ill. It is such a struggle to breathe through her worn-out frame. I sit constantly by her side, and chafe her hands and bathe her forehead, and can be quite cheerful for her sake; and she smiles to see me always there whenever she wakes.

Wednesday, Oct. 19.—At night she was terribly worse. Oh, it was so hard to see her suffer,—so very, very hard. Soon after midnight I gave dose after dose of laudanum, and when she was still, lay down—sank down, utterly worn-out. At 3 A.M. I heard Harriet's voice, 'Aunt is gone.' All was still then—the agony lived through, the fight fought. As I rushed into the room, the colour was fading out of my darling Pettie's cheeks, but her face and hands were still warm. A wonderful look of rest was stealing over the beloved features. I knelt down and said the bidding prayer. Truly we 'gave thanks' that our dearest one was at rest. Yet I felt—oh, so stunned, so helpless!

Oct. 23.—In the morning I went into her room to see my dearest Pettie for the last time. Lady Darnley had sent a box of lovely flowers, and I laid them round her. At eleven I set off alone, in a little carriage, by the familiar lanes. It was the loveliest of autumnal days, and all was in its richest, most touching beauty.

Soon after 2 P.M. the little procession appeared over the brow of the hill, the bearers, in white smock-frocks, walking by the carriages. I followed the coffin alone first, then all the servants from Holmhurst and many poor women from Lime Cross. The grave was by my Mother's side, in the same little garden enclosure. It was strange to feel that the next funeral there must be my own, and to look down upon her coffin on which my own will rest some day.

After the others were gone I walked in the old deer-park. I felt as if I was a spirit haunting the place. All was peace and loveliness, but how great the change from the time when I was there so constantly! All the familiar figures of my childhood are swept away—all the uncles and aunts, brothers and sister; all the old neighbours; nearly all the old friends; all the old homes too are broken up, pulled down, or deserted; only I and the ruins of the castle seem left.

VIII

IN THE FURROWS OF LIFE

1883–85

❧

JOURNAL.

June 19.—Dined with Lady Airlie, only meeting Mrs. Duncan Stewart and Lady De Clifford. Mrs. Stewart talked much of Mr. Carlyle.

'Mr. Hannay[1] knew Carlyle very well, and often went to see him, but it was in his poorer days. One day when Mr. Hannay went to the house, he saw two gold sovereigns lying exposed in a little vase on the chimney-piece. He asked Carlyle what they were for. Carlyle looked—for him—embarrassed, but gave no definite answer. "Well, now, my dear fellow," said Mr. Hannay, "neither you nor I are quite in a position to play ducks and drakes with sovereigns: what *are* these for?"—"Well," said Carlyle, "the fact is, Leigh Hunt likes better to find them there than that I should give them to him."

'I was sitting once by Mr. Bourton,' said Mrs. Stewart, 'and he was talking of Leigh Hunt. "He said, 'He is the only person, I believe, who, if he saw something yellow in the distance, and was told it was a buttercup, would be disappointed if he found it was only a guinea." '

Lady Airlie said she had known Leigh Hunt very well when she was a child. He had taken her into the garden, and talked to her, and asked her what she thought heaven would be like, and then he said, 'I will tell you what I think it will be like: I think it will be like a most beautiful arbour all hung with creepers and flowers, and that one will be able to sit in it all day, and read a most interesting novel.'

Of her early acquaintance with Washington Irving, Mrs. Stewart said, 'It was at Havre. My guardian was consul there. People used to say, "Where is Harriet gone?" and he answered, "Oh, she is down at the end of the terrace, busy making Washington Irving believe he is God Almighty, and he is busy believing it." '

June 21.—At Madame du Quaire's I met Oscar Wilde and Mrs. Stewart. He talked in a way intended to be very startling, but she startled him by saying quietly, 'You poor dear foolish boy! how can you talk such nonsense?' Mr. M. L. had recently met this 'type of an aesthetic age' at a country house, and described his going out shooting in a black velvet dress with salmon-coloured stockings, and falling down when the gun went off, yet captivating all the ladies by his pleasant talk. One day he came down looking very pale. 'I am afraid you are ill, Mr. Wilde,' said one of the party. 'No, not ill, only tired,' he answered. 'The fact is, I picked a primrose in the wood yesterday, and it was so ill, I have been sitting up with it all night.' Oscar Wilde's oddities would attract notice anywhere, but of course they do so ten times more in the *plein midi* of London society, where the smallest faults of manner, most of all of assumption, are detected and exposed at once.

[1] James Hannay, novelist and essayist, 1827–1873.—*Ed.*

180

July 2, 1883.—I have just heard again the ghost story so often told by Mrs. Thompson Hankey:

Two beautiful but penniless sisters were taken out in London by an aunt. A young gentleman from the north, of very good family and fortune, fell in love with one of them, and proposed to her, but she was with difficulty persuaded to accept him, and afterwards could never be induced to fix a date for their marriage. The young man, who was very much in love, urged and urged, but, on one excuse or another, he was always put off. Whilst things were in this unsettled state, the young lady was invited to a ball. Her lover implored her not to go to it, and when she insisted, he made her promise not to dance any round dances, saying that if she did, he should believe she had ceased to care for him.

The young lady went to the ball, and, as usual, all the young men gathered round her, trying to persuade her to dance. She refused any but square dances. At last, however, as a delightful valse was being played, and she was standing looking longingly on, she suddenly felt herself seized round the waist, and hurried into the dance. Not till she reached the end of the room, very angry, did she succeed in seeing with whom she had been forced to dance: it was with her own betrothed. Furious, she said she should never forgive him. But, as she spoke, he disappeared. She begged several young men to look for him, but he could not be found anywhere, and, to her astonishment, every one denied altogether having seen him. On reaching home, she found a telegram telling her of his death, and when the hours were compared, he was found to have died at the very moment when he had seized her for the dance.

Mrs. Thompson Hankey knew all the persons concerned.

During the summer of 1883, I left England to join my oft-times travelling companions, the Miss Hollands, for a tour in Russia. I did not greatly enjoy this tour, partly because I felt so terrible knowing almost nothing of the language of the country, not being able to read even the names of the streets. I also suffered from not having had time to teach myself anything of the country before I went there: for, after I came home, and tried to instruct my mind by every book I could get hold of about Russia, I found my travels had been much more interesting than, from the very intensity of my ignorance, I believed them to be at the time.

At Kieff I left my companions, and found my way home alone by Warsaw and by Cracow, with its curious monuments and odious Jew population. After the great discomforts of Russia, a very few days in Germany seemed very charming, and I was especially glad to see beautiful old Breslau, and afterwards Wilhelmshohe near Cassel, in a perfect conflagration of splendid autumnal tints.

To MISS LEYCESTER.

St. Petersburg, August 22, 1883.—A rest in the interesting group of North-German cities, Dantzic, Marienburg, Königsberg, prepared us for the thirty-six hours' journey through monotonous fir-woods and cornfields, unvaried through 1000 miles, till two great purple domes rose on the horizon—St. Alexander Newski and the Cathedral of St. Isaac.

It was difficult to believe we were in Europe on emerging from the station and seeing the endless droskies—sledges on wheels—drawn up, with their extraordinary looking drivers, in long blue dressing-gowns (wadded like feather-beds, so as to make the wearer look like a huge pillow), with a girdle, and low cap. Then the gigantic streets, each about as broad as St. James's Square, and the huge squares, in which the palaces, however vast, are so disproportioned to the immensity of space, that their architectural features are lost. Then the utter desolation, one carriage and two or three foot-passengers in the apparently boundless vistas. Altogether, St. Petersburg is quite the ugliest place I ever saw, even the Neva, huge as it is, so black and grim, and the smoke of the steamers giving the worst aspects of London.

Sept. 4.—We returned last night from Finland, of which I am glad to have visited a specimen, though there is not much to see, except gloomy little lakes, flat country, hundreds of miles of monotonous forests of young firs and birch, and little wooden villages. All is very much like an inferior Sweden, and the people understand Swedish,

CATHEDRAL OF ST. ISAAC, ST. PETERSBURG

and have the Swedish characteristics of honesty and civility, which, at so short a distance off, make them an extraordinary contrast to the Russians. Our journey was amusingly varied by endless changes of rail, steamer, walk, char-a-banc, as the country allowed.

Moscow, Sept. 9.—We left St. Petersburg on Monday, and went to Novgorod the Great, one of the oldest cities in Russia, once enormous, but now dwindled to a large village, with a decaying kremlin and a wonderful cathedral like a mosque, a blaze of beautiful ancient colour within, quite splendid in its gold and silver decorations, and the shrines of sixteen famous saints (the Greek saints are most puzzling) who are buried there, and whose mummified hands, left outside their cerecloths, are exposed to the kisses of the faithful. A journey of nineteen hours' rail brought us here on Thursday morning. The first impression of Moscow is disappointing—commonplace omnibuses at the station, ugly vulgar streets like the back-streets of Brighton, and, as the town is above twenty miles round and nine miles across, they seem endless. But you enter the Chinese town, in which we are now living, by gates in the strangest walls imaginable, and the street has all the crowd and clamour of Naples.

Kieff, 'The Holy City,' Sept. 21.—We made excursions from Moscow to all the great monasteries. There are few other sights of importance, but these, in Russia, are quite unique—immense spaces surrounded by walls, towers, and gates, which have stood many a siege, and which are like the towns in old woodcuts, and contain gardens, cemeteries, cathedrals, usually six churches with gilt domes and minarets, besides accommodation for 600 or 800 monks and nuns, who have their wells, gardens, farms, &c. Then we went to the New Jerusalem, where the famous Nikon lived and is buried —many hours jolting along a no-road through the forests in a rough tarantass, but a beautiful place when you get there.

The journey to Kieff by a slow train was terrible, lasting two days, and a night and awfully hot—across a hideous brown steppe the whole way, with scarcely a tree to vary it. To-day, however, has quite satisfied me that it was worth while to come, It

THE HOLY CHAPEL OF KIEFF

is a most unique and beautiful place, the vast town, or rather three great towns, so embosomed in trees and gardens, that the houses are almost lost. But the greatest charm lies in the constant view over the glorious Dnieper, and the immense aërial plain beyond, with its delicate pink lights and blue shadows. Then Kieff is the Mecca of Russia, full of tombs of saints and holy images, and, though this is no special season, the thousands and thousands of pilgrims are most extraordinary—in sheep-skins and goat-skins, in fur caps, high-peaked head-dresses and turbans; in azure blue, bright pink, or pale primrose colour. I never could have believed without seeing it the reverence of the Russian religion, and it has seemed the same everywhere and in all classes. The bowing and curvetting and crossing before the icons is most extraordinary, and still more so the three prostrations which all make on approaching any holy place, bending down and kissing the dust in a way worthy of an acrobat, though treated as a matter of course by the devotees themselves.

In the Warsaw train, Sept. 25.—In this smoothly gliding train, which takes one in fifty-four weary hours across the steppes, it is as easy to write as in the study at home. I should be most comfortable if it were not that my companion (in the compartment for two) is the most odious type of American I ever came across. 'I guess you will not want to have the windows of this carriage opened till you get to Warsaw, because I will not submit to it: I am in my right, and I will *not* submit to it.'

We were arrested again yesterday at Kieff, though then only by priests—veiled priests—for daring to sketch the outside of one of their sacred chapels; but after being hurried about from place to place for an hour, and shut up in a courtyard, with a wooden bench to sit upon, for another, we were regaled with a pile of beautiful grapes and apples, and sent about our business.

Warsaw, Sept. 27.—We arrived at the junction station of Brest more than two hours late, for on some of the Russian lines no hours are obligatory, and you are quite at the mercy of conductors and their whims for spending ten, thirty, or even forty minutes in gossiping at side stations. So the Warsaw train had left Brest, and we had five hours to wait for another. Ill and wretched, I left the horrible room where a crowd of people were smoking, spitting, and *smelling*, and made my way to a sort of deserted public garden, where cows were browsing on the lilacs. Here, from mere want of something to do, I began to sketch some cottages and bushes, when I was suddenly seized by two soldiers and carried off to the guard-house. Here a very furious bombastical old major cross-examined me, and went into a passion over each sketch in my book, with volleys of questions about each, and then he sent me with a military escort to the station to fetch my passport. It was right, of course, and at last, after several hours, I was dismissed with '*Maintenant c'est fini;*' but after a quadruple walk of two miles each way, and over such a pavement as only Russia can supply.

I never was at Warsaw before, and should not care to stay.

I spent the autumn of 1883 very quietly at Holmhurst, but paid some visits in the winter.

To Miss Leycester.

London, Feb. 23.—My dear Mrs. Duncan Stewart is dead. Her last words were 'Higher, higher!' and we may believe that she has passed into those higher regions where her thirst after life, not repose, meets it full fruition. There were few equal to her. Mrs. Proctor is most so. I met her the other day, and some one made her a pretty speech. She said, 'When I was very young, Sydney Smith said to me, "My dear, do you like flattery?"—"Very much indeed," I answered, "but I do not like it put on with a trowel." What I really do like is—in the words of Sterne—a few delicate attentions, not so vague as to be bewildering, and not so pointed as to be embarrassing.'

Ill-health in June made a happy excuse for my spending a delightful month abroad. I saw first the group of towns around Laon, charming old-fashioned Noyon, beautiful Soissons, and Coucy, with its grand castle. Then Alick Pitt met me at Thun, and we spent a delightful time at Mürren and Rosenlaui, sketching and flower-picking, and reawakening every slumbering sense of the delights of Switzerland.

JOURNAL.

Oct. 10.—Since I returned from Switzerland, my home life has been quite happy and uneventful. Only ten days ago I had a telegram from 'my Prince' (of Sweden and Norway), asking me to come and spend Sunday afternoon and evening with him at Eastbourne, as he was only there for two days. He met me most cordially and affectionately, making me feel as if the seeming neglect of several years was only 'royalty's way,' and pleasantly taking up all the dropped threads of life. We were several hours together, and while we were talking a sweet-faced young lady looked in. 'I must come in: you are such a friend of the Prince: I have heard of you, too, all my life. I am so very glad to see you at last,'—and I felt at once that the Crown-Princess was a friend. She wanted to know what I thought of the Prince—the Prince wanted to know what I thought of her: I was glad to be able to answer both most satisfactorily.[1]

NOYON

Highcliffe, Oct. 26, 1884.—Lady Waterford says that the father of that Thérèse Longworth who called herself Lady Avonmore was a young clerk at Bordeaux at the time of the Noyades. Two beautiful young girls were tied together, and were going to be drowned. Suddenly a poissarde, seized with compassion from their looks, jumped upon a barrel and shouted 'Are there no young men here who will save the lives of these two beautiful girls by marrying them?' Longworth and another young fellow were looking out of a window at the time and heard it, and said to one another, 'Shall we do it?' It was rather a gulp, for they were both very young at the time; but they went down and said they would, and they were both married there and then, by joining hands after the fashion of the Commune. The daughter of one of those marriages was Thérèse Longworth.[2]

[1] Crown Prince Gustav married Victoria, the daughter of the Duke of Baden.—*Ed.*

[2] Maria Thérèsa Longworth married William Charles Yelverton in Ireland in 1857. Yelverton (later Viscount Avonmore) repudiated the marriage and afterwards married the widow of Professor Forbes. The validity of the first marriage was upheld in Ireland, but it was annulled in Scotland, and the Scottish verdict was confirmed in the Lords.—*Ed.*

G*

Goldings, Herts, Nov. 20.—Isabel Smith says that a lady in Wales, a friend of Miss Frances Wynne, looked up suddenly one day after reading the obituary in the *Times*, and exclaimed, 'Now, at last, my lips are unsealed.' Then she told this:—

One day she had been alone at her country-house in Wales, with her son and a friend of his. She had received all the money for her rents that day—a very large sum—and put it away in a strong box. Being asked, she said she did not mind the least having it in her room, and should sleep with the key under her pillow.

When she had been in bed some time, she was aware that her door opened, and that a man in a cloak came into her room with a candle. He passed the candle before her face, but she lay with closed eyes, perfectly motionless. Then he felt for the key; he felt for a long time, but somehow he failed to find it. At last he went away.

As soon as the door closed, she sprang out of bed, intending to go to her son's room to warn him that a robber was in the house. But his room was a long way off, and she thought it would be better to go instead to the friend, whose room was nearer.

As she opened the door suddenly, she saw a figure muffled up in a long cloak put down the candle. It was the same figure who had come into her room. She looked at him fixedly. 'To-morrow at 9 A.M.,' she said, 'the dogcart will come to the door which was to have taken my strong box to the bank: you will go in that dogcart, and you will never enter my door again. If you never attempt to do this, I will never say a word on what has happened as long as you live.' And she never did, even to her son.

Nov. 21.—We have spent the day at Knebworth, an interesting place, though full of shams—a sham old house, with a sham lake, sham heraldic monsters, sham ancient portraits, &c. Lord Lytton,[1] with his velvet collar and gold chains, recalled his father, who is represented on the walls, with his boots pointed like a needle, in a picture by Maclise. Lady Lytton, beautiful, charming, and courteous, looked like a queen in the large saloons and galleries.

I wish one did not know that the real name of the Lyttons is Wiggett. William Wiggett took the name of Bulwer on his marriage with Sarah Bulwer in 1756, and his youngest son (the novelist) took the name of Lytton on succeeding to his mother's property of Knebworth, she being one Elizabeth Warburton, whose very slight connection with the real Lytton family consisted in the fact that her grandfather, John Robinson was cousin (maternally) to Lytton Strode, who was great-nephew of a Sir William Lytton, who died childless in 1704.

I have had the small trial of another 'call' of £300 on those unfortunate Electric Lights in which St. George Lane Fox involved me. I had saved up the money, so it was there, but it was provoking to have to pay what is almost certain to be lost, yet to be obliged to do so, as the only chance of seeing again any part of the £7000 which had gone before it. However, I am never more than very temporarily troubled by such things—there is no use. All I have ever made by my writings in fourteen very hard-worked years is gone now through St. G. Lane Fox—there is nothing else left to lose.

Babworth, Dec. 14.—Mrs. Drummond Baring has been most agreeable in her talk of the society at Paris under the Empire, the *soirées intimes*, at which all etiquette was laid aside, and Prosper Merimée, Théophile Gautier, &c., were seen at their best. No one knew so much about the Empress as Merimée. He had known her well

---

[1] Edward Robert Bulwer-Lytton, statesman, diplomatist and poet, 1831–91, first Earl of Lytton and son of the novelist. Was Viceroy of India from 1876–80 and Ambassador in Paris, 1887–91. Proclaimed Queen Victoria Empress of India at Delhi. Published various volumes of verse and his official despatches are examples of an exquisite prose style.—*Ed.*

as a girl, and all the letters about the marriage had passed through his hands. Nothing could be more naïve than the Empress in her early married days. She *would* go shopping. She clapped her hands with delight at the opera-bouffe, and the Emperor took them and held them, to the great delight of the people, who applauded vehemently.

In the last days at the Tuileries, all the court ladies were only occupied in packing up their own things; all deserted their mistress except Madame le Breton. She and the Empress stayed to the last. The Empress asked General Tronchim how long the palace could hold out. He said, 'Certainly three days.' It did not hold out three hours. They fled as the people entered, fled precipitately by the long galleries of the Louvre, once in agony finding a door locked and having to look for the key. The Empress had no bonnet. Madame le Breton, with a bit of lace, made something for her head. They reached the street and hailed a cab. '*Eh! ma petite mère*,' said the driver, '*il parait que nous nous sauvons: où est el papa donc* [Well, little mother, it seems as if we're running away: but where's papa]?' But he took them and did not recognise them. They went in the cab to the Boulevard Haussmann. Then they found that they had no money to pay it, and Madame le Breton took off one of her rings. 'We have forgotten our money,' she said, 'but you see how suffering my friend is. I *must* take her on to the dentist, but I will leave this with you; give me your address and I will redeem it.' And he let them go.

They took a second cab to the house of Evans, the American dentist, and there found he was gone to his villa at Passy. They followed him there, but when they reached the villa, the servant said he was out, and positively refused to let them in. But Madame le Breton insisted—her friend was so terribly ill; Mr. Evans knew her very well: she was quite certain that he would see her: and at length she almost forced her way in, and, moreover, made the servant pay the cab. At last Mr. Evans came in. He had been to Paris, in terrible anxiety as to the fate of the Empress, knowing that the mob had broken into the Tuileries.

Hickledon, Dec. 17.—Mrs. George Portal of Burgclere told Charlie Wood that when Allan Herbert was so ill at Highclere—ill to death, it was supposed—the nurse, who was sitting up, saw an old lady come into the room when he was at the worst, gaze at him from the foot of the bed, and nod her head repeatedly. When he was better, and after he could be left, the housekeeper, wishing to give the nurse a little distraction, showed her through the rooms, and, in Lord Carnarvon's sitting-room, the nurse suddenly pointed at the portrait over the chimney-piece and said, 'That is the lady who came into the sick-room.' The portrait was that of old Lady Carnarvon, Allan Herbert's mother, and the servants well recollected her peculiar way of nodding her head repeatedly.

Mount St. John, Dec. 20.—To-day was Lord Halifax's birthday.[1] The hounds met at Hickledon, wishing to do him honour, but it was almost too much for him. With me, I think it has been a pleasure to him to go back into old days, old memories, old sketchbooks, &c. I cannot say how much I enjoyed my visit to the kind old man, as well as to my own dear Charlie—better, dearer, more charming than ever, and more in favour, one feels sure, with God as well as with man. Yet Charlie does not wish to die: his life here is so perfectly happy and useful, but he says that it must be 'very unpleasant to God to feel that His children never wish to come home: he is sure *he* should feel it so with his children.' He says he is quite certain what the pains of

---

[1] His eighty-fourth. He died the following year.—*Ed.*

Purgatory will be—'they will be the realising for the first time the love of God, and not being able to do anything for Him: this life is our only chance.' He says he is 'sure that the next life will be in a more beautiful world, like this, only glorified, and so much, oh? so much better in everything. "Such cats!" my Uncle Courtenay says, "*such* cats!" '

Young Charlie came home yesterday, a most delightful boy, only less engaging perhaps than little Francis.[1] To me, these children of my dear brother-like friend are what no other children can ever be.

Whitburn, Dec. 28.—I stayed a few hours in Durham as I passed through, and found what is so picturesque in summer unbearably black and dismal in winter. The present Dean (Lake), who has so spoilt the cathedral, is most unpopular.[2] One day he had taken upon himself to lecture Mr. Greenwell, one of the minor canons, for doing his part in the service in thick laced boots. Greenwell was furious. Rushing out of the cathedral, he met Archdeacon Bland, the most polite and deliberate of men, and exclaimed, 'I've been having the most odious time with the Dean, and I really think he must have got the devil in him.'—'No, Mr. Greenwell, no, no, not that,' said Archdeacon Bland in his quiet way; 'he is only possessed by three imps: he is imperious, he is impetuous, and he is impertinent.'

Brancepeth Castle, Jan. 3, 1885.—Mr. Wharton dined. He said, 'When I was at the little inn at Ayscliffe, I met a Mr. Bond, who told me a story about my friend Johnnie Greenwood of Swancliffe. Johnnie had to ride one night through a wood a mile long to the place he was going to. At the entrance of the wood a large black dog joined him, and pattered along by his side. He could not make out where it came from, but it never left him, and when the wood grew so dark that he could not see it, he still heard it pattering beside him. When he emerged from the wood, the dog had disappeared, and he could not tell where it had gone to. Well, Johnnie paid his visit, and set out to return the same way. At the entrance of the wood, the dog joined him, and pattered along beside him as before; but it never touched him, and he never spoke to it, and again, as he emerged from the wood, it ceased to be there.

'Years after, two condemned prisoners in York gaol told the chaplain that they had intended to rob and murder Johnnie that night in the wood, but that he had a large dog with him, and when they saw that, they felt that Johnnie and the dog together would be too much for them.'

'Now that is what I call a useful ghostly apparition,' said Mr. Wharton.

March 19.—Edward Malet[3] was married to Lady Ermyntrude Russell in Westminster Abbey at 4 P.M. Seldom was there a greater crowd in the streets near Westminster. I met Lady Jane Repton in the crush, and we made our way in together through the Deanery. The glorious building was crowded from end to end, and the music most beautiful. Perhaps the greatest of smaller features was Lady Ermyntrude's dress, which the papers describe as 'more pearly than pearl, and more snowy than snow.'

[1] The third boy, Henry Wood, died in London, June 6, 1886. The second son, Francis, died at Eton, March 17, 1889. The beloved eldest son, Charlie, died at Hickledon, September 1890.—*Ed.*

[2] Much damage was done by Jas. Wyatt's earlier restoration of 1778–80. The restoration referred to here was carried out by Sir George Gilbert Scott and in very doubtful taste.—*Ed.*

[3] Later Sir Edward Malet, 4th baronet, diplomatist and envoy to Berlin, 1884–95.—*Ed.*

March 28.—Dining at Mrs. Quin's, I met Mrs. Ward, who was very amusing. She described the airs of Frances-Anne, Lady Londonderry.[1] One day she was extremely irritated with her page, and sent him to Lord Londonderry with a note, in which she had written in pencil, 'Flog this fellow well for me: he has been quite unendurable.' But the page read the note on the way, and meeting one of the great magnificent flunkeys, six feet high, said, 'Just oblige me by taking this note in to my lord: I am forced to do something else.' The flunkey brought out the answer, and met the page, who took it in to his lady. She was rather surprised, for it was— 'I'm afraid.' Mrs. Ward was in the house when this happened.

On the 1st of May 1885 I set off on the first of a series of excursions in France for literary purposes, oftentimes of dismal solitude, and always of weary hard work, though full of interest of their own. I found then, as I have always done, how different seeing a thing with intention is to ordinary sight-seeing. As usual, I found that the ordinary English travellers, who are always occupied in playing at 'follow my leader' all the time they are abroad, had missed the best part of France. In the central provinces the accommodation was very good in its way, and the food always excellent, but in some of the places in the Eastern Pyrenees the dirt was scarcely endurable. The excellent hotel at Montpelier came as a real respite. Whilst there, I made some acquaintance with a banker of the place, who had a poetic Ruskin-like way of describing the wildness of the Cevennes, the grey rocks, desolate scenery, long lines of russet landscape. This so took hold of me, that I went to Lodève and engaged a carriage for several days to explore the Cevennes thoroughly. It was wild enough certainly and rather curious, but an unbroken monotone; every view, every rocky foreground, even each dreary ruinous village, repeated the last, and after eight or nine hours I was utterly wearied of it; thus it was an intense relief when my driver came in the evening, with no end of apologies, and said he had received a telegram, bidding him return at once to Lodève; and I was free to jump into the first diligence and reach the nearest station. Railway then took me to Mende, an exceedingly beautiful place, and afterwards to Rodez. Hence I went south again by S. Antonin and Bruniquel, whence beautiful recollections of the spring verdure and clear river come back to me. I made a little tour afterwards to Luchon and other places in the Pyrenees which I had not seen before, and returned straight home from Bordeaux. During this two months' tour I do not think I ever saw an English person, even in the railway, and I made no acquaintances.

[1] Frances-Anne, daughter and heiress of Sir Henry Vane Tempest, who (1819) became the second wife of the 3rd Marquis of Londonderry, Charles William Stewart, who thereupon changed his name to Vane.—*Ed.*

To Miss Leycester.

Brive, May 15.—I feel like a child eating through a cake, feeling it a duty not to leave anything remarkable unseen in this part of France, so little known to the English. How unfairly those judge this country who measure France by what they see from the well-known railways to Strasbourg or Marseilles. Nothing can be more beautiful than these hills and valleys of the Creuse and Correze, nothing more rich than the forest-clad country, besides the interest of endless castles and later châteaux, of old towns where the greater proportion of the houses date from the thirteenth century, and of perfectly honest, primitive, and unspoilt people.

I came to Limoges last Friday, and remained there five days, that is to say, was scarcely there at all, but returned to a good hotel there at night. I saw the great castle of Chalusset; the romanesque Abbey of Solignac; S. Junien, a most grand church; Le Dorat, almost as fine; Montmorillon, full of curiosities; and Chalus, where Richard

LE CROZANT

Cœur de Lion was killed, and where, under the old castle he was besieging, the stone called Rocher de Malmont still rises in the water-meadows, upon which he was standing when the fatal arrow struck him.

Then I came here, and am staying here in the same way, breakfasting daily at seven, off at half-past seven, and only returning to go to bed. All yesterday I was at the wonderful sanctuary of Rocamadour—the La Salette of these parts—a most curious place, beautiful exceedingly; indeed, though it sounds a very grand comparison, rather like—Tivoli! But it poured all day, with a bitter wind, and this has been the case every day, only this afternoon there have been lovely lights at the falls of Gimel in the exquisite mountain forests. I am so glad I have no companions: they would never have endured the discomfort. No words can say how tired I am every day, nor how wet, nor how dirty; but I shall be glad afterwards to have done it all.

Carcassonne, May 28.—On Friday 23rd it poured in torrents, but I could not give in, so went by the earliest train as far into the hills as it penetrated, and then by omnibus to Souillac, one of the grand and glorious abbey churches, now parochial, which are so common in that part of France and nowhere else—full of colour and solemnity, though rugged to a degree, and into which you descend by long flights of steps.

It poured in returning too, but I stopped at a wayside station, and a long walk through chalky mud and a ferry over the Dordogne took me to Fénelon, which is a noble old château splendidly placed on a peninsula looking down upon the meeting of many valleys and streams.

Saturday I was up at five, and off by rail and road to Cadouin, another of those grand abbey churches, of the same character as the rest, but with the addition of a splendid gothic cloister. I arrived at nine, perished with wet and cold, but was resuscitated by the kind woman at the little inn, who made a hot fire on the great dogs of her hearth, and soon had hot coffee ready. It was, however, a long day, and I did not arrive till near midnight at Montpazier. This curious Bastide was built by Edward III of England, and has never been touched since his time, and, whilst all is so changed in England, it was interesting to find in this remote French hill-country a town the same as when the Black Prince lived there, with old walls and gates, gothic house-windows, rectangular streets, and in the centre of all the market, surrounded by arcades like those at Padua, only here the arcades are so wide that you can drive *in* them.

Narbonne, June 4.—The wet weather has changed to intense heat. . . . Yesterday was an interesting day, spent entirely at the great convent of Fontefroide, in the mountains nine miles from hence, spared at the late suppression of monasteries on account of the beneficent and useful lives of its monks—of whom there are still more than fifty—the benefactors of the whole of this part of the country, not only in teaching and preaching, but by taking the lead in all industrial and agricultural work. They receive all strangers, and gave me an excellent luncheon, though, being Wednesday, they had only boiled beans for themselves. The mountains all round the monastery were ablaze with cistus—white, pink, and rose-coloured, with yellow salvia and honeysuckle in masses.

Lexos, Aveyron, June 15.—Anything so cheap as 'Untravelled France' it is impossible to imagine. Even at Mende, where it is quite a good hotel, prices were: room—very good, 1 fr., dinner 2 fr., breakfast 50 c., service 50 c., bougie never anything, and these are the usual prices.

Nothing can describe what the delicious sweetness of the acacias has been, so abundant in all these town-villages, and now it is giving way to that of the limes.

This is a wooden inn of the humblest kind, close in the shadow of a great junction station, at which I am for convenience, but the pleasantness of the people gives it a charm. This solitary existence is a placid, peculiar halt in life.

I was the greater part of July in London.

JOURNAL.

Campsea Ashe, Suffolk, August 22.—This place, which the William Lowthers have bought, in the flat corn-lands of Suffolk, has a fine old garden, with clipped yew hedges and long tanks like Wrest. It has been a most pleasant visit. I heard some one say once, 'Mrs. Lowther is a most extraordinary woman: she never will let the grass grow under any one of her children's feet even for a single instant;' but it has made them all very agreeable, from the immense variety of occupations in which they are interested, and in which, consequently, they interest others.

We spent a long interesting day at the noble old moated house of Helmingham, where Lady Tollemache apologised amusingly for only having nine of her sons at home to assist her in doing the honours! It is a delightful place, with beautiful old gardens, and its inhabitants are delightful too. Lord Tollemache especially brims with goodness to all around him. He was very amusing in urging Miss Lowther, when she had as many sons as he has (!), to make their home pleasanter to them than any other place in the world, so that they should always prefer it to everything else. He showed us all his relics, especially his Anglo-Saxon MS. of the time of Alfred the Great, and several beautiful Bibles of the time of Edward I.

In the church is the tomb of Colonel Thomas Tollemache, who was distinguished in the wars of Queen Anne's time. The Duke of Marlborough ordered him to attack Brest. There were reasons which made him very doubtful of success, and he represented to the Duke that the only chance of it lay in a surprise: still the Duke ordered

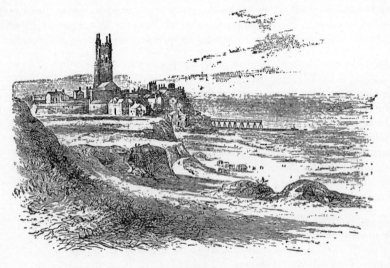

CROMER

him to attempt it. Brest was found thoroughly prepared, the hoped-for surprise was an utter failure, and Tollemache fell in the attack. The French Government had been forewarned, and it was afterwards found that it had been forewarned by Marlborough! When the Duc d'Aumale came to Helmingham, he said that the thing he was most anxious to see was the monument of this unfortunate officer, and that he had himself read, in the archives at Brest, the letter of the Duke of Marlborough warning the garrison of the coming attack.

Drayton House, Northamptonshire, Sept. 20.—I have been spending several days in this most pleasant old house, which is full of charm and interest. The gardens are full of terraces, staircases, fountains, pleached walks, avenues, and leaden statues— beautiful exceedingly. There is a gallery of Mordaunt portraits in the house; in the old library at the top are no end of treasures, and out of it opens the Duchess of Norfolk's boudoir, with old Japanese ornaments. Through a plank missing in the floor of an upper gallery you can look into quite a large room which no one has ever entered. Its windows are darkened by the overgrowth of the creepers outside, and the only object in it is a large box like a portmanteau. The Sackvilles have always lived here, yet not one of them has had the curiosity to descend into that room or to look into that portmanteau!

Then we have been to Boughton, the Duke of Buccleuch's great desolate house, which contains two cartoons attributed, without any cause, to Raffaelle. The house was built by the Duke of Montagu, who was ambassador to Louis XIV, and the king lent him a French architect and gardener. He made it as like a French château as possible. Then he told his friends that he must plant an avenue to drive to London by, and when they remonstrated that an immense part of the way to London did not belong to him, he said, 'Well, at any rate I will have an avenue of the same length,' and he planted seventy-two miles of it in his park. These trees, hemming in the view in all directions, make the place indescribably dull.

Cromer, Sept. 25.—Mrs. Ritchie (Miss Thackeray) is here [at the Laker-Lampsons], most charming and interesting, as I have always thought her. She describes Tennyson and Mrs. Kemble as the noblest man and woman she knows.

Mrs. Kemble found, when in England, that her husband was going to take advantage of an American law which allowed him to obtain a divorce if she was away from him two years. For her children's sake it was imperative that she should prevent this. She hurried back, and just arrived in time by two or three days. Afterwards she herself quietly obtained a divorce in some way which gave her the charge of her children.

Now, Mrs. Kemble is generally to be found knitting by her fireside. One day Mrs. Ritchie took her little girl to see her. 'Here I am,' Mrs. Kemble said to the child, 'an old woman who never allows another person to put in a word when she is talking; and now, what do you think of me?' The little girl, who was shy, did not know what to say, and looked as if she was going to cry. Mrs. Ritchie, to fill up the gap, said, 'Oh, she thinks, Mrs. Kemble, that no one could possibly wish to put in a word when they could listen to you.' *'Ma fille, ne dites pas des choses comme ça* [My girl, don't say things like that],' cried Mrs. Kemble furiously; and then, more quietly, 'You should not say such things before the child: it is not right to teach her to be artificial.'

'One day,' said Mrs. Ritchie, 'I found Mrs. Kemble sitting by her fireside looking rather disconsolate, and asked her what she was doing. "Oh, I'm knocking my head against the wall, my dear; that man who was here was so dreadfully stupid, I'm obliged to knock it out of me." '

For her own sharp sayings, Mrs. Kemble is repaid by her grandchildren. She wrote to one of her grandsons that she did not care for Wagner's music, she could not understand what he meant by it. He answered, that a fly crawling up the wall of Cologne Cathedral might as well presume to judge of its architectural glories as she of Wagner! She did not seem to know whether to be angry or pleased at this.

To MISS LEYCESTER.

Nov. 22, 1885.—Mother's birthday! on which for so many years we have been through the Catacombs (lighted up this one day of the year) to visit the grave of S. Cecilia. My pleasant holiday and happy visits are already becoming dreamlike, and it is as if my last time alone here going on still, as I sit in my hill-set solitude. The wind whistles in the fir-trees; a cow lows in the meadow for a lost calf; Rollo snorts with fat, but is always ready to play with Selma the cat, though greatly annoyed at her having given birth to a numerous progeny *in* his bed; new pigstyes are built, and a

Lawsoniana hedge is planted round the little garden up the steps. . . . and for myself, there is constant work to be done on *Paris*, where, as I labour down the highways, a thousand by-ways of interest and instruction are ever opening up.

I have, however, a little disappointment in Smith and Elder's account, nearly £300 to the bad again this year, and no gain whatever: so much for the supposed riches of 'a very successful author.'

Powderham Castle, Nov. 14.—I have been spending a week with Charlie Halifax[1] in this beautiful place, which recalls the Little Gidding of *John Inglesant* in its intense, its real saintliness—in the constant chapel services with wonderful singing of the servants, in the commemorative hymns for such saints as Martin and Bricius, in the spirit of harmony and universal love, which rules everything. Lord Devon is absolutely seraphic. Charlie says he [Devon] knows only two perfect forms of happiness, reciting the Holy Office or attending the Board of Guardians. 'I know one thing troubles you in respect of heaven,' says Charlie, 'it is, that there are no boards of guardians there; but, dearest Lord Devon, if they are quite essential to your happiness, I am sure that a board will be created in some planet, with celestial paupers for you to relieve.' When with the Halifaxes, I always become brimful of good intentions.

The latter months of 1885 found me quietly at home, exceedingly busy over my work on France.

---

[1] Succeeded his father as the second Viscount in this year.—*Ed.*

BEYOND THE TOP OF THE HILL

1886–87

ʑɛ

THERE is an old print at Holmhurst which represents life in its successive stages as the ascent and descent of a hill. At fifty the top of the hill is reached and the descent begins. I have passed the top, and every year must bring less power of work and action, though I scarcely feel older now than I did at five-and-twenty. But certain marks in the forehead show that age has left his card upon one; we do not know when he called, but the visit has been paid.

I have endless compensations for a lonely life in my pretty little home, my sufficient means, my multitudes of friends. I often feel, however, that this book would give a very false idea of my life. I recount my many visits and what I hear there because it is amusing, and I leave unnoticed the months and months when nothing happens, and in which I am probably employed in quiet work at Holmhurst. This, however, is enough of sentimentalising. I will return to facts.

On the 9th of February [1886] I went up to London for Miss Jolliffe's wedding, and came in for a revolution! On returning from the City, I found Trafalgar Square one mass of people, and many orators addressing them, but expected nothing more. Soon, however, a Socialist leader named Burns suggested a reign of terror and offered himself as captain. Thousands of men—well fed, well dressed, but still the scum of London— rushed down Pall-Mall, breaking windows as they went—a very carnival of outlawry. Their passions grew with their progress, and in St. James Street they wrecked the University Club, which had expelled Hyndman, one of their leaders, from its society. They seized certain carriages, turning out the ladies they contained, and stripped a footman of his livery. They pulled Lady Claude Hamilton out of her carriage and boxed her ears, but when, *after* this, she denounced them as dogs who ought to be flogged as curs, they applauded her courage, and let her go on. Breaking windows and wrecking many shops in Piccadilly, they entered the Park at Hyde Park Corner and left it at Stanhope Gate. Then they rushed on through South Audley Street, which they left much like Paris after the excesses of the Commune.

I went the next day to see Lady Foley, whose house in Grosvenor Square had been on their line of route. It had not only no pane of glass unbroken, but not even fragments of glass left, and stones heaped in the library enough to mend a good piece of road with. Lord Percy's house, next door, was so ruined that they went away next day.

For the two following days London had indeed a miserable aspect— windows all broken, streets littered with fragments, shops shut, streets paraded constantly by bands of entirely victorious and triumphant ruffians, and shopkeepers, in some cases, guarding their property with revolvers.

The call for a fresh edition of my *Walks in Rome* made me suddenly determine to go to Italy at the end of February. At Florence I was the constant guest of the ever-kind Duchess Dowager of Sermoneta, with whom I made delightful excursions in the hills.

To Miss LEYCESTER.

Hotel Paoli, Florence, March 7, 1886.—France was covered with snow from end to end, yet next day we were speeding through lemon-groves laden with fruit, and carpeted with a blaze of iris and scarlet geranium in full flower. Here, after reading about the snowstorms in England, I am glad in the gardens of Arcetri to sit to draw in the shade of the cypresses, and all the hills are pink with almond-blossom. I spent one evening with the Duchess at Palazzo Torrigiani, alone with the family there, which is the most perfect type of a grand old Italian household, consisting of between eighty and ninety persons. The kind and charming old Marchesa Elisabetta has four sons, who have all married as soon as they came of age, yet none have gone farther than to an apartment of their own under the maternal roof, and eighteen children and grand-children dine with her daily, besides other guests. The four daughters-in-law all live in the utmost harmony; the Marchesa Giulia, wife of the eldest son Pietro, and the Marchesa Margherita, who was a Malespina (which in Italy means great things), quietly giving precedence to the Marchesa Cristina, who is a princess (Scilla) by birth. All sat with work round a table, visitors dropped in, and it was most easy and pleasant.

I reached Rome on the 10th of March, warmly welcomed by a large circle of friends. Sir John Lumley was now reigning at the Embassy and making it delightful to his countrymen.

To Miss LEYCESTER.

Hotel d'Italie, Rome, March 17,1886.—What lovely June weather this is, so very hot, so unspeakably beautiful. . . . I find an immense deal to do in correcting and writing, chiefly, however, in taking away from my *Walks in Rome*, so very much is destroyed; indeed, Lanciani, the archaeologist in power, says, 'If they go on like this for twenty years, there will be nothing left of older Rome but St. Peter's and the Coliseum—*if* those.'

March 21.—What expeditions we have had! On Monday we walked through the glen at Ariccia and round the glorious old woods of the Parco Chigi, full of cyclamen, cytisus, blue squills, green iris, and masses of dark violets. Then, whilst the others went on to the convent of Palazzuola, I sat to draw above the still lake, and, when they came back, we went to the grand pine-groves of the Villa Barberini, to Castel Gandolfo, and through the ilex galleries in time for the evening train.

March 31.—I wish I could transport you suddenly into the glorious radiance of this cloudless sunshine and deepest of blue skies. To me Rome has never seemed so delightful in climate as after three months of fog and sleet at Holmhurst. . . . Amid all the changes elsewhere, I can always turn with comfort to the Palatine, and have spent many happy mornings there amongst the gigantic ruins, and the groves of laurustinus and lentisc, and the huge fenochii, meditating on my past and its past.

As to some of the most restful and happiest days of my later years, I look back to the extreme comfort of Perugia, and the perfect view from the windows of my room, unspeakably glorious at all hours, but most of all when the rising sun was lighting up the tops of the distant mountains, whilst all the details of the intermediate plain was lost in soft white haze. Equally delightful was the old-fashioned inn at Orvieto, and the drives into the hills and to Bagnorea and the Lago di Bolsena, returning in the carriage laden with branches of honeysuckle and masses of anemones, violets, cyclamen, and other spring flowers.

Nearly the whole of June I stayed in Paris, working at the archaeological details of the town for my book, and seeing no one. In July I was in London.

JOURNAL.

August 13, 1886.—Two days ago Lady Ossington took me to Lady Evelyn Campbell's wedding with James Baillie Hamilton in Henry VII's Chapel. They have married on his vocalion, which played all the time of the ceremony, and on which their future depends for the bread and butter of life, at present supplied to them by America for looking after it. They have also a camp, in which they propose to train boys for hardships in the colonies, and the sweet little bride began her own hardships by having to walk two miles to this, through the wet grass and fern of a desolate moor, carrying in a basket the cold chicken and bread which her sisters had put up for her supper.

I have been reminded how James Baillie Hamilton was at Harrow at Hayward's house, which in my time used to be Harris's, and to have then the reputation of being haunted. He told Catherine Vaughan that one night whilst he was there, Albert Grey, also a senior boy in the house, rushed into his room wild with horror, and said that when he was in bed he had seen by the moonlight a most terrible figure come in, a kind of nondescript, and that as it approached a chill as of death came over him. Eventually it had seemed to go into a corner of the room and disappear there. Something was arranged for Albert Grey for that night, and the friends never told at Harrow what had occurred. Years afterwards, at his camp, Baillie Hamilton met a boy called Anderson, who had been in Hayward's house. He told how he and another boy slept in the same room. One night he heard his companion in an agonised tone say, 'Oh *do* light the candle: there is something most dreadful in the room.' He lighted it, and found his friend sitting on the edge of his bed, trembling from head to foot. He said that the door had opened, and a horrible nondescript figure had come in, when the most terrible chill, as of death, had come over him. After a time, all seeming as usual, the boys put out the light. They had hardly done so, when Anderson himself saw the figure—the appalling figure, come towards him, and the same deathly icy chill seized him. They lighted the candle again, when the apparition vanished.

One of the curates at Llandaff was going to the place where Miss Hayward, sister of the Harrow Master, lived, and Catherine asked him to inquire if she remembered the circumstance. 'Yes,' she said, 'that is exactly what happened; and that room is never used now.'

With the Bishop [of Chichester] and his party I went to Midhurst, a most attractive old town in lovely country, and we walked through an ancient wood above the Rother to the grand ruins of Cowdray, full of recollections of the Poyntz family, who, as its possessors, came in bitterly for the curse of sacrilege. When Mr. Poyntz went out in a boat at Bognor with his two sons, and the boat upset whilst Mrs. Poyntz was watching it from the hotel-window, the boys clung to the tail of their father's coat as he held the side of the boat in the waves, and he—who could not swim—had the agony of feeling one after the other leave go and sink, without being able to help them. He himself was eventually saved by the boatmen.

Lychett Heath, Poole, August 30.—This is the beautiful house of the Eustace Cecils. The modern house is exquisitely placed amongst sandy, heathery hills, with a lovely view, across a rich wooded foreground, of the various reaches and windings of Poole harbour. I have had much pleasant talk with Lord Eustace, and like him immensely. We had a delightful excursion to-day, taking the train to Wool, and then driving in a car to Lulworth Cove, and walking up the fine wild hills, with noble sea-views, behind it. Then we went on to Lulworth Castle, stern and stately, quadrangular with round towers at the corners, standing on a terraced base, with beautiful park and woods around. We saw the pictures, a few good family portraits of the Welds, and Charles X's room which he inhabited when in exile.

Thomas Weld of Lulworth, who took orders after the death of his wife, became a bishop, and finally (1830) a cardinal. As a layman he had been perfectly devoted to hunting, and, on establishing himself at Rome, the first thing he did was to procure a very nice horse and hunt vigorously. The Pope (Pius VIII) sent for him and said, 'Cardinals must not hunt.' So, for his health's sake, Cardinal Weld took to a vehement course of walking; but the Pope sent for him again and said, 'Cardinals must not walk' —adding, 'If it is necessary for your health that you should walk, there is a place outside the walls where cardinals do walk up and down; you can go there.' But Cardinal Weld died of it.

Nov. 18.—An agreeable party at Worth (Mrs. Montefiore's), the most luxurious of modern houses, where a bit of the Law in a little bottle is screwed upon the door of every bedroom.

London, Dec. 6.—Luncheon with Miss Seymour to meet Madame du Quaire, who talked of the Praslin murder. She was with the old Duchesse de Grammont soon after, and Madame Alfred de Grammont was there. They began to discuss the division of money apportioned to different members of a family according to the French system, and they spoke of a member of the Praslin family whom they thought stingy. One of them added up her different expenses, ending with—'*et puis les dix-mille francs pour l'Angleterre.*' At this Madame Alfred, who is *très-bête*, suddenly broke in with, '*Avez vous été au Bois de Boulogne ce matin?*' 'It was then,' said Madame du Quaire, 'that I first learnt that the Duc de Praslin was alive, and that they knew it.' The next day the Duc de Grammont came to call upon me, and I told him of the conversation, adding—'I know now that the Duke is alive.' He neither allowed it nor denied it. A few days after, however, the Duke came again and said, '*J'ai une petite faveur à vous demander.*' It was that I would never repeat to his mother what I had said to him: it might upset her. Of course I promised, but then I *knew* the Duke was alive.'

'The Duke did not wish to marry Mademoiselle de Luzy: that is an invention. He only murdered the Duchess because she was such a bore. He certainly did not wish to marry any one else.'

Miss Seymour said that the Queen of the Belgians, speaking of the Praslin murder to Mrs. Augustus Craven, said, 'How dreadful to find one was being murdered by one's husband: one could not even cry out.'

Madame du Quaire was reminded of her friend Madame Solkoff, whose hair was quite snow-white whilst she was still quite young. 'She was a Miss Childe, you know, a daughter of that Mrs. Childe who had a salon—*un salon très répandu*—at Paris. She eloped with a Polish Count, to whom her family objected most intensely, and she was disinherited. Very soon after her marriage it became known that it had turned out very ill, and that the young Countess was very unhappy. Eventually it became impossible for her to remain with her husband, and she went to live at Cracow with her mother-in-law, who had a very fine old palace there, and was very kind to her. She had a large apartment of her own in her mother-in-law's house, her bedroom being approached through her sitting-room. She was still only twenty-two, when she was found one morning insensible on the floor of her sitting-room in her night-dress, and with the floor all around her saturated with blood from a terrible wound in her head. Her cabinets and jewel-cases were all broken open and rifled. The *interrogatoire* came, and she was examined. She said that in the night she heard a noise in her sitting-room, and going to see what it was, had found a man breaking open her drawers; that she had received a blow, and knew no more. It was in vain that she was questioned as to whom she had seen; she affirmed that she could not possibly tell who it was. But her hair was turned snow-white from that night. It was not till she knew he was dead that she allowed it was her husband she had seen.'

Madame du Quaire had met Lady Colin Campbell at dinner and sat opposite to her, but she did not know her. She could not help being attracted by the necklace she wore, it was so very extraordinary. After a time it seemed to be moving by itself. She fancied at first that this must be a delusion, but, putting up her glasses, she certainly saw the necklace writhing round Lady Colin's throat. Seeing her astonished look, Lady Colin said, 'Oh, I see you are looking at my snake: I always wear a live snake round my throat in hot weather: it keeps one's neck so cool'; and it really was a live snake.

Dec. 8.—Sat by Sir George Dasent[1] at breakfast. A Mr. Frere passed through the room. 'He comes from Roffham,' said Sir G., 'one of those places of which the name has such a rough East Anglian sound, and he is member of the family which possessed the Paston Letters without knowing it. There were six volumes of letters. Two of

---

[1] Sir George Dasent (1817–1896), Scandinavian scholar; British envoy to Stockholm; assistant editor of *The Times*; professor of English literature at King's College, London; Civil Service commissioner; translated various works from the Norse.—*Ed.*

them were sent up, by request, for Queen Charlotte to look at, and they were lost. She was very accurate herself, that old woman, especially about things that were lent to her, and there is no doubt that she had given them to one of her ladies to return: anyhow they were lost. Afterwards, however, duplicate copies of many of the lost letters were found to be still in the possession of the family, and their existence quite disproved an assertion that the letters had been forgeries.

'They were wonderful people, those old Pastons. They used to thrash their daughters like anything if they did not behave themselves, and then, when they had flogged them well, they would say, "And now they must have silk dresses, rich, red, and beautiful!"'

Dec. 9.—Dined with M. B., who told me of Lady Vane being quite worn-out by the ghastly noises at their place in Cumberland: it was as if some one were always trying to climb up a disused chimney in the wall, and then falling violently down again. But lately, when Sir Henry Vane was away, she had the wall opened. Inside she found a wide and very lofty closet, narrowing into a funnel as it reached the roof, where it opened by a very small hole to the sky. In it were human bones, a broken water-bottle, and the cover of an old Bible, which bore a date. Lady Vane had the bones gathered up and put into a box, which was left in a corner of Sir Henry Vane's room till his return.

When Sir Henry Vane came home, he was exhausted by a long journey and went at once to rest. Lady Vane did not intend to tell him of her discovery till the next day. But suddenly, late in the afternoon, she heard a tremendous noise in her husband's room. She rushed in, and found Sir Henry in a state of the greatest agitation. He said, 'I have seen the most frightful apparition—a woman in that corner,' pointing to where the box of bones had been deposited.

From old family archives they found that, some years before, exactly at the date upon the Bible cover, a woman had been walled up in the house. She had made desperate efforts to escape up the funnel of the disused chimney, and had always fallen down again. Sir Henry and Lady Vane themselves buried the bones in the churchyard, and the house has been at peace ever since.

On the 26th of February 1887 I left England again for my French work, and spent a month in Paris at a primitive and economical inn in the Rue d'Amboise. Living here, I spent my days entirely amongst the historic quarters, seeing nothing of the Boulevards or Rue de Rivoli, but making great progress with a work—my *Paris*—which had no interruptions, and in which I became increasingly interested as I knew more of my subject. On the fine days of early March many excursions were very pleasant, involving long walks to the Abbaye du Val, Nogent les Vierges, &c. Unfortunately the weather changed before I set out on a tour through the Bourbonnais; and in Provence, where many long excursions were necessary, the mistral was quite terrific. Mounting into the wild fastnesses of the Maritime Alps above S. Maximin, to visit the cave in which the Magdalen is believed to have died, I caught a terrible chill, from which I was afterwards very ill at Manosque. But the kindly though rough proprietors of the inn persuaded me to try the remedy of taking no nourishment whatever except hot tea, and letting nature lie absolutely at rest for forty-eight hours, and, as often since, I found this quite answer, though during that time I drove in an open carriage for eight hours to visit the Roman remains at Riez.

To MISS LEYCESTER.

Avignon, April 3, 1887.—It has been a suffering week, owing to the biting, rending, lacerating mistral, which has seemed perpetually to tear one's vitals inside out, and to frizzle them afterwards. Thursday I went by rail to Montelimar, and then in a carriage with a horse which either galloped furiously or would not go at all, over the sixteen miles of mountain-road to Grignan, where Madame de Sévigné lived so much with her daughter, and where she died. It is a really grand and striking place—the

LES BAUX

immense château rising on a solitary rock, backed by a lovely mountain distance, and the town at its foot surrounded by cork forests. All was ruined at the Revolution, but the shell of the rich palace-castle remains—'*un château vraiment royal,*' as Madame de Sévigné calls it. In a solitary spot near is the cave, with old ilex-trees, where she used to sit, and, even with blinding dust and wind, the colouring was most beautiful.

On Saturday, I had to spend five hours at Cavaillon, and wondered how to dispose of myself. But, on reaching the cathedral, the whole population was pouring in to take part in the funeral of a famous doctor who had been a great benefactor of the place. Every one there was presented by the family with a huge wax-candle, as long as a walking-stick, and asked to 'assist.' I had one, and walked and stood with my burning candle for two hours! It was a striking sight, thousands taking part, and the old bishop pronouncing the elegy of the deceased, whom he described as quite a saint. But oh! how it poured, and blew, and swelched, and how deep was the white mortar-mud of Provence!

Aix en Provence, April 15.—All Provence, as you perhaps know, is full of the same very early Church legend, that a number of the earliest Christians, escaping from Jerusalem after the Ascension, landed here on the coast and became the earliest missionaries of Gaul. Of these, Mary Salome and Mary Cleopas are supposed to have stayed at Les Saintes Maries in the Camargue, Lazarus to have gone to preach at Marseilles, Restitutus at S. Restitut, Maximin at S. Maximin; but Mary Magdalen went farther, spent years of penitence, and died in a cave at the top of the mountains, which is certainly one of the most curious places of pilgrimage in Europe. So it was to La Sainte Baume that I went yesterday, starting at 6 A.M. by rail to S. Maximin, and there engaging a carriage to Nant, where the road comes to an end. Thence it is an ascent of an hour and a half through the steep lonely rocky forest, covered with blue hepaticas, over stones, rocks, and quagmires. Near the top it began to hail and rain furiously, and the cold was most intense, snow still lying in great masses; but the cave is very curious, and the view magnificent over the lower mountains, beyond the masses of Alpine forest. How it poured! I sheltered at the worst times under some rocks, and got safely down to the sunlit valley about five, then had to wait at S. Maximin till nine o'clock for a train, and did not get back here till nearly one.

Grenoble, April 22.—On Wednesday evening, after returning from Briançon to Gap, I engaged a carriage thence to Corps, at the foot of the mountain of La Salette It was supposed to be three hours' drive, but took five and a half hours, and we did not arrive till nine o'clock, having spent the last two hours in pitch darkness, with a single lanthorn, driving along the edge of the most terrific precipices, with a driver who had never been there before! Still we arrived at last at the very miserable inn. On Thursday morning I set off early on foot to La Salette, three hours of weary steep ascent of the mountains, rather fine in their snowy solitudes, but affording just a slight panic to a solitary traveller owing to the bears which still prowl about there. In the latter part of the way the snow was above my waist, but a little gulley (turned into a watercourse from the meltings) was cut through it. When at length I reached the convent, I was received with great astonishment, as no one had visited those solitudes since April 6. All around, and up to the first floor of the building, was deep massy snow, not a rock to be seen. I was comfortably fed, however, and saw the strange place to which 15,000 pilgrims come annually. You know the story, how two children declared that the Virgin had appeared to them, and told them that the bad language of the neighbouring villages was so shocking that she could no longer restrain the avenging hand of her Son unless a church was built.

During the latter part of this French tour I had an unpleasant adventure, which excited more attention than I ever anticipated at the time. On April 19 I had gone from Gap to visit Embrun. I had not long left the station before I was aware that I was followed. I contrived to dodge my pursuer, and made, from behind a wall, the sketch of the cathedral which I wanted, and then had dinner at the hotel. When I was returning to the station I saw, by the faint waning light, the same figure following wherever I went. It was dark when the train by which I was to leave was to start. I had taken my place, and the train was already in motion, when it was stopped, and an official accompanied by a gendarme entered the carriage and demanded what I had been doing at Embrun. 'Visiting the cathedral.' 'Why should I visit the cathedral?' and so on, through a long series of questions of the same kind. My passport was demanded, and, though not usually considered necessary for English travellers, I happened to have one. It was, however, refused as an identification, not being dated in the present year. Fortunately, I recollected having in my pocket-book an order from the Préfet de la Seine authorising me to draw in all the palaces in Paris and elsewhere in France, and this was considered sufficient. The train was allowed to move on just as a crowd was collecting.

EMBRUN

At Briançon (where I spent the following day), I carefully abstained from drawing, as it was a fortified town. But on April 23 I left the station at Vizille to visit the old château, two miles distant. I had seen the château and began to occupy the quarter of an hour which remained before the omnibus started for the station by sketching it from the village street, when I was pounced upon by a gendarme. 'Who has authorised you to sketch the château of Vizille?'—'No one.'—'If you can draw this, you may also have drawn other places. You will go with me to the gendarmerie'; and I was marched through the long street of Vizille, followed by a crowd. At the gendarmerie a superior officer appeared, and, with the most extreme insolence of manner, demanded what I had been doing in France, &c. What had I drawn?—'Churches and mountains.'—'Ah!

mountains! then it has been very easy for you to make a little mark in the drawing, known only to yourself, meaning here is a fortress, and there a fortress.'—'But I am an Englishman.'—'Oh, you are, are you? Then I am all the more glad that we have taken you, for we shall probably soon be at war with England, and then you will make your sketches useful to your Government; so you will consider yourself under arrest.' The letter of the Préfet de la Seine was treated as worthless because it had no seal. The passport was rejected altogether with contempt. After this, all further protestations and remonstrances were answered by an insolent shout of—'Be quiet now, you're under arrest.'

Then the first gendarme was sent with me to the station, where my portmanteaux were opened and ransacked, the contents being tossed upon the platform. Two suspicious articles were found. First, a slight sketch of the gorge at Sisteron (not the fort; the fort is on the other side of the rock), and, far worse, three volumes of the *Guide Joanne* for France. 'What did I want with guidebooks?'—'To study the country.'—'Ah! that is just what I thought;' and all the officials of the station were called in to witness the discovery. The gendarme then declared that I must return with him and be locked up at Vizille, but a train coming up at that moment, I made a dash into it, and probably thinking a public scrimmage impolite, the gendarme allowed the station-master to fasten my boxes and bring me a ticket. The gendarme then took his place opposite to me in a first-class carriage.

At 5 P.M. the train arrived at Grenoble. At the station the gendarme of Vizille summoned a gendarme of the town, and I was conducted as a prisoner by the two to the Hotel Monnet. The gendarme of Vizille then left me in care of the other, shut up in a room of the hotel, where the gendarme of Grenoble sat silent opposite to me till 6.30. I thought that then the other gendarme would come back from the Préfecture with an order that I was to be freed from further annoyance. Not a bit of it! He came back with an order that all my possessions were to be carefully ransacked, and all the contents of my boxes were turned out upon the floor. All suspected articles were then put into my smallest portmanteau, and I was marched between the two to the old palace of the Dauphins, where the courts are. Here two clerks subjected me to a long examination. All my drawings (chiefly of church architecture) were examined in detail, and their objects inquired into. The terrible *Guides Joanne* were passed in review and, after an hour, I was told I was free, but without a single word of apology or regret. Indeed, I should not have got away then if at last one of the clerks had not said in his insolent manner, 'Are you such that there is not a single person in the whole of this part of

France who will answer for you?' And goaded to desperation I answered, 'Well, yes, there is one person, it is a lady: she is only a few miles from here now (at Aix les Bains): it is the Queen of England.'

I wrote this story in the train, and posted it at one of the stations to the editor of the *Times*, who inserted it in the paper, so that when I reached home I found England ringing with it, and a question asked in the House about it. I also complained to the Foreign Office, and Lord Salisbury sent me afterwards the French answer to the inquiries made. They allowed the facts of the examination, but denied that I had ever been arrested.

I returned home on May 3, and at the beginning of June was at Scotney Castle.

SCOTNEY CASTLE

JOURNAL.

Scotney, June 1, 1887.—Mrs. Papillon had been telling the Husseys of a very famous female mesmerist living in Park Street. Late one night this person had a visitor who urged her very much to consent to go at once to a mysterious patient, to whom she could only travel blindfolded. She hesitated for some time, but finally, being very much urged, she assented. A well-appointed carriage was at the door, in which she was driven to the railway. In the train she was blindfolded. Several hours were passed in travelling by train. Then she was taken out to a carriage and driven some distance. On arriving at a house, she was led up a staircase and into a large room. As her bandage was removed, she saw two ladies in black just leaving the room. A gentleman was lying in bed, very dangerously ill of typhoid fever. She mesmerised him and he fell asleep. When he awoke, a great change for the better was perceptible. He said, 'I feel better; I could drink a glass of beer.' She said, 'Give him the beer.' He drank it, and fell into a restful, natural sleep.

Then the lady was blindfolded again and conveyed back in the same way in which she came. When she reached her own house in Park Street, a cheque for a very large amount was left in her hands. The next day she read in the paper that the Prince of Wales—then most dangerously ill at Sandringham—had rallied, and fallen into a deep natural sleep from the moment of drinking a glass of beer.

Mr. Hussey told me that an old Mr. and Mrs. Close of Nottingham were very rich and great misers, and they both made wills leaving all they possessed each to the other. However, as they died within a few hours of each other, that made very little difference to anybody.

When the heirs-at-law arrived at Nottingham—young people full of spirits—they were greatly excited and brimming with curiosity. It was known that there were splendid diamonds, and that vast wealth of every kind existed, but at first nothing seemed to be forthcoming. Cupboards and drawers were ransacked in vain. Nothing particular was found.

At last, in a room at the top of the house a great trunk was discovered. 'Here,' they said, 'it all is; we shall find all the treasures now.' But when the trunk was opened, the upper part was found to be full of nothing but scraps of human hair, as if for years the off-scourings of all the old hair-brushes had been collected; then below that was a layer of very dirty old curl-papers; and the bottom of the box was full of still more dirty old corsets of ladies' dresses, and—the box was alive! When young Mrs. Close had dived into the box, she exclaimed, 'What disgusting old creatures our relations must have been! This horrible mess might infest the whole house; we must have it burnt at once.' So she had some men up, and the trunk carried down into the courtyard of the house, and a huge bonfire made there, and the trunk upset into it.

As it was burning, she stood by, and heedlessly, with her stick, pulled one of the curl-papers towards her, and poked it open at her feet. It was a £50 note! In an agony, she scrimmaged at the fire, and raked out all she possibly could, but it was too late; most of the notes were burnt; she only saved about £800.

Naturally her husband was furious, and of course he was very unjust. 'Any one but you would have examined the box carefully; there never was such an idiot of a woman,' &c. And every time he saw the burnt heap in the courtyard, he burst forth afresh. So she sent for the dustman round the corner, and had all the ashes carefully cleared away.

Still nothing had been found of the diamonds. They had certainly existed; there were always the diamonds to fall back upon. But though they searched everywhere, nothing could be found of them. At last they asked the only old lady with whom Mrs. Close had visited if she knew of any one who could help them. 'Yes, certainly,' she said; 'there's old Betty Thompson at the almshouses, she was always in and out of the house as charwoman; she knew more of Mrs. Close and her ways than any one else.' So away they went to the almshouses, and asked Betty Thompson. 'Oh, yes,' she said, 'she knew very well that there were diamonds, very fine diamonds indeed, but small good *they* ever did to old Mrs. Close, for she always kept them sewn up and hidden away in her old stays.'

The stays had all perished in the fire; the diamonds would not have burnt, but then the very ashes had been thrown away; there was no trace left of them. The bank-notes were all very old—the few that were saved—but they were quite good; but there was very little else left of the great inheritance.

To Louisa, Marchioness of Waterford.

Jermyn Street, June 16, 1887.—London is in gala costume,[1] the streets flooded with flowers, and the West End thoroughfares lined by stands, with seats covered with red and gay awnings. I am perpetually thinking of what Arthur Stanley's ecstasy would have been on looking forward to having so many kings and queens, besides no end of other royalty, in the Abbey at once. On Saturday I was at Osterley, where the gardens were quite lovely and delicious in the heat, and yesterday there was a pleasant party at Lord Beauchamp's,[2] with little comedies to amuse Princess Mary, who was exceedingly gracious and kind to me.

June 20.—The streets are all hung with scarlet and blue draperies, and Waterloo Place is embowered in a succession of triumphal arches. The crowds are tremendous. The foot-passengers have already expelled the carriages from the principal thoroughfares, and two million more people are expected to arrive to-day.

I dined last night with Charlie Halifax, meeting Lady Morton, the Arundel Mildmays, and Sir Hickman Bacon—a pale frail youth, so High-Church that he could not take part in any julibee gaieties whilst ———— (one of their especial clergy) was imprisoned. Charlie was very funny in his tantrums against the bishops. 'I hate them all except Lincoln, and—as cowards—I despise them.' He said he would not go to the service in the Abbey, because he considers it desecrated by having seats erected over the altar!

To Miss Leycester.

June 21, 1887.—Nothing can have been more sublimely pathetic than the whole ceremony (of the Jubilee)—more inexpressibly touching and elevating. The Abbey, too, did not look spoilt: all the tiers of seats, all the galleries disappeared utterly: nothing was visible between the time-worn pillars and under the grey arches but the masses of people they contained.

I went at 8 A.M. It was not a moment too soon. Cabs charged two pounds to the Abbey, but I walked very comfortably. The tickets had little maps of the Abbey, with the entrance for the bearer marked on each. Mine was by a door on the north-east behind St. Margaret's, and there I waited, with a small crowd, till nine struck, and some iron gates were opened by the police, when we ran down an awned passage to where a staircase of rough timber led up by the great Norris tomb to our places.

Mine was simply perfect, a splendid place, from whence 'To see the lords of human kind go by,' as Goldsmith says. I would not have changed it with any other in the building—a little red gallery to hold four, over the tomb of Aylmer de Valence; close above the princesses of Austria, Spain, and Portugal; opposite the kings; with a view of the peers and peeresses in the right transept, and so near the Queen that one could see every play of her expression. The Abbey blazed with colour—crimson uniforms, smart ladies, ushers stiff with gold embroidery, yeomen of the guard in plumed helmets.

Every moment the vast edifice became more filled with colour, but the peers and peeresses arrived very gradually. Lady Exeter, beautiful still, sat long alone in the marchionesses' seats, Lord and Lady Cross in the ministerial benches, and two or three duchesses in that appointed for them. Then the Argylls came in, he gorgeous in the uniform of—MacCallum More. Behind I recognised the Spencers, Powerscourts,

---

[1] For the Jubilee celebrations on the 21st and thereafter.—*Ed.*

[2] Frederick Lygon, sixth Earl Beauchamp, 1830–91, lord steward of the household 1874–80; paymaster of the forces 1885–7.—*Ed.*

Stanhopes, Charlie Halifax, and Lord Londonderry with the white ribbon of the Order of St. Patrick. The Lord Chancellor, preceded by mace and bag, now came in and took his place in the centre of the front row, with Lord and Lady Salisbury and the Duchess of Marlborough on his right hand. A figure which attracted more attention than any other was that of Maria, Lady Aylesbury, except her three Cambridge cousins and her two pages, the sole survivor of all those represented in the great picture of the Queen's coronation.

At 11.15 a burst of music announced the first procession, and the Princess Frederica, and the Tecks were conducted to the stalls, with two of the Edinburgh children, and three gorgeous Eastern princes[1] to the places immediately below us. Then the Queen of Hawaii, in a black dress covered with green embroidery, and with the famous yellow feathers only allowed to Sandwich Island royalty, was seated just opposite to us, with her princess-sister[2] (the heiress of the throne) in black velvet covered with orders, and with a great white ostrich fan:—not together, however, as every one was to sit according to rank, and an intermediate place after queens had to be reserved for the Duchess of Mecklenbourg-Strelitz.[3]

A long tension of waiting followed, but at twelve a rising of the white-robed choristers in their south-western gallery announced the second procession, and a flood of royalty poured in beneath us. Opposite sat the kings of Greece, Denmark (his father), the very handsome king of the Belgians, whose beard is beginning to turn grey, the king of Saxony, the Crown Princes of Austria, Portugal, Würtemburg, and Sweden, the Duc d'Aosta, and Prince George of Greece—a charming boy in a naval uniform. Beneath us were the Crown Princess of Portugal, Dona Eulalia of Spain, the hereditary Duchess of Mecklenbourg, and Princess Philip of Saxe-Coburg. But really one of the finest features of the whole was the coming in of the Queen of the Belgians[4] saluting everybody in comprehensive though slight inclination, infinitely graceful and regal in every attitude.

At last a blaze of trumpets announced the Queen's procession. It was headed by canons, the Bishop of London, the two Archbishops in most gorgeous copes, and the Dean of Westminster in a heavy old embroidered cope to his feet, which made him look like a figure risen from one of the old altar-tombs. Then—alone—serene—pale (not red)—beautifully dressed in something between a cap and bonnet of white lace and diamonds, but *most* becoming to her—perfectly self-possessed, full of the most gracious sweetness, lovely and lovable—the Queen! All the princesses in the choir, with the Queen of the Belgians at their head, curtseyed low as she took her place upon the throne, from which the long robe of state trailed so that it looked part of her dress.

When she was seated in lonely splendour, the princes poured in upon her right, and the princesses on her left, and took their places on gilt chairs on either side—a little behind. The bevy of grand-daughters, in white and pale blue, was very pretty—so many, all curtseying as they passed the Queen, and she smiling most sweetly and engagingly upon them with the most loving and motherly of looks.

[1] Prince Abu'n Nasr Mir Hissanum, Sultanah of Persia; Devawongse Varspraker of Siam; and Komatsu of Japan.

[2] Princess 'Liliuokalani.' Queen Liliuokalani was deposed January 1893, after a reign of only two years.

[3] Augusta, elder daughter of Adolphus, Duke of Cambridge, and therefore aunt to Queen Mary. She died in 1916, aged 94.—Ed.

[4] Marie Henriette, daughter of the Archduke Josef of Austria; known for her beauty as the 'Rose of Brabant.'—Ed.

MARY LEA GIDMAN

CHARLOTTE LEYCESTER

Then came the burst of the 'Te Deum.' The silver trumpets at St. Peter's seemed as nothing to the trumpet-shout which gave effect to the exultant sentences, pealing triumphantly through the arches, and contrasting with the single voices of solitary choristers thrilling alone at intervals—voices far, far away, like the tenderest echo. The Queen did not shed a tear, and held a book all the time, but once sat down as if it was too much for her, and often looked round at the Crown Princess—who stood nearest, very sweet and sympathetic—with a look of '*What* this is to us!' Princess Beatrice and the Grand Duchess Sergius cried the whole time.

A striking figure throughout the entire service was the Crown Prince of Germany,[1] especially when kneeling erect like a knight, in jackboots, but with folded hands and a simplicity of unwavering devotion.

Very solemnly, audibly everywhere, the Archbishop of Canterbury read the prayers —thanksgiving for all the mercies of the reign, the petition for eternal life. There was another psalm, sung most gloriously, then an anthem, with a burst of trumpets in the 'To be king for the Lord thy God.' Lastly, the benediction, in which the Queen bent low, lower, lower, as the 'Amen,' sung over and over again, died away in vanishing cadences.

When it was quite silent, in a great hush, she rose up, and a beautiful ray of sunshine shot through the stained windows and laid itself at her feet, and then passed on and gilded the head of the Prince of Wales.

She beckoned to him afterwards, and he came and kissed her hand, but she kissed him twice most affectionately. Then came the Crown Prince and the Grand Duke of Hesse, who kissed her hands, and then the Duke of Connaught. When the Queen saw him, maternal feelings overcame those of royalty, and she embraced him fervently, and then, evidently fearing that the last two princes might be hurt, she called them back, and kissed them too, and so all the princes, who came in order. She was especially cordial to Prince Albert Victor,[2] and heartily kissed Lord Lorne, who had bent down, as if he did not expect it.

Meantime the Crown Princess[3] stood by the step of the throne on the other side, and I think the most touching part of the whole was when she bent low to kiss her mother's hand and was folded in a close embrace, and so all the daughters and the grand-daughters—such a galaxy of graceful girls—bent to kiss the hand, and were kissed in turn.

Then the Queen went away, bowing all down the choir, and the flood of her youthful descendants ebbed after her.

I felt I scarcely cared to see the procession afterwards, but it was very fine. I am one of the 400 asked to meet the 100 royalties at the Foreign Office, but cannot manage arranging levée dress properly in time.

June 23, 1887.—Yesterday I went at 3 P.M. to Hyde Park. A dense mass of people walled in the vast enclosed space, but all in the utmost good-humour, though many came forward with—'Oh, do give me your ticket: oh, do now, just for once.' Inside the outer barrier was a second, within which people walked, and whence they saw. I was indignant at first at not being admitted farther, but when I saw the Archbishop of Canterbury refused, was quite contented to share the fate of the first subject in the

---

[1] Who, in March the following year, became the Emperor Frederick, and died three months later.—*Ed.*

[2] Eldest son of Edward VII., who died in 1892.—*Ed.*

[3] Victoria, the Princess Royal.—*Ed.*

H

realm. However, eventually we were both passed into the immense space where the children were playing, not apparently the least overdone by the hot sun, or tired from having been on the move since 10 A.M., and having been provided, on arriving, with nothing but a bag containing a meat-pie, a bun, and an orange, with instructions to put the bag in their pockets when done with! Each of the 30,000 children also had a 'Jubilee mug' of Doulton ware. Every now and then volleys of tiny coloured balloons were sent up, like flights of bright birds floating away into the soft blue, and, as the royalties arrived, a great yellow balloon, with several people in its car, bore a huge 'Victoria' skywards.

Between half-past four and five lifeguards heralded a long procession of carriages, with the Indian princes, the foreign queens and kings, and our own royal family in force. A number of Eastern chieftains were riding six abreast, and very like Bluebeard one or two of them looked. Finally came the Queen, smiling, good and gracious beyond words, and with a wonderful reception everywhere.

Having escorted Lady Normanton to the safe solitudes of Wilton Place, I rushed off to Windsor, arriving at nine. Certainly the grandeur of the London illuminations paled before the intense picturesqueness of those in the old royal city. I had no time to go to Eton, where the Queen had entered—like Queen Elizabeth—under an arch on the battlements on which Eton boys were lustily trumpeting. But the bridge, brilliant in electric light, also ended in an arch, kept dark itself, beyond which every house in the steep, sharply-winding street was seen adorned with its own varied devices of coloured light, from basement to attics, whilst the walls were hung with scarlet draperies, and brilliant banners of scarlet and gold waved across the roadway.

I stayed on the bridge to see the thousand Eton boys cross, marching in detachments, with white and blue uniforms alternately, carrying their (then unlighted) torches, and then went after them to the castle, where I was one of the few admitted, and pushed on at once to the inner court under the Queen's apartments.

Most unspeakably weird, picturesque, inspiring, beautiful, and glorious was the sight, when, with a burst of drums and trumpets, the wonderful procession emerged under the old gate of Edward III, headed by a detachment of the Blues, then the boys, six abreast, carrying lighted torches, till hundreds upon hundreds had filed in, singing splendidly 'God save the Queen.' All the bigger boys formed into figures of blazing light in the great court, weaving designs of light in their march—'Welcome,' 'Victoria,' &c., in radiant blaze of moving living illumination; whilst the little boys, each carrying a coloured Chinese lantern on a wand, ascended in winding chains of light the staircases on the steep hill of the Round Tower opposite the Queen's window, till the slope was covered with brilliancy and colour. The little boys sang very sweetly in the still night their song of welcome, and then all the mass of the boys below, raising their flaming torches high into the air, shouted with their whole hearts and lungs, 'Rule Britannia!'

It was an unspeakably transporting scene, and I am sure that the beloved figure in the white cap seated in the wide-open central window felt it so, and was most deeply moved by the sight and sound of so much loyal and youthful chivalry.

Then, in a great hush, she almost astonished them by leaving her place and suddenly reappearing in the open air in the courtyard amongst them, and making them a queenly and tender little speech in her clear beautiful voice—'I do thank you so very very much,' &c.

And then, in figures of light from their torches, as she reappeared at the window, the vast assembly formed the word 'Good night.' Nothing could possibly have been more picturesquely pretty.

JOURNAL.

July 6.—Yesterday I went with the Indian princes by special train to Woburn. Everything was arranged *en grand seigneur*—nothing to be paid anywhere—a train with saloon carriages, in which we floated into Bedfordshire without stopping, and thirty-two carriages, beautifully equipped, sent to meet us at the station. In one of these I drove through the lanes lined with dog-roses with Lord Normanby and Miss Grosvenor. 'I am always mistaken for Princess Mary, so must keep up her character,' said the latter, and bowed incessantly, right and left, to the village crowds, who were quite delighted with her. We had a long wait before luncheon, Europe and Asia separated by a great gulf which no one seemed able to bridge over. Lady Tavistock did her best, but the party hung fire, and, though a magnificent banquet, with all the gold plate displayed, took part of the time, there was not much to animate us, and we lounged on the lawn, tried to be agreeable and were not, and admired the beautiful Indians, with their gorgeous dresses and languid eyes, till another chain of carriages took us back through the Ampthill woods to another station.

July 7.—Miss Holford was married this afternoon to Mr. Benson at St. George's before an immense crowd. There was a great breakfast afterwards—though so late —at Dorchester House, where all London flocked through the rooms to admire the presents, which were indescribably splendid. The scene on the beautiful white marble staircase was charming, especially when the bride went away, her father and mother leading her down on either side, and all the tiny bridesmaids and pages—nieces and nephews between six and seven—gambolling in front, with huge baskets of dark red roses. Above, under the circular arches, between the pillars of coloured marbles, and against a golden wall background, the overhanging galleries were filled with all the most beautiful women in London leaning over the balustrades.

To LOUISA, MARCHIONESS OF WATERFORD.

June 30.—On Saturday I went to Osterley, meeting beautiful Lady Katherine Vane[1] with her brother and sister at the Victoria Station, and going down with them. Troops of people emerged from the train close to the gate in the park wall, and we all flocked together along the gravel walks through the hot meadows to the house, where the shade was very refreshing. Lady Jersey was receiving under the portico, and groups of Indian princes with their interpreters were busy over strawberries and cream in the corners of the great stone hall. I went, with several people who had an equally tender remembrance of the kind old Duchess of Cleveland, who lived there so long, to visit the little library where she always sat in winter—quite deserted now, and all the books sold—and then joined the many groups of people on the lawns and the green glade which ends in a porticoed summer-house like a Claude-Lorraine picture.

On Sunday I had luncheon at Lord Breadalbane's, to have a quiet sight of my Prince. It is a wonderful house—deeply covered ceilings with frescoes like those in an old Venetian palace, and wide spaces round the outside planted with groves of plane-trees. . . . The Duchess of Roxburgh, an Indian prince, and several other ladies dropped in, so there were three tables for luncheon. In the middle, Lady Breadalbane[2]

---

[1] Fourth daughter of the 3rd Marquis of Exeter, afterwards Lady Barnard.
[2] Lady Alma Graham, youngest daughter of the 4th Duke of Montrose.

got up and went round to each table, almost to each guest, to see that they had all they could possibly want, and to say the pleasantest things to them in the prettiest way: she certainly is a queen of hostesses. Afterwards my Prince came to me, and we walked up and down upon the terrace. He was most affectionate, as he always is when we meet, and talked of all people and things as if we had never parted, but reproached me much with never coming to him in Norway, urging very much that I should write at any time, or even telegraph that I was coming for any length of stay. Some day, when I am free from my French work, I will go.

At a quarter to five yesterday I went to Buckingham Palace—no string, no crowd, no difficulty. By my ticket I had to enter through the hall and rooms beyond it—the most picturesque way. The terrace was already full of people, but the space is so vast there never could be a crowd, and the scene was beautiful, looking down upon the sunlit lawns, the lake and fountain, and the thousands of gaily-dressed people—the splendid uniforms and lustrous robes and sparkling jewels of the Indians glistening amongst them. It was impossible to find any one one looked for, but one came upon hundreds of unexpected friends. Very few young men seemed to have been asked, but there were galaxies of pretty girls. One ancient Indian chief in white, with a flowing beard and a robe of cloth of gold over his shoulders, was told he might salute the Queen. He said he must do it after his fashion, which was to wipe the dust from her feet with his handkerchief, and then kiss it.

The beloved Queen, though very hot and tired (she had been before to revisit her birthplace at Kensington), looked very sweet and smiling, and walked indefatigably from side to side of the long avenues of people, shaking hands with different ladies. There was the usual procession of princes and princesses, including the white-haired Duchess of Mecklenbourg and the ever-pretty group of Hesse princesses.[1] The Princess Beatrice's baby assisted at the party in her perambulator, pushed by a nurse in white. A good deal of my time was taken up by the Duchess of Cleveland insisting that she could have no refreshment but lemonade, and that being quite a quarter of a mile off; but I could not get it after all, through people ten deep in the refreshment tents. Some of the guests were rowed by the Queen's boatmen in their gorgeous mediaeval costume upon the lake, with very pretty effect.

Sunday, July 10.—Sat in the afternoon in the garden at Lowther Lodge, seeing a long diorama of people drop in and have tea. Afterwards I ascended the great brick mansions close by to see Mrs. Procter (Barry Cornwall's widow), who is not the least aged in mind, and apparently not in body. People thought she would be broken by her daughter's death; but constitutions, especially of the old, seldom take any notice of heart-blows, though there is something touching in the way she speaks of her lost daughters as 'my Edith,' 'my Adelaide.' People call her 'Our Lady of Bitterness,' but her words have no touch of sharpness. No one is more agreeable still: no one has more boundless conversational powers: indeed, she often says of herself that 'talking is meat, drink, and clothing' to her. Her sense of humour is exquisite; she never speaks bad grammar herself, so she can never tolerate it in others She wears a front of *blonde cendré*, and boldly speaks of it as a wig. Mr. Browning came in, and they were most amusing together. 'My wife thought you would not perhaps like to meet Mr. Labouchere, Mrs. Procter?' said Mr. Thompson of the *Pall Mall Gazette*, rather interrogatively. 'Your wife was quite right: had I found, on coming to dine with you, that Mr. Labouchere was expected, I should have been compelled to ask you at

---

[1] The children of Princess Alice.—*Ed.*

once to call me a cab.'—'Ah! Labby, Labby!—Hie, cabby, cabby!!' cried Mr. Browning in the quaintest way. Mr. Browning goes to see Mrs. Procter every Sunday afternoon, giving up all else for it.[1]

Mrs. Procter has the almost lost art of conversation in the fullest degree. Lord Houghton recollects how she was asked to meet Macaulay at one of Rogers' breakfasts. Afterwards she said to Rogers, 'But where was Macaulay?'—'Why, he sat opposite to you!'—'Was *that* him?' Why, I always heard he was such a tremendous talker.'— 'So he is,' said Rogers; 'but you see I talked so much myself, I only left one opening, and that *you* took.'

July 11.—There was a beautiful ball at Lowther Lodge—the Princess Christian[2] there and the garden illuminated, and looking, in that dress, as big as the Green Park. I sat out with Lady Strathmore, full of all the discomforts of a great inheritance—such endless details to be filled up: such endless new responsibilities; and just what seems the wrong things always left away.

July 17.—A most pleasant dinner at Charlie Balfour's, meeting a group of real friends. Lady Heathcote Amaury, whom I took down to dinner, said, 'You know young Lady Onslow was a daughter of Lord Gardner. She told me that her father rented a place called Chilton from Colonel ——. When he took it, Colonel —— said, "As you are taking the place for some time, I think perhaps it is my duty to tell you that the state bedroom is haunted. A young ancestor of mine, dressed in a blue coat and breeches, with a rose in his buttonhole, comes in, arranges his hair at the mirror, looks at the occupant of the room, throws up the window, and vanishes through it. He does nobody any harm, and is excessively pleasant-looking, still I ought not to let you take the place without telling you.

'Lord Gardner said he did not care a bit; but the state bedroom had very remarkable furniture,—a magnificent bed with curtains looped up by gilt cherubs, and, after Lady Gardner heard the story, she got leave to change the furniture, and the old hangings were carefully put away, and modern furniture used instead.

'Soon after some cousins of Lord Gardner, two ladies belonging to the elder branch of the family, came from Scotland to stay, and were put into that room. When they came down next morning, Lord Gardner asked the elder if she had rested well after her journey. She answered, "Yes, indeed, and I have had the most delightful dream: I dreamt that the room I was in was furnished in the most beautiful way, with gilt cupids, hangings, &c.,—and really what I dreamt was so charming that I longed for you some time to be able to furnish the room just in that way. And then—I seemed to be awake, but of course I could not have been—I saw a young man of most beautiful countenance come into the room, dressed in a blue coat, &c., which was quite in keeping with the room, and he went up to the glass and arranged his hair, then he looked at me with a charming expression upon his face, but just when he seemed going to speak, and I was longing to know what he would say, he threw open the window, and disappeared through it.'

[1] Mrs. Procter—Anne Benson Procter—was born Sept. 11, 1799, being the daughter of Mr. Skepper, a small Yorkshire squire. Her mother, a Benson, who was aunt of the Archbishop of Canterbury of that name, married, as her second husband, Basil Montagu, Q.C. In 1823, Miss Skepper married Bryan Waller Procter, known as Barry Cornwall, described by Patmore as a 'simple, sincere, shy, and delicate soul,' well known to his contemporaries for his songs set to music by popular composers. He died in 1874.

[2] H.R.H. Princess Helena Augusta Victoria, fifth child of Queen Victoria, who married Christian of Schleswig-Holstein in 1866.

July 20.—At luncheon at Lady Airlie's I met Henry Cowper [who] talked of the friendship between Bright and Tuke. They had always been intimate. Then they loved the same woman. In his great friendship Tuke gave way, and the lady became the first Mrs. John Bright. Afterwards they were greater friends, and saw more of each other than ever: Bright would do anything for Tuke.

Tea with Mrs. Ford—always interesting. She talked much of Dr. Morell Mackenzie —well known to her. When he arrived at Berlin, he found six great doctors waiting for him at the palace. They took him to a room filled with knives, &c. 'What are these for?'—'For your choice in operating upon the Crown Prince [Frederick].'—'But I can only operate upon him in one way, that is my own;' and he explained it. Four of the doctors agreed with what he said, two violently opposed it. He was taken at once to Bismarck, who said, 'Do not consult me: ask me as many questions as you like about *la haute politique*, but about this I can say nothing.' Then he was taken to the Emperor, to whom he explained his views. The Emperor listened to all, and then only said quietly—turning to those who were with him—'Let the Englishman act.' He then went at once to the Crown Prince. He performed the operation with his own forceps, steeped in cocotine, which deadens, absolutely paralyses the throat, and seizing the wart, dragged—not cut—it out. It seemed like a terrible responsibility for England, as if the life of the Crown Prince was in its hands.[1]

Mr. Browning described how he had been asked to dinner by two elderly ladies —sisters. He did not know them, but it was very kind of them to ask him, and he went. He met a very singular party at their house—Gladstone, Mrs. Thistlethwayte, and others. Going down to dinner, the lady who fell to his share suddenly said to him, 'You are a poet, aren't you?'—'Well, people are sometimes kind enough to say that I am.'—'Oh, don't mind my having mentioned it: you know *Lord Byron was a poet!*'

Browning is unlike Tennyson; he does not write from inspiration, but by power of work. He says he sets himself a certain number of lines to write in a day, and he writes them. Sometimes he says, 'To-morrow morning I will write a sonnet; and he writes it. Nevertheless he is always greater in aspiration than achievement. Mr. Carlyle could not bear his poems. 'What did the fellow mean by leaving that cart-load of stones at my door?' he said to Alfred Tennyson when Browning left one of his poems there.

Woodlands, Glassbury, Sept, 7.—I came here through the lovely Church Stretton country, stopping at picturesque Shrewsbury on the way to stay with the Bishop of Lichfield and Augusta.[2]

Augusta had many interesting reminiscences of Lord Beaconsfield. One day, at luncheon, she offered him the mustard. 'I never take mustard,' he replied in his sepulchral voice. 'Oh, don't you?' she said airily. 'No,' he continued in solemnest tones. 'There are three things I have never used: I have never touched mustard; I have never had a watch; and I have never made use of an umbrella.'—'Well,' said Augusta, 'I can understand the mustard—that is a mere matter of taste; but surely going without the other things must have been sometimes rather inconvenient.'—'And why should I want them?' continued Disraeli more sepulchrally than ever. 'I live under the shadow

[1] Dr. Morell Mackenzie, who specialised in throat diseases, and helped to found the Golden Square Hospital, was severely censured by the Royal College of Surgeons for writing and publishing an account of his treatment of the Crown Prince.—*Ed.*

[2] William Dalrymple Maclagan became Archbishop of York in 1891 (see page 243). He married, secondly, Augusta, the youngest daughter of the sixth Viscount Barrington. Augusta's mother was a cousin of 'Italima'.—*Ed.*

of Big Ben, and there is a clock in every room of the House of Commons, so that I cannot possibly require a watch; and as I always go about in a close carriage, I can never want an umbrella.' Disraeli was always full of these small affectations.

To Miss Leycester.

Sept. 22.—Yesterday we went to Houghton, in a well-timbered park—a house full of stately magnificence. The present Lord Cholmondeley has sold many of its treasures, but, though much has been taken away, it is especially interesting because nothing has been added since the time of Sir Robert Walpole. George, Lord Walpole, destroyed the grand staircase of the house, so that you now have to enter through the basement, instead of in state by the grand hall on the first floor, where Sir Robert and his companions used to carouse, and where the chairs which they used still remain, with the rings in the ceiling which supported the scales for weighing deer.

In one of the drawing-rooms is a glorious picture of the Duchess of Ancaster, who was sent to bring Princess Charlotte of Mecklenbourg-Strelitz to England when she came to marry George III. 'Pug, pug, pug!' cried the people when they saw her appearance as she was entering London. 'Vat is dat they do say—poog?' said the Princess, 'vat means poog?'—'Oh, that means, God bless your Majesty,' promptly replied the Duchess, without the slightest hesitation.

Journal.

Oct. 2.—Again at Highcliffe with Lady Waterford, whose conversation is as charming as ever. 'And thy eternal summer shall not fade,' is a line of Shakespeare which seems ever to apply to her. Here are some fragments from her lips:—

'When I was young, I delighted in Tittenhanger. We used to post down from London—a most delightful drive then. I thought it all charming—the old house, and a wood with bluebells, and the Colne, a mere dull sluggish stream, I suppose, but it had frogs and bulrushes, and I found it enchanting. A few years ago I thought I would post down to Tittenhanger in the old way, but it was a street all the way to Barnet, and when the people saw the white horses and postillion in blue, they came crowding round; for, though it was only my little maid Boardman and me, they thought, "Now we shall see them: now we shall see the newly-married pair."

'The Duc d'Aumale is married. He married Mademoiselle Clinchamps, who was lady-in-waiting to the Princess of Salerno, the Duchesse d'Aumale's mother. She does the honours of his house, but it is a sort of morganatic marriage. . . . Madame Adelaide was married too to one of the generals. . . . I remember the Aumales riding through the green avenues near Ossington; Mary Boyle was with them. She was a most excellent horsewoman, but a great gust of wind came, and the whole edifice of her chignon was blown off before she could stop it. The little Prince de Condé was very young then, and he was riding with her. He picked it up and said, "I will keep it in my pocket, and then, when we reach Thoresby, you can go away quietly and get it put on;" and so she did.

Whilst I was away on my visits, I had left my dear old cousin Charlotte Leycester provided with companions at Holmhurst during the annual summer visit of several months, which had never failed since my mother's death. I felt that thus my mother's home, thus her own especial room, were fulfilling what she would most have wished for them. And (though, unlike my gentle mother, Calvinistic, vehement, with a habit of con-

stantly 'improving the occasion' and utterly intolerant still of all that did
not agree with her in religious matters), the beloved and beautiful old
cousin, at nearly ninety, was this year more than ever occupied by plans
and thoughts for the good of all around her, more full of spiritual meditation herself, lifting her own heart and mind into celestial dwelling-places.

When turned to her reminiscences of the past, her conversation was
often very interesting. I remember her telling me this summer of her
visit to Paris in 1827, and going to the Royal Chapel, into which came
the king, Louis XVIII, and the Duchess d'Angoulême with full evening
dress in the morning and feathers on her head. When the king entered,
a great picture of our Lord hung opposite where he was to sit, to which
the master of the ceremonies seemed to introduce him—'Le roi.' At
Rosny, a beautiful old château with chestnut avenues, to which we drove
out one October evening after dining at Mantes, we saw the Duchesse
de Berry. Most amusing the travelling then was, with the postillions in
blue and in great jack-boots, into which they had to be lifted, with the
blowing of their horns at every village we passed through.

A few days after I reached home, two more volumes of mine were
published, *Paris* and *Days near Paris*. They had been the engrossing
work of the last two years. My hourly thought had been for them, and
I had taken all the pains I could with them. I knew their faults, and know
them still; but all the same I am conscious, and I am sure it is not conceit,
that no better general books on those subjects have ever been written,—
certainly in French there is nothing of the kind. I suppose it is one of the
penalties of a lonely life that no one spoke of them; that day after day
passed on, and no one ever mentioned their existence. And then came a
review-leading article indeed—in the *Athenæum*, not of mere abuse of the
books, though no words were strong enough for that, but of such bitter
personal malignity against myself, as gave one the shuddering conviction
that one must indeed have an enemy as virulent as he was unscrupulous.
'Turn author,' says Gray, 'and straightway you expose yourself to pit,
boxes, and gallery: any coxcomb in the world may come in and hiss if
he pleases; ay, and what is almost as bad, clap too, and you cannot hinder
him.' Most of the reviews of my books have been unfavourable, but
the books have always contrived to outlive them; and generally, when
they have been found fault with, I have felt almost grateful for such lessons
of humility. Even honest reviewers, however, seldom read beyond the
first chapter of a book; *that* they usually read, and occasionally criticise;
but even then the tendency to save themselves trouble generally causes a
great deal of copying.

X

IN PLEASURE AND PAIN

1887–90

୬୰

In the middle of October I went North for a short time.

JOURNAL.

Thoresby, Oct. 20, 1887.—A visit here has been charming—its inmates all so filled with kindness and goodness of every description, and Lady Manvers so very agreeable. Nothing could exceed the dying splendour of the autumnal tints in the forest, of which we saw a great deal, as we sat out through the whole of each morning drawing amongst the tall golden bracken, over which the great antlers of a stag were now and then uplifted.

Southwell, Oct. 21.—Lord Manvers—kindest of hosts—sent me here, fourteen miles. It is a tiny town clustered around its—chiefly Norman—minster. The beautiful chapter-house has a wreathed door, before which Ruskin stood for an hour when he was here, motionless in rapt contemplation.

We went from Thoresby to Rufford,[1] a curious old low-lying house containing much fine tapestry, but where the old furniture is greatly made up. The house has an obstreperous ghost, that especially haunted the room which Augustus Lumley chose as his own, and frightened his pug-dog out of its wits; for beyond that room is a little chamber in which a girl was once shut up and starved to death; but since some bones have been found under one of the passages and received christian burial, the ghost has been laid. There is a portrait of a boy who was taken as a baby from gipsies and brought up in the house, but who disappeared after he grew up and never was heard of again: it was supposed that the impulse was too strong, and that he rejoined the tribe he came from.

Raby Castle, Oct. 25.—The Duchess of Cleveland has been describing Lord Crawford's interview with a famous clairvoyant. Lord Crawford saw the medium go and hold his head in the fire: the flames played round him and he was quite unhurt. Then the medium said he could make Lord Crawford impervious to fire: 'Would he like it?' He said 'yes,' and the medium took a large live coal from the fire and put it on the palm of one of his hands, which was entirely unhurt, though the coal was left upon it, and Lord Crawford was told to light his cigar at it, which he did. The clairvoyant then said, 'Your other hand is not impervious: touch the coal with it,' and he touched the coal which lay in the palm of his left hand, and one of the fingers of his right hand bears the marks of it still.

[1] Home of Sir John Savile, first Baron Savile of Rufford, diplomatist; British Minister in Rome, 1883.—*Ed.*

Oct. 26.—It has been a great pleasure during this visit that the Duke[1] has come in each morning for talk, generally more or less narrative—in which he rises suddenly from his chair, walks rapidly backwards and forwards to the fire, and then sits down again, always with his sharp fiery restless look; but all he says most interesting. To-day he told of his father's early life,—sent to Oxford with a tutor, Mr. Lipscombe, then abroad for three years, spent chiefly at Orleans learning French with John, Duke of Bedford (the father of Lord Russell). The Duke of Dorset was ambassador then, and took the two young men to Versailles, where they played billiards with Marie Antoinette. The French aristocracy were quite unconscious then of the coming danger, and would not believe in the serious state of politics. The Duc de Bouillon was the great person, and they stayed with him in the country. They went on to Rome, where Cardinal York was then living. They went to his weekly receptions, where he was always treated as royalty. 'The Duchesse d'Albanie gave my father a ring,' said the Duke, 'but after my father's death it was stolen from the Duchess Elisabeth by her maid. All young men stayed abroad their three years at that time, and so did my father, then as soon as he came home he was married to my mother, who was the Duke of Bolton's daughter.

'For myself, I went to Paris at eighteen in diplomacy, and was there for many years. I spoke French better than English, and lived entirely in French society. Thiers I knew intimately in all the different phases of his life. He was said to have had an intrigue with Madame Dombes. I don't know how that may have been, but he married her daughter, and she made him a very good wife. He always began his writing at six, when he had a cup of coffee, and he wrote on—no one being allowed to disturb him— till 12 A.M., which was the hour of *déjeûner*, and it was this which enabled him to write his histories; when he was in office he had not time. He and Guizot were always rivals.

'I was in Paris in Louis Philippe's time, but not under the Restoration. Many of the Dames de la Cour of the older time, however, were still in Paris, and had *salons*— Madame de Noailles, &c. I used to see much of Princess Charlotte de Rohan, who had been privately married to the Duc d'Enghien, and whose excitement was great when Louis Philippe was appointed. I was at Marienbad when the news of that revolution came, and posted back to Paris at once: we expected great difficulty on the way, but there was none. I saw the barricades, however, in the early *émeute* of Louis Philippe's time, and the people with their passions roused, and the *gamins* who used to come under the windows of the Palais Royal and call for the king till he came out and made them a bow: it was the regular thing that was done.

'I was at Coppet with Auguste de Staël a few years after Madame de Staël died: he asked Sismondi to meet me there and several others. Old Madame Necker—Madame de Staël's mother—had a very remarkable *salon* in Paris: her daughter was Duchesse de Broglie and her granddaughter married the Comte d'Hausonville, whom I knew very well: but, oh! it is more than half a century ago now that I was at Coppet.'

Oct. 27.—Mrs. Forester, wife of the Duke's nephew, who is here, has told me much that is curious.

'An old Mrs. Sauchiehall, unfortunately dead now, told Lady Vane that when she was a girl at Doncaster, at a famous school of that time, she made a very intimate friendship with two other girls, and when they parted, they made each other a solemn

[1] Harry George Powlett, 4th Duke of Cleveland, who died August 21, 1891. He died without heirs, as did his two brothers before him.—*Ed.*

vow that if either of the three were in any real trouble in after life, the others would do all they could to help her.

'They parted, and Mrs. Sauchiehall married in Cumberland—married twice, and became a second time a widow. Life had seemed constantly to drift her away from her old friends. At last, at Marienbad, she met one of them, then Mrs. A., and spent some weeks there with her, renewing all their old intimacy.

'Mrs. A. told her that she had always continued to be on terms of the most extreme intimacy with their third friend—Lady B. Her own story had been a very sad one. She had been left a widow with several children, and almost in a state of destitution. In all her troubles, she had continued to confide in Lady B., who never lost sight of her. At one time especially, Lady B. was perplexed as to how she could help her, and spoke of it to her husband, who said, "Well, there is at least one thing I could do for her: there is that old place of ours in Dorsetshire, where nobody lives. It is all being kept up for nothing, so if Mrs. A. likes to go and inhabit it, she is quite welcome; only, you know, she ought to be told that it is said to be haunted.'

'Lady B. made the proposal to Mrs. A., who was enchanted, and she moved at once with her children to the house in Dorsetshire, where she seemed to find a refuge from her troubles and every comfort. She asked the servants whom she found in the house about the ghosts, and they said, "Oh, yes, the great hall and the rooms beyond it are said to be haunted, but we never go there, and the ghosts never come to our part of the house, so we are never troubled by them in the least." For several years Mrs. A. lived most happily in the old house, and nothing happened.

'At last, on one of her children's birthdays, she invited some children from the neighbourhood to come and play with her own children, who begged that, after tea, they might all go and play hide-and-seek in the great disused hall. The children had finished their games, and Mrs. A. was alone in the hall setting things to rights after-wards, about 8 P.M. in the evening, with an unlighted candle in her hand, when she heard some one call out loudly, "Bring me a light! bring me a light!" Then, almost immediately, the door from the inner passage leading to the farther rooms opened, and a lady rushed in, beautifully dressed in white, but with all her dress in flames. She ran across the hall screaming "She's done it! she's done it!" and vanished through a door on the other side. Mrs. A. instantly lighted her candle, and ran with it up the passage from which the lady had emerged, but she found all the doors locked. The next night, at exactly the same hour, she came again to the hall, and exactly the same thing happened. She then wrote to Lady B. that she should be obliged to leave the place, unless Lord B. could explain the mystery.

'Lord B. then said that an ancestress of his—a widowed Lady B.—had an only son, who fell in love with the charming daughter of a neighbouring clergyman. The young lady was lovely, fascinating, and very well educated, but the mother regarded it as a mésalliance and would not hear of it. The young man, who was a very dutiful son, consented to gratify his mother by waiting, and went abroad for two years. After that time, as their attachment was unbroken, and he was of age, he married the young lady.

'It was with joyful surprise that the young married pair received a very kind letter from the mother, saying that as all was now settled, she should make a point of wel-coming the bride as her daughter, and always living happily with her afterwards. They went home to the mother at the old house which Lord B. had lent to Mrs. A., and were most kindly received. All seemed perfectly smooth. At last a day came on which the mother had invited an immense party to be introduced to and do honour to the bride

The evening arrived, and the young lady was already dressed, when her mother-in-law came into the room, kissed her affectionately, and then said to her son, 'Now that she is indeed my daughter, I am going to fetch the family diamonds, that I may have the pleasure of decorating her with them myself.'' The diamonds spoken of were really the property of the son, but he had never liked to irritate his mother by claiming them, and rejoiced that his wife should accept them from her.

'The mother then went to fetch the diamonds, the son lighting her. As they were coming back, they heard the voice of the young lady calling to her husband to bring her a light. "Oh, I will take it to her," cried the mother suddenly, and snatched the candle out of his hand. In another instant the girl rushed by with her white dress enveloped in flames, screaming "She's done it! she's done it!" The mother confessed that her hate and jealousy had been too much for her.

'Now the house is pulled down, and a railway passes over its site.'

The Duchess of Cleveland says that when the Sultan was at Buckingham Palace, one of his servants offended him, and he condemned him to death. The Sultan was informed that he could not execute him in this country; then he said he should do it on board his own ship. One of his wives also is said to have been executed whilst he was here, 'because, poor thing, she had been so dreadfully sea-sick, that it was quite disgusting,' and she is said to be buried in the palace garden.

Raby Castle, Oct. 28.—A pleasant Mr. and Mrs. Wilkinson—neighbours—came to stay yesterday. He told me a very remarkable story.

One day last year, Mr. Gurdon, an excellent Catholic priest belonging to a mission in the East End of London, had come in from his labours dreadfully wet and tired, and rejoicing in the prospect of a quiet evening, when the bell rang, and he was told that a lady wanted to see him on most urgent business. He said to a friend who was with him, how sincerely he dreaded being called out again into the wet that night, and how he hoped that the visit meant nothing of the kind; but he admitted the lady. She was a remarkably sweet, gentle-looking person, who told him that there was a case in most urgent need of his immediate ministrations at No. 24 in a street near, and she implored him to come at once, saying that she would wait to point out the house to him. So he only stayed to change his wet things, and then prepared to follow the lady. He took with him the Host, which he wore against his breast, holding, as is the custom, his hand over it. It is not considered right for a priest carrying the Host to engage in conversation, so Mr. Gurdon did not speak to the lady on the way to the house, but she walked a little way in front of him. At last she stopped, pointed to a house, and said, 'This, Father, is No. 24.' Then she passed on and left him.

Mr. Gurdon rang the bell, and when the servant came, asked who it was who was seriously ill in the house. The servant looked much surprised and said there was no illness there at all. Much astonished, Mr. Gurdon said he thought the servant must be mistaken, that he had been summoned to the house to a case in most urgent need. The servant insisted that there was no illness; but Mr. Gurdon would not go away without seeing the owner of the house, and was shown up to a sitting-room, where he found the master of the house, a pleasant-looking young man of about twenty-five. To him Mr. Gurdon told how he had been brought there, and the young man assured him that there must be some mistake—there was certainly no illness in the house; and to satisfy Mr. Gurdon, he sent down to his servants, and ascertained that they were all perfectly well.

A tea-supper was upon the table, and very cordially and kindly the young man asked Mr. Gurdon to sit down to it with him. He pressed it, so they had tea together and much pleasant conversation. Eventually the young man said, 'I also am a Catholic,' adding, in an ingenuous way, 'but I fear you would think a very bad one;' and he explained that the sacraments and confession had long been practically unknown to him. 'As long as my dear mother lived,' he said, 'it was different: but she died three years ago, and since her death I have paid no attention to religion.' And he described the careless life he had been leading.

Very earnestly and openly Mr. Gurdon talked with him, urging him to amend his ways, to go back to his old serious life. At first he urged it for his mother's sake, then from higher motives. He seemed to make an impression, and the young man was touched by what he said, and said no one had spoken to him thus since his mother died. At last Mr. Gurdon said, 'Why should you not begin a new life *now?* I might hear your confession, and then be able to give you absolution this very evening. But I should not wish you to decide this hurriedly: let me leave you for an hour—let me leave you perfectly alone for that time—you will then be able to think over your confession, and decide what you ought to tell me.' The young man consented, but urged Mr. Gurdon not to leave the house again in the rain: there were a fire and lights in the library, would not Mr. Gurdon wait there?

Mr. Gurdon willingly went to spend the time in the library, where two candles were lighted on the chimney-piece. Between these he placed the Host. Then he occupied himself by examining the pictures in the room. There were many fine engravings, and there was also the crayon portrait of a lady which struck him very much. He seemed to remember the original quite well, and yet he could not recall where he had seen her. On going back to the other room, he told the young man how very much he had been struck by the picture. 'Ah!' he said, 'that is the portrait of my dear mother, and it is indeed the greatest comfort I have, it is so very like her.' At that moment Mr. Gurdon suddenly recollected where he had seen the lady: she it was who had come to fetch him to the house.

Mr. Gurdon heard the young man's confession and gave him absolution; he seemed to be in the most serious and earnest frame of mind. He could not receive the sacrament, because it must be taken fasting, so the evening meal they had had made it impossible. But it was arranged that he should come to the chapel at eight o'clock the next morning, and that he should receive it then. Mr. Gurdon went home most deeply interested in the case, and truly thankful for having been led to it; but when morning came, and the service took place in the chapel, to his bitter disappointment the young man was not there. He feared that he had relapsed altogether, but he could not leave him thus, and as soon as the service was over he hastened to his house. When he reached it, the blinds were all down. The old female servant who opened the door was in floods of tears: her master had died in his sleep.

On the last evening of his life his mother had brought Father Gurdon to him.

Muncaster Castle, Oct. 30.—What a gloriously beautiful place this is!—an ascent from the station, and then a descent through massy woods, till the castle appears on the edge of a gorge, wooded on both sides, and which now has every tint, from the dark blue-green of the hollies and the russet of dead fern, through crimson, scarlet, orange, to the faintest primrose colour of the fading chestnut leaves. Then behind are the finest of Cumbrian mountains, and in front terraced gardens, and the not far distant sea. . . . I sleep in 'the ghost-room,' and in a red silk bed used by Henry VI when he was here, and when he gave 'the luck of Muncaster' to the family—an old Venetian glass bowl, from which every child of the house has been christened since. Once it was thrown from an upper window: the owners never had the courage to hunt for and examine it, and it remained buried in the earth for some years: then it was dug up quite uninjured.

Alnwick Castle, Nov. 4.—Lady Airlie and Lady Griselda Ogilvy were at the station, and I travelled with them as far as Naworth. On arriving here, it was pleasant to be met by the cordial welcome of Duchess Eleanor, always most genial and kind. The actual Duchess [of Northumberland][1] did not appear till dinner, when she was wheeled into the room in a chair, very sweet and attractive-looking, but very fragile. The Duke[2] looks wiry, refined, rather bored, and some people would find him very alarming. Lord and Lady Percy seem to be two of the most silent people in the world—she pretty

ALNWICK CASTLE

still in spite of her ten children. We played at whist in the evening, but it was broken at ten by going to prayers, which the Duke reads in the chapel. It is the only time I have seen evening prayers in any country-house for the last fifteen years.

This morning Duchess Eleanor showed me the rooms—the magnificent Italian rooms, which owe their glory to her husband, Duke Algernon, who, when remonstrated with for thus changing a mediaeval fortress, said, 'Would you wish us only to sit on benches upon a floor strewn with rushes?' He purchased the whole of the great Camuccini collection at Rome, because of his great wish to have one single picture, which they would not sell separately. . . . The magnificent decorations of the rooms are by Canina. But the most lasting attraction of the castle is the library, with the really splendid collection of books formed by Duke Algernon.

The Percies are Irvingites now, as well as the Duke and Duchess. Her father, Mr. Drummond, was 'one of the twelve apostles,' in whose time it is a tenet of faith that

[1] Louisa, daughter of Henry Drummond, Esq., died 1890.
[2] Algernon-George, 6th Duke of Northumberland.

the Lord must return. Now only one 'apostle' is alive, and when he dies what will happen? Meantime, though a very old man, he is hard at work beating up recruits and inciting proselytism. The family go to the church here, but then the vicar of Alnwick is also an Irvingite. All the gibberish which the Irvingites talk when seized by the spirit is taken down and treasured up as 'prophecy.'[1]

Nov. 5.—This Irvingite family is constantly waiting and looking out for the millennium: it is terribly anxious work. But their faith is most simple and touching. When one of the Percy boys was very ill, they had him anointed with oil: after that he recovered. 'We had no doubt it would be so,' said Lady Percy, 'no doubt whatever.' After the anointing, the friends of a patient have altogether done with human agency, and leave everything in the Divine hands. It is curious to hear members of this family say casually—'The angel was here on Monday, and will be here again on Friday.'

To Miss Leycester.
Dec. 24.—The dreary Christmas season of damp and dyspepsia, bills and bother, is less odious than usual this year, as the day itself is swallowed up in Sunday.

Journal.
Holmhurst, Feb. 10, 1888.—The news of Lady Marian Alford's sudden death removes from the cycle of life one whom I had felt to be a true friend for more than thirty years. Our meetings were at long intervals, but when we met, it was as more than mere acquaintances. With a grace which was all her own, she often unfolded beautiful chapters in her own life to me, and she was one of the very few person who have read in manuscript much of these written volumes of my past. She was a perfect *grande dame*, unable to harbour an ignoble thought, incapable of a small action. Regal, imperious, and extravagant,[2] she was generous, kind, and personally most unselfish, and, had the real greatness and goodness that was in her been regulated and disciplined by the circumstances of her early life, she would have been one of the noblest women of her century.

March 14.—Met Lady Fergusson Davy (*née* Fortescue). She told me that when Lady Hills Johnes, the friend of Thirlwall,[3] was twenty-four, she was once in society with the late Lord Lytton, who was talking of second-sight, and of his own power of seeing the future of those he was with. She urged him very much to tell her future, but he was very unwilling to do so. Still she urged it so much that at last he did. He did it after the manner of the Chaldees—told it to her, and wrote it down at the same time in hieroglyphics. He said, 'You will have a very great sorrow, which will shake your faith in man: then you will have another even greater sorrow, which will come to

---

[1] Irvingites: religious body properly known as the Catholic Apostolic Church, named after the Rev. Edward Irving, who from 1829–1834 preached at the Regent Square Presbyterian Church, London. Henry Drummond, a wealthy banker, was a leading supporter. In 1831 some of the congregation began to 'prophesy' and to speak in 'unknown tongues'. The hierarchy consisted of 'Apostles', 'Prophets', 'Evangelists', and 'Pastors'. An 'Angel' was the equivalent of a bishop. The last 'Apostle' died in 1901, Since only 'Apostles' could ordain, there have been no additions to the ministry since then.—*Ed.*

[2] How well I remember, when somebody remonstrated with Lady Marian for 'burning the candle at both ends,' the quickness with which she answered—'Why, I thought that was the very way to make two ends meet.'

[3] Connop Thirlwall, 1797–1875, historian and Bishop of St. David's. Wrote a *History of Greece* in 4 vols. Buried with Grote in Westminster Abbey.—*Ed.*

you through an old and trusted servant: you will marry late in life a king among men, and the close of your existence will be cloudlessly happy.' All the first part of the prophecy has come true—the breaking off of her first engagement; the terrible murder of her father by his servant; her marriage with Sir James Hills; all that remains now is happiness.

Holmhurst, May 14.—I have just returned from an interesting month in London seeing many people delightfully and making some pleasant new acquaintance. In going to London, I first saw, on a placard at the station, that Matthew Arnold was dead. It seemed to carry away a whole joyous part of life in a moment—for I have known Matthew Arnold ever since I remember anything, though I did not know till I lost him that his happy personality and cordial welcome had made a real difference to me for years, especially in the rooms of the Athenæum, where I have spent so much time of late years. He had an evergreen youth, and died young at sixty-six, and he was so impregnated with social tact and courtesy, as well as with intellectual buoyancy, that he was beyond all men liveable with. . . . I went on April 19 to his funeral in the graveyard of the ancient church at Laleham. It was a day of pitiless rain, which pelted upon the widow and sisters and crowd of mourners round the grave, and on the piles of exquisite flowers beneath which his coffin was hidden.

At dinner at the Miss Monks' I was interested to find myself sitting next to Lady Sawle, who told me that she was niece of the Rose Aylmer who was the love of Landor's youth. It was on her that he wrote the lines which Archbishop Trench declared to be better than many an epic, and which Charles Lamb said he lived upon for a fortnight. Lady Sawle was herself one of the three Roses to whom Landor afterwards addressed a poem, the third Rose being her mother. She described the death, when she was at Rome, of Miss Bathurst—beautiful, radiant, and a splendid horsewoman, riding along the narrow path between the Acqua Acetosa and the Ponte Molle. The horse suddenly slipped backwards into the Tiber. She called out to Lord Aylmer, 'Uncle, save me!' but he could not swim, nor could any of the gentlemen or the groom who was present. Another groom, who was a good swimmer, had been sent back to Rome with a restive horse. She sank in her long blue habit, and her body was never found. All Rome mourned '*La bella Inglesa*,' and the little party of friends, closely united and present at her death, dispersed sadly. One of them alone, Mr. Charles Mills (of the Villa Mills), returned to Rome in the autumn. As he was about to enter the city, he sent his carriage on to the gate from the Ponte Molle, and walked slowly along the Tiber bank by what had been the scene of the accident six months before. As he walked, he saw two peasants on the other side of the river catch at something which looked like a piece of blue cloth on the mud, and pass on. A sudden impulse seized him, and he got some men to come at once with spades and dig there in the Tiber bank. There Miss Bathurst was found as if she were embalmed, in her blue riding-habit, perfectly beautiful, and with her long hair over her shoulders. There was only one little mark of a wound in her forehead. For a minute she was visible in all her loveliness— a minute only. She was buried in the English cemetery.

On 28th May 1888 I went abroad to my French work, feeling as usual greatly depressed at leaving home and going off into solitude, but soon able to throw myself vigorously into all the interests of my foreign life and its work. How full each week seemed!—the two first alone amongst quiet villages and churches in Picardy and afterwards in Auvergne, and many others after my friend Hugh Bryans joined me at wild S. Flour, in the hill country of Auvergne, at beautiful Obazine, and at Rocamadour again, then at beautiful S. Emilion, in wandering amongst the innumerable historic relics of La Vendée; lastly by the Loire and its surroundings. Three places especially come back to me with pleasant memories—the homelike inn at S. Emilion, its beautiful old buildings radiant with the blossom of pinks and valerian, and the sunset walks on its old walls looking into the vineyards and cornfields:—the little fishing port of Le Croisic, with its gay boats, its snow-white houses, and its windy surroundings:—and charming Clisson, with its pleasant inn and its balconies overhung with rose and wistaria.

To MISS LEYCESTER.

Clermont Ferrand, June 9.—Oh, it has been so hot! Never in my life have I been so grilled, roasted, boiled, and melted down; and it has been hard having to work on all day, whatever the intense exhaustion from the heat. But I have kept up to exactly the tale of work measured out for each day before I left home.

Le Puy, June 13.—We had an exquisite journey on Tuesday by rail down the valley of the Alagnon to Neussargues, the quantity of old castles on the rocky hills as striking as those on the Rhine were forty years ago, and the mountain flowers lovely. Then we drove up through the cool forests to the high plateau which is under snow nine months of the year, and which was quite chilly even now. Here, in the evening, we reached the old episcopal town of S. Flour, on a great basaltic rock, the most wonderfully placed of all French cities, and much recalling Orvieto. Everything seemed to belong to another world. From my window I could throw anything sheer down the most tremendous of quite perpendicular precipices, and the view was magnificent. The house has been in the same family for four hundred years, and the landlady showed with pride the dark passage where her ancestor intercepted the Protestants when they were trying to take the city by stealth, the stone on which they were beheaded, and the drain by which their blood flowed away.

S. Nectaire le Haut, June 28.—It was dark and raining in torrents before we arrived here, and the driver suddenly announced not only that he had lost his way, but that one of our wheels was likely to come off! We were skirting a precipice by a rocky road without any parapet, and at last, by holding the carriage lamps low, found that we had somehow got into a very ancient churchyard, where stone coffins were strewn all about. At last we knocked up a woman at a farmhouse, who guided us back to the hotel, which we had long passed in the dark. This is an enchanting place, beautifully situated in a wooded gorge below the old romanesque church, where the Sunday congregation—from many far-away villages—winding up the hill with baskets of food for the day, has been most picturesque. There are lovely walks in all directions, and Switzerland at its best never had more beautiful flowers, fields covered with lilies, orchis, narcissus, globe ranunculus, pansies, pinks, &c.

I returned to England on August 7th.

To Miss Leycester.

Sept. 17.—It was a great pleasure to find Sir Howard[1] and Lady Elphinstone at the Eustace Cecils'. I like them both so very much. They say the Queen is much occupied in learning Hindustanee and speaks it now quite well—a great delight to her Indian subjects. She has three Indian servants in constant attendance, and converses fluently with them.

Journal and Letters to Miss Leycester.

Ford Castle, Northumberland, Nov. 26.—Mr. Bellairs, the Highcliffe agent, who is here, said—

'My grandfather was both at Trafalgar and Waterloo, for he was wounded as a middy at Trafalgar, and then went into the army. It was odd when, long afterwards, some one said about Trafalgar, "It was so and so" and he said, "No, it was not, for I was there," and that the conversation then went on to Waterloo, "It was so and so." —"No, I beg your pardon, but I was *there*."

'Afterwards he fell in love with Miss Mackenzie, one of two heiress sisters. He had nothing to marry upon, and the father forbade him the house, but he was allowed one interview, and in that he found out that the butler was just leaving, and the family would be wanting another. He dressed up and came and applied for the place. He got it, and it was three weeks before he was found out, and then Mr. Mackenzie allowed that he was too much for him, and allowed that he should marry his daughter. But he insisted that my grandfather should leave the army. "Very well," he said, "if you like I will go into the Church." So it was agreed to, and in time he became a Canon. He was as earnest in the Church as everywhere else. Soon after his appointment to a country living, as he was crossing some fields on a Sunday, he found a number of miners crowding round some prize-fighters. "Come," he said, "I can't have this: I shall not allow this." "But you can't prevent it," they cried. "Can't prevent it! you'll soon see if I can't fight for my God as well as for my king: I'll fight you all in turn," and he polished off the two strongest miners in fair fight, and then the others were so pleased, they chaired him, and carried him through the village to his church, which they filled from that time forward.'

Dec. 11.—My old cousins, Mr. and Mrs. Thurlow, who had often invited me before to their house of Baynards, wrote that this week was my last chance of going, as Baynards was just sold, so I have been for one night. Mrs. Thurlow says that Cardinal Wiseman went to dine with some friends of hers. It was a Friday, but they had quite forgotten to provide a fast-day dinner. However, he was quite equal to the occasion, for he stretched out his hands in benediction over the table and said, 'I pronounce all this to be fish,' and forthwith enjoyed all the good things heartily.

Jan. 10.—To tea with Mrs. Humphry Ward, almost a celebrity now as authoress of 'Robert Elsmere,' at her house in Russell Square. She said it tried her somewhat to receive from an American 'Whiteley' his circular with—'for economy in literature we defy anything to beat our Elsmere at six cents.'

On Shrove-Tuesday, March 6, I left home for the south, and spent a fortnight at Mentone. On the 22nd I reached Rome, where I spent six

[1] Sir Howard Crawford Elphinstone, 1829–1890, major-general; served in Crimea; appointed aide-de-camp to Queen Victoria, 1877.—*Ed.*

weeks, seeing many friends, correcting my *Walks in Rome*, and drawing a great deal.

JOURNAL.

April 7.—On Friday I went with some friends to Albano, and, whilst they drove to Neni, drew in the glen at Ariccia, and never was I so tormented by children as by a beautiful little cowherd—Amalia Maria—who, on my refusing her demand for *soldi*, vowed she would 'lead me a life,' which she did by fetching six other little demons

PONT S. LOUIS, MENTONE

worse than herself, when they all joined hands and danced round me and my campstool, kicking and screaming with all their might. Then they fetched a black *pecorello* [sheep], and having tried to make it eat my paints, danced again, the *pecorello*, held by a string, prancing behind them. Happily at last the cow which Amalia Maria was supposed to be chaperoning made its escape over a hedge, and whilst she was pursuing it over the country, I fled, and joined my companions at a little caffè, where we had a delicious luncheon of excellent bread, hard-boiled eggs—painted purple for Lent—and sparkling Aleatico, for fourpence a head. Afterwards we sat to draw, looking down upon that loveliest of lakes and woods full of cyclamens and anemones.

The crowds in the Roman galleries are endless. Whole families arrive together, every member of them carrying a campstool, and they will sit down opposite each of the statues in turn, and move onwards gradually, whilst the father reads aloud from a guide-book, and they all drink it in. He often begins the description at the wrong end, but they do not find it out, and . . . it does not signify!

April 18.—Caught in tremendous rain and hail near a warehouse at the back of the Palatine, and took refuge under a rude porch with a number of peasants and was kept there an hour. One of the men described his life as a soldier when his battalion was sent against the brigands near Pescara. Of these, the famous Angelo Maria was so horrible a monster, that his own mother determined to rid the world of such a fiend and to deliver him up. He discovered this, seized his mother, laid her on a table, ripped her up, and taking out her steaming heart—ate it! Words cannot describe the horrible gestures with which the peasant told this story, or the dramatic power with which he described the sister seeing the terrible scene through a chink in the door, and coming afterwards to the guard-house, saying that she wished to betray her brother. 'Oh,' said the officer, 'you need not suppose that we trust you; this is a trap you have laid for us.'—'Yesterday,' she answered, 'I might have laid a trap, but I had not then seen that monster eat my mother's heart.' And he was taken.

But Capolo Roscia was worse. He came one night to a *masseria* [farm]. The doors were barred, but he forced his way in with his band. The head of the farm hid himself in the straw, but he was found and dragged out. All the men in the *masseria*, eighteen in number, were brought out and made to sit in a row. 'Now you must all be shaved,' said Capolo Roscia, and he cut all their eighteen heads off and put them in a basket.

'Oh, in that time when we were brigand-hunting we did not stop much to inquire how far they were guilty. "*A ginocchio: avete cinque minuti* [on your knees, you have five minutes]," we shouted to a peasant if we caught him. "*Oh, ma signori, signori!* [Oh, but gentlemen, gentlemen]" he would say." *A ginocchio! Un minuto, due, tre, cinque—bo-o-o-ah* [On your knees! one minute, two, three, five—bo-o-o-ah]!" and he was done for; for he had given the brigands provisions, and so he was as bad as themselves. Even with *i sindaci* [the mayor], well, we often did the same; but—we got rid of the brigands.'

Easter Sunday, April 21.—To St. Peter's. The service was under the dome, but the group around the shrine would not call up even a reminiscence of the glorious services under the Papacy. The relics were shown afterwards from a high gallery—the spear-head of Longinus, the bit of the true cross, the napkin of Veronica, to the sight of which seven thousand years' indulgence is attached. I gazed hard, but could only see its glittering frame, nor could any other member of the congregation see any more.

After leaving Rome, I spent ten days with a pleasant party of friends at beautiful Perugia, and then went on to Venice. I was at the Pension Anglaise, crowded with lively, kindly ultra-English people, whose mistakes were amusing. 'Gesu-Maria!' suddenly exclaimed the gondolier on narrowly escaping a concussion at a sharp corner. 'Why on earth does he say '*Je suis marié* [I am married]'? said a Mrs. R. Afterwards I had a week's hard work in intense heat in Eastern France, and reached home on May 27.

JOURNAL.

July 18.—With troops of the London 'world' to a garden-party at Hatfield to meet the Shah of Persia (Nasr-ed-Din), who looks most savage and unimpressionable. He is, however, preferred to his servants, who give themselves endless airs, refusing the rooms prepared for them, &c., and their hosts are afraid to complain of them to the Shah, for fear he should cut off their heads! He is a true Eastern potentate in his consideration for himself and himself only: is most unconcernedly late whenever he chooses: utterly ignores every one he does not want to speak to: amuses himself with monkeyish and often dirty tricks: sacrifices a cock to the rising sun, and wipes his wet hands on the coat-tails of the gentleman next him without compunction. He expressed his wonder that Lord Salisbury did not take a new wife, though he gave Lady Salisbury

THE ROCKY VALLEY, HOLMHURST

a magnificent jewelled order. He knows no English and very few words of French, but when the Baroness Coutts, as the great benefactress of her country, was presented to him by the Prince of Wales, he looked in her face and exclaimed, '*Quelle horreur!*'

To MISS LEYCESTER.

Holmhurst, August 15, 1889.—I wish you were here this morning. A delicate haze softens the view of the distant sea, sprinkled over with vessels, and the castle-rock rises up ink-grey against it. Far over-head, the softest of white clouds float in the blue ether. In the meadows, where the cows are ringing their Swiss bells, the old oak-trees are throwing long deep shadows across lawns of the most emerald green, and the flower-beds and the terrace borders are brimming with the most brilliant flowers, over which whole battalions of butterflies and bees are floating and buzzing; the little pathlet at the side winds with enticing shadows under the beech-trees, whilst the white marble Venetian well, covered with delicate sculpture of vines and pomegranates, standing on the little grassy platform, makes a point of refinement which accentuates the whole. Selma steals lazily round the corner to see if she can catch a bird, but finds it quite too hot for the exertion; and Rollo raises himself now and then carelessly to snap at a fly. The doves are cooing on the ledge of the roof, and the pigeons are collecting on the smokeless chimneys. Upstairs Mrs. Whitford and Anne are dusting and laughing over their work, with the windows wide open above the ivied verandah, and Rogers is planting out a box of sweet-scented tobacco-plants which has come by the post.

To Louisa, Marchioness of Waterford.

St. Michael's Mount, Sept. 7, 1889.—This is a wonderful and delightful place. It was nearly 10 P.M. when I reached the Marazion station. The day had been very hot, and the evening lights and reflections perfectly lovely; but night had quite closed in. Lord St. Levan's carriage met me at the station, and stopped at the head of a staircase leading to the sea, where four sturdy boatmen took possession of me and my things, and rowed away on a waveless sea, following up the long stream of brilliant light which fell from one of the upper windows of the castle on the sacred mount, grim and black in the still night. An old man with a lanthorn met me at the landing-place, and guided me up a steep pathlet in the rocks.

It is a life apart. The chapel-bell rings at nine, and I always meet Mrs. Lowther on the staircase hurrying up to the service, which is reached by an open-air walk at the top of everything. Then, before breakfast in the 'Chevy Chase Hall' (surrounded by old stucco hunting scenes), we linger on the grand platform, looking down into the chrysoprase waves with sea-birds floating over them, and across to the mainland with its various bays, and its fleeting golden lights and purple shadows.

This truly aquatic family bathe together from a raft at 7 A.M. most mornings. To-day they were all rowed in their scanty bathing costumes, looking like Charon's souls being ferried to purgatory, into the little port, and there (at twelve mid-day) one after the other took a header into the sea, and swam—many of the guests with them— to the main-shore at Marazion, to the great astonishment of the natives on the beach there.

In quoting so constantly from journal and letters, I do not think I have mentioned how much poverty had been pressing upon me in the last few years. Not only had Messrs. Daldy and Virtue, representing my first publishers, ceased to pay even the interest of their large debt, or paid it most irregularly, but under my second set of publishers I had made *nothing whatever* during the seven years I had been with them. Their accounts showed that 28,000 of my books had been sold in the time, but the innumerable percentages, &c., had swallowed up the whole of the profits, leaving me nothing but the loss of money expended on woodcuts, &c.

Whilst I was at Muncaster, however, Mrs. Arthur Severn came to the castle, and told me how Mr. Ruskin also had made nothing by his books in the hands of my then publishers, but that they had brought him in a good income since they were removed to the hands of Mr. Allen of

Orpington. To his hands, therefore, I soon after removed all my books.[1] I had no complaint of unfairness to make against those I had lately employed; they only acted according to their agreements and their usual method, which I had long hoped against hope might eventually result to my advantage: and they behaved very handsomely about parting with the books, though it must have been both a loss and disappointment to them.

From Christmas 1889–90 people were already beginning to talk a great deal about the 'influenza epidemic' which was spreading over Europe, and was like a malarial fever. I was in London for a few hours on January 11, and bringing it back to Holmhurst with me, was very ill for nearly a month, but with the comfort of being in my own home, and, to me, the great comfort of being alone.

Feb. 26, 1890.—Went to see Lady De Ros,[2] aged ninety-five. . . . Lady De Ros was very full of her dispute with Sir William Fraser[3] about the house in which the ball was given at Brussels by her father, the Duke of Richmond, on the eve of the battle of Waterloo. She was quite certain of her facts and that the house was now gone. She had been living in the house itself, in the Rue de la Blanchisserie ('where the Duke would direct to me "in the wash-house" '), and cited as a proof that the ball was given in her own house, the fact that her youngest sister, who had been sent to bed, stole out, and watched the company arrive through the banisters. 'I believe Sir William Fraser asserts,' said Lady De Ros, 'that I am confused and doting now through my great age, but you know very old people remember the long-ago as if it was to-day, and that is the case with me. In 1860 I went back to see Brussels, and I could not find our house then; the whole street was swept away. At last, as I was walking up and down, I was attracted by the name on a pastry-cook's shop: it was a name I remembered in that long-ago time. So I went in and asked if they knew anything of our house. "Oh, a house in the Rue de la Blanchisserie," they said; "it has been pulled down years and years ago." '

---

[1] Publication with Mr. George Allen was on a profit-sharing basis: two-thirds of the profits to the author and one-third to the publisher. This arrangement produced a fairly considerable income, amounting to well over £1,000 in one particular year, a sum which in those days of low living costs and low taxation was worth a very great deal. Mr. Allen published also from his London address in Bell Yard and subsequently in Charing Cross Road. In 1914 the business became a constituent part of George Allen & Unwin Ltd., who have republished this volume. The accounts covering the Hare books are still in existence.—*Ed.*

[2] Georgiana, third daughter of Charles, 4th Duke of Richmond.

[3] Sir William Augustus Fraser (1826–1898) politician and author of several gossipy volumes on contemporary history. He was the son of a colonel on the staff at Waterloo and one of his works was wholly devoted to the Waterloo Ball.—*Ed.*

XI

AT HOME AND ABROAD

1890

⊱⊰

WHEN my friend George Jolliffe had passed his diplomatic examination, I promised him that I would go out and pay him a month's visit wherever he was sent to. Thus I came to set out for Constantinople on April 10, 1890. At Vienna I spent several days with the Lützows, who showed me the sights in the most agreeable way. The town was full of grand-dukes or exiled princes—Cumberland, Parma, Tuscany, &c., all very rich and adding to its prosperity.

To MISS LEYCESTER.

British Embassy, Constantinople, April 22, 1890.—We came straight through from Vienna. There were vast plains of corn till Belgrade, a poor town hanging shaggy on the hillside: then we entered low wooded hills like the Sabina. In the Servian villages of rude huts and ruder fences we could see the swarming people, men and women in loose folds of white linen, the former with the air of princes. All seemed remote and unreal, and the shadows, as in Syrian clearness, fell pure blue upon the dusty hills. By the second morning we were passing through Roumelia. All had become poorer. The villages, of wretched huts, stood in wattled enclosures of thorns, inside which all the domestic animals are driven. Now, the men were seen in crimson and green, with magnificent mahogany-coloured faces beneath their turbans, and the women, all closely veiled, moved like masses of dark drapery; a little mosque appeared, with a delicate and refined minaret; a little fountain-cistern with a gothic arch in a grove of thorns; marshes with storks; plains with buffaloes.

About 3 P.M., the lovely Sea of Marmora gleamed upon the right, with a variety of inlet bays of solitary beauty, and, in the distance, the aërial mountains of Asia. Then a succession of battlemented towers rose on the left from the untrodden plain—the walls of Stamboul! Through these the train passes. We were far from the station still, but what a change from our two days' desolation! We rushed across many shabby courts, paved either with mud or rough stones. The old houses, with their projecting lattices, were veiled in a web of flowering wistaria, and shaded by pink Judas-trees in fullest bloom. Then above us rose the mosques with their slender minarets and huge storm-blasted cypresses. St. Sophia itself, Achmet, Suleiman, Mahmoud were passed, with many a strange gothic fountain or decorated cistern, before we reached the shed-like station, where George was a most welcome sight, armed with an Embassy cavass to extricate us from the mass of yelping, screaming natives.

Off we went across the creaking, rocking, timber bridge over the Golden Horn, thronged by the strangest of multitudes. Then up the steep street of Galata, where the lattices project until they almost obliterate the sky, and the pavement is made of rough stones set edgeways, up which the horses scrambled like cats. A road succeeded, a dusty deep-rutted track, overlooking an old burial-ground without barriers, where, amid the immemorial cypresses, thousands of battered tombstones remain, neglected, ruined, but never wilfully destroyed; and so we reached the handsome palace of the Embassy, with its delightful garden, overlooking the valley of the Golden Horn.

April 27.—I have been suffering terribly from rheumatic fever, but am better to-day, and have been to St. Sophia. The carriage stopped at an obscure door on the N.W., where the cavass took off his boots and fetched some of the Turkish guardians of

CEMETERY OF PERA, CONSTANTINOPLE

holiness, who, for a very large consideration of baksheesh, put slippers over ours. Then we passed the curtain, and found ourselves at once at the northern extremity of the great western narthex, like that of St. Mark's at Venice on a huge scale, and—almost immediately—from a side-door, in the church itself.

It is so unspeakably, overwhelmingly, indescribably, entrancingly, bewilderingly glorious, words can give no idea of it.

Of the immense space—a St. Mark's lifted into the heavens, soaring far above in the mystic involutions of its entwining arches and the delicate nuances of its grey-golden colouring, never sufficiently defined to be obtrusive in any special point, only melting and harmonising into a whole as tender and glorious as the hues in a dove's back.

We drove by the tomb of the Sultan Mahmoud the Reformer, where we stared through a metal screen at his sarcophagus, to the finest of the great mosques or *djami*, the glorious Suleimanyeh, which Solyman the Magnificent intended to surpass St.

Sophia. On its giant dome is the truly catholic inscription (Sura xxiv. 36), 'God is the light of heaven and earth. His light is in the windows on the wall, in which a lamp burns covered with glass. The glass shines like a star, the lamp is lit with the oil of a blessed tree. No Eastern, no Western oil; it shines for whoever wills it.' On the ever-clean matted floor of this mosque of glorious proportions numbers of barefooted children were sporting as in a playground, and very pretty and graceful were the interlacing groups which they made. Behind is a curious burial-ground, crowded with tombs, chiefly of women, marked by a sculptured rose, whilst the headstones of the men are crowned by a turban or fez. In two great sepulchral chapels or *turbé* lie Solyman the Magnificent and his immediate family and successors. The sarcophagi are covered with splendid embroideries and delicate muslins, those of the sultans being often shrouded by their favourite wives with their shawls—most precious of their possessions. At their heads are their tall white turbans, with bunches of peacocks' feathers on either side.

But all through the streets of Stamboul the greatest feature is the little burial-grounds, with their closely packed tombs and their huge cypresses or tamarind trees, which always give them picturesqueness, between the houses, at the angles of the streets, everywhere—the dead forced, as it were, into the very life of the living, and never to be forgotten for a moment.

The next great feature—and an odious one—is the swarms of dogs, like little foxes, which lie about everwhere in the sun, encumbering the footways, and refusing to move for any one. They are the friends of cats, but if a strange dog enters their quarter, they demolish him at once. They never bite a human being, at least they have never been known to bite more than one, and that was—the Russian ambassador! Successive travellers have given the idea that they are scavengers, but it is quite false: a man goes round at night with a cart and takes everything undesirable away. All night the air resounds with the yells of the dogs. The English doctor is obliged to poison them by hundreds near the hospital, or all the patients would die of the noise.

May 12.—As I have felt stronger, each day here has been more full of interest. On alternate mornings I stay quietly in the Embassy garden or the adjoining cemeteries and have luncheon with my kind hosts, with whom I have several times been out afterwards to the bazaars, steep, rugged, stony lanes, arched overhead, and a blaze of colour from their shops and costumes. Here we have been served with cups of coffee in the inner den of Marchetto, the tradesman of *Paul Patoff*,[1] whilst going through the wearisome routine of bargaining for old silver, weighing and re-weighing, and only discovering one had concluded a purchase when one had utterly despaired of it. How forcibly the truth of that verse of Proverbs strikes one here—'It is nought, it is nought, saith the buyer, but when he goeth his way, he boasteth thereof.' The whole bazaar seems like an inextricable web to outsiders, yet any one or anything can be found there in ten minutes by one who knows the place; and, amid all the bustle and confusion, one sees many a charming picture of an old Turk with snowy beard and robes, sitting cross-legged at an angle of his counter, poring over an ancient parchment Koran, and as utterly absorbed in it as if he were in the Great Desert.

On other days I have gone off immediately after breakfast with a cavass from the Embassy—Dimitri—as my guard, making much use of the trams, from which one sees so much that is curious, and in which one has so many experiences of Turkish

---

[1] Marion Crawford's novel.

life, from the ladies like bundles of green, brown, or shot silk, who are huddled behind the curtain at the end of the carriage, to the child-pasha well provided with copper coins to quiet the numerous clamourers for baksheesh. Thus I have twice reached Yedi Kouli, the Seven Towers, where the triple walls of the town make their farthest angle close to the Sea of Marmora—bluest of blue waters melting into chrysoprase-green near the shore. Here I was drawing an old gate in pencil in my little book, heedless of an old Turk who had been cursing the 'christian dog' as a breaker of the second commandment, when suddenly, with a spring, he flew upon me, and in an instant his long talons would have torn out my eyes, if Dimitri, throwing himself upon him, had not hurled him on his back in the gutter, after which he got up, and went away quite quietly.

All around the walls are tombs: the woods are filled, the hillsides are powdered, with them. The woods are all of cypress, which is supposed to neutralise effluvia. When a death occurs, a body is hurried to the grave as soon as possible, for the soul is always in torment, it is believed, between the death and burial. Little parcels of food are laid in holes by the side of the grave, and large headstones are always erected, stones on which the angels Nebir and Munkir sit to judge the souls of the dead. We saw many touching little funerals—young girls being carried to the grave without any coffin or shroud.

We all went by carriage with an order to the Seraï or Seraglio near St. Sophia, which occupies at least two-thirds of the ancient Byzantium, selected by Constantine for his capital. By an unkempt ascent we reach the Bab-el-Sélam, or Gate of Safety, which had doors on either side, and in the intermediate space of which high officials condemned by the Divan were executed. Passing an avenue of cypresses, we reached a second gate, the Bab Seadet, or Gate of Happiness, guarded by white eunuchs. It was here that the sultans used to give up their unpopular ministers to the popular fury; that Murad III gave up his favourite falconer, Mehemet, to be cut to pieces before his eyes; that Mahomet III gave up his three chief eunuchs, and Murad IV his grand-vizier Hafiz, who was killed by seventeen wounds. Many old aunts and cousins of sultans still reside in the inner apartments, guarded by numbers of eunuchs, the historic criminal figures of Turkish history, whose existence is expressly condemned by the Koran, and who are generally bought or stolen as children from Syria or Abyssinia. Without name, family, or sex, they often marry, and even have harems for the sake of feminine friendship.

Another day we went to the mosque of Selimyeh, beautifully situated, and afterwards I sat to draw under a bower of banksia roses, surrounded by a marvellous group of Turkish figures, in the Saddlers' Bazaar (*seera-jobane-jamissi*). Here the people were good to us, as there are so many Christians in that quarter of the town, but generally the natives never cease cursing those who are breaking the second commandment by making a likeness of something in heaven or earth. In the courtyard of Suleimanyeh I was less fortunate: a number of soldiers crowded in front, wholly obstructing all view, and on Dimitri remonstrating, their officer came up quite furious, with 'My men shall stand where they like, and if they wish to hide the man's view they shall certainly do so.'

We went to the evening service at St. Sophia, three white-turbaned figures receiving us in the dark at a postern door, and—after exacting ten francs apiece—conducting us by a winding stair to the broad gallery, far beneath which the great chandeliers gleamed like flower-beds over the immense grey space, intersected by long lines of black figures—all males, for women are soulless—bending, curvetting, prostrating symmetrically like corn in a wind, and with the same kind of rush and rustle. It is a curious but monotonous sight, a repetition of the same movement over and over again, and the shrill harsh cry of the swaying and falling lines, even more discordant in its echo by the choir, soon grates upon one: especially as the priests never cease whispering and worrying for extra baksheesh.

After waiting one morning for a weary time with an order at the 'Selamlik,' we saw the Sultan go to the Yildis mosque. The coachman was gorgeous in his golden livery, but the 'Sultan of Sultans, the King of Kings,' was a piteous sight, a mixture of boredom and terror. Cringing cowardice prevents his going to Stamboul more than one day in the year, and this occurred lately. It is a great day for the court ladies, who are all allowed to accompany him in three hundred carriages, and avenge themselves for veiled faces by exhibiting their bare arms covered with bracelets and as much else as they dare.

Almost every night through the streets there is a rush of the Talumbodgi or firemen—half-naked savages with primitive engines, who scurry to save the valuables of burning houses, not for the owners, but for themselves, so that they are far more dreaded than the flames. In recent conflagrations in Galata and Pera it is certain that the fire began in three or four places at the same moment; for when a street in Constantinople is wholly bad or unsafe, the authorities do not scruple to set fire to it, regardless of the consequences, though the people are such fatalists that they will not leave their dwellings till the last moment, and then fly, leaving everything behind them.

May 23.—My last hours at Constantinople were spent in an expedition with the Whites in their picturesque state barge to the Sweet Waters of Europe. I believe I have said nothing of Sir William White, though he is the ambassador in whose house I have been living so long. His simple manners are full of bluff humour. He is said to understand the Turk perfectly, and rose entirely by his own merits, with the help of a lucky appointment to the Conference [of Constantinople] of 1876–77.[1]

To LOUISA, MARCHIONESS OF WATERFORD.

Ober-Ammergau, June 2.—We have seen the Passion-Play. It is a day to have lived for: nothing can be more sublimely devotional, more indescribably pathetic.

Yesterday morning, I imagine, no visitor could sleep after four, when their peasant hosts began to tramp overhead and clatter down their narrow oak staircases. Then, after an excellent breakfast of hot coffee, cream, eggs, and toast, many visitors and all the people of Ober-Ammergau hurried to the six-o'clock service in the church, where all the five hundred actors knelt with their pastor in silent prayer, and many of them received the Sacrament. At eight all were comfortably placed in their seats in the open-air theatre, and the soft wild music of Schutzgeister, which seems to come from behind the hills, preluded the performance.

One might be seated in the Piazza del Popolo at Rome with one's back to the gate. There is the same vast intervening space, and the same three branching streets (the central closed by an inner theatre for tableaux), with marked buildings at the entrance. Only here those buildings are the houses of Annas, Caiaphas, and Pilate, and the streets are those of Jerusalem, lined with Eastern houses, domes, and here and there a palm-tree, and they melt far away into lovely ethereal mountain distances, the real mountains of the Bavarian Alps. The performance begins when the spirit-chorus of eighteen

[1] Sir William White died the following year.

persons, male and female, in many-coloured tunics and mantles, advance in stately lines from either side of the stage, and in a chaunt, weird but most distinctly audible, explain what is coming, and urge those present to receive it in a humble spirit of reverence and adoration of God. Then, on the central stage, begin the strange series of types and antitypes, and, as the veil falls the second time, the vast Hosanna-procession of five hundred men, women, and children, singing, shouting, and strewing palm-branches, appears down the distant streets, and, as it draws nearer, and the mountains resound with jubilant shouts and the whole air is ablaze with life and colour, the serene, rapt, stately figure of the Christus, riding upon the ass, but even then spiritualised into absolute sublimity by the sense of his divine mission, comes for the first time before us. Afterwards, through the long eight hours of thrilling tension which follow, overshadowing the endless, almost wearisome, series of Old

OBERAMMERGAU

Testament scenes, drawing every heart and eye nearer to himself through the agony of the trial, the cross-bearing, the crucifixion, does that sublime figure become more familiar; never again can the thought of the God-man be severed from it. And in the great drama itself one sees all the rest, but one feels with, one lives for, the Christ alone; and the dignity of his lofty patience, unmoved from the holy calm which pervades his whole being even when four hundred savage Jews are shouting and jibing round in clamorous eagerness for his death, must be present with one through life.

Of the New Testament scenes, the leave-taking with the family of Bethany is perhaps the most pathetic. It is an exquisite sunset scene. Huge olive-trees stretch their gnarled boughs overhead and are embossed against the amber sky, in the distance the village of Bethany stands out in the soft blue mists of evening. Through the sunset comes the Christ in lingering last words with the sisters and Lazarus, and there, under the old trees, is their last farewell, touching indescribably, after which the weeping family return to Bethany, and he goes away, a solitary figure upon the burnt hills in the twilight, to his death at Jerusalem.

The evening shadows are beginning to fall as we see Christ raised on the cross. He hangs there for twenty minutes, and most indescribably sublime are the words given from thence. When all is over, it is so real, you think that *this time* death must really have taken place. The three crosses, the bound thieves, the fainting women, the mounted centurion, the soldiers drawing lots, all seem to belong to real events, enacted, not acted. The deposition of the dead Christ on the white sheet is a vast Rubens picture.

The resurrection is more theatrical, but in the final scene, where the perfect figure of the spiritual Christ is seen for the last time, he goes far away with his disciples and the Marys, and then, upon Olivet, in the midst of the group relieved against the golden sunset, he solemnly blesses his beloved ones, and whilst you gaze rapt, seems to be raised a little, and then you look for him and he is not.

Each one of the four thousand spectators then sits in a vast sense of loneliness amid the silent Bavarian hills. The long tension is over. The day is lived out. The Master we have followed we can follow no longer with material sight. He has suffered, died, and risen from the grave, and is no longer with us; in the heavens alone can we hope to behold Him as He is.

During the varied occupations of this summer of 1890 I was asked to write biographies of several members of my family for the *Dictionary of National Biography*, and did so. My articles appeared, but greatly altered. The editor had a perfect right to condense them at his pleasure, but I was astonished to find *additions*. Bishop Hare was saddled with a third son, Richard Hare, 'an apothecary of Winchester,' who was the father of James Hare, afterwards called the 'Hare with many friends.' This son of my great-great-grandfather is entirely imaginary; our family was never in the remotest degree related to Richard or James Hare.

To Miss Leycester.

Sept. 6.—I have enjoyed a visit to Holmbury (Mr. Leveson Gower's), now let to Mr. Knowles of the *Nineteenth Century*—a lovely place with a delightful view over Surrey plains. He has talked much of Tennyson, with whom his family are very intimate, and who used often to stay with him when he first married and lived on Clapham Common. Tennyson speaks every thought without respect of persons. 'What fish is this?' (at dinner).—'Whiting.'—'Yes, the meanest fish there is.' Yet his kindness of heart is such, that when his partridge was afterwards given him almost raw, he ate steadily through it, for fear his hostess might be vexed.

After dinner Tennyson will sit smoking his pipe by the chimney-corner. That is his great time for inspiration, but he will seldom write anything down. 'Thousands of lines just float up this chimney,' he said one day. Sometimes he will go into the drawing-room and recite something he has just composed. Some of these poems Mr. Knowles has written down. If asked to repeat them again, Tennyson can never do it in the same way, something is always altered or forgotten: so hundreds of his poems are lost. One day lately, when he was unusually melancholy, his nurse, whom he greatly likes (he always has a nurse now), took him to task. 'Mr. Tennyson, you ought to be ashamed of yourself for grumbling in this way: you ought to be expressing your gratitude for your recovery from your bad illness by giving us something—by giving it to the world.' And he took her reproof very well, and went away to his own room, and in half-an-hour had written his lines 'Crossing the Bar', which he gave to her.

Tennyson was very rude to Mrs. Brotherton, a neighbour at Freshwater. The next day he came to her house with a great cabbage under each arm. 'I heard you liked these, so I brought them.' It was his idea of a peace-offering.

My *France* is just appearing, under the guardianship of Ruskin's friend Allen. I think it is good. I have certainly worked hard at it. The woodcuts are beautifully engraved, and with the letterpress I have even more than usual followed Arthur Young's advice to authors—'To expunge as readily as to compose.'

To Miss Leycester.

Oct. 14, 1890.—I went on the 27th to Worth, the ultra-luxurious house of the Montefiores, where the servants have their own billiard-tables, ballroom, theatre, and pianofortes, and are arrogant and presumptuous in proportion. . . . I was put down at the station on my way to Highcliffe, to which I hastened in answer to an unusually urgent and affectionate invitation from its dear lady, bidding me on no account to miss coming at that time; at another time it might not be possible. I found the dear Lady Waterford sadly ailing, but I hope I was able to be useful to her during some days of extreme quietude and much reading aloud. She had lately been to the Queen at Osborne, crossing the Solent in the *Elfin*, seated between the two great bags—'as big as large arm-chairs'—containing the Queen's letters for the day. 'The Queen would have my drawings in. It was dreadful! for you know how a big portfolio slides off the table, and the Queen looked at them all so closely, and I was afraid the portfolio would slip and catch hold of her nose, and then I should have been sent to the Tower or something. There was one of the drawings she liked so much that I gave it to her. It was of Time with his scythe over his shoulder. A quantity of little children were gambolling and sporting in front and beckoning him onwards, but behind were a number of old people trying to hold him back; for one wanted to go on with his book, another to finish a drawing, and so on, and so they were clinging to his skirts as he was striding away.'

I felt sadder than usual in leaving Highcliffe this time, as if it might be a last visit, yet it is difficult to imagine life without what has given its greatest interest and charm. The dear lady was down before I came away, though it was very early, and I retain a beautiful picture of her standing in the conservatory under the great brugmantia laden with its orange flowers. She came with me through the rooms, and I looked back at her, and found her still looking after me, and so, somehow walked away sadly down the dewy lanes to the station, with a desolate feeling that I might see her no more.

To Louisa, Marchioness of Waterford.

Nov. 10, 1890.—On October 20 I went to Tatton, meeting a large and pleasant party for the week, and one sees every one there to perfection, Lady Egerton knowing so well how to unlock a portal of communication—often of friendship—with just the right key. Little Knutsford was sanded all over in patterns (as in India) for a wedding: it is a custom which dates from King Alfred, who met a wedding-party as he was passing through the town and threw down some sand, saying that he hoped the descendants of the marriage might be as numerous as its grains. The patterns of sand—flowers, love-knots, &c.—are made through the spout of a teapot.

Lord Donington told Lady Egerton that when he went to live where he does now, his two young boys were taught by an admirable English governess. One day, having observed the housekeeper carefully locking the door of a spare bedroom, she casually said, 'Do you always keep the doors of the unused bedrooms locked?'—'No,' said the housekeeper, 'only this one;' and she invited the governess to look into it, saying that there was a mystery about it. Some one always seemed to come to sleep there, whom she could not imagine, and she believed some trick was being played upon her. As an experiment, she said she would be very much obliged if the governess would take away the key after the room was locked, and keep it till the following morning. The next day they went together to the room, which showed every appearance of having been slept in, yet the window was carefully fastened inside, and there was no other possible entrance.

Some time after, a young man came to shoot with the boys, and was put into that room. In the morning he came down with a very scared look, and said he was very sorry, but he must leave. Being much pressed, he allowed that he had been dreadfully frightened. He had kept his candle by his bed to finish a book he had been reading, and, looking up, he saw an old man sitting by the fire, who eventually rose, came, looked into the bed, and seeing him there, walked away. 'And,' said the visitor, '*that* is the man!' pointing to a picture on the wall of an ancestor who had died centuries before.

To Louisa, Marchioness of Waterford.

Nov. 30, 1890.—I had a pleasant visit at St. Audries, Sir A. Acland Hood's beautiful place. In a corner of the hall are baby-clothes of three boys beneath the portrait of another remote ancestor, Edward Palmer of Ightham Mote. One Whitsunday morning a servant came in and said, 'Sir, your lady has presented you with a son.'—'The most joyful news you could have brought me!' said Mr. Palmer. The following Sunday the servant came again: 'Sir your lady has presented you with another son.'—'Oh, God bless my soul! you don't say so!' exclaimed Mr. Palmer. But the third Sunday the servant came in with 'Sir your lady has presented you with another son.' It seemed quite too much; but the babies all lived, and grew up to be very distinguished men, being all knighted for their valour by Henry VIII.[1]

From Somersetshire I went to Hatfield, arriving just after sunset. You could only just see the red colouring on the majestic old house, but all the windows blazed and glittered with light through the dark walls; the Golden Gallery with its hundreds of electric lamps was like a Venetian illumination. The many guests coming and going, the curiously varied names inscribed upon the bedroom doors, give the effect of having all the elements of society compressed under one roof. It was pleasant to meet Lady Lytton,[2] beautiful still, and with all the charm of the most high-bred refinement. Another guest was Count Herbert Bismarck. Lady Salisbury had spoken of him as a fallen power, greatly broken by his fall, and so had enlisted our sympathies for him, but he quenched them by his loud authoritative manner, flinging every sentence from him with defiant self-assertion. He was especially opinionated about Henry VIII's wives, utterly refusing to allow that Anne of Cleves did not precede Anne Boleyn. He is a colossal man and a great eater, and would always fill two glasses of wine at once, to have one in reserve. At dinner he was rather amusing about the inefficiency

---

[1] The birth of John, Henry, and Thomas Palmer is perhaps the only well-authenticated instance of a fortnight intervening between the eldest and the youngest child produced at a birth. It is described by Fuller [in *The Worthies of England*, a reprint of which—the first for more than a century—is being produced by George Allen & Unwin Ltd. in 1952.—*Ed.*]

[2] Wife of the first Earl of Lytton, son of the novelist.—*Ed.*

THE HON. CHARLOTTE CANNING AND
THE HON. LOUISA STUART
the "Two Noble Lives"

of doctors, and said that the only time when cause follows effect was when a doctor follows the funeral of his patient.

The life of a Prime Minister's family is certainly no sinecure. Lady Salisbury and her daughter have constantly to go off to found or open charities of every description. Lord Salisbury is occupied with his secretaries to the very last moment before breakfast and luncheon, into which he walks stooping, with hands folded behind him, and a deeply meditative countenance, and by his side the great boar-hound called 'Pharaoh' —'because he will not let the people go'; but when once seated as a host, he wakes up into the most interesting and animated conversation.

To LOUISA, MARCHIONESS OF WATERFORD.

Dec. 7, 1890.—How interesting is the Parnell crisis![1] At Miss Seymour's I met a Countess Ziski, who talked of how curious it was that abroad, if a woman misconducts herself, she is boycotted, but no notice is taken of the misconduct of the man: here, if a woman misconducts herself, an easy-going society makes excuses for her, but the man is cashiered for ever.

Alas! the shadows which I had observed during my last visit to my dear friend Lady Waterford were now gathering very thickly around her. She had failed rapidly from the time of her removal from Highcliffe to her Northumbrian home, and was no longer able to answer me; but I still wrote to her. It was on [the 1st of March] that I first truly realised that my dearest Lady's illness must be fatal. Our Lady was told that it must be so, that the end might come any day, any hour. At first she shed a few natural tears, and said, 'I thought I should have lived to seventy-seven, as my mother did, and then added sweetly, 'But why should I mind, since God so wills it? tell me how it will be.'—'Perhaps in your chair, just as you are sitting now.'—'Oh, that will be well—so quiet, so well.' . . . One heard of the gradual increase of the disease: of her laying aside all painting and writing: of her reading prayers to her servants for the last time; but still talking in her wise and beautiful way of all things 'lovely and of good report.' laughing brightly over old recollections: then of her lying constantly on a sofa, always rejoicing to see those she loved, but mistaking her younger relations for their mothers, dear to her in the long ago. Often also others, those dearest to her, who had gone before, appeared to be present with her as angel ministrants to cheer and comfort.

Mr. Neville, the rector of Ford, prayed with her daily. 'How I wish that others might have the solace this is to me,' she said, with her peculiar emphasis on the word 'solace.' And so, peacefully, radiantly, our dearest Lady fell into the ever-smiling unconsciousness, in which, on May 11th, she passed away from us to join the beloved and honoured who are at rest with Christ.

[1] It was in November 1890 that Parnell appeared as co-respondent in O'Shea's divorce suit; in December he was deposed from the leadership of the Irish party.—*Ed.*

I

I should have gone to Ford afterwards, but our Lady only died on Monday, and it was late on Wednesday night before I heard that she was to be buried on Thursday afternoon, so to arrive in time was impossible. Miss Lindsay wrote to me how her coffin was carried on the shoulders of her own labourers to the churchyard, how all the village and all her tenantry came to her funeral, with the few intimate friends within reach, and how Helmore's music was sung.

XII

SOCIAL REMINISCENCES

1891–92

To the HON. G. JOLLIFFE.

Holmhurst, August 1891.—I enjoyed my months in London at the time, yet was very glad to come away. It is a terrible waste of life. The size and lateness of dinners have killed society. Scarcely any one says anything worth hearing, and if any one does, nobody listens. People love talking, but not talk. Dinners are rather display than hospitality, supplying abundance of sumptuous viands, but no *esprit.* I heard pleasanter conversation in one quiet luncheon at the Speaker's from his delightful family than at a hundred parties: as a social art it is extinct. One never hears such conversationalists as gathered round my aunt Mrs. Stanley's homely table long ago, or as, in later times, round Arthur Stanley, Mrs. Grote, Madame Mohl, the first Lady Carnarvon, Lord Houghton, Lady Margaret Beaumont. The dinners, in food sense, have never any attraction to me. L. and I dined out together at —— and I think it was an even match which of us suffered most, L. or myself: myself, because the dinner was too good; L., because it was not good enough.

I saw the Emperor (of Germany)[1] several times, a fat young man with a bright good-humoured face, though apparently never free from the oppression of his own importance, as well as of the importance of his dress, which he changes very often in the day. And I went, one glorious afternoon, when the limes were in blossom, with several thousand other people to Hatfield to meet the Prince of Naples, whose intelligence (especially on subjects connected with Natural History) seems to have pleased everybody. He is very small, but has none of the aggressive ugliness of his father and grandfather. One day I went to luncheon with Miss Rhoda Broughton, who is seen at her very best in her little house at Richmond, most attractive in its old prints and furniture and lovely river view.

To W. H. MILLIGAN, *and Note-book.*

Holmhurst, Oct. 1891.—I have returned from my autumn visits, which had been delightful.

I arrived at Bishopthorpe the day before the Archbishop's enthronement, and found a large party of relations assembling; but it would be difficult to crowd the house, as there are forty bedrooms and the dining-room is huge. The palace lies low, and out of the dining-room window you could very nearly fish in the Ouse, which often floods the cellars. The ceremony in the Minster was very imposing, the more so as a military escort was given to the Archbishop, as having been an old soldier. Most moving was his address upon the responsibilities, and what he felt to be the duties, of his office.

---

[1] William II, then aged 31.—*Ed.*

The ebb and flow of processional music was beautiful, as the long stream of choristers and clergy flowed in and out of the Minster.[1]

Most happy and interesting were my four succeeding days at Hickleton, where I met one of the familiar circles of people I always connect with Charlie Halifax. More characteristic still of the host was the presence of a nun in full canonicals—Sister Caroline—'this religious,' as Charlie called her—who appeared at meals, though only to partake of a rabbit's diet. In the churchyard a great crucifix, twelve feet high is being erected, and the people of Doncaster do not come out to stone it; on the contrary, the crucifix and its adjuncts attract large congregations of pitmen, who would not go to church at all otherwise; and the neighbourhood is beginning to wonder how long the Church of England can dare to deny its Lord by condemning the crucifix, the vacant cross being but the frame of the picture with the portrait left out, and in itself an eloquent protest against the omission. Another smaller crucifix commemorates the three dear boys who have 'gone home.' The shadow of their great loss here is ever present, but it is truly a sanctified grief. Only a deep sudden sigh from the father now and then recalls all he has undergone.[2]

To the COUNTESS OF DARNLEY.

Hotel d'Italie, Rome, March 30. 1892.—I have been abroad since November 16, beginning by a week at Paris, and a month spent at Cannes in visits. How civilised and be-villa'd Cannes is now, almost the least pretentious house remaining in it being the little Villa Nevada, where the Duke of Albany died,[3] which was close to us, and which was so often visited by 'Madame d'Angleterre,' as the people of Cannes call our Queen.

I spent a week at Bordighera. George Macdonald, a most grand old patriarch to look upon, is king of the place. He writes constantly, and never leaves the house, except to see a neighbour in need of help or comfort. One after another of his delicate daughters has faded away, but his sons seem strong and well, and there are several adopted children in the house, half in and half out of the family, but all calling Mrs. Macdonald 'Mama.' It is a very unusual household, but ruled in a spirit of love which is most beautiful. I dined with them, the dining-table placed across one end of the vast common sitting-room. On Sunday evenings he gives a sort of Bible lecture, which all the sojourners in Bordighera may attend.

Then I was a month in a palatial hotel at S. Remo, and greatly enjoyed bright winter days of quiet drawing in its ravines with their high-striding bridges, by its torrents full of Titanic boulders, or on its pathlets winding through vine and fig gardens or along precipitous crags; most of all in a delicious palm-shaded cove by the sea, where I spent whole days alone with the great chrysoprase waves breaking over the rocks in showers of crystal spray.

But it is in changed, spoilt Rome that I have spent the last two months. All picturesqueness is now washed out of the place, so that people who have any interest about them now usually give it only a glance and pass on. It has been delightful for me, however, that Miss Hosmer[4] is settled in this hotel, and that we dine together

[1] William Dalrymple Maclagan, 1826–1910, bishop of Lichfield, 1878–91, and Archbishop of York, 1891–1908. Crowned Queen Alexandra in 1902.—*Ed.*

[2] See note on p. 188.

[3] In 1884, the fourth and youngest son of Queen Victoria. He was then 31 years old, father of the Princess Alice, Countess of Athlone.—*Ed.*

[4] Pupil of Gibson, the sculptor.

daily at a little round table, where she is a constant coruscation of wit and wisdom. All day she is shut up in her studio, which is closed to all the world, but she cannot have a dull time, by the stories she has to tell of the workmen and models who are her only companions. Here are a few of them:—

'Minicuccia was an excellent model, but very jealous. "Have you seen Rosa? What fine arms she has!" I said to her one day. "I have seen *Rosaccia*," she replied, "and I should have thought Signorina, that a lady of your taste would have known better than to admire her arms. What are they in comparison with really fine arms—with mine, for instance?"

'One day Minicuccia was at a café, and some one admired the legs of another model. Forthwith she gathered up her petticoats, and danced with her legs perfectly

S. REMO

bare all about the place. She was not a bad woman; on the contrary, she was a very moral one, and there was never a word against her, but she wanted to show what fine legs were. The police, however, heard of that escapade, and she was put in prison for a month afterwards for such an offence against the *decenza pubblica* [public decency]. Poor Minicuccia!

'Then there was Nana, whom Lady Marian (Alford) painted so often, and whom she was so fond of. She was a magnificent woman. Dear Lady Marian used to say, "I would give anything to be able to come into a room with the grace and dignity of Nana." Her dignity was natural to her. Another model once said to me, "I met that Nanaccia; she was walking down the Via Sistina as if it all belonged to her."

'Mariuccia lived to be old, and many is the dinner and *paolo* I have given her; but when she was fifteen or so, she was the model for Mr. Gibson's 'Psyche borne by the Zephyrs.' She was always a wonderful model: no one could act or stand as she did.

'Then there was that woman who had the drunken husband, who used to beat her. One night he came in late and fell down dead drunk across the bed. She took her needle and thread, and sewed him up in the sheets so that he could not move, and then she took a stick, and beat him so that he died of it: she was imprisoned for some years for that, though.'

You may imagine how entertaining stories like these—traits from the life around one—make our little dinners, and afterwards we often go into the Storys' apartment close by, where the easy intellectual pleasant talk and fun are always reviving.

Mrs. Story was very amusing about an Italian who wanted a portrait of his father very much, and came to an artist she knew and asked him to paint it. The artist asked, 'But when can I see your father?'—'Oh, you can't see him: he's dead.'—'But how can I paint him, then?'—'Well, I can describe him, and he was very like me: I think you can paint him very well.' So the artist painted away, according to the description, as well as he could. When he had finished the portrait he sent for the son, anxious to see if he would find any likeness. The son rushed up to the picture, knelt down by it, was bathed in tears, and sobbed out, '*O padre mio, quanto avete sofferto, o quanto siete cambiato: O non l'aveva mai riconosciuto* [Oh my father, how much you have suffered, how much you have changed: oh, I cannot recognise him any more].'

My room in this hotel looks out on the Barberini gardens, and the splash of its fountain is an enjoyment. Its being lighted by electricity for the King's visit the other day was a type of the times, rather a contrast to twenty years ago, when there were torches on every step of the great staircase to welcome even a cardinal, and when not only the staircase, but the whole street as far as S. Teresa, was hung with tapestries for the Prince's funeral.

On Ash-Wednesday I went, as I have always done here, to the 'stations' on the Aventine. It is still a thoroughly Roman scene. Before one reaches S. Sabina, one is assailed by the chorus of old lady beggars seated in a double avenue of armchairs leading up to the door, with '*Datemi qualche cosa, signore, per l'amore della Madonna, datemi qual' co* [Give me something Sir, for the love of the Madonna, give me something]'; and behind them kneel the old men in brown gowns and with arms stretched out *alla maniera di S. Francesco*. Spread with box is the church itself, with its doors wide open to the cloistered porch and the sacred orange-tree seen in the sunny garden beyond. The Abbot is standing there, and has his hand kissed by all the monks who arrive for the stations, till a cardinal appears, after which he takes the lower place and is quite deserted. Then we all hurry on to S. Alessio and its crypt, and then to the Priorato garden, where, by old custom, we look through the keyhole of the door, and see St. Peter's down a beautiful avenue of bays.

The passage of the Pope to the Sistine on his coronation anniversary was a very fine sight. Borne along in his golden chair, with the white peacock fans waving in front of him, and wearing his triple crown, Leo XIII looked dying, but gave his benediction with the most serene majesty, sinking back between each effort upon his cushions, as if the end had indeed come. Only his eyes lived, and lived only in his office; otherwise his perfectly spiritualised countenance seemed utterly unconscious of the thundering *evvivas* with which he was greeted, and which rose into a perfect roar as he was carried into the Sala Regia. The potency of 'Orders' here is so great, that my Swedish decoration not only gave me the best place, but I took in two young men as my chaplain and equerry! After the Pope had entered the Sistine, we sat in great comfort in the Sala Regia till he returned, and then, as there was no one between us and the procession, we saw all the individual faces of the old cardinals—how few of them the same now as those I remember in the procession of Pius IX.

There are no *evvivas* now for the comparatively young king with the white hair and the ever-tragic countenance: the taxes are too great. I believe that he can read, if no one else can, the handwriting on the wall which foretells the doom of his southern kingdom. And yet personally no one could be braver or more royal, and, where they detest the king, the people honour the man.

To HUGH BRYANS.

Rome, April 26, 1892.—There is little to admire now in this much-changed Rome beyond the extreme loveliness of the spring, with its Judas and May flowers, and the golden broom of the Campagna. I have just been, with my old friends Mrs. Ramsay and Miss Garden, to the Villa Doria to pick anemones. There were thousands of them, and the ladies gathered them in like a harvest.

I have seen little of the Easter ceremonies. On Holy Thursday I went to St. Peter's, and watched in the immense crowd for the extinction of the last candle and beginning of the Miserere; but all the effect was lost and the music inaudible from the incessant moving and talking. Afterwards there was a fine scene at the blessing of the altar in the already dark church—the procession, with lights, moving up and down the altar-steps, and then kneeling all along the central aisle, whilst the relics were exhibited from the brilliantly lighted gallery.

It has been a great pleasure to see a good deal of 'Mark Twain' (Mr. Samuel Clemens) and his most charming wife. He is a wiry, thin old man, with abundant grey hair, full round the head, like an Italian *ʒaʒʒara*.[1] He speaks very slowly, dragging his words and sentences laboriously, and is long in warming up, and when he does, he walks about the room whilst he makes all his utterances, which have additional drollery from the slowness with which they are given. He began life as a wharfinger, throwing parcels into barges, and as he threw them the overseer called out 'Mark one, Mark twain,' and the chime of the words struck him, and he took the name. Speaking of the Catacombs he said, 'I might have hooked the bone of a saint and carried it off in my carpet-sack, but then I might get caught with it at the frontier. I should not like to get caught with a thing like that; I would rather it were something else.'

To the HON. G. H. JOLLIFFE *and* JOURNAL.

Rome, April 27.—All the features of this Roman spring have been American. Mrs. Lee was in this hotel. 'I was just raised in the South,' she said, 'and I'm a Southerner to the backbone. Some one wanted to be complimentary, and wrote of me in a newspaper as one raised in the lap of luxury, but I was just raised in the lap of an old nigger.' She was very full of having been to the masquerade ball at La Scala. 'It was awfully indecent. I could not have let my daughter go, but for me it did not matter; so I just went, and stayed to the end, for I thought some one might come along and say, "Ah! you don't know about that, because it happened after you left," so I thought I'd just see what was indecent for once; it might be my only chance; and I made quite sure nothing should happen after I left.'

'I promised to tell you about the siege of Rome,' said Miss Hosmer the other day. 'All that year we knew it was coming, and at last it came. The Italians had 70,000 men, and the Pope had only 11,000, so of course all effectual resistance was out of the question; but it was necessary to make a semblance of defence, to show that the Romans

[1] Actually, Mark Twain was almost the same age as Hare himself.—*Ed.*

only gave in to force. September came, and the *forestieri* [foreigners] who remained in Rome were all urged to leave, but Miss Brewster and I elected to stay. We were not likely to have another chance of seeing a bombardment, so we just hung an American flag out of our windows; that we were told we must do, as it might be necessary to protect us from pillage. All the other *forestieri* left, and most of the Roman aristocracy. In the last days, when the Sardinians were just going to enter, there was a solemn Mass in St. Peter's for the Pope, to implore protection for him against his enemies. I went with Miss Brewster. It was the most striking sight I ever saw. Every corner of the vast church was filled. Every one was in black—every one except the Pope in his white robes, and when he appeared, a universal wail echoed through the church. It was not a silent cry; it was the wail of thousands. There was not a dry eye in the church. The Pope passed close to me. His face was as white as his dress, and down his face the large tears kept rolling, and all his clergy, in black, were crying too. Oh, it was a terrible sight. I am not a Catholic, I am much the contrary, but I sobbed; every one did. Well, the Pope passed into the chapel where he was to say Mass, and he said it, and he walked back again; but he was still crying. It was very piteous, and when we went out into the piazza, there was Monte Mario white with the tents of the Italians, waiting, like vultures, to descend. It was uncertain, for the last few days, by which gate they would enter. It was thought it would be by the Porta Angelica, then by the Porta del Popolo; finally, it was by the Porta Pia.

'We were told that there would be no bombardment, but at five in the morning we were waked by the cannon, and they went on till ten. Shells came flying over our house, and one of them struck the church near us, and carried part of it away. At ten there seemed to be a cessation, so I sallied out as far as the Quattro Fontane, with my man Pietro behind me. When I got into the Via Pia (now Venti Settembre), I heard a cry of "*In dietro! in dietro!*" and the people ran. I thought I might as well get out of the way too, but indeed, any way, I was carried back by the crowd. I heard what I thought was a scampering of feet behind me, and when I reached the Quattro Fontane, I looked back, and seeing a man I knew, I said, "Why, what is the matter with you?" for he was covered with blood, and he said, "Why, Signorina, did not you know that a shell burst close behind you, and it has carried off several of my fingers, Signorina?" So I just took him into my house and gave him some wine, and bound his hand up as well as I could, and then sent him on to a surgeon. Then I went up to Rossetti's house beyond the Cappuccini, because I thought from his loggia I should be able to see all that was to be seen; but as soon as we reached the roof a musketball grazed my face, and others were playing round us, so I said, "We had better get out of this," and we went down.

'After the firing finally stopped, we went to Porta Pia to see the damage. The house which is now the British Embassy was completely riddled. Six dead Zouaves were lying in the Villa Napoleone opposite, and though the statues of S. Peter and S. Paul, which you will remember at the gate, were otherwise intact, both their heads were lying at their feet.

'At four, we went out again to see the Italian troops march into the city. There was no enthusiasm whatever. The troops divided, some going by S. Niccola, others by the Quattro Fontane, to their different barracks.'

No one who did not know the 'has been' can believe how the sights of the Rome of our former days have dwindled away. All is now vulgarity and tinsel: the calm majesty of the Rome of our former winters is gone for ever.

To MISS LEYCESTER.

Cadenabbia, May 13.—At Venice, I went to see 'Pen Browning,' at the Palazzo Rezzonico, his most beautiful old palace, full of memorials of Pope Clement XIII. The son Browning has no likeness to either father or mother: he has worked hard, both as painter and sculptor, and has a good portrait as well as a bust of his father, from his own hands. There were many relics of his parents and their friends, amongst them a sketch by Rossetti of Tennyson reading one of his own poems to them, with an inscription by Mrs. Browning. 'Pen' was going off to his house at Asolo, a place which his father first brought into notice when he walked there and wrote 'Pippa Passes.'

Venice is still as full of odd stories as when my sister went to a party there, and was surprised because the oddly dressed old lady by her side never answered when she spoke, and then found she was made of wax. Most of the company were, being ancestors present thus in the family life of the present. Recently a lady named Berthold has lived at Venice who was of marvellous beauty and charm. All the society flocked to her parties. One evening she invited all her friends as usual. They found the palace splendidly lighted, and listened to the most exquisite music. At the close of the evening, curtains which concealed a platform at the end of the principal room were drawn aside, and within, the beautiful hostess was seen, seated on a throne, and sparkling with jewels, in all her resplendent loveliness. And then, as she waved a farewell to all present, the curtains were suddenly drawn, and she disappeared for ever. No human eye has seen her since. She had observed signs, unperceived by others, that her beauty was beginning to wane!

Here, at pleasant Cadenabbia, I have been glad to fall in with Lord[1] and Lady Ripon. He said, 'Do you know that *you* have been the cause of my buying a property in Italy?' It was in consequence of the sentence in my *Cities of Central Italy* beseeching some Roman Catholic nobleman to save such a sacred and historic place, that he had bought S. Chiara's convent of S. Damiano near Assisi, giving its use to the monks on the sole condition that it was never to be 'restored.'

---

[1] In his early years was with F. D. Maurice in the Christian Socialist movement; served under Palmerston and Gladstone; became a Roman Catholic in 1874; Governor-General of India, 1880; led the Liberal party in the Lords, 1905–8.—*Ed.*

I*

XIII

A KNOCKING AT THE DOOR

1892–93

ﾍﾞ

T
HE summer of 1892 was full of quiet pleasures. Visits leave little
to be remembered except the pleasant parties and the extreme
kindness of hosts and hostesses everywhere. I am indeed glad
that my visiting-lines are cast in such pleasant places, that I so seldom
have to consort with the drearier part of human nature. In these houses,
where the conversation is perfectly charming, yet where no evil is spoken
of any one or by any one, one sees truly how a christian spirit will chris-
tianise everything it touches.

To VISCOUNT HALIFAX.

Nov. 9.—I have been very ill. It was a bad chill at first, followed by most terrible
pains, which I thought were part of the chill, and struggled against them, moving about
when I ought to have kept perfectly still. When at last I sent for a doctor, he said I
had been in most imminent danger for several days, and that I must have died before
another forty-eight hours were over if he had not come just then. A slight operation
was necessary at once to re-arrange an internal misplacement, and this relieved the
agonising pain. I have not often been before so immediately, never so suddenly, face
to face with possible death. For some hours no one knew how it would go, yet I
have often *felt* more ill. . . . How strange it is when one knows, when one is told,
that one is almost in the valley of the shadow of death! I felt more surprised than
frightened; indeed, I do not think I felt frightened at all, I could leave it so completely
in wiser Hands. . . . I may not always go on feeling so; but I feel now as if I had left
my long youth on the other side of this illness.

To the HON. G. H. JOLLIFFE.

Dec. 21, 1892.—You know how ill I was in November, but you do not know all
the serious thoughts it awakened. I have a great deal to say about it, but as you will
like facts better, I will only tell you that since I recovered I have been quite a tour of
visits, beginning with Lady Beauchamp,[1] and meeting charming Lady Granville and
a party of sixteen young men and maidens at Madresfield Court, a moated house with
a lovely view of the Malvern Hills, and full of precious collections of every kind—
old books, old music, old minatures, ivories, enamels, &c. There is a chapel, where
Lady Mary Lygon watches over the musical part of the services, aided by a footman
who sings splendidly and plays five instruments well!

  [1] Lady Emily Pierrepont, daughter of Earl Manvers, widow of Frederick Lygon, 6th Earl Beauchamp.

I had a happy week at beautiful old Blickling, with Constance, Lady Lothian, who —though no blood relation to her—reminded me more than any one else of my dear Lady Waterford, with much the same charm of manner and power of enjoyment of all the smallest things of beauty. The park, gloriously wild, belonged to Harold, and endless illustrious owners since. The house is a dream of beauty externally, and is full of ghost-stories. It was the family home of the Boleyns, and in the tapestried drawing-room Anne Boleyn is still supposed to walk at night with her head in her hand. In the present serving-room the devil appeared to Lord Rockingham, who threw an inkstand at him, which missed, and marked the wall. When Lord[1] and Lady Lothian first came to Blickling, they altered the house and pulled down partitions to make the present morning-room. 'I wish these young people would not pull down the partitions,' said an old woman in the village to the clergyman. 'Why so?'—'Oh, because of the dog. Don't you know that when A. was fishing in the lake, he caught an enormous fish, and that, when it was landed, a great black dog came out of its mouth? They never could get rid of that dog, who kept going round and round in circles inside the house, till they sent for a wise man from London, who opposed the straight lines of the partitions to the lines of the circles, and so quieted the dog. But if these young people pull down the partitions, they will let the dog loose again, and there's not a wise man in all London could lay that dog now.'

Lady Lothian took me to Mannington, Lord Orford's curious little place. It was here that Dr. Jephson saw his much-talked-of ghost. He had been sitting up late over the MSS., when an old man appeared to him. He spoke to the figure, and, though it did not answer, he was for some time quite certain of the apparition. Whilst I was at Blickling, however, Dr. Jephson[2] was one of my fellow-guests, and he now thinks the vision was an optical delusion. On the outer wall of the house of Mannington are a number of Latin inscriptions, put up by the present owner. They are all most bitter, vehement, and incisive against women. But in a distant part of the grounds there is also a monument to 'Louise,'[3] with *'Pensez à lui, et priez pour elle.'* This is in a little wood, close to an old ruined chapel, within which Lord Orford has already placed his own sarcophagus, with an inscription (saying nobody else would ever do it), and around which he has collected a vast number of architectural fragments from destroyed churches. Lord Orford seldom comes to Mannington now, but till five years ago he was much here in strictest seclusion, with his adopted son and his wife, who were much tried by the dinner at half-past six, always of exactly the same food, after which he would talk to the lady with incessant quotations from the Latin poets, of which she did not understand a word. Every Saturday he used to pass Blickling on his way to Norwich, where he used to see his doctor, play a game of whist, and hear a mass, returning next day.

To W. H. MILLIGAN *and* JOURNAL.

Belvoir Castle, Jan. 6, 1893.—'Be firm with the weather, and it's sure to clear up,' said old Miss Hammersley, and, after the terrible early winter, the weather, though

---

[1] Schomberg Henry Kerr, the ninth Marquis of Lothian, 1833–1900, diplomat and, later, Secretary of State for Scotland.—*Ed.*

[2] Arthur Jephson, 1858–1908, explorer who accompanied Stanley to Lake Albert, 1888.—*Ed.*

[3] I have since heard that this was Louise de Rohan Chabot, whom his father forbade Lord Orford to marry, because she was a Roman Catholic. She was the love of his life, which was wrecked, and he became a Roman Catholic himself—such is Nemesis!

bitterly cold, is most glorious. My arrival at this stately castle was a fiasco. The Duchess had forgotten that she had told me to come to their little station of Redmile, and when I arrived at that desolate place, with deep snow on the ground and night fast closing in, there was nothing to meet me. The stationmaster sent his little boy to the next village, and in an hour he returned with an open waggonette, agonisingly cold across the open plain. But I was repaid when we entered the still loveliness of the ice-laden woods, every bough sparkling in the moonlight like crystallised silver; and still more when we emerged upon the plateau at the top of the hill, and the mighty towers of the castle rose pale grey into the clear air, looking down into the wooded frost-bound gorges like the palace of the ice-queen. I found the Duchess [of Rutland] waiting for me in the corridor, with that genial solicitude for one's comfort which goes straight to the heart when one does meet with it, which is so seldom.

How I like all the mediaeval ways—the trumpeters, who walk up and down the passages and sound the dressing-time; the watchman, who calls the hours through the night; the ball-room, always ready in the evenings for those who want to dance; the band, in uniform, which plays soft music from an adjoining room during dinner, at which all the hunting men appear in their red coats, and add brilliancy and colour to the immensely long table with its glorious old silver ornaments.

On the first morning, I went after breakfast with the Duchess to her private rooms, filled with comfort and sunshine, where she fed thousands of birds upon the little platform outside her windows, and the Duke,[1] amongst other treasures, showed me a deed of King John conferring Haddon upon Richard Manners. At 12, I met the Duke and Duchess again, and walked alone with them on the terraces and along the exquisitely beautiful wood walks, all glistening in silvered splendour, whilst the sun was bright and the air quite still. The Duke told me how he had the bill—at £60 a piece—of those curious statues by Cibber which are such an ornament to the garden. When we reached a little garden where there is a slab inscribed with verses by Mrs. Kemble, he was tired and returned. I went on with the Duchess, a long and most attractive path through the woods, and she talked of her real devotion to the Queen, and of the Queen's extreme kindness to her.

Yesterday the Duchess was ill, and I went out alone with the Duke to the kitchen-garden and to the fine stables, of Charles II's time, where there are still sixty horses, over which Edward Manners presides as 'field-master.' The Government gives £5 annually as a retaining fee for ten of the best horses being always entered to serve in case of an invasion.

JOURNAL.

Jan. 1893.—Mrs. Kemble was certainly the living person I most wished to see, but I have let too many opportunities slip, and she has passed away without my knowing her. She must have been a great and generous woman, and those who knew her always loved though they feared her. Miss Hosmer has often told me how dearly she and her companions loved Mrs. Kemble when she was at school in America near the place where she lived. But her severe manner terrified those who were given that way. 'We had some private theatricals,' Mrs. Story told me, 'and Mrs. Kemble came to look on at the rehearsal, at which a girl was acting who was supposed to do it very well. Afterwards, when she came in, Mrs. Kemble walked up to her, and '*Are* you a fool?' was all she said.

---

[1] John James Robert, Lord Manners, seventh Duke of Rutland; statesman. Made Baron Roos of Belvoir in 1896. Born 1818, died 1906.—*Ed.*

To some Americans she met she said, 'We hate you for your politics: we hate you for your prosperity: we hate you for your manners: and . . . I don't wonder at it.'

Mrs. Sartoris[1] had more talent, but Mrs. Kemble had the greater genius. Those who met her recognised it at once. I heard one who loved her best say, 'She married Mr. Butler because, for once in her life, she was a fool. He was very faulty as a husband, but she was so imperious, *no one* could have lived with dear Mrs. Kemble.'

When Mrs. Cummings was taking the duty in the chapel at Dresden, they lived in the same house. Mrs. Cummins wishing to be civil, after some time sent her card, and asked is she might wait on Mrs. Kemble. The daughter came up at once and explained, very civilly, that her mother now saw no one, so Mrs. Cummings thought no more about it. But some time after, as she was sitting alone in her room, came a tap at the door, and on her opening it, she saw a lady in black velvet and lace, closely veiled, who startled her by saying in sepulchral accents, 'I'm come to say that I shall never come again.'—'Oh, is that really you Mrs. Butler?' said lively little Mrs. Cummings, and the sound of her real name, unheard for years, made her quite pleasant, and she came in, and was glad to hear of many mutual friends in the Berkshire of Massachusetts. But unfortunately Mrs. Cummings made some allusion to Shakespeare, and 'I did not come here to speak of Shakespeare,' said Mrs. Kemble in her most awful accents, and the charm was broken.

When in Boston long ago, while she was reading in public, she ordered dresses, pink and blue satin, at the great shop, the Marshall & Snelgrove of the town, but gave no address. The shopmen were afraid to ask her. The manager felt he must run after her and ask where the things should be sent. Unfortunately, to attract her attention, he touched her. 'Unhand me, ruffian,' she shouted in her most ferocious tone. 'And such was the man's terror,' said my informant, 'that, though he was quite young, his hair was turned white that night.'

A lady was once alluding to the hope she entertained of reducing her figure. In her most tragical voice Mrs. Kemble said, dwelling on every syllable, 'With a hereditary tendency to fat, nor exercise, nor diet, nor grief may avail.'

To Mrs. C. Vaughan *and* Journal.

Longford Castle, Salisbury, Jan. 18.—I have been five days in this magnificent old place, and it has been a very interesting visit—and weird, from being with people[2] to whom the other world is so very near, who seem to be as intimate with the dead as with the living, and who think no more of 'receiving a message' from one of their 'guiding spirits' than we should of a note from an ordinary acquaintance. These spirits, the wise 'Huldah,' the scientific 'Iganesis,' the sympathetic 'Echord,' the evangelistic 'Ernest,' and 'Semirus,' the wise physician, are the friends of the Radnor's daily life. There comes a rap, such a noise as we should speak of as 'only the furniture,' and then it is supposed that one of the spirits has something to say, and a pencil is put into the hand of a medium. One cannot say that she writes, for she often even goes fast asleep! but *it* writes, frequently volumes—not the sprawling incomprehensible stuff which I have often seen before from 'Planchette,' but clear MS. in different handwritings, and purporting to come from one of the spiritual friends. Personally, I should say that most of these communications were not the least worth the immense amount of time and thought given to them. The letters—'messages'—from Echord and Ernest, are

---

[1] Younger sister of Frances Kemble.
[2] The Earl and Countess of Radnor.

excellent certainly, but mild and affectionate religious platitudes, such as might be written by an Evangelical clergyman of rather poetical tendencies. They all, however, speak of the dead as not asleep, but in action: of there being no 'place,' but 'a state' after death: of existence after death being a process through gradations. None of the spirits have seen 'God,' but 'the dear Master,' 'the sweet Master,' is ever with them and amongst them. The communications from Semirus are most important. He is the great physician, and his advice has provided means of healing and safety for numbers, where earthly physicians have proved powerless or helpless. The Bishop of Salisbury has been scandalised at the state of things at Longford and felt impelled to come and testify against it. He recognised all that happened as fact, as every one must, but denounced it as 'devilry,' saying that the owners of the castle were risking their own souls and all the souls around them. They answer: 'It was said to Christ, Thou hast a devil.'

The really remarkable communications are those which have reference to History. In August 1889, Sir Joseph (then Mr.) Barnby,[1] came down to Longford to play the organ at Lady Skelmersdale's marriage. One day at this time Miss Wingfield's [the medium's] hand wrote a communication in strange old-fashioned characters, which purported to come from one 'John Longland.' When asked why he came, he said that he had been brought 'by the influence of Mr. Barnby, whose music he had heard in Eton College Chapel, where he was buried.' Later in the day, the party went to Salisbury Cathedral, and while Lady Radnor and Miss Wingfield were sitting in the Hungerford Chapel (the freehold family pew of the Radnor family), Mr. Barnby played. Whilst he was playing, Miss Wingfield saw, as in a vision, various scenes enacted, culminating in a procession of monks and other ecclesiastics with banners and canopies: one of these, a grave-faced man, came up to the chapel and looked in at her through the bars. At the same time he announced (by loud raps on the wainscot, which is the ordinary means of communication) that he was John Longland, that it was he who had written in the morning, and that he had come to the cathedral because he had been Dean there in 1514, and that he had more to tell. Another vision in the cathedral showed the gorgeous ceremonial of a consecration, which was announced to be that of one Brian Duppa, Bishop of Salisbury: in a third vision, Brian Duppa was again seen, lying in his coffin.

On reaching Longford, Miss Wingfield received more writing from John Longland, who described himself as anxious to confess how faithless he had been to his intimate friendship with Thomas Bullen (Anne's father); that he had been instrumental in persuading Henry VIII to divorce Catherine and to marry Anne, thus advancing his friend's daughter, and that afterwards—entirely from motives of personal pique against his former friend—he had influenced Henry against Anne, and fostered suspicions which led to her execution. He again said that he was buried in Eton College Chapel.

Anxious to verify these statements, Mr. Wingfield purposely went to Eton to search for the tomb of John Longland, and nowhere could it be found. The Radnors and Miss Wingfield then thought that John Longland must be a 'lying spirit.' and not finding any records of his being Dean of Salisbury either, they tore up his writings.

After Mr. Barnby had left Longford, John Longland came again, but no one would listen to him. He was, however, so persistent, that the Radnors decided to have a hunt for a list of officers of the cathedral. In a lobby cupboard they discovered some

[1] Composer and conductor; second principal of the Guildhall School of Music. In 1889 he was precentor of Eton.—Ed.

old volumes of county history, uncut and covered with dust. In one of these they found that John Longland had been Dean of Salisbury at the date mentioned, and that he was translated to Lincoln in 1521. Turning to 'Britton's Lincolnshire,' equally covered with dust, showing it had not been moved for months (so that there was no possibility of Miss Wingfield having seen the statement), it was found that Bishop John Longland was a person of great learning and piety, &c., that he was confessor to Henry VIII, and suspected of having unduly influenced the King with regard to Catherine and Anne, &c. He died at Woburn, and was privately buried in Eton College Chapel, of which he was 'visitor,' his heart being sent to Lincoln. The Radnors afterwards learnt that the tombstone of Longland was removed from Eton College Chapel during a 'restoration.'

On the 17th of February 1893, my dear old cousin Charlotte Leycester died peacefully at her house in London. For months past she had been failing in her great age (ninety-five) as to physical powers, but her mind was as much alive as ever, and her affection and sympathy as warm and ready. She has had a home at Holmhurst every summer, and I have never allowed a week, generally not three days, to pass without writing to her. She carries away with her my closest link with the past, but no one could wish to keep her here. Better that she should go in her great age before the suffering of age came.

To HUGH BRYANS.

June 20, 1893.—I was in London a long time, but saw and heard little of interest. At Mr. Knowles's one day I met the honest sturdy Miss Octavia Hill,[1] and another day Bret Harte, a young-old man, with white hair and an unwrinkled rosy face. It was odd to hear him called 'Mr. Harte.' After luncheon Mr. Knowles read Tennyson's 'Boadicea' in a weird monotonous kind of chant, imitating him exactly, I should think. He said that was the way Tennyson always wished his poems to be read—straight on, without emphasis or any change of voice.

To VISCOUNT HALIFAX.

October 20, 1893.—I have been little away from home all summer, being so busy with my Waterford Memorial, at which I have certainly worked *con amore*.[2]

I was three pleasant days with Lord Arthur Hervey, the delightful old Bishop of Bath and Wells, in his moated fortified palace, as picturesque and as beautiful as it could possibly be. The Bishop talks freely on all subjects with perfect ease and simplicity, in the repose of a mind at rest and the humility of real knowledge. He was much occupied with the question as to whether the children of Israel were 200 or 400 years in the wilderness, all depending upon where a stop ought to be placed.

At Holmhurst I have been much alone, and I feel, with Carlyle, that 'the memory of many things which it is not at all good to forget rises with strange clearness on me in these solitudes, very touching, very sad, out of the depths of old dead years.'

---

[1] Octavia Hill, co-founder of the National Trust. Was early influenced by F. D. Maurice; philanthropist and social reformer, especially interested in housing.—*Ed.*

[2] *The Story of Two Noble Lives*, a biography of Lady Waterford and of her sister, Lady Canning, published in Dec. 1893.—*Ed.*

In December I sat for my portrait to Mr. Eddis.[1]

JOURNAL.

Dec. 5, 1893.—I had a delightful morning with Mr. Eddis, now eighty-three, but full of vigour and vivacity, and still more of reminiscence. He said, 'You would not have been here now having your portrait painted if it had not been for the Athenaeum. When I was a very young man, one Magrath, who was secretary there, told me he wanted a sketch made of himself, and that he would give me £5 for one. So I did it, and it was such a success, that no fewer than sixty members of the club put their names down to be drawn by me. I was doubtful if I should do them, for I wanted to study, and I had not studied enough, but I asked Hilton, who was a very good artist then, and he told me it would be folly to refuse what came so easily; and so I did the portraits, and from that time orders have poured in all through my long life, and so I have never had time for real study since: I have only learnt through my work. . . .

'Sydney Smith did not make at the time all the jokes which were attributed to him: he thought of them afterwards, and circulated them. He told me once, for instance, that Landseer had asked him to sit for his portrait, and that he had answered, "How could I possibly refuse a chance of immortality," which was perhaps a very natural thing to say. But it was reported afterwards in London, and reported with at least his consent, that he had answered, "Is thy servant a dog, that I should do this thing?"

'Macaulay, it is true, talked incessantly—talked like a machine, but he had his attractive points. I found this out especially when he brought the present Lady Knutsford, as a very little girl, to me to be painted, and talked nonsense to her the whole time, but it was always nonsense which had a lesson in it.'

This afternoon Victoria took me to see Mr. [G. F.] Watts. A drive through wooded lanes and water-meadows; then the carriage stopped at the foot of a wooded knoll, and we walked up little winding paths through the bracken and Scotch firs to the house—a rustic hermitage. You enter directly upon the principal dwelling apartment—two low rooms, with old carved furniture and deep windows, and much colour and many pictures. The ceiling is in panels, decorated in stucco by Mrs. Watts. At least she has finished one room, and is going to do the other with an epitome of the religion of all the nations of the earth—'A work,' she said, 'which gives me much study.'

Soon Mr. Watts came in, like a pilgrim, like a mediaeval hermit-saint, in a brown blouse and slippers, with a skull-cap above his white hair and beard, and his sharp eager features, in which there is also boundless tenderness and refinement. He sat by me on the window-sill, and began at once to talk of Lady Waterford—of her wonderful inspirations, her unrivalled colouring, her utter unconsciousness of self, and her majestic beauty—how, when he first saw her out walking at Blickling, with her grand mien, he could not but exclaim—'It is Pallas Athene herself!'

Mr. Watts took us into his studio, an immense and beautiful room added to the cottage. Here were many of his pictures, the work of years, on which, from time to time, he adds a few touches. He likes to have many of his works around him, and to add to them thus. At the end of the room hangs his vast 'Court of Death,' which can be lowered by pulleys whenever he wishes to add to it. He was greatly pleased with a photograph of it, which has the effect of a Tintoretto, and which, while preserving the grand masses, blots out the detail. 'Death' is throned in the upper part of the picture. 'I have given her wings,' said Mr. Watts, 'that she may not seem like a Madonna.

---

[1] Eden Upton Eddis, 1812–1901, exhibited at the Royal Academy from 1834–81.—*Ed.*

In her arms nestles a child—a child unborn, perhaps, who has taken refuge there. By her side the angels of silence guard the portals of the unseen. Beneath is the altar of Death, to which many worshippers are hastening: the old mendicant comes to beg; the noble offers his coronet; the warrior does not offer—but surrenders—his sword; the sick girl clings for refuge to the feet of Death. I have wished to paint Death entirely without terrors.

'You wonder what that is, that other picture of a figure of a rich man in Eastern dress whose face is half-hidden, buried away in the folds of his garment. I meant that for the man who was "very sorry, for he had great possessions." He cannot give them up. He has tried, but he *cannot*. He is going out into the world again, and yet—and yet he is very sorry.'

He said, 'I am within two years of eighty, and I have worked all my life, but I do not feel old or feeble. I do not even use a maul-stick, and I intend to do my best work yet.' He said he had no wish to go into the world again. Living was outliving. Holland House, the second home of many years, was swept away from him, and all its intimates were passing away, and its memories perishing. Nothing else in London could attract him.[1]

He had wished to make large pictures of Hope, Charity, and Faith. With the two first he had no difficulty, but he lingered long over the third. He showed us the picture he had done—of a woman seated, looking upwards, an Amazonian woman, sheathing her sword, and bathing her blood-stained feet in a brook of clear water. 'She had found out that all that was no use—no use at all.' His words, his thoughts, his works, all seemed imbued with the truest spirit of religion. 'With theology,' he said, 'I have nothing to do.'

Dec. 7.—Another delightful sitting with Mr. Eddis. I told him of our visit to Watts, and he said how he felt, on seeing his pictures and those of Alma Tadema, that Watts was the head, while Tadema was only the hand.

He talked of his own early life as a student. At that time, Fuseli[2] had recently been the head of the Academy—the very fierce head. He used to say to his pupils, "You may be very good buttermen, you may be very good cheesemen, but students of Art you will never be; and now, give me my umbrella, and I'll go and look at Constable's pictures."

'Turner [J. M. W.] often used to come in and look at us and our work. There was a student amongst us who had painted in a red background, and he painted it the crudest, brightest red he could manage. Turner came in and said, "Come now, this will never do; give me your palette and brush," and in a few minutes he had toned and mellowed it down with a hundred delicate gradations of tint. "Well now, don't you think it's improved?" said Turner. "No, I don't," answered the man; "I think it it was much better before," which annoyed Turner rather. I remember that he came to me that day. I was copying a Vandyke, and he looked at my work. "Part of that is very good," he said; "why isn't all the rest as good?"—"Because," I said, "all

[1] Watts was introduced to Lord and Lady Holland at Florence in 1843 and remained their guest until 1847. Lived at Little Holland House in Kensington from 1850 until 1875. In this period he moved among the most distinguished men and women of his time and painted the portraits of many of them, including Lord John Russell, Thiers, Prince Jérôme Bonaparte, Lord Stratford de Redcliffe, Tennyson, Lady Margaret Beaumont, etc. Married Ellen Terry in 1864 but separated in 1865; secondly, in 1886, Mary Fraser Tytler. Born 1817, died 1904.—*Ed.*

[2] Henry Fuseli (or Füssli) died in 1825. Füssli was of Swiss origin, became an R.A. in 1790 and Professor at the Academy in 1799. He is buried in St. Paul's.—*Ed.*

the rest is me, and that part is an accident."—"Well, let that accident to-day become principle to-morrow," said Turner, and we were always rather friends afterwards.

'Turner was proud of his picture of Carthage. He had received many mortifications about his pictures, and people had haggled about the prices—very small prices too—that he asked for them. When Lord Francis Egerton came and told him that a subscription was on foot to buy that picture from him and present it to the National Gallery, he burst into tears, he was so moved. But he said, "No, I will not sell it, but I will leave it to the National Gallery." Afterwards, however, he changed his mind, and wished to be buried in that picture. He spoke of it to Chantrey, who was his executor, and begged that he would see that it was done, urging him to promise that it should be done. "Yes, since you wish it, I'll see you buried in that picture," said Chantrey, "but, as sure as you're alive now, I'll see you dug up again." Eventually the picture was left to the National Gallery.'

In December 1893 my *Story of Two Noble Lives* appeared, and was warmly welcomed by the upper classes of society—'the public' for whom it was especially written. It was curious, on going to London, to see how opinions differed about the book—how one heard, 'Oh, all the interest is confined to Lady Canning,' or, 'Of course all one's sympathies are with Lady Waterford; it is only Lady Waterford one cares for,' or, 'The old French history is the only point of interest.' The Reviews were just the same, wishing that the first, or the second, or the third volume were excluded—'the general public would have been sure to welcome the book if it had been much shorter.' But that was exactly the welcome I did not care that it should receive. The general public had no interest in, could not understand, and was not constituted to benefit by such 'noble lives,' while the inner circle for whom they were intended could always skip—skip a whole volume if it pleased, just as suited the reader. Lady Cork was furious because the married life of Lord and Lady Canning had not been painted as cloudlessly, beatifically happy. But how could I do this with all the written evidence before me? And, after all, what made Lady Canning's so perfectly 'noble' a life was that, however much she suffered, she allowed her mother and sister to live and *die* under the impression that she was the happiest of wives.

A very large first edition—5,300 copies—was produced. I felt these would be called for, and that such an edition would probably cover the very heavy expenses. But the sale of the book is not likely to go on; the generation contemporary with the two sisters will have passed away. For myself, if I like a book, I prefer that it should be very long. It enables you to make a real acquaintance with the people described, to learn to love them perhaps, and to be very sorry to part with them. I wonder if it will be so if some of these—very long—journals are ever made public.

XIV

WRITING THE GURNEY MEMOIRS

1894-95

༚ঌৎৎ

I HAD frequently been urged by my friend Madame E. de Bunsen to write the lives and edit the letters of her family—the Gurneys of Earlham; but I had long declined. But towards the close of 1893 it was again urged upon me—urged with great persistency; and when I had taken many of the Gurney journals and letters home, a memoir seemed gradually to unravel itself in my mind, and at length I promised to do my best.

To the HON. G. HYLTON JOLLIFFE.

London, April 1894.—I have had a pleasant time here, and as usual have found that there is more to be learnt by enduring the ups and downs of social pleasures than by withdrawing from them, while in the mornings I have been very busy at the Athenaeum with a new edition of *Walks in London* and the production of my little *Sussex*. There is no place where Death makes a stranger impression than at the Athenaeum. You become so accustomed to many men you do not know, to their comings and goings that they become almost a part of your daily life. You watch them growing older, the dapper young man becoming grizzled, first too careful and then too neglectful of his dress: you see his face become furrowed, his hair grow grey, then white, and at last he is lame and bent. You become worried by his coughs, and hems, and little peculiarities. And—suddenly—you are aware that he is not there, and all your little annoyances immediately seem to have been absurd. For a time you miss him. He never comes. He will cough no more, no longer creak across the floor. He has passed into the unseen; gradually he is forgotten. His place knows him no more. But the wheel goes on turning; it is others; it is oneself perhaps, who is waning away.

To the HON. MRS. W. LOWTHER.

Holmhurst, May 21, 1894.—You said you would like to hear about Belvoir. . . . At Grantham was a quantity of red cloth, and crowds of people to see the Princess (Louise),[1] and a string of carriages from the castle, and George Manners to show us which we were to go in. The Princess was already at tea when we arrived, and very gracious and kind. But though she is such a really charming person, the conversation had the effect of muffled drums, which always accompanies the presence of royalty. Lord Lorne is much improved in appearance by age—a good Rubens, as his uncle, Ronald Gower—also at Belvoir—is a bad Bronzino. The Duke, as always, was most

---

[1] Sixth child of Queen Victoria; Duchess of Argyll, who died in 1939, aged 91.—*Ed.*

delightful, so courteous, considerate, and full of interesting information. In the mornings we walked, drew, or sat in the gardens—a many-hued carpet of spring glories. In the evenings most of the company danced. . . .

Holmhurst is now a nest of spring blossoms, the azaleas glorious, and the gold of the laburnums quite hiding the leaves.

It had weighed upon my mind for the last two years that my *France* remained unfinished. There was still another volume which could not be written without personally visiting all the places of interest in Normandy and Brittany, and my publishers were constantly urging its completion. The book has always been utterly unremunerative, very much the contrary, which is very depressing in its way, but '*on ne vit dans le mémoire du monde que par ses travaux pour le monde.*[1] So I determined to give up London and home pleasures this summer, and to set about it, taking my young cousin Theodore Chambers as my companion and guest.

We left Holmhurst together on the first of June, and spent June in Normandy and July in Brittany. It was one of the most laborious journeys I ever made—eight or nine hours a day of walking, standing, collating, correcting, simmering in the relaxing western heat, and constantly soaked by the Scotch mist which pervades that district five days out of seven. Thus my associations with North-Western France are not transcendent. Places, even the most beautiful, are innutritious to the mind in the long run; one needs people with mental life and enthusiasm to see them with.

To the cloudiest days, however, come gleams of sunshine. I remember with great pleasure the Abbey of S. Waudrille near Caudebec, restored once more to the Benedictines, ejected at the Revolution. We were cordially pressed to go and stay there, and shown the charming rooms we might have, and I should really have liked it. Then five days at Mont S. Michel were enchanting, and the invigorating air, which the hundred and thirty steps to our bedrooms gave us full opportunity of benefiting by. And then from Brittany came recollections of many wonderful calvaries; of Tregastel and its golden rocks; of S. Jean du Doigt in its deep hollow, lovely in spite of soaking rain; and of Carnac and its wild moorland, redolent of sweet basil and thyme. It was enchanting to reach home again at the end of July. My companions said the journey had turned my hair grey, and so it really had—rather.

JOURNAL.

August 16.—The natural beauty of the garden here is a never-failing delight to me. Most people seem to be so full of expectations from the future that they do not

[1] Chateaubriand.

allow themselves to enjoy the present; but when I am at home, I am sure that is not the case with me. On the prettiest site in the grounds I have just finished putting up the statues of Queen Anne and her four satellites by Bird, which formerly stood in front of St. Paul's. They were taken away four years ago, and disappeared altogether till last spring, when my friend Lewis Gilbertson discovered them in a stonemason's yard on the point of being broken up for the sake of the marble. I found they belonged to three people—the Archbishop of Canterbury, the Bishop of London, and the Lord Mayor, and all these were persuaded to resign their claims to me. The statues were brought down to Holmhurst at great expense, and put up, at much greater, on a home-made pedestal like their old one; and now I hope they are enjoying the verdure and sea-breezes after the smoke of the City.

Bishopthorpe, Oct. 16.—I have had a delightful long drive with Augusta to Bramham. The old house was burnt down sixty years ago, and has never been rebuilt. But its glorious old gardens are kept up. There is nothing like them in England. They were laid out by Le Nôtre when he laid out Versailles, and are more like that than any other place. Eighty acres are intersected by grand avenues with immense walls of clipped beech, ending in summer-houses, statues, vases, or tanks walled in with stone and surrounded by statues and vases of flowers. Mr. Fox, a most grand old man, showed me everything, and talked of the change from the old times of his youth, when Yorkshire country visits were so cheery, and the chief dissipation of the county people was a ball at York. 'Now every man with three hundred a year and a daughter thinks he must go to London.' He talked of the degeneracy of Temple Newsam from the time when three litters of cubs were regularly brought up in the woods near the house. His sitting-room is full of hunting pictures and caricatures of his old friends —a great enjoyment to him.

I asked Augusta much about Mrs. (Adelaide) Sartoris,[1] whom she had known well. She said: 'Edward Sartoris did not go with Adelaide when she went to Vichy. Leighton,[2] who was always as a slave to her, went with her, took her lodgings, and did everything for her. Then he said, "You will be very dull, knowing no one here; I know some young men here, and I will introduce them to you. They are Burton[3] and Swinburne, but you know one is a believer in Buddhism, the other in nothing; so you must not mind what they say." Then Leighton left.

'The next evening Adelaide was having her coffee in the gardens, when the two young men came up and sat down by her. At first they made themselves very agreeable. Then at length they began to air their opinions, and to say things evidently intended to shock. Adelaide laid down her cup, looked at Burton, and said very slowly, "You believe, I think, in *Juggernaut*, therefore, with regard to Juggernaut, I shall be very careful not to hurt your feelings. And you, Mr. Swinburne (turning to him), believe, I think, in *nothing*, but if anything is mentioned in which you *do* believe, I shall be very careful not to hurt your feelings either, by abusing it: now I expect that you will show the same courtesy to me."

[1] Mrs. Kemble's sister, also an actress.

[2] Frederick, Lord Leighton, the painter and President of the Royal Academy, 1878–96. His more famous works included 'Hercules Wrestling with Death,' 'The Bath of Psyche', 'Perseus and Andromeda,' and other classical subjects. Raised to the peerage on the day before his death and buried in St. Paul's.—*Ed.*

[3] Sir Richard Burton, explorer, orientalist and eccentric, translator of the *Thousand and One Nights,* as well as the *Pentamerone* (Basile), Catullus and Camoens, etc.—*Ed.*

'The young men laughed, and for some days all went well. Then the impression passed, and one day they began to talk as before. Adelaide again laid down her cup, and began again in the same slow tones—"You believe, Mr. Burton, I think, in Juggernaut" . . . Then they burst out laughing, and they always behaved themselves in future.'

'When I was a girl,' said Augusta, 'I was with Mary at Madame de l'Aigle's near Compiègne. There was to be a little function in the village, and some music was got up for it. We assisted at the practices, and Leighton also, who was there as a beautiful young man. But before the day of the function came he had to go. "Oh, Fay, why should you desert us? what can we do without our tenor?" said Madame de l'Aigle. But she implored him in vain; he said he *must* go. We all continued, however, to urge him, and at last he said, "Well, I'll tell you what I'll do: I must go, but I'll come back." —"What! all the way from London?"—"Yes." And he did. It was not long after that we found out why he thought himself obliged to go: it was because the sale of the pictures of that poor artist, Mason,[1] who had died leaving his wife and children terribly unprovided for, was going to take place, and Leighton thought that if he were present at the sale, and seen bidding for the pictures, they would fetch higher prices. It was only one of a thousand kindnesses Leighton has done. . . . People have sometimes called him affected, but he was not. His manners were perfectly natural: he could not help being the spoiled darling of society.

'George IV, as Prince Regent, was very charming when he was not drunk, but he generally *was*. Do you remember how he asked Curran to dinner to amuse him—only for that? Curran was up to it, and sat silent all through dinner. This irritated the Prince, and at last, after dinner, when he had had a good deal too much, he filled a glass with wine and threw it in Curran's face, with "Say something funny, can't you!" Curran, without moving a muscle, threw his own glass of wine in his neighbour's face, saying, "Pass his Royal Highness's joke."[2]

'That story reminds me of the old Queen of Sweden. She was furious at the appointment of Bernadotte, and would have nothing to do with him; at which people congratulated him rather, because if she had seen him, they said, she would certainly have killed him. But at last she seemed to get tired of her estrangement, and she invited Bernadotte to a banquet. He was delighted—so glad to be friends; but as he was going to her palace, a paper was put into his hands inscribed—by whom he never knew—with the words, "If she offers you food or drink, as you value your life, refuse it." He arrived, and the Queen was most affable, courtesy and kindness itself. After dinner a cup of coffee was brought on a golden salver, and, with the most exquisite grace, the Queen offered it to Bernadotte. He was just about to drink it when he remembered the warning, and he returned it to her, saying, "*Après vous, Madame.*" The Queen turned deadly pale, looked him full in the face, and—drank it. Next day Stockholm was agitated by terrible news. The Queen-Dowager had died in the night.'

Nov. 16.—At Letton, the pleasant house of the Gurdons in Suffolk, I have met a large party, including the Hamonds of Westacre, into whose courtyard an invisible horse and rider clatter whenever any death is about to occur in their family. Mrs. Hall

[1] George Henry Mason, 1818–1872, went to Rome in 1845 and picked up a living there painting the portraits of English residents. Met Leighton there and they remained friends for life. He returned to England in 1858 and exhibited regularly at the Academy till his death. His subjects in England as in Italy were mainly rural.—*Ed.*

[2] John Philpot Curran, Irish judge and famous orator.—*Ed.*

Dare had told of a young girl friend of hers. She was with a number of other girls, foolish and frivolous, who went to consult an old woman who had the reputation of being a witch, and who was supposed to have the power of making them see their future husbands. She said they must say their prayers backwards, perform certain incantations with water, lock their doors when they went to bed, and then they would see whom they were to marry, but they would find their doors locked in the morning.

The girl followed all the witch's directions. Then she locked her door, went to bed, and waited. Gradually, by the firelight, a young man seemed to come in—to come straight through the locked door—a young man in uniform; she saw him distinctly. He went to the end of the room and returned. As he passed the bed his sword caught in the curtain and fell upon the floor. Then he seemed to pass out. The girl fainted.

In the morning at first she thought it was a dream, but there, though her door was still locked, lay the actual sword upon the floor! Greatly aghast, she told no one, but put it away and kept it hidden. It was a terrible possession to her.

The following year, at a country-house, she met the very young man she had seen. They fell violently in love and were married. For one year they were intensely—perfectly—happy. Then her husband's regiment had to change its quarters. As she was packing up, with horror which was an instinct, she came upon the sword put away among her things. Just then, before she could hide it, her husband came in. He saw the sword, turned deadly pale, and in a stern voice said, 'How did you come by that?' She confessed the whole truth.

He was rigid. He said, 'I can never forgive it; I can never see you again;' and nothing she could say or do could move him. 'Do you know where I passed that terrible night?' he said; 'I passed it *in hell*!' He has given up three-quarters of his income to her, but she has never seen him since.

A Miss Broke, a niece of our host, told me even a more curious story. A few years ago there was a lady living in Ireland—a Mrs. Butler—clever, handsome, popular, prosperous, and perfectly happy. One morning she said to her husband, and to any one who was staying there, 'Last night I had the most wonderful night. I seemed to be spending hours in the most delightful place, in the most enchanting house I ever saw—not large, you know, but just the sort of house one might live in one's-self, and oh! so perfectly, so deliciously comfortable. Then there was the loveliest conservatory, and the garden was so enchanting! I wonder if anything half so perfect can really exist.'

And the next morning she said, 'Well, I have been to my house again. I must have been there for hours. I sat in the library: I walked on the terrace; I examined all the bedrooms: and it is simply the most perfect house in the world.' So it grew to be quite a joke in the family. People would ask Mrs. Butler in the morning if she had been to her house in the night, and often she had, and always with more intense enjoyment. She would say, 'I count the hours till bedtime, that I may get back to my house!' Then gradually the current of outside life flowed in, and gave a turn to their thoughts: the house ceased to be talked about.

Two years ago the Butlers grew very weary of their life in Ireland. The district was wild and disturbed. The people were insolent and ungrateful. At last they said, 'We are well off, we have no children, there's no reason why we should put up with this, and we'll go and live altogether in England.' So they came to London, and sent for all the house-agent's lists of places within forty miles of London, and many were the places they went to see. At last they heard of a house in Hampshire. They went to it by rail, and drove from the station. As they came to the lodge, Mrs. Butler said, 'Do you know, this is the lodge of my house.' They drove down an avenue—'But this *is* my house!' she said.

When the housekeeper came, she said, 'You will think it very odd, but do you mind my showing *you* the house: that passage leads to the library, and through that there is a conservatory, and then through a window you enter the drawing-room,' &c., and it was all so. At last, in an upstairs passage, they came upon a baize door. Mrs. Butler, for the first time, looked puzzled. 'But that door is not in my house,' she said. 'I don't understand about your house, ma'am,' said the housekeeper, 'but that door has only been there six weeks.'

Well, the house was for sale, and the price asked was very small, and they decided at once to buy it. But when it was bought and paid for, the price had been so extraordinarily small, that they could not help a misgiving that there must be something wrong with the place. So they went to the agent of the people who had sold it and said, 'Well, now the purchase is made and the deeds are signed, *will* you mind telling us why the price asked was so small?'

The agent had started violently when they came in, but recovered himself. Then he said to Mrs. Butler, 'Yes, it is quite true the matter is quite settled, so there can be no harm in telling now. The fact is that the house has had a great reputation for being haunted; but you, madam, need be under no apprehensions, for you are yourself the ghost!' On the nights when Mrs. Butler had dreamt she was at her house, she—her 'astral body'—had been seen there.

Ashridge, Nov. 19.—I arrived here by tea-time, passing in the beech woods Lady Lothian, who reminded me of Lady Waterford, as I saw her in her long black dress and black hat, backed by the leafless trees against the golden sunset. The dinner was lighted from brilliant sconces on old boiserie from a Flemish sacristy. In the evening 'Critic' was acted as a charade, led by Lady Jersey.

Breakfast was at small tables. Lord Brownlow, at ours, talked of a neighbouring house where a Lady Ferrers, a freebooter, used to steal out at night and rob the pilgrims coming from St. Albans. She had a passage from her room to the stables. In the morning one of the horses was often found tired out and covered with foam: no one could tell why. At last the poor lady was found dead on her doorstep in her suit of Lincoln green. She constantly haunts the place. Mr. Ady, who lives there now, meets her on the stairs and wishes her good night. Once, seeing her with her arms stretched out in the doorway, he called out to his wife who was outside, 'Now we've caught her!' and they rushed upon her from both sides, but caught—nothing.

It was Sunday, but I did not go to church, and walked with Lady Lothian through the sunlit green glades and russet woods of autumn. The house is of immense length of frontage, and behind it rises the chapel like a great church. In the evening we went to service in the chapel through the splendid conservatory, with long falling festoons of Ipomea. There was a full congregation and singing.

Middleton, Dec. 9.—A very agreeable visit to Lord and Lady Jersey. The country is hideous, but the house pleasant and comfortable, and a large new ball-room is hung with many fine portraits. . . .

Conversation fell on Christine, Lady Saye and Sele, who had three husbands. When she married the first surreptitiously, she took the bull by the horns, and said to her father at dinner, 'Father, I'm married!'—'Well, my dear, but at least wait till

Thomas has left the room.'—'No father, Thomas need not leave the room, for Thomas is the man I've married.'

My home life this year was very quiet and uneventful, only marked by my books. The Edgeworth family had placed Maria Edgeworth's letters in the hands of Lionel Holland, now a publisher, and desired him to find an editor. He asked me to accept the office—certainly not a remunerative one, as I only received fifty pounds for it, the whole large profits of the book falling to the publishers. The book at once became popular, and had a very large circulation. But *The Life and Letters of Maria Edgeworth* was rather a by-play. Most of my time was given to *The Gurneys of Earlham*, which gave me plenty of very hard and anxious work. I could not help feeling, as I attacked the mines and mountains of self-introspection in the form of religious journals which each one of the Gurney brothers and sisters left behind them, how unsuited I was for the task, how little I could enter into their feelings.

At Christmas I was with the Halifaxes.

To W. H. Milligan.

Hickleton, Dec. 28, 1894.—Can it be I? I say to myself, when I am called in pitch darkness in these winter mornings, and hurry in the dawn through the still dark shrubberies to the brilliantly lighted church, where, amid clouds of incense and the chanted salutation of the Blessed Sacrament, I receive 'the mass,' kneeling under the shadow of a great crucifix. Then, after breakfast, there is matins, what we should call early morning service, at which there are few worshippers; but when it is over, and you think you are going away, not a bit of it; there is a sound like the sea rushing in, and instantly the church is filled—thronged with people—and these come, not to receive the Sacrament, but to adore it! Charlie Halifax says, 'How strangely things come round. My uncle, a lawyer—who had his home here with my father and mother, and died when I was five years old—used to be a great friend of Newman and Lord Devon, and others who thought as they did, and his beautiful spiritual letters and his religious sonnets remain to us. He longed for what he thought was the impossible; he longed to have it here, and now here it is. At that time there was only celebration here four times in a year; he never hoped it could be otherwise, and yet what he so longed for—what I, too, so longed for as a boy—has been all realised.'

Hatfield, Jan. 30.—After a visit to Lord and Lady Knightley at Fawsley, in bitter cold and snow, I came here to meet a huge party—Cadogans, Iveaghs, Hampdens, and very many others. Most of the company have skated in the morning, but I have thoroughly enjoyed the equably warm passages and rooms of this immense house. Arthur Balfour is here, with charming manners, quite unspoilt. He stays in his room and does not appear till luncheon-time, so getting many quiet hours for work. Lord Rowton[1] also is here, and most agreeable in his natural ripple of pleasant talk. He says that he once asked Disraeli what was the most remarkable, the most self-sustained

[1] See note on p. 114.

and powerful sentence he knew. Dizzy paused for a moment, and then said, 'Sufficient unto the day is the evil thereof.'

Lady Salisbury said that her *masseuse* went constantly to the Queen. She told Lady Salisbury that what appeared to be lameness in the Queen was merely that her feet were too small to support the weight of her body.   Her hands are those of a little child. . . .

I said how one of the things I most wished to see, Lady Anne Grimston's tomb, was in Hertfordshire. 'Oh,' said Lady Salisbury, 'I will drive you there in my sledge;' and so she did, across the snow-laden roads. It is the most extraordinary sight. Lady Anne Grimston was a sceptic, and when she lay upon her deathbed in 1717, her family were most anxious to make her believe in a future state, but she wouldn't. 'It is as likely,' she said, 'that I should rise again as that a tree should grow out of my body when I'm dead.'

Lady Anne Grimston died, and was buried in Tewin churchyard, and over her grave was placed a great altar-tomb, with a huge massive stone slab on the top of it. In a year or two, this slab showed signs of internal combustion, and out of the middle of it—out of the very middle of it—grew a tree (some say six different trees, but one could not see in winter), and increased, till, in the time which has elapsed, it has become one of the largest trees in Hertfordshire. Not only that, but the branches of the tree have writhed about the tomb like the feelers of an octopus, have seized it, and lifted it into the air, so that the very base of the tomb is high up now, one with the tree or trees, so are they welded together. Then a railing was put round the tomb, and the tree has seized upon it in the same way, has twisted the strong iron rails like pack-thread, and they are to be seen tangled and twirled high in the branches of the tree. Another railing has now been put, and the tree will behave to it just as before. 'I have brought back Mr. Hare a most firm believer in a future state,' said Lady Salisbury as we re-entered the Golden Gallery at Hatfield, where all the guests were sitting.

To W. H. MILLIGAN.

July 20, 1895.—I have come away from London because all that was interesting in the season seemed to be at an end; but I enjoyed it to the last, though certainly what I find to delight in would not please many others. Most of all I have liked my quiet writing-table at the Athenaeum, and the silence, not the society, of the club, where no one, except Lord Acton[1] and myself, seems to work in the mornings. Then, after two o'clock, I never go back, but see people for the rest of the day. The garden-parties make this delightful, and I had charming afternoons at Osterley, at Roehampton, and at Sion, where the brilliant groups of people are so picturesque under the great cedar-trees. It was a great pleasure once more to be welcomed to Holland House, and to find how much those who possess it appreciate its great interest and charm. Once a week the writing-time was broken into, and I went with drawing-parties to the garden at Lambeth, to Waltham Abbey, and to the roof of the Record Office, whence we tried to paint St. Paul's and all the satellite City churches reared up against an opal sky. In the evenings there was less of interest, and a great party at Devonshire House left more to recollect than the daily dinners, with little real conversation. I think it is Bacon who says, 'A crowd is not company, and faces are but a gallery of pictures, and talk but a tinkling cymbal, where there is not love.' The last day, however, a dinner at Lady Audrey Buller's was most pleasant. It was

[1] Sir John Emerich Edward Dalberg, Lord Acton, historian, 1834-1902.—*Ed.*

in honour of her cousin Captain Townshend,[1] the hero of Chitral, who gave me a most graphic description of lying all day smoking behind a barrier of earth, with a spyhole through which he could fire at any man who showed himself, hearing the thud of the return shot against his barrier afterwards. Returning to England, he was shocked to find no one but boys at the balls—'boys who shake hands with a movement like that of kangaroos.' I sat by —— the widow of the historian, who talked of other historians, especially of Mr. Freeman—how he had the head of a Jupiter on the body of a gorilla: how he did not eat, but devour; it was no use to put anything less than a joint before him: how scenery never gave him the power of realising an event which he could not read of. One day at dinner Mr. Parker was within one of him. To him Freeman talked incessantly across the lady who was next him. At last there was a pause. The lady thought she would have her innings. 'It has been very hot weather lately, Mr. Freeman,' she said. 'Stuff and nonsense,' said Freeman. 'Parker you were saying,' &c.[2]

To VISCOUNT HALIFAX.

Penrhyn Castle, Sept, 22, 1895.—I left home in the case of one 'Chi per lungo silenzio parea fioco,'[3] and have much enjoyed my holiday talking-time. How many delightful people there are in the world. I so seldom see any one I cannot care in the least about. One side, one aspect, seems unprepossessing, but then, if one takes the trouble to go round on the other side, one is sure to find something. . . . I saw no end of people in Shropshire when I was at Buntingsdale—so familiar in my long-ago—for Gertrude Percy's wedding at Hodnet. After that I was in quieter scenes, but oh! how lovely, on Wenlock Edge, with such fine views over the rich plain below.

Penrhyn Castle has been delightful, and my room, with its exquisite views over sea and mountains, the most delightful thing in it. Lady Penrhyn presides over the great place with the calm of perpetual moonlight: sunlight is left to her beautiful and impulsive step-daughter Miss Alice (Pennant), who orders out no end of carriages to take guests up into the hills or wherever they want to go.

Do you know that *The Gurneys of Earlham* is out? You will not like it, I think, and indeed I feel myself, that Carlyle would be justified in saying it was 'a very superfluous book.' Still, I will anticipate your asking me, and tell you that, up to its lights, it is not a bad piece of work.

To W. H. MILLIGAN.

Garrowby, Yorkshire, Oct. 4.—The glorious weather which illuminated Wales continued at Lyme, which was still in the full splendour of summer flowers. . . . I went on to flattest Lincolnshire, to Revesby Abbey, to visit my distant cousin, dear Edward Stanhope's[4] widow. . . . The house at Revesby was full of interesting objects. Amongst them was a magnificent repeater watch which belonged to the old Lord Stanhope. One night, when he was out late, a man pounced upon him with pistols and

---

[1] Sir Charles Vere Ferrers Townshend, 1861–1924, major-general, K.C.B. 1917. After Chitral, he saw service in the S. African war and in Mesopotamia in the first World War. Captor of Kut, but after his failure to capture Baghdad he was himself forced to surrender Kut and was interned by the Turks until 1918.—*Ed.*

[2] It will be recalled that it was Freeman who accused Hare of literary robbery in using, without express permission, so much of Freeman's writings in *The Cities of Northern Italy*. See page 83.—*Ed.*

[3] 'Whose voice seemed faint through long disuse of speech.'

[4] Edward Stanhope, 1840–93, second son of the fifth Earl, President of the Board of Trade, Colonial Secretary, Secretary for War.—*Ed.*

'Your money or your life.' Always imperturbable, Lord Stanhope replied very slowly, 'My friend, I have no money with me.'—'No,' said the robber, 'but you have your watch; I must have your watch.'—'My friend, this watch was given to me by one very dear to me, and I value it extremely. It is considered to be worth £100. Now, if you will trust me, I will this evening place a hundred-pound note in the hollow of that tree.' And the highwayman trusted him and Lord Stanhope placed the note there. Very many years after, Lord Stanhope was at a public dinner in London, and opposite him sat a City magnate of great wealth and influence. They conversed pleasantly. Next day Lord Stanhope received a letter from him, enclosing a hundred-pound note, and saying, 'It was your Lordship's kind *loan* of that sum many years ago that started me in life, and enabled me to rise to have the honour of sitting opposite your Lordship at dinner.'

Here, at Garrowby, I have been very happy with the Halifaxes. I always feel better for the life with them, and I have especially liked the spiritual part of it here, where there is no chaplain, as at Hickleton, and where the services in the beautiful little chapel are led by Charlie Halifax himself. Everybody joins, and a footman sings gloriously at the very pitch of his voice. In everything Charlie recalls to me something which I have read with a higher reference—'Not by his doctrines has Christ laid hold upon the heart of men, but by the story of his life.'[1] He has 'under all circumstances that just admixture in the moral character of sweetness and dignity' which Marcus Aurelius speaks of. Unlike everything else is the simplicity and singleness of heart and purpose written so distinctly on everything he says and does. Action is easy and natural where faith is so absolute. 'At all times a man who would do faithfully must believe firmly,' was a saying of Carlyle. And though religion pervades everything, no house was ever so gay as that of which Charlie is master. What merriment we have had over our games in the evening: what fun over the mysterious disappearances by day into the four secret chambers which make this house so curious: what admirably good stories have been told: and while the loss of the dear boys who are gone ever leaves a blank in the parents' hearts, how happy life is made for the children who remain!

---

[1] Jerome K. Jerome.

XV

IN MANY PLACES

1895–1900

❧

GREATLY as I always enjoy my little home of Holmhurst, dear as every corner of it is to me, I never feel as if it was well to stay there too long in winter alone. In summer, Nature itself can give sufficient companionship; but when earth is dead and frost-bound, the silence in the long hours after sunset becomes almost terrible, and I increasingly feel that late autumn and winter are the best time for visits.

To VISCOUNT HALIFAX.

Holmhurst, Nov. 25.—I have much enjoyed a visit from Mr. and Mrs. Cummings, the Americans who were so kind to us on our terrible return journey from Italy in 1860, and of whom the wife, at least, is so clever, that she is suffering—as Mrs. Kemble said once of some one—from a constipation of her talents. They came here fresh from a visit to Haworth, much impressed with its severe desolation,—'that any one should be able to have any hope, or look forward to a future life, on the top of Haworth hill is nothing short of a miracle.'

Mrs. Cummings says we should not like America; 'it is a country utterly without perspective; one must go up to the Indians and the Jesuit missionaries for that.' She has been describing Miss Louisa Alcott, the well-known authoress. 'She lived with her old father and her beautiful mother and her three sisters. They used to write little stories. One day her sisters said, "Louisa, you must write something more than these." —"I would, but I can't do it here," she answered. So the sisters clubbed their little savings together, and they sold a few things, and Louisa went to Boston. There she called upon Roberts, the publisher of all American good things, and said, "I want to write a story."—"Very well," he answered; "what kind will you take?"—"Oh, I can't make up anything," said Louisa; "I can only just write what I know."—"Oh, you can just write what you know," said Roberts; "then don't stay talking here; go away at once and begin." So she went and lived by herself and wrote, and in five weeks she brought him her *Little Women.* He took it and said, "Come again to-morrow." And when she went next day he said, "Well, I will take your story, and I will offer you one of two things; either you can take two hundred dollars down for it, or you can take your chance."—"But what would you do if you were me?" asked Miss Alcott. Roberts said he had never been placed in such an awkward predicament in his life, but he spoke the truth and said, "I would take my chance," She did, and soon after he had to pay her 10,000 dollars. She wrote *Little Men* afterwards, but it did not answer as well; boys do not take books to their pillows as girls do.'

To HERBERT VAUGHAN.

Kingston Vicarage, Wareham, Nov. 10.—You would have liked going with us to Wool, on a *Tess of the D'Urbervilles* pilgrimage, for there, rising by the reedy riverside, is the old gabled house to which Tess was taken after her marriage. It is exactly as Hardy describes it; even the plank bridge remains across which Angel carried her in his sleep to the stone coffin at Bindon Abbey. The two old pictures mentioned in the book really hang at the top of the staircase, and the lady in one of them is supposed to blow out the candle of any one who ventures up the stairs after midnight.[1]

To VISCOUNT HALIFAX.

Elvedon, Thetford, Nov. 14.—All the way back from Dorsetshire did I come for the pleasure of meeting the Duchess of York here (at Lord and Lady Iveagh's); but that was not to be, as an impending event is considered too near for her to travel with safety.[2] The Duke[3] is here, and very unaffected and pleasant, really a very nice prince, and quite good-looking. He never fails to be punctual to the moment—a grand quality for a prince, and due, probably to naval discipline. He talks a great deal, and talks well, but in reality princes have no chance—no chance at all—conversationally, as no one ever contradicts them, however much they disagree; no subjects are aired but those which they choose for themselves, and the merest commonplaces from royal lips are listened to as if they were oracles.

I floated here in the luxurious saloon carriage of a special train, but felt rather shy, because whereas all the rest of the party were on terms of christian-name intimacy, I knew none of them before except Lord Rowton, who is, however, always very kind and pleasant. But I was interested to see those who are so frequently part of the royal circle, and liked them all, especially and extremely Lord and Lady Carrington; but then—everyone does!

I wonder if you know this house of Elvedon. It was Duleep Singh's, and he tried to make it like an Indian palace inside. Much of his decoration still remains, and the delicate white stucco-work has a pretty effect when mingled with groups of tall palms and flowering plants. Otherwise the house (with the kindest of hosts), is almost appallingly luxurious, such masses of orchids, electric light everywhere, &c. However, a set-off the other way is an electric piano, which goes on pounding away by itself with a pertinacity which is perfectly distracting. In the evenings singing men and dancing women are brought down from London, and are supposed to enliven the royal guest.

You know, probably, how this place is the most wonderful shooting in England. The soil is so bad that it is not worth cultivating, and agriculture has been abandoned as a bad business. Game is found to be far more profitable. Each day I have gone out with the luncheon party, and we have met the shooters at tents pitched at different parts of the wilderness, where boarded floors are laid down, and a luxurious banquet is prepared, with plate and flowers. The quantity of game killed is almost incredible, and the Royal Duke shot more than any one, really, I believe, owing to his being a very good shot, and not, as so often is the case in royal battues, from the birds being driven his way.

---

[1] *Tess of the D'Urbervilles* had been published in 1891.—*Ed.*

[2] The birth of Prince Albert (subsequently Duke of York and King George VI), exactly a month later.—*Ed.*

[3] Subsequently H.M. King George V.

A great feature of the party is Admiral Keppel, kindest, most courteous, and most engaging of old gentlemen, so captivating that there is always a rivalry amongst the ladies as to who shall walk with him, and amongst the men to get hold of his stories. He described the prayers at Holcombe on Sunday evening in his boyhood. After dinner the men were allowed an hour or two over their wine. Then the prayer-bell rang, and they all went in. Afterwards an old servant stayed to take up those who could not get up from their knees, and carry them to bed by turns when they were too drunk to go by themselves. He remembered Charles James Fox reeling down the corridor at Holcombe, falling helplessly from side to side. His father followed him, and he followed his father, who kept exclaiming, 'Good God! drunk! Good God! drunk again!' for the expression had not gone out then.[1]

To W. H. Milligan *and* Journal.

Nov. 27, Hornby Castle, Bedale.—I came here yesterday. Several people were in the castle omnibus when I got into it at the station, of whom a grand lion-like old man turned out to be Mr. Bayard, the American Ambassador. He gave an interesting account of the allotment of land in America: how a reserve was left to the Indians, but they were dying out, chiefly because of their catching all the vices of Europeans, especially their love of alcohol. He said they were like the buffaloes. These used to come down and swoop through the country in vast herds, and devour all the spring produce; and later, in their vast battalions they would swoop back again; but now, fettered and shut in by barriers and fences, they pined, starved, and died; and so it was with the Indians. He described how, after an unjust woman had published a libel on her country,[2] the greatest suffering had resulted to the slaves, who would follow their former masters to suffering, wounds, imprisonment, and death.

Nov. 29.—At breakfast, at one of several little round tables, Mr. Bayard talked pleasantly of a grave in the cemetery at Nuremberg. It is one of Adam Kraft's iron tombstones, and it bears no name. Affixed to it is a human skull, exquisitely modelled, with a jaw which opens and shuts. In the forehead—the bronze forehead—is a white patch of some other metal. The story is that the owner of that skull was very unhappily married. His misery drove him from home, drove him into very bad company, and he sank lower and lower. One day he suddenly died and was buried; but soon afterwards his family began to suspect foul play, and he was exhumed. At first his body seemed to bear no witness, but then, in his forehead, under his hair, a large nail was found, buried up to the hilt, hammered in so accurately that no blood had come. Every one believed that it was his wife who had done it, but it could not be brought home to her; his associates were too bad for their evidence to be trusted. But the model of his skull was laid upon his grave, and his wife left the place; she could not continue to exist near it.

Hams, Birmingham, Nov. 30.—This is a large house of extreme comfort, and its owner, Lord Norton, who looks sixty, though he is eighty-two, is one of the most agreeable hosts in England.[3] Walking on the terrace this morning, he said he ought to put up a slab to record how the whole constitution of New Zealand was settled

[1] Sir Henry Keppel (1809–1904); served in the China War 1841–2, and the Baltic campaign 1854; was C.-in-C. Devonport, 1872, and Admiral of the Fleet 1877. Wrote a four-volume *A Sailor's Life under Four Sovereigns.*—*Ed.*

[2] Mrs. Beecher Stowe in *Uncle Tom's Cabin.*

[3] Charles Bowyer Adderley, first Baron Norton, 1814–1905, a pioneer of town planning at Saltley, President of the Board of Trade, a musician and art critic.—*Ed.*

on that terrace: that which was arranged while walking up and down there had never been altered. The view of the pretty windings of the Thame recalled the exclamation of a famous landscape-gardener when he saw it—'Clever!' 'It was not made, it is natural,' said Lord Norton. But no, his friend could not regard it except from the gardening point of view, and 'clever' was all he could say.

Dec. 2.—A walk amidst the remnants of the Forest of Arden led to much talk about trees. 'When Gladstone meets any one new,' said Lord Norton, 'his first thought is, "What does he know? what can I get out of him?" When he met Lord Leigh, he had heard of Stoneleigh, that it possessed some of the finest oaks in England; so, when he sat down by him, he began at once, "Lord Leigh, have you any theory as to the age of oaks?"—"Yes, certainly I have; I possess several myself that are above a thousand years old."—"And how do you know that is so?" said Gladstone. "Well," said Lord Leigh, "I have several that are called 'Gospel Oaks,' because the old Saxon missionaries used to preach under them more than eight hundred years ago, and they would not be likely to choose a young oak to preach under: we may suppose that they chose an oak at least two hundred years old."—"Well, that is a very good reason," said Gladstone.'

While talking of hunting as conducive to the manliness of Englishmen, Lord Norton said, 'When I was hunting with Charlie Newdigate, a boy almost naked, not quite, came out of a coal-pit, and on a donkey, without saddle or bridle, hunted with us all day, not going over the hedges, but through them. Newdigate was delighted. "*That's* the stuff English heroes are made of," he said, and he had a long talk with the boy afterwards, and explained to him all about the field, &c. . . . In Northumberland there was a boy who would ride one of his father's bulls. His father cut him off at last, and would have nothing more to do with him. 'I'm not a bad father,' he said, 'and I don't mind his riding my bull, but when he takes him out with the hounds it's too much.'

To VISCOUNT HALIFAX.

Rome, April 23, 1896.—I wonder if you know that I have been abroad since the first of February. At first, for a month, I was on 'the Rivieras,' finishing up a little volume which will be so called, and which will appear before next winter. . . .

At Nice, I was not in the town, but at the old Villa Arson, which you will remember. It was all beautiful, and the sky was cloudlessly blue for a month; and I lingered at Bordighera with the Strathmores and my dear old friend Emilia de Bunsen, and then at Alassio with my cousin Lady Paul, and at beautiful Rapallo. But oh! the difference on entering real Italy, and finding oneself in the delightful old-world streets of Lucca, with their clean pavements and brown green-shuttered houses, with the air so much more bracing, the sky so much more soft, and the pleasant manner and winning tongue of the Italian people.

My last six weeks have been spent in Rome,—spoilt, destroyed, from the old Rome of our many winters here, but settling down now into the inferior mediocrity to which the Sardinian occupation has reduced it. And, though one does not see them every hour as one used to do, there are still many lovely and attractive corners to be hunted up. The Italian archaeologists (so called) are also finding out that they have made a great mistake in tearing away all the plants and shrubs which protected the tops of the ruins, and are comically occupied in planting little roots of grass and chickweed on their barren summits.

The ruin of the great families here is depressing. There has been a sale at the old historic Orsini palace, at which a marble statue holding a baton behind the auctioneer seemed to repeat his action and to preside coldly over the ruin of his house and dispersion of its treasures. And on the floor of the hall, appropriately surrounded by overthrown marble pedestals, lay the great bust of the Orsini Pope, with a look of unutterable disgust upon his face at having been just sold for £6. I bought a little Madonna, which will adorn Holmhurst, if I can get it out of the country.

To-day—a desperately wet day—has been enlivened by a summons to luncheon with the Crown Princess of Sweden, whom I think one of the most charming, natural, and attractive of human beings; and oh! how simple, how utterly without affectation is that sort of person who can have nothing to *pretend* to. It is that, I suppose, which makes such people so much the easiest to talk to, which makes one feel so far more at rest with them than with persons of another, even of one's own class.

To Miss Garden *at Rome.*

Viterbo, May 1, 1896.—Yesterday went to Toscanella. The landlord of the hotel was to engage a little carriage for me, which I found at the door when I went down, but with a horse which was an absolute skeleton. Still they declared it could go, and it *could.* How it rushed, and tore, and swung us down the rose-fringed descent to the great Etruscan plain, where the faint dome of Montefiascone rose in the blue haze against the heavens, beyond the aërial distances of burnt grass, broken here and there by Etruscan caves and ruins. Then how the skeleton horse still galloped into the uplands, till great towers appeared grouped like ninepins, or rather like S. Gemignano. It is yet a long circuit to the town, a descent into a rocky gorge, then a steep ascent winding round the hill outside the walls, a sort of Calvary to this Jerusalem, where the great churches stand, S. Pietro like the most magnificent cathedral, girdled by huge walls and towers, with a ruined episcopal palace beside it, and a triumphal arch, like like those of Brittany, in front of the east end.... The city of Toscanella scrambles, a mass of brown towers, golden roots, and grey houses, along the opposite hill, and has a thousand corners which are enough to drive an artist frantic—such gothic windows; such dark entries; such arcaded streets, with glints of brilliant foliage and flowers breaking in upon their solemn shadows. At a little inn I had luncheon—a dish of poached eggs, excellent bread, cheese, and wine, and all for forty centimes, so living is not dear in Toscanella.

Then oh! how the skeleton horse galloped home under the serene loveliness of the pellucid sky, over the plain where all the little grasses and flowers were quivering and shimmering in golden sunset ecstasy.

I cannot say the food here is delicious; it would be an exaggeration. All the little somethings and nothings a butchered calf is capable of, and vegetables lost in garlic and oil. The host's name is Zefferino; he is a very substantial zephyr. He arranged for my going this morning to S. Martino, which I was most anxious to visit, for love—or was it hate?—of Donna Olimpia Pamfili.[1] I so longed to see where the great 'papessa' died; and how the plague got hold of her on that most grand height, overlooking

---

[1] Olimpia Maidalchini was born in 1594 and married Count Pamfili, over whose brother she obtained an astonishing ascendency. Under her guidance he eventually became Pope (Innocent X) in 1644 and as her husband was then dead, she went to live in the Vatican and there, in her brother-in-law's name, spent the rest of her life selling benefices and offices at the highest possible prices. When Innocent died in 1655 she had acquired fabulous wealth in estates and gold and precious stones, and although Pope Alexander demanded their surrender, it was not done. When she died, her son, who had been a cardinal, inherited all her riches.—*Ed.*

K

seventy miles of pink and blue distances, one cannot imagine. Rocky honeysuckle-hung lanes lead up to it—a little brown-walled town, with gates and fountain, and just one street—the steepest street in the world, up which the great white oxen can only just struggle—leading up to the palace and church. Before the high altar of the latter is Olimpia's tomb, providently placed in her lifetime, with, I thought, a rather touching inscription, saying that she had really tried to do all the good she *could*.

To W. H. MILLIGAN.

Abbazia di S. Gregorio, Venice, May 17.—On arriving here, I was persuaded to go to one of the principal hotels, sumptuously luxurious, and consequently intensely unsympathetic and unattractive. The mass of Americans, travelling like their own trunks, and with as much understanding of the place, drove me away at last, and I was enchanted to find a refuge in this dear little abbey, with its venerable court full of flowers and beautiful decorated gateway, outside which the green waves of the Grand Canal sparkle and dance. I have enjoyed Venice more than any other part of this time abroad—have had very happy times with friends in the afternoons, and in the mornings by myself drawing in desolate but lovely corners, unknown places, quite overlooked in what Symonds calls 'Ruskin's paint-box of delirious words.' Yet I find colouring here very difficult, and quite a new style necessary, where *every* shadow is transparent.

August 1, 1896.—I have enjoyed my six weeks in London with their much people-seeing. People laugh at me for liking it all so much, and still more for expressing my liking for it; but I believe I shall never turn out to be 'one of those whom Dante found in hell-border because they had been sad under the blessed sun.'[1] How many people in 'the world,' so called, are perfectly charming! Surely if there are many like the Woods, Jerseys, William Lowthers, Pennants, Ilchesters, and oh! how many others, good must far predominate over evil in society.

I was two days at Hatfield—days of brilliant sunshine, glowing gardens, scent of lime-flowers, great kindness from host and hostess, and much pleasant companion-ship. Most of the guests did nothing but talk and enjoy the summer beauty. Madame Ignatieff, coming to Hatfield, said, 'Ah, I see what your life in great country-houses is—eat and doddle (dawdle), doddle and eat.' Dear Sir Augustus Paget, of many pleasant Roman memories, sat out by me part of the time, and on the Monday morning kept me after breakfast talking of how very happy he was, how many enjoyments in his life. I could not help feeling afterwards what characteristic 'last words' those were. I went into the drawing-room to take leave of Lady Salisbury, and in an instant Lady Cranborne ran in saying that Sir Augustus had fallen in the hall. He scarcely spoke again, and on Saturday his bright spirit had departed.[2]

Lady Salisbury is delightful, not only to listen to but to watch. She is so young in her spirit. All she does, as all she says, is so clever, and her relation to her many daughters-in-law, to the great variety of her visitors, to her vast household, is so un-failingly sagacious. Even 'to know her is a liberal education,' as Steele said of a lady he admired. She is a great contrast to Lord Salisbury: I watched him solemnly and slowly walking up and down the rooms with his hand on the head of his great dog Pharaoh.

[1] George Eliot's Letters.

[2] Sir Augustus Berkeley Paget (1823–96). Diplomatist. Served in Paris, Athens, Egypt, the Hague, Berlin and Scandinavia. Was in 1867 appointed Envoy Extraordinary at Rome at the most critical period of Italian history. He remained in Rome many years and was appointed Ambassador in 1876. From 1884 to 1893 he was Ambassador in Vienna.—*Ed.*

The next Sunday I was at Osterley, in intensely hot weather. Sir E. Burne Jones was there (as well as at Hatfield), the painter of morbid and unlovely women, who has given an apotheosis to ennui—the Botticelli of the nineteenth century. He is very agreeable naturally, and made infinitely more so by his seductively captivating voice. He described going to dine with the Blumenthals, where the footman at the door presented him with a gilt apple, and informed him that he was Paris, and would go down to dinner with whichever of the Graces he presented it to. 'I knew I must make two deadly enemies,' said Sir Edward, 'so I shut my eyes and stretched out the apple into space; *some one* took it.'[1]

Here is a delightful story of the present Bishop of London for you, which is *molto ben trovato*, at any rate. One day, he took a cab home to Fulham from the City, and wishing to be liberal, gave the man sixpence beyond the full fare. The man looked at it. 'What, aren't you satisfied?' said the Bishop. 'Oh, yes I'm *satisfied*,' said the man; 'but if I might, I should like to ask you a question.' 'Oh certainly,' said the Bishop, 'ask whatever you like.' 'Well, then, if St. Paul had come back to earth and was Bishop, do you suppose he'd be living in this here palace?' 'Certainly not,' replied the Bishop promptly, 'for he'd be living at Lambeth, and it would be a shilling fare.'

To FRANCIS COOKSON.

Sept. 7.—Is it a sign of old age coming on, I wonder, when one has the distaste for leaving home by which I am now possessed? I simply hate it. When one has all one wants and exactly what one likes, why should one set off on a round of visits, in which one may, and probably will, have many pleasant hours, but as certainly many bare and dull ones, often in dreary rooms, sometimes with wooden-headed people, and without the possibility of the familiar associations which habit makes such a pleasure? I cannot say how delightful I always find my home life—the ever-fresh morning glories of the familiar view of brilliant flowers, green lawns, and oak woods; and then the sea, which to me is so much more beautiful in its morning whiteness with faint grey cloud-shadows, or smiling under the tremulous sun-rays, than in the evening light, which brings a lovely but monotonous blueness with it: the joyous companionship of my little black spitz Nero ('Black,' not the wicked emperor): the regularity of my proof-sheet work, and other work, till luncheon-dinner, after which there are generally visitors to be attended to; and then quiet work again, or meditation on the long-ago and the future.

I wonder if you ever saw Coventry Patmore[2] here, who died lately. He often came to Holmhurst during the latter part of his residence at Hastings, where he wrote 'The Angel in the House' in memory of his first wife, and in memory of his second spent most of the large fortune she had brought him, £60,000, in building a beautiful church, S. Mary Star of the Sea; and whilst building it, though always a devout Catholic, imbibed, from being brought into close contact with them, a hatred of priests which never left him. The existence of 'In Memoriam' may be said to be due to Patmore. When young, he and Tennyson lodged together at some house in London, where they had a violent quarrel with their landlady, and left suddenly in a huff. Once well away, they recollected that the MS. of 'In Memoriam' was left in the cupboard of their room with the unfinished ham and the half-empty jam-pot. The timid Alfred would not face

---

[1] Sir Edward Burne-Jones died in 1898, aged 65, one of the last of the pre-Raphaelite painters, specialising in legendary and mythological subjects.—*Ed.*

[2] Coventry Patmore, 1823–1896, poet. The four parts of the long poem, *The Angel in the House*, were written between 1854 and 1862. Turned Roman Catholic in 1864.—*Ed.*

the wrath of the landlady, but Patmore went back to get it. He found the woman cleaning her doorstep and told her that he was come to get something he had left behind. 'No,' she said, 'there was nothing, and she had seen quite enough of him, he should not go upstairs.' But the slim Patmore took her by surprise, slipped past her, rushed up to the room, and from the jam cupboard extracted the MS., and made off with it in spite of her imprecations.

Tennyson recognised what Patmore had done at the time, and said he should give him the MS. But he never did; he gave it to Sir J. Simeon, who left it to his second wife. When Tennyson's MSS. rose so much in value, his family asked for it back, and Lady Simeon has promised that it shall go back at her death. In another generation, if Tennyson's fame lasts so long, it will probably be sold for a large sum.

JOURNAL *and* LETTERS.

Chesters, Northumberland, Oct. 6.—One thing a man who pays a good many visits should always be certain of—*never* to outstay his welcome. It would be dreadful to see one's hostess begin to have the fidgets. It is safest—at latest—to go by the eleven o'clock train, but a good and pleasant plan is to take leave overnight, and *be* gone the next morning. I was full of enjoyment at Penrhyn Castle—the genial and charming family, the great variety of the guests, and the excursions, in spite of furious storms, into the Welsh hills. Then I was with a most kind bachelor host, Fred Swete, at Oswestry, and spent the day at Brogyntyn with Lord Harlech, a perfect example of old-fashioned courtesy and kindness. Then I was at Ridley Hall, full of—oh! how many memories of my long-ago. But it was the greatest pleasure to see Frank and Lady Anne Lyon there, and how much they appreciated and cared for the place. Lord and Lady Wantage were at Ridley, and I went with them to Hexham Abbey, once a most grand church, but utterly ruined by an ignorant restoration. And now, wandering still on the footprints of past days, I am at Chesters with the widow and children of my dear old friend George Clayton, and Miss Annie Ogle, whom I knew so well in those far-away days, here as a delightful *old* lady, with snow-white hair, but the same winning character and ways as in her youth.

Airlie Castle, Oct. 18.—Monday was fearfully cold, and it was a pleasure to see the beautiful face of Lady Airlie—more picturesque and distinguished in late middle life than any one else—looking out of a close carriage come to meet me. Her most poetical home is just suited to her—the tiniest castle in the world, with its one noble gate-tower giving access to a little green plateau beneath which the Melgum and the Isla rush through deep wooded gorges to their meeting-place. In the serene beauty of her age [Lady Airlie] lends a lustre to her surroundings; quietly, contentedly severing most links with the great world in which she has so long been a star.

We drove to Cortachy through woods laid prostrate by the great storm of 1893, which has left the trees piled on one another, like the dead of a vanquished army on a battlefield. Lady Airlie made the whole of the weird desolate country live through her interpretation of it:—

'Those are the black hornless cattle of Angus. That is the hill of Clota, on the top of which is the old tower where the last witch was burnt. In the church books there is an entry that on a particular day there was no service, because all the congregation were gone to the burning of the witch. That village in the hollow, which is so red and striking in the sunset, is Kirriemuir: it is the "Thrums" of Barrie's novel. Now we will leave the carriage at "the Devil's Stone": it is just a stone which the devil threw at the kirk, but it missed and fell into the stream: it rests the opposite way to all boulders, and it is of a different formation from all the other stones in the district. Dicky Doyle[1] loved the story and the stone, and used to paint it. And now we will go into the "Garden of Friendship". I made it when I first married out of an old kitchen-garden, and I cut down a belt of trees and let in the view. Over there is our deer-forest. Charlotte, Lady Strathmore, took me up to the tower of Glamis once, and stretched out her hand towards our hills—"You have a deer-forest, and a river, and *scenery*," she said, "and I have *nothing*."

'Here is King Charles's room. Charles II was here for the gathering of the clans, but they did not gather as they ought, and he went away disappointed. He left a Prayer-book and a Euclid here: he was a great scientist. Under the floor at that corner is a secret room: we have never seen it. Some workmen found it after the great fire here whilst every one was away, and before we came back it was walled up, and it has never been thought worth while to disturb it again. . . .'

All evening Lady Airlie has talked delightfully:—

'We were a very quarrelsome family as children. At Gosport, whilst we were at church, my next sister, Cecilia, who had been left at home, fell out of the window She lived for some days, very suffering and scarcely conscious, but she used constantly in her half-delirium, to say, "Oh, don't quarrel, don't quarrel;" and it made a very great impression upon me, and afterwards I always tried never to quarrel. My father never let us complain. If anything unpleasant happened and my mother murmured, he would always say, "Oh, don't; we have so much more than we *deserve*." He always thought it so ill-bred—so ill-bred towards God—to murmur. . . . As soon as I came out, I went with my parents to the Grange, where the first Lady Ashburton was very kind to me, and I passionately adored her. There I first saw Carlyle and Mrs. Carlyle, but he had known my mother very well before. Mrs. Carlyle really loved Lady Ashburton, yet she was madly jealous of her. When they were at home, and Carlyle would come in quite tired out with a long day's work, she would say, "Now just walk down to Bath House and see Lady Ashburton, and that will refresh you." She meant him to go, but as soon as he was gone her grief was passionate, because she felt it would not have been the same thing to him if he stayed with her. He was always pleasant, but to a few—to my mother especially—he never failed to show the most intense delicacy of feeling.'

Bishopthorpe, Oct. 23.—This house has a charm from the great variety of its styles, even the gingerbread-gothic is important as being of a date anterior to Horace Walpole, who has the reputation of having introduced that style.

Lord Falkland has been here. He had been lately at Skelton Castle. His hostess, Miss Wharton, took him to his room, down a long passage—a large room, panelled with dark oak and with a great four-post bed with heavy hangings. It was very gloomy and oppressive, Lord Falkland thought, but he said nothing, dressed, and went down to dinner. When he came upstairs again, he found the aspect of the room even more oppressive, but he made up a great fire and went to bed. In the night he was awakened by a pattering on the floor as of high-heeled shoes and the rustling of a stiff silk dress. There was still a little fire burning, but he could see nothing. As he distinctly heard the footsteps turn, he thought, 'Oh, I hope they may not come up to the bed.' They *did*. But then they turned away, and he heard them go out at the door.

[1] Richard Doyle, artist and caricaturist, contributor to *Punch*. Illustrated Ruskin's *King of the Golden River*.

With difficulty he composed himself to sleep again, but was soon reawakened by the same sound, the rustling of silk and the footsteps. Then he was thoroughly miserable, got up, lighted candles, made up the fire, and passed a wretched night. In the morning he was glad to find an excuse for going away.

Afterwards he heard an explanation. An old Wharton, cruel and brutal, had a young wife. One day, coming tipsy into his wife's room, he found her nursing her baby. He was in a violent temper, and, seizing the baby from her arms, he dashed its head against the wall and killed it on the spot. When he saw it was dead, he softened at once. Even in her grief and horror Mrs. Wharton could not bear to expose him, and together they buried the child under the hearthstone; but she pined away and very soon she died. She used to be heard not only rustling, but weeping, wailing, sobbing, crying. At that time the Whartons were Roman Catholics, and when the family were almost driven from their home by its terrors, they got a priest to exorcise the castle and to bury the baby skeleton in consecrated ground. Since then, there have been no sobs and cries, only the rustling and pattering of feet.

To Miss Garden *at* Rome.

Oct. 26, 1896.—The first three volumes of the *Story of My Life* are come out, and I send them to you. Even the favourable reviews complain vehemently about their length. But after all, it was not written or printed for the public, only for a private inner circle, though I am sure that, in return for having been allowed to read it, 'the public' will kindly be willing—well, just to *pay* for the printing! Then it is funny how each review wants a different part left out—one the childhood, one the youth, one the experiences of later life: there would be nothing left but the little anecdotes about already well-known people, which they all wish to keep, and, in quoting these, they one and all copy each other; it saves trouble. . . . As you know, I never intended the book, written seventeen and printed two years ago, to appear till after my death, but this year it was so strongly represented to me that then all who would care to read about my earlier years would then be *dead too*, that I assented to the story up to 1870 being published. To tell the truth, I feel now how sorry I should have been to have missed the amusement of hearing even the most abusive things people say. . . . Yet, yet, just for the sake of variety, I should like some day, as a change to the unknown, to read a really favourable review of *something* I have written, though I read somewhere, 'To like to be right is the last weakness of a wise man: to like to be thought right is the inveterate prejudice of fools.'

To Viscount Halifax.

Jan. 9, 1897.—Some people are very angry with me for telling the truth in the *Story of My Life* about these young years, when I was suffering 'from an indiscriminate theological education,' as Mr. Schimmelpennick calls such, and when I was made so constantly to feel how '*l'ennui n'a pas cessé d'être en Angleterre une institution religeuse* [boredom has not ceased to be in England a religious institution—Elisée Reclus].' And it is not merely the 'canaille of talkers in type [Carlyle]' who find fault, but many whose opinion I have a regard for. . . .

One of my reviewers says he would like to read a truthful word-portrait of Augustus Hare by one of the persons he describes in print: so should I exceedingly, and most appallingly horrible it would be! . . . Most extraordinarily *virulent* certainly reviews can be! Really, 'hurricanes of calumny and tornados of abuse'[1] have been hurled at

---

[1] John Bright.

me. *Blackwood* (*i.e.* the Maurice spirit in *Blackwood*), in an article which breathes of white lips, after dwelling scornfully upon 'the sickening honey of the "Memorials," ' writes: 'What is Mr. Augustus Hare? He is neither anybody nor nobody—neither male nor female—neither imbecile nor wise. . . . As we wade through this foam of superannuated wrath . . . this vicious and venomous personal onslaught . . . Mr. Hare's paragraphs plump like drops of concentrated venom over the dinted page. . . . Such a tenacity of ill-feeling, such a cold rage of vituperation, is seldom to be met with.'

I wonder a little if any one can really from his heart have offered such 'a genuine tribute of undissembled horror,' or whether these sentiments were only written to order?

To Mrs. C. Vaughan.

May 8, 1897.—Last night I dined with Lady Ashburton, a quiet party, with all the beautiful Kent House pictures lighted up. Mr. Henschel whistled like a bullfinch at dinner, and sang gloriously '*Der Kaiser*' afterwards. Mrs. F. Myers, who sate by me, was most agreeable. Amongst a thousand interesting things, she told me that, at Cambridge, she found Lord De Rothschild's son especially difficult to get on with, till one day he startled her by asking, 'Have you got any fleas?' She was surprised, but found that special point of Natural History was just the one thing he cared about, knew about, and would talk on for ever; and she was able to get him some rare fleas from a friend in India, with which he was greatly delighted.

I also sate at dinner by —— whose father was ambassador at Vienna. He rented Prince Clary's house. One day, as a little girl, she was at the end of the drawing-room with her mother, when they both saw a chasseur—their own chasseur, they supposed—standing in an alcove at the end of the room. 'Oh, there is Fritz,' said her mother. 'What can he be doing there? Run and tell him to go downstairs.' She ran across the room, but as she came up to the alcove the chasseur seemed to vanish. This happened three times; then the mother said, 'If we were superstitious we might say we had seen a ghost, but it can be only a question of angles.' Soon afterwards her father met Prince Clary at dinner and began, 'Have you ever been troubled by any appearance?' &c. 'Oh, don't speak of it,' exclaimed Prince Clary; 'it is a most painful subject: the fact is, that, in a fit of anger, my father killed his chasseur on that spot.' Sir Augustus Loftus, who succeeded at the Embassy, took the same house, and reproached them much for not warning him of the apparition, on account of which he soon left and went to live in a hotel.

At Easter I was with the Carysforts at Elton, and was taken to see Castor, with its fine Roman and Norman remains, and Stobbington, a very interesting old house, with with a most curious collection of rare living fish, the pets of its owner. Lady Alwyn Compton, who was at Elton, told me a curious story. It was one of the great commentators—Calamy, she thought—who had occasion to go to a market-town in Devonshire, and take a lodging there whilst the assizes were going on. In the evening a servant came to his room and said that the master of the house hoped that he would do him the honour of coming down to supper with him. He said, 'Oh, pray thank him very much, but say that I never take supper.' But the servant came three times with the same message, and at last he said to himself, 'Well he seems so anxious to have me that it is rather churlish not to go,' and he went. There were many people in the room, quite a number of guests, and a great supper prepared. But, being a religious man, before sitting down he said grace aloud, and, as he said it, the whole thing vanished.

To HUGH BRYAN *and* JOURNAL.

Castle Hale, Painswick, June 17.—. . . Just before her marriage, H. went to see Lady Burton at Mortlake, and was taken to Burton's mausoleum as a natural part of her visit. Afterwards Lady Burton wrote to her saying that she wanted to ask a very great favour. It was that she would never wear again the hat in which she had come down to Mortlake. H. liked her hat very much—a pretty Paris hat in which she fancied herself particularly, but she said she would do as an old friend of her future husband wished, though utterly mystified. Afterwards Lady Burton wrote that when H. had come into the room on her visit, she was horrified to see three black roses in her hat; that they were the mark of a most terrible secret sect in Arabia, mixed up in every possible atrocity, and that—especially as worn by a girl about to be married—they were a presage of every kind of misfortune; that, in another case of the same kind, she had given the same warning, and the girl, who disregarded it, died on the day before her wedding. H. wore her hat again, but took out the black roses.

Sir Richard Burton died of syncope of the heart—died twenty minutes before Lady Burton's priest could arrive; so her report of his having been received into the Roman Catholic Church was a complete delusion.[1]

H. says that Count Herbert Bismarck went lately to a great function in Russia. While he wished to be incognito, he still did not see why he could not have the advantages of his cognito. 'Stand back; you must keep the line,' said an official as he was pushing through. 'You do not know who I am: I am Count Herbert Bismarck.' 'Really? Well that quite *explains*, but it does not *excuse* your conduct,' rejoined the officer.

To the COUNTESS OF DARNLEY.

Holmhurst, June 29, 1897.—I said I would tell you about the Jubilee. For the first few days I was with the hospitable Lowthers, and thence, on Sunday, went to the Thanksgiving service at St. Paul's. Going very early, I had perhaps the best place in the choir, and enjoyed seeing the gradual gathering of so much of the bravery, learning, and beauty of England beneath the dusky arches and glistening mosaics. When the long file of clergy went out to meet the royal procession at the west door, the faint distant song was very lovely, gradually swelling, and lost in the blare of trumpets, the roll of drums, and the triumphant shout of welcoming voices as the clergy re-entered the choir. The most important figure was the Bishop of Finland in a white satin train with two gorgeous train-bearers; but the newspapers tell this, and how the lines of royal persons sate on crimson chairs opposite the entrance of the choir, and how the Bishop of London preached touchingly, not effusively, about the Queen and her reign, and officiated at the altar in a gorgeous mitre and cope.

On Monday Miss Lowther and I went to tea with my friend (minor-canon) Lewis Gilbertson at his lovely little house in Amen Court, and then were taken, by one of the many secret staircases of the cathedral, to emerge over the portico for the rehearsal of the next day's ceremony. Perhaps, in some ways, this was more impressive than

[1] Lady Isabel Burton, who shared to some extent her husband's travels and interests, especially in the Near East, but did not approve many of his activities, died in 1896, six years after her husband. They are buried together at Mortlake in a fantastic mausoleum, carved in marble after the pattern of an Arab tent.—*Ed.*

the reality, as none of the vast surrounding space was kept clear; all was one sea of heads, whilst every window, every house-top, even every chimney-pot, was crowded with people. Never was anything more jubilant than the 'Te Deum,' more reverent than the solemn Lord's Prayer in the open air—every hat off. When the appointed programme was over, the crowd very naturally asked for 'God save the Queen,' and after some hesitation, and goings to and fro of dean and canons, it was begun by the bands and choristers, and taken up vigorously by the mile of people as far as Temple Bar. How grand it was!

That evening the dear Queen said to Miss——'To-morrow will be a *very* happy day for me;' and I think it must have been. Where are anarchists and socialists before such a universal burst of loyalty—not of respect only, but of heartfelt filial *love?*—Nowhere! Their very existence seems ridiculous. I saw all from the Beaumonts' in Piccadilly Terrace, where a most kind hostess managed all most beautifully for us, and, entering through the garden, we had neither heat nor crowd to fear. No small part of the sight was the crowd itself—the unfailing good-humour increased by the extreme kindness of the police towards fainting women and all who needed their help. The Colonial procession was charming—its young representatives rode so well, and were in themselves such splendid specimens of humanity, and so picturesquely equipped. Then the group of old English generals on horseback drew every eye, and the sixteen carriages of princesses, amongst whom the Duchess of Teck was far more cheered than any one except the Queen herself.[1] And lastly came the cream-coloured horses with their golden-coated footmen, and the beloved Lady herself—the 'Mother of the Land,'—every inch a queen, royal most exceedingly, but with an expression of such love, such gratitude, such devotion, such thankfulness! Oh, no one felt for and *with* her only as a sovereign; it was a far closer tie than that.

In the evening, Mrs. Tilt and her sister went with me to the Maxwell-Lytes on the top of the Record Tower, whence we saw the bonfires round London light up one by one, and St. Paul's in silver light—a glorified spiritual church rising out of the darkness of the city against the deep blue sky. Far more than the illuminations of the noisy streets, it was a fitting end to so solemn and momentous a day.

And on Wednesday I was in the Green Park, and heard the thousands of school-children sing their farewell to the Queen as she went away to Windsor.

To MRS. C. VAUGHAN.

March, 1897.—I think the reviews of the first three volumes of my *Story* must be coming to an end now. I have had them all sent to me, and very amusing they have been, mostly recalling the dictum of Disraeli, that 'critics are those who have failed in art and literature.' Many criticisms have been kind. One or two, but not more, have been rather clever, and some of the fault-finding ones would have been very instructive if I had not so entirely agreed with them at the outset on all their main points—that I was a mere nobody, that my life was wholly without importance, and that it was shocking to see parts of the story in print, especially the painful episode which I called 'The Roman Catholic Conspiracy'; for reviewers, of course, could not know the anguish it cost when I was led to publish that chapter, by its being my *one* chance of giving the true version of a story of which so many false versions had been given already. Some of the reviews are very funny indeed. The *Saturday Review* of 'A Monument of Self-Sufficiency' contrives to read (oh! where?) 'how sweet and amen-

---

[1] The Duchess of Teck died later the same year.

K*

able and clever Augustus was,' but is so shocked by a book 'wholly without delicacy'
that it—'cannot promise to read any more of it'!! The *Athenæum* describes me as a
mere 'literary valet.' Yet I am glad that most of the more respectable reviews say
exactly the opposite, and certainly the public does not seem to agree with those I
have quoted; it would be terribly expensive if it did.

Did you see Mr. Murray's letter to the *Times*, which certainly gives a touching
picture of the spirit of self-sacrifice which actuates publishers in their daily life, for he
announces that my *Handbook of Berks, Bucks, and Oxon*, which had three editions
before his father's death, and on which the author was only paid *altogether* £152,
left, at that death, a deficit of £158!! I was sorry, all the same, that he was annoyed
at my description of his father wrapt in his *enveloppe de glace*; for old Mr. Murray (who
had cut me dead for all the years since the appearance of my Italian Handbooks) asked
me to shake hands with him once again a few months before he died, which I did most
cordially.

WARBLETON PRIORY

To FRANCIS COOKSON.

Holmhurst, August 29, 1897.—Last week I was for three nights at Hurstmonceaux,
actually—for the first time in thirty-seven years—at my old home of Lime. What a
mixture of emotions it was; but within all is so changed, I could not recall my mother
and Lea there; and the present inhabitants, the young Baron and Baroness von Roemer,
were boundlessly good to me. Outside, there were many spots alive with old memories,
especially in the garden, where my mother and I lived so much alone.

We made a little excursion. In my very early childhood I was once at the ever-
haunted Warbleton Priory, and the recollection of its utter weirdness and of the skulls
kept there had always so remained with me that I had quite longed to see it again. The
many stories about it are such as ought never to be told, only whispered. The very
approaches have a mystery. No one will stay there now, even by broadest daylight;
so we went to an old manor near Rushlake Green for the keys, but found even that
so bolted and barred that we were long in obtaining them. 'Oh no, there is never any
one there,' said the servant, 'but you must go on till you come to a black gate, then

drive in.' To reach this, we followed a lane with well-built cottages, but they were deserted, their windows broken and their gardens overgrown; no one could live so near the accursed spot. Through the black gate we enter dark woods. A cart-track exists, winding through thickets with fine oaks interspersed, and by reedy ponds dense with waving cotton-plants. Then we cross open fields entirely covered with thistles—enough to seed all Sussex—for no one will work there. Then, through another black gate, we enter a turf-grown space, with lovely distant views between old trees, and there, with high red-tiled roofs, golden here and there with lichen, is a forlorn and mossy but handsome old stone house, built from and rising amidst other remains of an Augustinian priory. In its little garden are roses, and box bushes which have once been clipped into shape. Inside, the mildewed rooms have some scanty remnants of their old furniture. In one of them, where a most terrible murder was committed, the blood then shed still comes up through the floor—a dark awful pool which no carpenter's work can efface. The most frightful sounds, cries, and shrieks of anguish, rumblings, and clankings, even apparently explosions, are always heard by night, and sometimes by day. In the principal room of the ground floor, in the recess of a window, are two skulls. They are believed to be those of two brothers who fought here and both fell dead. From one, the lower jaw has fallen down, increasing its ghastly effect. Successive generations of farmers have buried them, and instantly everything has gone wrong on the farm and all the cattle have died: now they have altogether abandoned a hopeless struggle with the unseen world. Besides this there is a tradition—often verified—that if any one touches the skulls, within twelve hours they pass through the valley of the shadow of Death. So naturally Warbleton Priory is left to the undisputed possession of its demon-ghosts.

JOURNAL *and* LETTER *to* W. H. MILLIGAN.

Thoresby, Oct. 22, 1897.—I began my little tour of visits at Maiden Bradley. . . . You know how it is almost the only remnant the title possesses from the once vast Somerset estates. The 12th Duke left everything he possibly could away, and when the present Duke and Duchess succeeded, they were pictureless, bookless, almost spoonless. Still they were determined to make the best of it. 'He could not take away our future: we will not lament over all that is lost, but enjoy to the very utmost what we have'; this has been the rule of their existence, and so 'Algie and Susie,' as they always speak of each other, have had a most delightful life, enjoying and giving enjoyment. No one ever looked more ducal than this genial, hearty, handsome Duke: no one brighter or pleasanter than his Duchess.

Next, I visited Lady Margaret Herbert (daughter of my dear Lady Carnarvon) as châtelaine at Teversal manor in Notts, a smoky wind-stricken country, but with Hardwicke and other fine houses to see. The charming aunt of my hostess, Lady Guendolen, was living with her as chaperon, none the worse in body for being a strict vegetarian, and in mind the sunniest of the sunny, delightful to be with. I was glad to be taken to spend the day at Bestwood, the Duke of St. Alban's modern place, its woods an oasis in the wilderness, and its honours were charmingly done by Lady Sybil Beauclerk and her good-looking brother Burford. The Ladies Herbert sometimes, but in a far-away sense, remind me of their mother, who was quite the most perfectly brilliant person I have ever known. I have always heard that she was this even as a girl, and that it was a perpetual surprise to her parents, who were very inferior people. Lady Dufferin used to say that they were like savages who had found a watch.

To MRS. C. VAUGHAN.

Holmhurst, Nov. 16, 1897.—I went to stay with 'the richest man in the world,' genial unassuming Mr. Astor, in his beautiful Cliveden, much improved since he bought it from its ducal owners. We had a charming party—Jane, Lady Churchill, retaining in advancing years '*sa marche de déesse sur les nues* [the step of a goddess upon the clouds—St. Simon],' for which she was famous in her youth; the Lord Chancellor,[1] Lady Halsbury, and a daughter; pretty gentle Princess Löwenstein; the Duchess of Roxburghe, ever wreathed in smiles of geniality and kindness, with two very tall agreeable daughters; Lord Sandwich, as bubbling with fun as when he was a young man; Lord and Lady Stanhope—always salt of the earth; with Mr. Marshall Hall[2] and Sir Arthur Sullivan[3] as geniuses. Every one of these delightful people, too, was simplicity itself, rare as that virtue is to find.

On Sunday morning we all went to the beautifully situated little church at Hedsor, arriving early and seeing the congregation wind up the steep grassy hill as to a church in Dalecarlia. In the afternoon we were driven about the grounds of Cliveden to the principal points—Waldo Story's grand fountain in the avenue and his noble landing-place on the river. Exquisitely beautiful were the peace of the still autumn evening, the amber and golden tints of the woods, and the wide river with its reflections. Mr. Astor has attended to all the historic associations of the spot.

Now, I am enjoying the time alone at home, with its much-reading opportunity, and I often think that my natural bent would have been to enjoy it quite as much as a boy, when all the family except you treated me not only as a consummate dunce, but a *hopeless* dunce; and when almost every book was thought wicked, or at best quite unsuited for a boy's digestion. Now, eyes ache often, but I may say with Lady M. Wortley Montagu, 'If relays of eyes were to be ordered like post-horses, I would admit none but silent companions.'

To MISS GARDEN *at* LUCCA, *and* JOURNAL.

Holmhurst, August 1, 1898.—I have been much in London since I wrote last, enjoying the garden-parties at Sion, Osterley, Holland House, Hatfield, Lady Pen-rhyn's, Lady Portman's, &c., and seeing many pleasant people. Yet, in the season, it is all too great a hurry; one seldom has time to become really acquainted with any one. I dined out daily for two months, but how difficult it is to remember any dinner-party! 'Who cares for the whipped cream of London society?' was a saying of Walter Scott. I do recollect one dinner, however, at Mr. Knowles's, from the fine effect of light on Leighton's 'Clytie,' the principal ornament of his dining-room, all the illumination being given to one fold of the dress, and the rest effectively left in shadow. One charming person whom I remembered was Lady Blake, lately returned to England with her husband, who had been governor of Jamaica. She was fond of tame animals. 'In Jamaica,' she said, 'I often had a large snake coiled round my waist; my tiger-cat I generally led by a string, for I never knew what he might do, but my tame crocodile always quietly followed me.'

The nobly Christian death of Mr. Gladstone and the almost ludicrous apotheosis of one who, in his political life, did nothing and undid so much, were events of the spring. I have personally more individual recollection of his kindness to those who

---

[1] Lord Halsbury, after whom the great *Laws of England* is named, died in 1921, aged 98.—*Ed.*

[2] Who later became Sir Edward Marshall Hall, whose triumph was the Russell divorce case. He died in 1927.—*Ed.*

[3] The composer.—*Ed.*

needed it than of his witty sayings; but they were constant. 'What do you think of Purcell's *Life of Manning?*' some one said to him shortly before the end. 'I think that Manning need have nothing to fear at the day of judgment.' He was formidable to strangers, chiefly on account of 'those demoniac eyes of his,' as Cardinal Alcander said of Luther; and though in his private capacity he was all goodness, it seemed inconsistent with his public one. Yet what admirers he had! I remember his saying once to Lord Houghton, 'I lead the life of a dog,' and the answer, 'Yes, of a St. Bernard —the saviour of men.' Joseph Parker used to describe him as 'the greatest Englishman of the century, he was so massive, sincere, and majestic. If he had had humour he would have been too good to live, but eagles don't laugh.'

How much and long people have talked of him, and now what a silence will fall upon it all. An amusing breakfast at Mr. Leveson's has just been recalled to me, where Lady Marian Alford said, 'Gladstone really puts his foot in it so often, he is a perfect centipede.' Directly after, a wasp lighted on the breakfast-table and there was some question of killing it. 'Oh, don't; I can't bear killing anything,' cried Lady Marian. 'What! not even a centipede?' quietly said Lord Lyons, who was present.

While in London I went for two days to Bulstrode, which the late Duke of Somerset left to his youngest daughter, Lady Guendolen Ramsden, who is the most charming of hostesses, but the place is disappointing. . . . About Mr. L., who always speaks his mind, Lady Guendolen was very amusing:—'Mr. L. took me in to dinner, and I thought I was making myself very agreeable to him, when he suddenly said— 'Talk to your neighbour on the other side." I felt humiliated, but I thought he fancied I couldn't, so I did, and went on, and never spoke another word to Mr. L. I told him of it afterwards, that he had hurt me so much that I dreamt of it, and I told him my dream—that I said to him that I was considered to become very amusing after I had had two glasses of wine, and he answered, '*Then*, my dear lady, you must have been most uncommonly sober this evening.'

To Viscount Halifax.

Holmhurst, August 21, 1898.—I have been for three days at Hurstmonceaux, doubly picturesque in the burnt turf of this hot summer, upon which the massy foliage of the trees is embossed as in Titian's landscapes. It is a pleasure now to be there, though life there is living amongst the sepulchres. . . . How different everything is to the time which Hurstmonceaux recalls; all hurry now and energy and updoing, and then such an extreme quietude of intellectual pursuits, in which every uninitiated visitor was considered an unendurable bore, if, however interesting he might be in himself, he did not fall in with the mutual admiration society of which the Rectory was the axis. I remember how Thomas Carlyle and Monckton Milnes, with his 'gay and airy mind,'[1] were amongst those so considered, for they had naturally their outside views and intelligence, and the Rectory group never tried for a moment to penetrate '*l'écorce exterieur de leur vie* [the outer skin of their life];' and, while whistling with prejudices themselves, they always found much to be shocked at in every outside person they came across.

To W. H. Milligan.

Holmhurst, Sept. 29, 1898.—The building and changes here go on well, but very slowly, a result of having the work done with my own stone, and as much as possible by the men of our village. I think all will look well in the end. Where you will remem-

[1] Tennyson.

ber a steep grass bank, there is now a double stone terrace, with vases and obelisks, and luxuriant beds of brilliant flowers edged with stone, copied as a whole from the Italian Villan Lante near Viterbo. At the end are a staircase and gateway to the Solitude, the 'Ave-Vale Gate,' with 'Ave' on the outside and 'Vale' within. Cypresses are growing up beside it to enhance the impression of Italy, which is further carried out in a widening staircase from the centre of the terrace, with lead vases on the piers,

THE AVE-VALE GATE, HOLMHURST

copied in design and proportions from one at the Villa Arson near Nice. Just now, in this hot noonday, the gorgeous flowers against the stone parapet, and background of brown-green ilex and blue-green pine are really very Italian, while below in the meadows all is as English as it can be, the cows feeding in the rich grass, the heavy rounded masses of oak foliage, and the misty sea asleep in the motionless heat.

To MRS. C. VAUGHAN.

Holmhurst, Oct. 16, 1898.—My most interesting visit was that to Baddesley Clinton in Warwickshire, rising, with a fortified central gate-tower, from a deep still moat, and with an inner courtyard full of flowers. It has dark tapestried rooms, several priest's hiding-holes, ghosts of a lady and a child, and a murder-room, stained with the blood of a priest whom a squire of Edward IV's time slew when he caught him chucking his wife under the chin. Then there are all the refined luxuries of fast-day dinners, evening prayers in the chapel with a congregation of maids veiled like nuns, and a live Bishop (of Portsmouth), in violet robes and gold cross and chain, to officiate. Such a bishop he is! such a ripple of wit and wisdom! and so full of playfulness! I read and copied somewhere—'A man after God's own heart is never a one-sided man. He is not wholly spiritual, he is not wholly natural; he is not all earnestness, he is not all play; he cannot be all things at once, and therefore he is all things by turns.' Our Bishop at Baddesley was just like this in his fun, in his love of cats, and never more charming than when he gathered up all the scraps of toast left at breakfast, and throwing open one of the windows, called 'Quack, quack!' and crowds of ducks came rushing under the bridge over the moat to scramble for them, one brown duck, which the Bishop called 'the orphan,' being especially cared for.

To W. H. MILLIGAN, *and* JOURNAL.

Belvoir Castle, Nov. 18, 1898.—One of those kind and characteristic telegrams of the Duchess of Rutland, extending over a whole page, has brought me here, where there is a large party too, almost entirely composed of the Duke's innumerable nephews and nieces. As I do not either shoot or care for the regular evening ball in the gallery, what I like best is the daily walk with the Duke and Duchess, meeting them in the hall as the clock strikes 12.15, and wandering in the wood walks or on the nearer terraces, already fragrant with violets, listening to the Duke's reminiscences of his own past and Belvoir's past, always of endless interest. How I pity my host and hostess in their over-anxious cares about their immense estates; but they must be comforted themselves by the pleasure they are able to give.

There is a great charm in being made a sharer in what Disraeli called 'the sustained splendour of a stately life,' but much of the pleasure of a great country-house depends upon whom it falls to your lot to take down to dinner, and the Duchess attends to this with careful cleverness. I was especially amused by one sentence in that delightful 'Isabel Carnaby'—'There is one good thing in getting married. You know then that, whatever happens, there is one woman you will never have to take in to dinner again as long as you live.'

And what funny things people say at dinner. Lately—not here—a very 'great lady' said to me, 'I can assure you that the consciousness of being well dressed gives me an inward peace which religion could never bestow.'

JOURNAL *and* LETTERS.

Rome, March 10, 1899.—I was very ailing, and Catherine Vaughan insisted on my seeing Dr. Sansom, who found me so 'run down' that he insisted on my coming out here to my 'native air'; therefore here I am, and already it has done me good.

The other day I was with a circle of old friends who were discussing the *Story of My Life*. 'Surely the early part must have been exaggerated,' said one of them, 'that story of Aunt Esther hanging the cat, for instance, because the child loved it.' 'I can testify that that story was absolutely true, for *I was there*,' said an old clergyman present, 'and I have shuddered over the cruel recollection ever since.' It was Canon Douglas Gordon. I had quite forgotten that he was a pupil of Mr. Simpkinson, curate of Hurstmonceaux, at the time. Mr. Gordon also said, 'I can vouch, too, for the truth

of the story of the bullying at Harrow, for *I was myself the victim*'; and he told how
a brutal bully got a dead dog, and cut off its feet, ears, &c., and forced him to drink
them in coffee. That day he ran away. 'Alexander Russell' went with him. They had
only four miles to go to his father Lord Aberdeen's house at Stanmore. He and Lord
Abercorn were governors of the school. They happened to be together, and they sent
him back in a carriage that evening with a letter to the headmaster saying that, in the
interests of the school, what had happened had better be hushed up; but that it was so
dreadful, that he—the master—must be compelled to take the awful bullying in the
school seriously in hand. And he did. Mr. Gordon says that the wickedness of Harrow
at that time was quite appalling: things which could never be mentioned were then of
nightly occurrence all over the school. The masters were as bad, and would come into
the very pupil-rooms humming obscene songs.

March 24.—We have been to Tivoli on the most glorious day—a pellucid sky,
and exquisite blue shadows flitting over the young green of the Campagna. From the
station I went to S. Antonio, the old hermitage and shrine bought by the Searles. Mrs.
Searle met me most kindly. I said, '*What* a beautiful home you have!' 'Yes,' she answered, 'and the really delightful thing is that *the Lord* has given it to us.' I could hardly
help saying, 'I suppose that means you bought it.' Afterwards I found she was one of
the very few ladies who belong to the Salvation Army. She is kind and Christian
beyond words and her lovely home is a centre of thoughtful charity; but being in this
Catholic country gives her many qualms and shocks. One day lately she was alone
in a lane near her home, and came upon a shrine of the Virgin with her little statue,
and was filled with righteous indignation at 'that doll.' As she stood there, a number
of peasant women came up and knelt before the shrine and prayed most devoutly.
When they got up she said, 'How could you pray to that graven image? I wonder
what you were praying for.' 'Why, we were asking the Madonna to send us rain; our
land needs it so much,' said the women, much surprised at her wrath. 'How can you
pray to *her* for that?' said Mrs. Searle; 'let me show you how to pray,' and then and
there she knelt down in the dusty road and prayed aloud, prayed with her whole heart
to her Lord, that He would send them the rain they needed; and immediately, though
the sky had been quite clear till then, it *poured*.

April 1.—I have had one of my Palatine lectures quite in the old way, and a
luncheon with the charming Crown Princess of Sweden has been a great pleasure.

Dining at Palazzo Bonaparte, M. de Westenberg told me that one day when Madame
Mère was living there, a stranger came to the palace and insisted upon seeing her on
a matter of vital importance. He was evidently a gentleman, but would not tell his
name or errand. At last his urgency prevailed, and Madame Mère admitted him.
He gave her a crucifix and said it belonged to her son in St. Helena, and then he said,
'You need no longer be unhappy about him, for he has just entered into rest: his sorrows are over.' It was on that day that Napoleon died in St. Helena.

Palazzo Guadagni, Florence, April 17.—I have been here ten days as the guest of
the ever-kind Duchess Dowager of Sermoneta, and found Mrs. and Miss Lowther
here. It is an unusual life. We scarcely see our hostess till dinner-time, unless she asks
us to drive with her, and we have each a most comfortable apartment, with excellent
food and service, and the whole day to employ as we like. Many are the old friends
we have seen, but most frequently the Marchesa Peruzzi, Story's daughter, who has

all his agreeable power of narration. 'The reason why we loved Mrs. Browning so much as children,' she says, 'is because she always treated us as her equals, and talked to us as such. Pen and I used to sit at her feet, and she was just as courteous to us as to any of the grown-up people.'

Holmhurst, May 10.—Reached the dear home with great thankfulness, after a most severely hard-worked fortnight for a new edition of my *Paris.*

June 14, 1899.—At luncheon at Lady Constance Leslie's I met Mr. Holman Hunt,[1] a charming, simple, natural man. He spoke of the great difficulty of getting any one to do such work as is wanted for St. Paul's Cathedral; that few would give up the high prices paid now for other work for the small prices the Government would pay. He talked of Leighton,[2] whom he had known intimately in early life. Three tailors in Bond Street, thinking it might be a good speculation, clubbed together to buy one of his first pictures. They offered £100 for it: he stuck out for £200. Eventually it was arranged that they should pay £150, but a suit of clothes was to be thrown in. Then came the violent abuse of all Leighton's work, and the tailors got alarmed, and sold the picture for £100 without any suit of clothes. That picture was afterwards bought for thousands by the Gallery at Liverpool, and there it is now, unlikely ever to come to the hammer again.

After this, when Leighton's pictures were accepted for the Academy and he was hard at work for the next year, he was told by his studio-man that some one wanted to speak to him. He sent out word that he was very busy and could not see any one; but the man was pertinacious and would not go away. At last Leighton said, 'Well, he had better come in for a minute and say what his business is.' So he was let in. But it was a man who stood by the door and did not come further. 'Well,' said Leighton, 'what do you want?' 'To come straight to the point at once,' said the man, 'I want that picture' (pointing to the work upon the easel). 'You get £300 now for your pictures, don't you? Well, I will give you £700.' 'But you have not even seen the picture,' said Leighton; 'you don't even know what the subject is.' 'No, I don't,' said the man, 'and, if I did, I should know no more about it than I do now.' That man was Agnew.[3] He acquired the picture: it was his first venture.

JOURNAL.

Holmhurst, Sept. 31.—I have been a week at Swaylands to meet the Duchess of York, and as there were scarcely any other guests, saw a great deal of her, and was increasingly filled with admiration for the dignified simplicity and single-mindedness, and the high sense of duty by which her naturally merry, genial nature is pervaded, and which will be the very salvation of England some day. Before her scandal sits dumb: she has a quiet but inflexible power of silencing everything which seems likely to approach ill-natured gossip, yet immediately after she gives such a genial kindly look and word to the silenced one as prevents any feeling of mortification. All morning the Duchess was occupied with her lady in real hard work, chiefly letters, I believe; in the afternoons we went for long drives and sight-seeings—of Penshurst, Knole,

[1] William Holman Hunt, 1827–1910, pre-Raphaelite painter and founder of the Brotherhood; first exhibited at the Academy in 1847. Among his more famous pictures are 'The Scapegoat,' 'Nazareth,' 'The Ship,' 'The Hireling Shepherd.' Buried in St. Paul's.—*Ed.*

[2] See note on p. 261. Lord Leighton was in his early days somewhat influenced by the pre-Raphaelites, but denied he actively participated in the movement.—*Ed.*

[3] Sir William Agnew, the art dealer, 1825–1910.—*Ed.*

Groombridge, Hever, Ightham, and she was full of interest in the history and associations of these old-world places. At Hever the owners were away, but we got a table from a cottage, and an excellent tea-meal was spread upon it at the top of the high field above the castle. If the Duchess is ever Queen of England, that table will be considered to have a history.[1]

Dec. 22, 1899.—I am just at the end of a long retreat in a sort of private hospital, where I have been for the sake of the 'Nauheim cure' for an affection of the heart, from which I have now suffered for more than a year, and which was greatly increased by the anxieties and sorrows of last August. I am better since my 'cure,' but am seldom quite well now, and, as I read in a novel, 'my dinner is always either a satisfying fact or a poignant memory,' and generally the latter. The South African war news is casting a shadow over the closing year, and the death of Lady Salisbury has been a real sorrow —an ever-kind friend since my early boyhood. I went to the memorial service for her in the Chapel-Royal—a beautiful service, but a very sad one to many.

Holmhurst, May 23.—I found a very large party on Saturday at hospitable Mr. Astor's, and Cliveden in great beauty, entrancing carpets of bluebells under the trees. A telegram from the Queen of Sweden took me to Roehampton on Monday. It was twenty-two years since I had seen the King, and I thought him even handsomer and more royal-looking than of old. The Queen is not less fragile, and as full of good thoughts and words as ever. I had luncheon with the royal pair and their household, and a long talk with the Queen afterwards, who told me much of my especial Prince, now Regent in his father's absence.

---

[1] The Duke of Clarence had died in 1892. The Duke of York (afterwards George V) was therefore second in succession, after Edward VII. Queen Mary writes (1952) to the editor of this volume that she well remembers meeting Hare on this occasion; they quickly made friends, she says, because they found so many interests in common.—*Ed.*

XVI

FAREWELL

1900

꤮

I MUST close this book. Printers are calling for its last pages. It is like seeing an old friend go forth into a new world, and wondering if those who inhabit it will understand him and treat him well. Perhaps no one will read it except the intimate circle—a large one certainly—who have loved Hurstmonceaux, Stoke, and little Holmhurst at different times. But I can never regret having written it, and it has been so great an enjoyment to me, that perhaps others may like it; for I have concealed nothing, and Coleridge says, 'I could inform the dullest author how he might write an interesting book. Let him relate the events of his own life with honesty, not disguising the feelings that accompanied them.'

Except that I have seen more varieties of people than some do, I believe there has been nothing unusual in my life. All lives are made up of joys and sorrows with a little calm, neutral ground connecting them; though, from physical reasons perhaps, I think I have enjoyed the pleasures and suffered in the troubles more than most. But from the calm backwater of my present life at Holmhurst, as I overlook the past, the pleasures seem to predominate, and I could cordially answer to any one who asked me 'Is life worth living?'—'Yes, to the very dregs.'

In my quiet home, of which little has been said in these volumes, days succeed each other unmarked, but on the whole happy, though sometimes very lonely. The whole time passes very quickly, yet it is, as I remember the Grand Duchess Stephanie of Baden wrote to my aunt Mrs. Stanley—'In youth the years are long, the moments short, but in age the moments are long, the years short.' Really I have been alone here for thirty years, twelve in which my dearest Lea was still presiding over the lower regions of the house, and eighteen in absolute solitude. It is the winter evenings, after the early twilight has set in, which are the longest. Then there are often no voices but those of the past. People say, 'It is all your own fault that you are solitary; you ought to have married long ago.' But they know nothing about it; for as long as my mother lived, and for some time after, I had nothing whatever to marry upon, and after that I had very little, and I have been constantly reminded that people of the class in which I have always lived do not like to marry paupers. Besides, the fact is, that except in one impossible case perhaps, very long ago, 'I have never loved any one well enough to put myself in a noose for them: it is a noose, you know.' What I have to regret is that I have no very near relations who have in the least my own interests and sympathies, though they are all very kind to me.

The greatest of all the blessings I have to be grateful for is, that though, since my serious illness six years ago, I have never been entirely without pain, I have, notwithstanding this, good health and a feeling of youth —just the same feeling I had forty years ago. I suppose there will be many who will be surprised to see in these pages how old I am; I am unspeakably surprised at it myself. I have to be perpetually reminding myself of my years, that I am so much nearer the close than the outset of life. I feel so young still, that I can hardly help making plans for quite the far-distant future, schemes of work and of travel, and I hope sometimes of usefulness, which of course can never be realised. I have very good spirits, and I feel that I should be inexcusable if I were not happy when I remember the contrast of my present life to my oppressed boyhood, or to the terrible trial of the time when every thought was occupied by such tangled perplexities as those of the Roman Catholic conspiracy.

My next greatest blessing is my home, so infinitely, so exquisitely suited to my needs, and indeed to all my wishes. As I write this, and look from my window across the tiny terrace with its brilliant flowers to the oak-woods, golden in the autumn sunset, and the blue sea beyond, with the craggy mass of Hastings Castle rising up against it, I feel that there are few places more lovely than Holmhurst. And in the little circle of this pleasant home love assuredly reigns supreme. I look upon my servants as my best and truest friends; their rooms, in their way, are as pretty and comfortable as my own, and I believe that they have a real pleasure in serving me. We unite together in looking after our less fortunate friends, who come in batches, for a month each set, to the little Hospice in the grounds. I could not ask my servants to do this, but they are delighted to help me thus, as in everything. When one of our little household community, as has happened four times now, passes, in an honoured and cherished old age, from amongst us, we all mourn together, watch by the deathbed, and follow the flower-laden coffin to the grave.

My local affections are centred in Holmhurst now. Rome, which I was formerly even fonder of, is so utterly changed, it has lost its enchaining power, and, with the places, the familiar faces there have all passed away. I go there every third year, but not for pleasure, only because it is necessary for *Walks in Rome*, the one of my books which pays best.

In the summer I generally have guests at Holmhurst, but even then my mornings are passed in writing, and several twilight hours besides. Then the early months of spring are often spent abroad, and the later in London, and in the autumn I have the opportunity of far more visits than I like to pay: so that I have quite sufficient people-seeing to prevent getting rusty, or at any rate to remind me of my utter insignificance in every society except my own. However, reviews are a perfect antidote to all follies of vainglory. I used to be pained by the most abusive ones, though I generally learnt something from them. Latterly, however, I have been more aware of the indescribable incapacity and indolence of the writers, and have not cared at all. I a little wonder, however, why I have scarcely ever had a favourable review. My work cannot always have been so *terribly* bad, or it would not have had so wide a circulation —wider, I think, than has attended any other work of the kind.

When I look at the dates of births and deaths in our family in the Family Bible, I see that I have already exceeded the age which has been usually allotted to the Hares. Can it be that, while I still feel so young, the evening of life is closing in. Perhaps it may not be so, perhaps long years may still be before me. I hope so; but the lesson should be the same, for 'man can do no better than live in eternity's sunrise.'

APPENDIX

The reader who has pursued this autobiography to its end will have seen that Augustus Hare considered it to be complete. In his last pages he had tied up the loose ends and had drawn from his experience what conclusions he could. But the habit of keeping a journal was too deeply ingrained to be so easily broken, and Mr. Somerset Maugham, who visited him at Holmhurst during his closing years, tells us that 'Even after the publication of the second three volumes, undeterred he went on with the story, writing every morning, to the very end of his life. There was no one, however, with sufficient piety to publish what was doubtless a bulky manscript.'

Of any manuscript in a condition to be regarded as a formal sequel to the six-volume autobiography I can find no trace, yet I was most fortunate to be provided with the very last of Augustus's journals, the raw material of a sequel, which lacked only its author's interpolations and other editorial attention. This journal begins in May, 1902, and ends with the night of Augustus's death in January, 1903, and therefore leaves a gap in our record of two complete years. Of the intermediate journal nothing has come to hand despite advertisement, though there is reference to it within the black shiny covers of this one thick note-book: 'In case of my death, my executors are requested to send this volume, *with the red one preceding it*, to Messrs. Allen, 156, Charing Cross Road, London.'

The following are extracts from its pages, written in a remarkably uniform hand. The entries were not made daily, even at Holmhurst, but at irregular intervals. Certain passages were enclosed within red brackets, indicating evidently that these were not for publication; they include a few comments, for instance, on the character of Edward VII, perhaps injudicious at the time but now harmless, and on other persons then still living but long since dead. Such indications I have ignored. There were also extensive passages added to the entries as obvious afterthoughts, and these I have included as part of a continuous text. Otherwise I have applied the same principles of abridgement as to the main narrative.

MALCOLM BARNES.

JOURNAL.

Holmhurst, May 27, 1902.—The James Lowthers have been here for two days—delightful guests, bringing with them the pleasantest of whiffs from the outside world, from which little Holmhurst seems quite cut off. After a winter long drawn out, we are now in delicious summer weather, the little terraces brimming and bubbling over with flowers and the sea deep blue beyond the brilliant yellow-green of the young oak foliage.

May 28.—I cannot help being anxious, even so long beforehand, about next winter, whether I can get to Italy and do my work there. I suppose few ever leave and trust the future sufficiently in God's hands, simply ready to enjoy the pleasures, or face the trials as they are sent. 'God help me and all of us,' said Don Carlos de Seso, 'from the subtle snare of mixing with the question *What is his will?* that other question *What will be our fate if we try to do it?* All that really matters is to be found amongst those who follow the Lamb whithersoever He goeth. And He went—to Calvary.'

June 2.—The news of Lady Northàmpton's death fills me with sorrow. I had known her so well from her earliest childhood and, though I have scarcely seen her since her wedding day, I seem, through her mother, one of my oldest friends, to have followed every phase of her sad illness of years, borne with patience and heroic endurance.

June 4.—The proclamation of peace in South Africa is a relief to thousands. Besides the personal losses of many, all England is bored to death with the tiresome subject which has occupied three years, with the long delays, and battles with unseen foes, and above all with the expenses and taxation. Hastings fired guns and sent up fireworks far into the night after hearing of the peace.

8, *Amen Court, St. Paul's, June 15.*—I have had a delightful four days at the Barrows, near Farnham. We drove great distances in that lovely country, with especial enjoyment of the deep lanes overhung with noble beeches behind Pepperharrow. Great Tangley Manor is a very dream of loveliness . . . there is a garden of indescribable glory, a glen filled with rarest rock plants, and a mere with shallow reaches brilliant with every shade of iris, but mostly with the loveliest blue.

Several pleasant people came to dinner, amongst them Sir Henry Hildyard from Aldershot. He told me that Sidney Clarke, the chaplain of Chelsea Hospital, had lived long ago in an old château in Brittany. There the children were constantly joined in their play by a little boy in a red cap. They called him Caspar. He was a dwarf, but most pleasant in his ways and seemed to be able to ward off misfortunes from them and help them in various ways. They were very fond of him, but their parents never saw him except once: it was when one of the boys was drowned and Caspar broke it to the mother. Once, when the girls grew up, they persuaded Caspar to go to a ball with them. Then he vanished for ever.

Holmhurst, July 1.—I had the strongest presentiment that the coronation of Edward VII would not take place and had often said so. But when the day fixed for the ceremony was only one day distant, as a delightful place was offered me, I thought it was foolish not to go, and went up to kind Miss Sumners on Tuesday the 24th. The porter who opened the carriage door at Victoria Station said the Coronation was put off and the King was dangerously ill.

Everything had been outwardly glorious, inwardly inauspicious. From all parts of the earth princes and potentates had arrived to do the King honour. Every detail of the ceremony had been studied, thought out and rehearsed. London had expended vast fortunes in decorations for the triumphal progress through the streets. Private individuals had ruined themselves in the stands and seats which had spoilt the appearance of the capital for weeks. Armies were encamped in the surrounding parks, vast bodies of colonial troops had arrived to lend lustre to the royal progress. Everyone seemed inclined to forget all the evil—all the gambling and infidelities—and to praise all the good in the royal character; besides, the coronation was to be the beginning of a new, of a nobler life.

But the Indians all arrived with the conviction that nothing would take place. Their soothsayers had warned the different Maharajahs and Sultans that they might spare themselves their journeys. . . . The King is said to have looked to see his coronation in a magic crystal, and instead to have seen himself lying in a coffin. The day chosen for the ceremony was a day of ill omen, always avoided for public events by Queen Victoria, who had put off her own coronation from it, when she learnt that George IV had died on that day.

To the outside world all went well to the very last, more pomp, more splendour, more riches flowed into London and were more lavishly displayed everywhere. No one outside the Palace knew that the King was in mortal agony. . . . Then, at the last moment, when the chorus of praise, adulation, adoration almost, was at the very highest, when Edward VII seemed to have reached the highest point attained by any English sovereign, came the hand-writing on the wall. It was the story of Belshazzar over again. In the evening there had been a great banquet at Buckingham Palace, at which royalties innumerable were present; in the morning the King could no longer conceal the agonies he was enduring, and all the doctors and surgeons, suddenly called in, declared that an immediate and dangerous operation was the only chance of saving his life.

The report of the King's danger, of the operation in actual progress, and of the postponement of the Coronation, reached Westminster Abbey whilst the ceremonial was having its final rehearsal. The Bishop of London was there. It was evident that terrible news had arrived and all work suddenly stopped. The Bishop, in a few words, announced what had happened, and added 'And now let us pray for the King in his imminent danger.' Then and there the workmen dropped their chisels and hammers. All knelt just where they were—the greatest and the humblest. It was the most impressive sight.

Charlie Halifax drove me through the streets to see the preparations—the temporary west end of the Abbey, so really perfect in architecture and taste: the great arch given by Canada in Whitehall, chiefly formed by ears of wheat; the beautiful green avenue of arches in St. James's Street, with the strange stuffed doves floating in abundance in mid-air.

To CUTHBERT FRANKSON.

July 12.—Did I tell you of my audacious project of having an Exhibition of my Italian sketches? It is open now—at the Leicester Gallery, and really it looks much better than I expected. I asked 960 people to the 'private view' and did not know, till I came to hunt them up in the Red Book, that I had so large a London acquaintance. . . .

Mrs. Lowther was boundlessly kind, taking me to Osterley where the green glade under the fine old trees, filled with brilliantly dressed people, looked coolness and loveliness itself on a hot, dusty day. I always enjoy these parties—the turning into the park with the newly mown grass, and the masses of crimson rambler roses along the drive, the landing at the broad steps, and crossing the paved court to the door where Lord and Lady Jersey receive everyone—not hurriedly, but with the characteristic grace of an especially pleasant word of greeting to each; then the happy gatherings round little tables laden with tea and strawberries in the great hall, and the passing through the picture gallery to the sunlit perron beyond, and then the green lawns and groups of delightful friends, and beautiful music sufficiently soft to stimulate, not stop, conversation.

JOURNAL.

Holmhurst, July 14.—There have been endless newspaper notices of my little exhibition—interesting, because all those that enter into detail are abusive on such curiously different lines—'the artist has no knowledge whatever of architecture'—'so long as he keeps to architecture alone the artist's drawings are admirable' and so forth.

July 23.—The visit of my dear cousins Florentia Hughes and Constance Haldon has been a real delight. . . . We went yesterday to Hurstmonceaux and they enjoyed it all, and felt that no other place has the same weirdly picturesque beauty. Most grand is the ruined castle, but, like many human friends, it looks greyer every time I see it. After our luncheon in the ruins, we walked up to the church and the beloved resting-place, where the Mother and Lea rest beneath the Spina Christi from Calvary and the cypresses from Uncle Augustus's grave in the cemetery at Rome. How many of those whose tombs are now moss-grown have I known in their lifetime. There is a certain pleasure even in reading the all-familiar names in the epitaphs, which I know so well, and yet which I never can resist reading again.

July 29.—The Eustace Cecils have just driven away, after a visit which I have enjoyed exceedingly; he is so full of interesting anecdote, and she so pleasant and good. He walked to Battle, and returned full of admiration of Harold—'only he ought to have won the battle.'

Eustace Cecil talked of the ghost at Hatfield. It is his great-grandfather (James, 6th Earl of Salisbury), whose mother was a daughter of Lord Thanet. Her son ran away from Westminster and she sent him back with a request that he might be severely flogged. He was eighteen then and it soured him for life—drove him to the bad altogether. He gambled, lost enormous sums and plunged into every excess. He married a Miss Keet, sister of the rector of Hatfield, and his cruel treatment caused her to die of a broken heart. It is his ghost carriage that drives up at night, and he was often seen in the room which is now used as a smoking room.

Eustace Cecil said that, at dinner, Lady F. Trevanion had told him, as having happened at Glamis, a story which I have often heard without definition of place. Briefly, the story is that a gentleman, staying at Glamis, and unable to sleep, looked out of his window into the bright moonlit night. At the extreme end of the avenue he saw a dark object moving, and as it came nearer he saw it was a carriage, but there was no sound of wheels. Noiselessly, silently, it drove up to the door and, after a minute, drove away again. As it went off, the driver looked up—with a marked and terrible face, which the onlooker felt he should never forget. At breakfast the next morning, he said to Lord Strathmore, 'You had a very late arrival here last night.'—'No, there was no arrival.'—'But I saw a closed carriage drive up.' Lord Strathmore turned pale, said nothing, and his visitor at once changed the subject. Shortly after, he was at Paris. Thoroughly tired with a fatiguing day, he decided to go down from his third floor to the table d'hôte in the lift. It stopped at his floor and he was about to step in, when the man who guided it looked at him. It was the face he had seen at Glamis and he at once drew back. An instant after, there was a frightful crash, the lift fell and all its inmates were killed.

Eustace Cecil talked of his visit to Russia, the intense melancholy and monotony of the country and the utter and irreclaimable filthiness of the people. . . . In the Palace of Tzarskoe Selo he saw a magnificent room with a great gilt bed arranged for royalty, and, turning down the magnificent embroidered coverlet, saw it swarming —a vast colony of vermin.

August 9.—In spite of all the prophecies and prognostications the coronation is now well over. The glamour which had attended the June preparations had passed away, and Belgravia this morning looked like streets in a city of the dead, only a few belated peeresses were trying to get their carriages on as far as they could before falling into the line. . . . It remained fine. The Maharajah of Jaipur, seeing the frequent rainstorms of the last fortnight, thought it would always be so, unless the rain-goddess was appeased. So at great expense and trouble, he procured three black goats and sacrificed them in his garden on Campden Hill to his own rain-goddess, getting her to intercede with the English rain-goddess. He sent the King word of this, saying it was sure to answer; a sacrifice of black goats never failed.

The crowd seemed absolutely silent and unimpassioned. At 1.30 the procession began to pass, chiefly military, and some of the Indian officers' dresses most picturesque and magnificent. Then appeared the great Cinderella coach, with the King and Queen in their robes and crowns. He looked pale, almost grey from illness, with a white beard, but very royal, and in the Abbey they said he bore himself splendidly. All remembered that in the last month he had reached the gates of death, to look in, and then to be permitted to return, and they prayed that he might lay the great lesson to heart. After they had passed, there was a long pause until, when we had ceased to expect anything more, the Prince of Wales's part of the pageant came. Then—so did the procession fail in stateliness—there was another pause, so very long that most people went away. Even the soldiers left their ranks but were hurried back when all the princesses came in closed carriages *with two horses*, almost through an emptied street—Mecklenburghs, Coburgs, Battenbergs, Schleswig-Holsteins, and then the new King's three daughters, and his grand-daughter, Lady Alexandra Duff, in a great coach with six black horses, a difference which drew forth great sympathy with the daughters of Queen Victoria, in their first public deposition from the highest estate. The procession was interesting, but as to grandeur it was ill-managed and a failure.

The simultaneous putting on of coronets is said by those who were in the Abbey to have been far the finest scene in the Coronation. The Queen, at 58, bore herself with an incomparable dignity and majesty, enhancing her marvellous beauty in which absolute success excuses the triumph of art over the ravages of nature. By an error which gave great offence, the four duchesses who held the canopy over her were chosen not for their rank or their hereditary claims, but for their good looks. All the good-looking peeresses might as well have been selected for the front rows. . . . The Duke of Norfolk acted splendidly as the Earl Marshall. But compared with former ceremonials in the beloved queen's time, there was a general want of enthusiasm, owing partly to the presence of several individuals, whom his regretful subjects recognised in the gallery of 'the King's friends,' and whom many called his 'fallen angels.' No one tells the truth to the King on these subjects, unless—as is often vaguely reported—the German Emperor does. Minor catastrophes were that Lord Cadogan had sat down when there was no seat behind him, and came down upon the floor, and the Duchess of Devonshire had tripped over a step, fallen, and her diamond tiara had come off.

There had been endless rehearsals. At the last, Colonel Brocklehurst personated the King, and each order of peerage had to kiss him. The Archbishop did so, who had not met him since he had flogged him at Rugby for poaching.

Campsea Ashe, August 21.—Mrs. Capel Cure told me of her old Kentish home, Broom Hall, being haunted by two ghosts. One is a spurred cavalier who tramps up the stairs. The other is a lady in a white satin dress with a blue sash, often mistaken, even by her mother, for Mrs. Capel Cure before she married. 'Why, I not only saw, but touched her,' said Lady Oxenden. A great uncle, who had been Governor of Bombay, returned with a beautiful lady friend and an Indian. One night, the guests in the house, being aroused by a tremendous noise, rushed out of their rooms, but at the end of the corridor were stopped by their host, who refused to let anyone enter a particular room. From that time both the Indian and lady entirely disappeared, but two skeletons were found long afterwards and the lady has returned as a ghost.

To CUTHBERT FRANKSON.

The Pleasaunce, Overstrand, August 31.—This place is astonishing—a house infinitely picturesque as well as luxurious—extending year by year in gables and bays without, and more and more little rooms within, and gardens increasing in the same way till now there are seventy acres of them, with pergolas, arcades, fountains, terraces, and bosquets of beautiful shrubs and flowers. In the house itself are endless valuable pictures, cabinets, embroideries and books—a joyful surprise at every turn. Even the offices are walled with beautiful Spanish and Portuguese tiles. They surround a court—'a little Pieter de Hoogh' says Cyril Battersea. . . . Battersea, dressed in the evening in crimson velvet coat and trousers and white waistcoat—is unspeakable pleasant and amusing, and—with a truly marvellous memory—seems able to repeat endless poems by heart, whenever they are alluded to. I never saw anyone with such a bubbling spring of vitality.

Mr. John Hare (the actor) spoke of the respective merits of Dickens and Thackeray, and I was surprised to find he greatly preferred the former. Battersea said he found that to young men of the present generation Thackeray was practically unknown. Two young Cambridge men, a marquis and an earl, were here the other day and had never heard of him—to his name their countenances were an absolute blank.

To-day the Crown Princess of Austria came to luncheon, the widow of the tragic Prince Rudolph. She is tall, good-looking, with an admirable figure, and very pleasing. I was told to sit by her at luncheon and she talked very pleasantly of haunted castles in Austria and of her dogs. Her mother has never got over her marriage, yet it is a very happy one. Her husband, Count Lonyay, a Hungarian magnate, who was with her, is excessively handsome, with beautiful violet eyes. They both spoke English perfectly. After luncheon she smoked cigarettes.[1]

JOURNAL.

Sept. 1.—Miss Mary Higgins and Lady Alfred Paget and her daughters are very pleasant people who have come in and out daily or joined in our drives. The first,

---

[1] This is the widow of Rudolf, who committed suicide at Mayerling; Count Lonyay is the second husband. The Crown Princess was the daughter of the Queen of the Belgians who died three weeks later. Her relentless father is said to have driven her from her mother's deathbed.—*Ed.*

especially, has an inexhaustible fund of agreeableness. We are all sorry that the time here has come to an end. It is astonishing how a week's visit affords so very much more interest and pleasure in proportion than the usual conventional one of three days.

September 3.—I have received from Allen my publishing accounts for the last year. My many French volumes, on which I expended eight hard-worked years of my life, have never even begun to pay their very great expenses, and my English counties have also been a great loss of time and money.

At my little Hospice now are two 'sisters,' in feeble health, entirely due to insufficient food and over labour at trivial menial work to which they were not called ... shrinking from all their natural and family duties their life is one of entirely self-indulgent self-contemplation. It is impossible to help feeling that a religion which always looks to self must be valueless in God's sight.

September 6.—I have had such a sharp attack of heart-pain whilst dressing, that I feel death may come suddenly, at any moment. This great and unusual pain came to me as a surprise, as I had been very much better at Cromer and had renewed all my old enjoyment of life. Now I have been obliged to put off all visitors and visits and the doctor emphatically says I must not venture to go abroad. . . . Like Cardinal Manning, 'I like to talk about my end, it helps to make me ready and takes away all sadness and fear.'

September 7.—To-day I only hear a faint echo from the solemn warning voice of yesterday, when I felt, as the Queen of Roumania wrote of a great crisis in her life, 'all seemed trivial, all that people say and do seems so small and of so little importance when God Himself speaks to us.' Now, though very weak, I am quite out of pain and have telegraphed to beg Lady Hylton, whose visit I put off yesterday, to come all the same on Monday. The great thunderstorm of yesterday has annihilated many of the flowers, but it has been very lovely as I have been sitting out on the terrace—the long sharply cut shadows falling on the brilliant green meadows, the family of Indian cattle lying under the trees, the distant blue sea alive with white sails and the rich foreground of semi-tropical plants.

Temple Combe, September 20.—This is a lovely place in the chalk hills, so richly clothed with beeches, above the Thames near Henley. A delicious drive through the woods brought me here, to find my hosts [Mr. Denny and Lady Hope] and Lady Wynford at tea upon the lawn. After tea I went in a donkey chair and they walked to the head of the lovely combe, Sir Robert Anderson, 'the man of the criminal law,' is staying here, a tall spare man, very deaf but most excellent. His beautiful reading (of Titus II) and simple exposition of Family Prayers could not but touch anyone who heard it. For myself, I *felt* it, and long for more of it.

Yesterday we made a delicious excursion by river to Shiplake, where one of the Miss Phillimores met us at the landing stage and had a donkey chair to take me up to the house where we saw many Phillimore relics. Then we went on by water to dear beautiful Sonning. Here a young Mr. Hudson, editor and, I think, owner of *Country Life* has built, with the aid of Lutchens, an astonishing and delightful house, Elizabethan with Italian details and attractions. It is too medieval inside for comfort, whitewashed walls, no comforts, no arm chairs, the washing stands mere boards with jugs and basins upon them.

Baddesley Clinton, October 17.—There is a wonderful charm in this beautiful old moated house, and its presiding genius and mistress, my kind cousin Pysie Dering,[1] who makes it such a centre of beneficence and hospitality to those who need it. All the overworked priests who want rest and good dinners hover round it like a flock of ravens. I really believe also that there are a few of them who would not be ashamed to take an undue advantage of the utter simplicity of goodness which they find here.

Fifty years ago no road whatever led to Baddesley Clinton; it was absolutely isolated in its then double moat amid its green pastures. There are still few other houses where one drives by a road skirting parklike fields, descends upon the old house, and is set down at the entrance of a bridge over a wide deep moat which washes the walls of the house itself and keeps them dry. A courtyard, bright with flowers, and with turf intersected by little paved paths, takes one to the entrance lobby in a corner. This opens into the fine old hall—a low room with a grand stone chimney-piece and many arched windows filled with glorious armorial glass of the alliances of the Ferrers family. . . . The chair by the entrance is 'the ghost's chair,' where a spirit-lady, with her little girl, comes to sit for a time at four o'clock in the afternoon, not frightening or distressing anyone. Pysie says she has never seen her herself, but her niece has, and many others. Lady Chatterton often saw her. She also saw some of the other ghosts in the house, and the figure of the lady who appears in 'the ghost room' with the dawn of day. The 'Bishop's Room'—often assigned to Roman Catholic prelates—in which I sleep, has also its peculiar phantom visitant, but I have seen nothing unusual. It is a delightful room with panelling, a noble chimney-piece, the exquisite armorial glass windows which abound all over the house, and many of Pysie's portraits of her two husbands in the strange medieval dresses in which they delighted. . . . Though there is a shrinking from them, ghosts were the chief topic with Pysie and her friend Miss Throckmorton (Lady-in-Waiting to Empress Elizabeth of Austria) last night, till, at a quarter to ten, we were summoned upstairs to the chapel, where the housekeeper, veiled like all the maids, read, in a rapid monotone like the priests, a number of prayers and the litany of Jesus, to which we all responded. There was really nothing that could not be joined in by one far more Protestant than myself.

There is no artificial light in this house but that from masses of wax candles everywhere. Hundreds of pounds must be spent upon them annually.

October 18.—What strikes one most in the evening prayers in the chapel here is the *silences* in which all are asked to remember the faults for which they should especially ask forgiveness.

'That is the portrait of King James III,' said Pysie, in showing the house to Kate Grant who came over to luncheon. It is a thorough old Jacobite house, though it must be allowed that in the hall is a relief of James III on one side and George I on the other, which could be turned round according to who was arriving.

We had expected Mme. de Navarro, better known as the beautiful Mary Anderson, to come over from Broadway to luncheon in her motor-car, and this led Pysie to tell us her ghost story. She was in the habit of frequently visiting the Lyttons at Knebworth, and had always been given the same room there, a very pretty bright room with French furniture. But once, when she reached Knebworth, Lady Lytton said to her,

---

[1] 'Pysie' (Mrs. Rebecca Dulcibella Orpen) Dering first married Marmian Ferrers, the last of a famous Catholic family. Hare's cousin, Heneage Dering, was first married to Lady Chatterton, the novelist. The Ferrers and the Derings all lived together in the old house and when their respective spouses had died, Heneage and 'Pysie' married. Heneage died in 1892. In Hare's day the Catholic faith flourished at Baddesley Clinton, where there were 250 adherents.—*Ed.*

'I am very sorry that I cannot give you your usual room this time, as my mother is occupying it, and I must not move her.' And she was given a large panelled room with an old-fashioned four-poster bed. The party were late that evening, having been much amused by a game of questions and answers in rhyme, and, after reaching her room, Mme. de Navarro stayed up some time longer answering letters of urgency. When at length she went to bed, she remained awake thinking of much better answers she might have written to questions which had been asked. Suddenly, in the furthest corner of the room she heard a rustle, a sound which increased, as if a lady in a very stiff silk dress were passing down the side of the room. It seemed to bring with it the most intense sense of cold—an icy air—then it returned. Then it seemed to turn towards the bed. Mme. de Navarro sat up, when she felt, from the invisible presence, a violent pressure upon the shoulders, and was forcibly pushed back upon the pillows. At that moment the door of the dressing-room, in which her maid slept, opened and the maid rushed in—'Oh, I cannot stay in my room, there is something terrible there which has been trying to strangle me!' Mme. de Navarro went along the passage to the room where the French governess slept and asked her if there was no other room in the house in which she could possibly take refuge. She said there was only one room vacant—in a turret, and there Mme. de Navarro and her maid passed the rest of the night. In the morning, when Lady Lytton was told, she said that the thing often happened and that her mother's terror of it had led her to take the room Mme. de Navarro usually occupied.

October 20.—To this house of constant hospitality three Birmingham artists had been invited to spend the day. One of them, Mrs. King, told us her most extraordinary dream. She had been, with her husband, painting near Bala Lake and they had arranged to go on to Towyn. The night before they were to move, she dreamt that she went to a house most beautifully kept. In her dream she went up a staircase scrubbed to perfection. She entered a large fresh-looking room, well furnished and hung with very common scripture prints. It had a particularly curious carpet, made of large squares of carpet sewn together and involuntarily suggesting trapdoors underneath. The windows were fastened by a row of very large nails, sticking up but hammered in along the window sill. She went to bed in her dream but, when she was there, a terrible-looking woman with long black hair falling down on either side of her face came in and said rapidly—'You are in a very evil place, you must make your escape, now, at once, leave all you have, only escape.' And the woman touched her to hurry her and she woke with a scream. This aroused her husband, to whom she told all her dream in detail. The next morning her landlady, who had been very kind to her, observed upon her looking ill. She said, 'I am not ill, only somehow—I cannot tell why—I cannot bear to go to Towyn: I feel a strange sort of shrinking from it.' 'Well,' said the landlady, 'that is very odd: but I see no sort of reason why you should go to Towyn. Why not go to Aberdovey instead.' So they went to Aberdovey. There they saw that lodgings were to let in a house which looked very nice on the outside, and they went in. *There* was the staircase she had seen, and when they ascended it, *there* was the room—the same scripture prints, the same unusual carpet, the same tall row of nails along the window sill. On entering, they had ordered tea. 'Oh, who will bring it up?' said Mrs. King with horror to her husband. And it was brought up by the woman with the black hair, exactly the person she had vividly described to him. They were afraid to drink the tea. They paid their bill and left hurriedly. Years afterwards they were at Aberdovey again. The house was then a shop. They enquired about the former occupants and heard that the house had had a very mysterious and bad reputation and that the former owners had all left quite suddenly in the night.

Pysie told a story I have often heard before on the authority of her mother-in-law, Mrs. Cholmondley Dering, who often visited the old house of the Trenchards, then let to the Misses Foster. The staircase opened from the hall, and below it was a glass door leading to a passage. One day, coming down stairs, dressed for dinner, she saw through the glass door an old gentleman with a blue coat and pigtail, apparently attired for a masquerade in the dress of the last century. Going into the drawing-room, she told the Misses Foster what she had seen. 'Oh,' they said, 'you have seen the ghost of the house. He is perfectly harmless, but he often appears and was a Mr. Trenchard who was excessively cruel to his wife. This Mr. Trenchard, however, was very hospitable to his neighbours. One day the Colonel of a regiment quartered close by at Weymouth was dining there with a young subaltern. At dinner the young man's eyes seemed constantly fixed in a very odd manner on the lady of the house, and immediately after dinner he entreated, with great insistence, that they might leave. The Colonel was annoyed but, thinking he was ill, made an excuse and complied. In the carriage the young man said to him, "Is it possible that you did not see the figure, which was exactly the double of Mrs. Trenchard, standing behind her chair, and that every movement of Mrs. Trenchard was repeated by the figure." The Colonel was beginning to say "What nonsense," when a servant whom he knew rode by, just stopping to say, "I am going for a doctor, though it is no use, for Mrs. Trenchard has hanged herself." The appearance was several times seen before the death of a Mrs. Trenchard. Philip II of Spain slept at the house on his way to marry Queen Mary, and he saw it: Mrs. Trenchard of that time died the next day in her confinement.'

Holmhust, October 28.—The King has made two most successful visits to the city, tremendously well received by the people, who care more for behaviour than for conduct. As part of a pageant he never fails to excel both in tact and dignity. He might even be a great King, if he had anyone to speak truth to him, but even in the ordinary world few men have sincerity in their speech, and courtiers of the present age apparently have none at all.

November 20.—M. F. writes to me that everyone who is entering upon their closing years must feel the loneliness of life. I do. Up to the last few days, in the radiant beauty of surrounding nature, with the soft blue of the sky, the sunshine on the garden, the golden and crimson tints of the autumnal woods, I have not felt it at all, but indeed I have not been alone, for I have sat out for hours, watching my three young men planting crocus and snowdrop bulbs under the trees. But now all is changed; one night of arctic frost has blackened the flowers. With the haste of a flight from an enemy, all the great aloes and myrtles of the terrace have been hurried into winter refuges; the sky is drab, the winds are lacerating and howl piteously, snow falls at intervals, and as I sit alone in my pleasant upper chamber, I cannot help recalling how all who have really had an intimate part in my life have passed away—that I myself am on a desert island shore, though assuredly a very pleasant desert island, waiting to be taken away.

Bishopsthorpe, November 27.—I came here on Monday, as I had not seen the Archbishop and Augusta for so long, and was so much the worse for the journey that I feel I must resign all hope of reaching Italy this winter. I have been very weak and ill, but everyone most kind, in spite of the almost tumult of religious and semi-religious duties which pervade every corner of this great house.

Augusta has a delightful room on the ground floor. It looks out on the Ouse and is close to it. From its windows, if she thinks a book bad and worthless, she throws it into the river—'And it floats down the river to someone who reads it,' I said. 'No,' said the chaplain, 'the books sink; the bed of the river here is already paved with Mrs. Maclagan's books.'

The Archbishop says, 'In my late diocese of Lichfield—at Glossop—there were a clergyman and his wife whom I knew intimately—persons of most undoubted veracity. Constantly, as they both affirmed, when they were sitting together alone in the evening, a spirit lady in a brown dress would open the door and come in and take a vacant chair and sit with them for a time. She said nothing and they did not speak to her. After sitting for a time, she got up and went away. It happened continually.'

November 30.—This family is consumed by an absolutely insatiable passion for church services: Dona, the daughter of the house, has been to seven to-day, besides some little private rite of her own in between two of them.

41 *Seymour Street, December* 8.—A week in London always gives one more to think about than two months in the country, and, at the kind Shaw-Lefevres, I have seen an immense number of interesting and delightful people, and have been so much better that I have been able to enjoy them. I was glad to make the acquaintance of Miss Braddon,[1] whom the *Daily Telegraph* calls 'the queen of English novelists,' a pleasant elderly lady who seemed to know how to pick out all the best things in life to think of and dwell upon.

At a pleasant dinner at the Wilberforces, where one always meets people of good gifts and possibilities, the great success of Willie Maugham's new novel, *Mrs. Craddock*, was a topic. Both the Archdeacon and I much regretted the author's Zola-like realism and that his great talent was not devoted to nobler aims. 'What old maids you both are,' said a lady present, and I believe that would be the prevailing feeling now. How society has changed!

The Education Bill was going on in the House of Lords, and many were coming and going—amongst them the Bishop [Percival] of Hereford and Lord Stanmore, who were both going to speak. A young Munro[2] was introduced to me as one of the most gifted and promising young men of the time.

96 *Eaton Place, December* 11.—I am staying for a week with the ever kind Miss Sumner, the ancient sister-in-law who took such devoted care of my paralysed cousin Mr. Thurlow during the last years of his life. Now many of the fine contents of Baynards are transferred to Eaton Place, and the whole house is full of pictures, including a grand Vandyke of Charles I from Carisbrooke Castle, of which the hands were cut off by the Roundheads and put on again. There is also a curious screen containing a portrait of Queen Elizabeth, surrounded by the likenesses of all those supposed to have been in love with her.

Life here is like that in a French house. No one is expected to appear till luncheon,

[1] Mrs. Mary Elizabeth Maxwell, better known as Braddon, 1837–1915. Her most famous novel, *Lady Audley's Secret* was by no means her best, but it made a fortune for her publisher, who built a house from the proceeds and called it Audley Lodge. She married John Maxwell, a publisher, and apart from an immense amount of journalistic work, she wrote some eighty novels. She was bitterly and unjustly attacked as a 'sensationalist,' but her books were enjoyed by many of the great men of her day. She was the mother of the novelist W. B. Maxwell.—*Ed.*

[2] Probably Hector Munro, better known as 'Saki,' who was then making a name for himself as a foreign correspondent for the *Morning Post.* But there is nothing to prove this identification.—*Ed.*

till which Miss Sumner does not come down and at which extra places are laid for any friends who like to appear. Then all disperse again to their own pursuits. Dinner is at seven, and in the evening the kind old lady likes her guests to play at Ludo with her.

I am wearied by people in London—people who do not care in the least about the answer—constantly asking 'What are you writing now?' as if it was always necessary that you should have something you wished to say to others—on paper. It is happily only so sometimes—George Sands at seventy wrote: 'To write you must have lived and sought, you must have digested much, loved, suffered, waited, working always.'

Holmhurst, December 16.—A moist, dark, oozy, spongy day, all view blotted out by mist, and darkness and candles at 3 P.M. Yet—home, the drawing-room bright with flowers, the dear mother's chair and writing-table and little bookcase; the smiling faces of the welcoming servants; the little black spitz twirling round and round in his joy at getting me back.

I wonder if many people dream as I do. For me so much of actual life is passed in dreamland. My mother and Lea come to me every night and have done ever since they left me, and they come, not as passing flitting images, but to remain, I am convinced, for hours, in which we live through all the pleasures—none of the pains—of the past, and visit again in detail a thousand places we have loved—at Rome, Perugia, Assisi, Lucca, Heidelberg. And it is no hazy phantoms which I see with me, but the beloved ones, as clear and as tangible as I have ever known them. The whole barrier of separation is broken down by such dreams. The Hares and Maurices who oppressed my childhood never return—but my aunt, Mrs. Stanley, calm, beautiful, sparkling with intelligence, only gentler and softer than in life; Arthur Stanley at his best before the influence of the world and of the court had corroded him; Catherine Vaughan in her brightest youth; Hugh Pearson, Lady Waterford, the best ones connected with my happiest memories—they all seem to act and speak through the night with a background of indescribable beauty. I cannot speak of it often, or tell all that it means to me.

My last act in London, it is always my last there, was to go to see my mother's old friend Mrs. Woodward, still, at ninety-two, retaining all her mental and many of her physical powers. . . . One wonders in seeing all old people of intellectual powers and tastes, why they should be permitted apparently to have them all cut off. I see that George Eliot in her Letters says something of this: 'We are getting patriarchal, and think of old age and death as journeys not far off. All knowledge, all thought, all achievement, seems much more precious and enjoyable to me than it ever was before in my life. But as soon as one has found the key of life it opens the gate of death.' Yet perhaps none of it will really come to an end, only be expanded and glorified, all that one has learnt *here* being permitted to be useful *there*. How I hope that it may be so. It would be the greatest of undeserved rewards.

December 28.—I have just read a capital answer to the question 'What is a Lady?'— 'One who considers others, one who never by word or deed causes unnecessary pain, who listens sympathetically, talks pleasantly, never says a great deal even when she feels much and knows more. One who does her mental and moral washing in private, but is not afraid to do her duty in public; who respects the secrets of others, the honour of her family, and her own self more than all. One who speaks with tact, acts with discretion and places God before fashion without needlessly advertising the fact

L

to the annoyance of the rest of the world.' There are just a few left in England still who answer to this description, but they become fewer every year in a country which can admire such horrors as 'the Smart Set,' 'the Souls,' etc. 'The beautiful manners of the past are almost extinct,' wrote Lady Verney some years ago; 'It seems as if we could hardly grow them amidst the luxury, the struggle for existence, the zeal for getting on and up, of the present day: a certain repose of mind is necessary for perfect behaviour. Security of position is also a great help, which may be as much felt in a lower as in an upper class, but any aping of a superior class, or striving after a higher grade of society, is fatal to them.'

Last week Archbishop Temple died. It is strange to think that I have known well five Archbishops of Canterbury, five from whom I have had an ever-kind welcome to Lambeth.

December 29.—A very sudden fainting fit this morning without even a warning of being ill, makes me feel more than ever the uncertainty of life. . . . I say constantly, and I should like my last thoughts or words to be—'*Fiat voluntas tua, O Deus, in terris ut in coelo*'—the prayer which Pius IX taught me as including all others. When one comes to think of it, it is strange one should ever be afraid of death, when it is only going to God.

January 3, 1903.—Helen and St. Clair Baddeley are here. . . . How many little reminiscences have Helen and I called up together—of old Mrs. Sumner, who used to talk so funnily to her footman John, and if she heard boys shouting anything particularly horrible in the street, would send him out to find out all about it, and when he came in with the terrible details always said, 'Oh, how shocking, John, but human nature, John, human nature,' and he as regularly answered, 'You're about right there, mum,' and went away;—of Miss Bird whose friend had asked Swinburne to dinner, to which he had come and been most brilliant, the life of the evening, but the next day he had called and said, 'I cannot say how sorry I was not to be able to avail myself of your invitation last night'; he had forgotten all about it;—of her own little Eddie of six, from whom she had thought it necessary to take away some toys, and who had turned upon her with, 'I will never forget what you have done to me, never: I will never forget it when I am a very old man: I will never forget it when I am only a handful of ashes on a wave of the sea: I will never forget it when I am nothing but a wind whistling in the tops of the pine trees.'

January 21.—Just now I am busy mourning dear old Mme. Ernest de Bunsen, the kindest, staunchest and most hospitable of friends, whom I had known well and continuously since I was ten years old, when she rode up, with her father Samuel Gurney, to the doors of the inn at Patterdale, before her marriage with Ernest Bunsen. Her daughter had kindly sent me a warning of the approaching loss of this old friend. She was the axis around which the whole clan of Gurneys seemed to circulate and her house and heart were ever open to all of them. It was entirely owing to her kind insistence that I wrote *The Gurneys of Earlham*.

*   *   *

[These were the last words that Augustus wrote. The following morning his maid brought him his tea and found him dead.—*Ed.*]

INDEX

IN MY SOLITARY LIFE

This book is an abridgement of the second half of *The Story of My Life*, which was first published in 1900. The complete work originally consisted of six volumes, and an abridgement of the first three was recently published with the title *The Years with Mother*, which recorded the facts of Hare's ancestry, his childhood at Hurstmonceaux and Lime, his schooldays at Harnish and Southgate and Harrow, and his early travels with his adoptive mother in the more spacious days of the mid-century. Of his highly entertaining volume Miss Georgiana Battiscombe wrote in *Time and Tide*: 'Dickens in his wildest flights of imagination never conceived of anything so improbably bizarre as the sober truth here recorded.'

The book was also described by Peter Quennell (*Daily Mail*) as: 'A magnificent repository of bedside reading', to which Edward Shanks (*Daily Graphic*) added: 'His picture of one side of Victorian life is unique and enthralling.'

BOOK SOCIETY RECOMMENDATION

THE WORTHIES OF ENGLAND
By Thomas Fuller
Edited, with an introduction by John Freeman

Sm. Roy. 8vo   About 30s. net

The Worthies of England is a magnificent storehouse of biography,
topography and proverbial and other lore, spiced with many a good
anecdote heard by Fuller as he toured the country in search of information.
Fuller's humour, wit and liveliness, and his aphoristic style, made him a
favourite with our forefathers, and he was enthusiastically enjoyed by such
diverse temperaments as Pepys, Coleridge, Lamb and E. V. Lucas. The
Worthies has not been reprinted for over a century; this generation has
been deprived of a great and lovable work because of its rarity.

The aim of the present edition is to reduce and to knit together the
vast materials supplied by Fuller, whilst remaining faithful to the spirit
of the original, and to provide just enough annotation to help the reader's
enjoyment. The editor's introduction gives the life of Fuller, considers
his achievement, and places him in the context of his age.

THE VICTORIAN TEMPER
By Jerome Hamilton Buckley

Demy 8vo   30s. net

The literary scene in nineteenth-century England was crowded and
active, with movements, leagues, and coteries which included not only
the accepted major artists, but many an important figure underestimated
today and many an oddity now forgotten. What they were all talking
and writing about, the impulses that prompted their ideas and standards,
the forces that shaped their creative expression this—the Victorian temper
—is Mr. Buckley's main concern.

VINDICATION OF RUSKIN
By J. Howard Whitehouse

Demy 8vo   10s. net

'Now comes *Vindication of Ruskin* by the scholarly J. Howard Whitehouse,
a slim volume of an importance altogether disproportionate to its size. . . .
When Ruskin's wife Effie brought the famous nullity action, Ruskin prepared a statement in his defence for his proctor. This statement now given
in full is a prominent and illuminating feature of the Vindication, its publication being held necessary to protect Ruskin's good name, in a book
written with judicial restraint and reasonableness.'

Lancashire Evening Post

GEORGE ALLEN & UNWIN LTD.
LONDON: 40 MUSEUM STREET, W.C.1
CAPE TOWN: 58–60 LONG STREET
TORONTO: 91 WELLINGTON STREET WEST
BOMBAY: 15 GRAHAM ROAD, BALLARD ESTATE
CALCUTTA: 17 CENTRAL AVENUE, P.O. DHARAMTALA
WELLINGTON, N.Z.: 8 KINGS CRESCENT, LOWER HUTT
SYDNEY, N.S.W.: BRADBURY HOUSE, 55 YORK STREET